CREATIONISM IN THE CLASSROOM

CASES, STATUTES, AND COMMENTARY

■ ■ ■

By

Edward J. Larson

University Professor and Hugh & Hazel Darling Chair in Law
Pepperdine University

AMERICAN CASEBOOK SERIES®

A Thomson Reuters business

Mat #41266498

Thomson Reuters created this publication to provide you with accurate and authoritative information concerning the subject matter covered. However, this publication was not necessarily prepared by persons licensed to practice law in a particular jurisdiction. Thomson Reuters does not render legal or other professional advice, and this publication is not a substitute for the advice of an attorney. If you require legal or other expert advice, you should seek the services of a competent attorney or other professional.

American Casebook Series is a trademark registered in the U.S. Patent and Trademark Office.

© 2012 Thomson Reuters
610 Opperman Drive
St. Paul, MN 55123
1–800–313–9378
Printed in the United States of America

ISBN: 978–0–314–28100–5

In Memory of

Anne Proffitt Dupre
&
J. Douglas Toma

Two Esteemed and Beloved Colleagues
in Education Law and Policy at
The University of Georgia's
Institute of Higher Education

PREFACE

The American legal controversy over creation and evolution is primarily fought over what is taught in public high-school biology classes. Virtually no one disputes teaching the theory of evolution in public colleges and universities or using public funding to support evolutionary research in agriculture or medicine. There is little serious debate over the core evolutionary concept of common descent among biologists. For nearly a century, however, parents, teachers, students, and scientists have battled over how scientific and religious concepts of biological origins should be presented in the classroom. The dispute has legal, social, religious, historical, and political dimensions–and it is not going away. If anything, the controversy is growing in intensity as participant on both sides have become more sophisticated and nuanced in their public pronouncement and legal strategies. Although various constitutional arguments are invoked by partisans on the differing sides, the Establishment Clause typically stands at or near the center of most disputes: In any given situation, does teaching Darwinism or creationism, or disparaging them, in public schools have the sole purpose or primary effect of promoting or hindering religious belief in violation of the First Amendment? In grappling with this question in diverse forms as presented in differing fact situations over the past fifty years, American courts have examined the meaning of the Establishment Clause and sharpened their interpretation of it. Indeed, lawsuits over no other contested curricular subject-matter shed more light on the historical and current understanding of the Establishment Clause than the long line of evolution-teaching cases that began with *Tennessee v. Scopes* in 1925. By a focused examination of the cases, statutes, and judicial opinions generated by the creation-evolution legal controversy, this casebook explores Establishment Clause jurisprudence generally and fundamental issues in religious, academic, and individual rights.

Although the cases, statutes, and commentary in this collection could have been organized topically, ultimately an historical approach seemed best. Topically, the cases and statutes sorted themselves into four broad clusters based on the remedies sought, three different groups based on the types of litigants involved, and as many as six main categories depending on the constitutional principles invoked. As remedies, critics of Darwinian instruction typically asked for (1) removing the topic of evolution from the classroom, (2) balancing it with some form of creationist instruction, (3) depicting it as a theory rather than a fact, or (4) teaching why it is controversial. These remedies, although always under consideration to some extent, tended to play out chronologically as to when they have dominated so as to create discernible historical phases of the controversy. This observation suggested a historical approach to the presentation. The cases themselves most typically were brought by or against teachers, parents and students, or school districts, but these groupings are neither inclusive nor exclusive. Ultimately the parties involved revealed little about the underlying litigation because, depending on the case, teachers, parents and students, and school districts stood on all sides of every issue. Regarding the constitutional principles at stake, issues of anti-establishment, free speech, free exercise, due process, equal rights, and academic freedom were ever present to a greater or lesser degree and blurred together in many cases and statutes. A historical approach offered the advantages of exploring how these constitutional issues developed over time in the context of each other.

Using history as an organizing structure, the chapters fit into four groups. The first two chapters cover the phase of anti-evolutionism in American law characterized mainly by efforts to remove evolution from the high-school biology classroom altogether. This phase was highlighted by the 1925 trial of John Scopes and culminated in 1967 with the U.S. Supreme Court decision of *Epperson v. Arkansas*, which declared that states could not exclude Darwinism from the classroom for religious reasons. The next two chapters deal with cases and statutes mostly from the 1970s and early 1980s, as creationists explored various avenues to secure a place in public schools for their own theories. Chapter Five focuses on the 1990s when, among other approaches, some creationists sought to emphasize that Darwinism is only a theory, not a fact, and to question its scientific legitimacy. The final two chapters cover current and recent statutes and court opinions, as critics of evolutionary instruction struggled to incorporate into public education at least some discussion of the "controversy" over Darwinism. This historical approach should help illumine the legal topics and constitutional principles at stake.

Several stylistic conventions are employed throughout this casebook. In commentary, notes, and questions, the term Darwinism is used in its popular sense to mean the then-current scientific theory of evolution rather than the particular nineteenth-century ideas of Charles Darwin. To make them more easily readable and understandable, all of the judicial opinions are edited for instructional use. Deletions from the text of opinions are indicated by ellipses. These deletions range from a word to entire multiple paragraphs. Additions to the text are in brackets. There is no acknowledgement of omitted footnotes, appendices, parallel citations, or cited authorities. All included footnotes are numbered consecutively along with the commentary rather than by the numbers appearing in the original opinions. Within the body of opinions, ellipses in material quoted by the court appear as they do in the original source. Throughout, the style of this casebook follows the principle of function over form, with the sole function being to assist readers in comprehending the material.

As with any law-school casebook, various teachers, students, and other sources have contributed immeasurably to this work. In this instance, these contributions extend back nearly four decades to when, shortly after graduating from Harvard Law School, I resumed graduate studies in the history of science at the University of Wisconsin–Madison. My dissertation topic became the history of the evolution-teaching controversy in America. Starting with research for that dissertation and continuing through my subsequent work on numerous books, articles, lectures, courses, and conference presentations dealing with the topic, I have accumulated a lifetime of debts to those that have helped me along the way. Among the countless people who have suffered my questions or supplied me with information about this topic, I would be remiss not to acknowledge Michael Ruse, Kenneth Miller, Eugenie Scott, Glenn Branch, Henry Morris, Larry Witham, Phillip Johnson, William Dembski, John West, Judge John Jones, Barbara Forrest, Richard Cornelius, Tony Randall, Robert E. Lee, Wendell Bird, Nell Segraves, Kelly Segraves, Carolyn Agger, Robert Okazaki, John Ball, Robert M. O'Neil, Checker Finn, Edward Asner, Carl Henry, and Bernard Ramm. At Thomson Reuters, I have benefited from the encouragement, support and editorial assistance of Ryan Pfeiffer and Louis Higgins. I also wish thank the students in my 2012 Stanford Law School seminar on Creationism and Constitution, who served as guinea pigs for the first edited version of these cases, and the reference librarians at Stanford Law School who helped to prepare it, particularly Sergio Stone. Above all, credit goes to my major professor at Wisconsin, ongoing mentor, and treasured friend, Ronald L. Numbers, who is the premiere authority on the history of modern creationism and creation-science. Any complaints about this book should be directed to him.

EDWARD J. LARSON
Palo Alto, California

Summary of Contents

TABLE OF CONTENTS

―――――――

TABLE OF CASES

The principal cases are in bold type. Cases cited or discussed in the text are in roman type. References are to pages. Cases cited in principal cases and within other quoted materials are not included.

CREATIONISM IN THE CLASSROOM

CASES, STATUTES, AND COMMENTARY

CHAPTER 1

THE ANTI-EVOLUTION CRUSADE

■ ■ ■

I. ORIGINS OF THE LEGAL CONTROVERSY

"Darwinism" refers to a theory of organic evolution devised by the English naturalist Charles Darwin in the mid-Nineteenth Century. In his 1859 book *On the Origin of Species*, Darwin depicts all plant and animal species as evolving from pre-existing species over millions of years through the natural selection of variations that make some individual organisms better fitted to their environment than others of the same species. Individuals possessing fitter traits survive, reproduce, and propagate those beneficial traits into the next generation, displacing those with less-fit traits. As the process continues over generations—particularly in times of environmental stress, under the influence of changes in the local environment, or as individuals move into new environments—minor variations accumulate into major ones, ultimately leading to the evolution of new species. Extrapolating backward to the beginning of life, Darwin envisioned a branching "tree of life" in which all current species descended with modification from one or a few original types. Although disagreements emerged over what drove the process, the evidence for common descent assembled by Darwin and his followers quickly persuaded the European and American scientific community that all known past and present species evolved over time and were not specially created by God. By 1880, virtually all American botanists, zoologists, paleontologists, and other naturalists accepted the concept of organic evolution and were using it to understand natural processes of life.

As the Mendelian laws of genetics became widely understood and accepted during the early Twentieth Century, Roger Fisher, Theodosius Dobzhansky, and other biologists integrated them with Darwin's original theory to forge the Modern Neo–Darwinian Synthesis that has dominated scientific thought ever since. It holds that variations in the phenotype (or expressed traits) of organisms are caused by genetic combinations and mutations that occur at conception. Once fixed, these genetic factors—some dominant and some recessive—are inheritable under standard genetic laws and result in a pool of genetic diversity within populations that can respond rapidly to changes in the environment. In this manner, minute

1

variations in dominant and recessive genes have driven the evolution of living things since the first appearance of self-replicating molecules. At bottom, the process relies on random genetic variations and a competitive struggle for existence among individuals. In theory, it lacks purpose or direction.

Before the advent of Darwinism, scientists with strong religious convictions were among the staunchest defenders of the doctrine of special creation. Even after the general acceptance of evolutionism by scientists, those with conservative Christian leanings tended to hold out the longest for creationism or favor theistic theories of evolution that attributed beneficial variations to God's intelligent design. As scientific support for creationism waned, some theologians, ministers, and lay Christians took up its defense. In his 1874 book *What is Darwinism?*, for example, Princeton theologian Charles Hodge spoke for many conservative Protestants when he equated Darwin's denial of intelligent design in the origin of species with the denial of God. Beginning in the late nineteenth century, conservative religious publishers poured forth a steady stream of anti-evolution books and tracts for lay readers. After the popular evangelist Dwight L. Moody lent his voice to the choir denounced the doctrine of naturalistic evolution as demonic, his influential Chicago Bible Institute (renamed for him after his death in 1899) emerged as an institutional center for anti-evolutionism.

By the early twentieth century, theologically conservative Protestants in the United States had splintered into various self-identified groups. Evangelicals proclaimed the traditional Protestant gospel of personal salvation though faith in Jesus and upheld the Bible as God's inspired word. In the 1910s, some militant evangelicals began calling themselves "fundamentalists" to emphasize their commitment to what they saw as the fundamental tenets of biblical Christianity, particularly the inerrancy of scripture, the veracity of Old and New Testament miracles, and the trustworthiness of end-time prophecies. Pentecostals emerged about this time as a separate strain of conservative Christians who, based on their interpretation of scripture, claimed power through the Holy Spirit to heal, prophesy, and speak in tongues. By all accounts, most Americans who identified with these groups never warmed to the idea of organic evolution due to the difficulty of reconciling it to the biblical account in Genesis that speaks of God creating the earth and all the various kinds of animal, including humans, in six days. By the 1920s, many leading American evangelicals and fundamentalists had taken a public stand against Darwinism. Powerful Baptist and Presbyterian pastors launched drives to purge denominational colleges and seminaries of evolutionism and other supposedly corrupting modernist influences. Among those responding to a 1927 survey of American Protestant ministers, large percentages of Lutherans (89%), Baptists (63%), Presbyterians (35%), and Methodists (24%) answered yes to the question, "Do you believe that the creation of the world occurred in the manner and time recorded in Genesis?"

Notably, only about one in ten of the Episcopalian and Congregationalist ministers responding to this survey affirmed a belief in the Genesis account of creation. Except in the solidly Baptist South and the Lutheran strongholds of the Upper Midwest, Episcopalians and Congregationalists (because of their wealth and social standing) tended to carry weight in elite culture, higher education, and state politics disproportionate to their numbers. Evolutionism often became part of the religious world view for liberal theologians and ministers in these and other Protestant denominations. The renowned Congregational pastor Henry Ward Beecher blazed the trail in 1885 by publishing *Evolution and Religion*, in which he extolled evolution as "the method of God in the creation of the world" and the development of human society, religion, and morality. "Evolution is accepted as *the method* of creation by the whole scientific world," Beecher wrote. "It is the duty of the friends of simple and unadulterated Christianity to hail the rising light and to uncover every element of religious teaching to its wholesome beams."[1] Creation by wholesale is more impressive than creation by retail, he famously quipped.

By the 1920s, University of Chicago divinity school dean Shailer Mathews and New York's progressive Baptist minister Harry Emerson Fosdick assumed leadership roles in the fight for religious liberalism and against anti-evolutionism within the church. In his widely reprinted 1922 sermon, "Shall the Fundamentalists Win?" Fosdick contrasted the backward intolerance of fundamentalists with the openness to new scientific knowledge of the many progressive Christians who saw evolution and other natural processes as God's way of acting in the world. The battle over creation versus evolution took place as much within certain Protestant denominations, particularly the Presbyterian Church in the U.S.A. and the Northern Baptist Convention, and among various religious groups as between conservative Christians and secular scientists. Indeed, during the height of the creation-evolution controversy in the Twenties, such leading evolutionary scientists as Princeton University biologist Edwin G. Conklin, American Museum of Natural History president and paleontologist Henry Fairfield Osborn, and Johns Hopkins University zoologist Maynard M. Metcalf remained active church members even as they publicly defended Darwinism.

In 1922, the mounting concerns of American evangelicals and fundamentalists over the theory of human evolution and its implications for society and religion erupted into a nationwide effort to drive Darwinism from public education. More than any other individual, William Jennings Bryan transformed an inward-focused campaign to purify church doctrine into an outward-looking crusade to change government policy.

Bryan was a legend in his own lifetime. A political liberal with decidedly conservative religious beliefs, he entered Congress in 1891 as a young, silver-tongued Nebraska populist committed to defend rural and small-town Americans from economic exploitation by Eastern bankers and

---

1. HENRY WARD BEECHER, EVOLUTION AND RELIGION 51–53 (1885).

railroad barons. Rejecting the Social Darwinian government policies of his day, Bryan delivered his most famous speech at the 1896 Democratic National Convention, where he demanded an alternative silver-based currency to help debtors cope with the crippling deflation caused by exclusive reliance on limited gold-backed money. "You shall not press down upon the brow of labor this crown of thorns," he shouted in an address heard from Wall Street banking houses to Rocky Mountain silver mines, "you shall not crucify mankind upon a cross of gold."[2] The speech electrified the convention and secured him the party's presidential nomination at age 36, the youngest person ever nominated for president by a major political party.

A narrow defeat against a highly favored opponent in the ensuing bitter election did not diminish Bryan's standing in his party or with his people. He secured two subsequent presidential nominations as he fought against imperialism and militarism following the Spanish–American War and for increased government oversight of big business. Although trained as a lawyer, Bryan's vocation became speaking and writing, with his words coming from both the political left and the religious right. During the balance of his life, he delivered an average of over two hundred speeches a year, edited a progressive political journal with nationwide circulation, wrote a syndicated newspaper column, and published dozens of popular books. His only official position during this period was a two-year stint as Woodrow Wilson's Secretary of State, a post that he resigned in 1915 to protest the administration's growing involvement in the First World War. Early in the 1920s, Bryan began speaking out against Darwinism with a shrill tone of urgency.

As early as 1904, Bryan had criticized the theory of human evolution for the support that it gave to Social Darwinism. "The Darwinian theory represents man as reaching his present perfection by the operation of the law of hate," Bryan complained at the time, "the merciless law by which the strong crowd out and kill off the weak."[3] Although he repeatedly delivered the speech containing these words, he said little else publicly about evolution until 1921, when he began blaming Darwinism for the First World War and an a loss of religious faith among educated Americans. Following his customary practice, Bryan drew his evidence from a few semi-popular books, particularly biologist Vernon Kellogg's *Headquarters Nights*, which tied German militarism to a struggle-for-existence philosophy, and psychologist James Leuba's *The Belief in God and Immortality*, which presented survey data suggesting a decline in theism among college students and scientists. "To destroy the faith of Christians and lay the foundations for the bloodiest war in history would seem enough to condemn Darwinism," he argued.[4]

---

2. William Jennings Bryan, *In the Chicago Convention*, in 1 SPEECHES OF WILLIAM JENNINGS BRYAN 249 (William Jennings Bryan ed., 1909).

3. William Jennings Bryan, *The Prince of Peace*, in 2 *id.* at 268.

4. WILLIAM JENNINGS BRYAN, IN HIS IMAGE 94, 98, 100, 126 (1922).

Although Bryan railed against belief in the theory of human evolution and assumed a leadership role in trying to purge his own mainline Presbyterian denomination of Darwinian influences, he did not initially call for laws against teaching evolution. That changed in January, 1922, after he heard about such a proposal in Kentucky and made it his own. Within the month, Bryan was in Frankfort addressing a joint session of the Kentucky legislature on the matter. He spent the next month touring the state in support of the bill, which fell one vote short of passage in the House of Representatives. If public schools could not teach religious doctrines of creation, Bryan asked, why should they be allowed to teach anti-religious doctrines of evolution? Tax-supported schools should be neutral on the sensitive subject of human origins, he argued.

The crusade for anti-evolution legislation spread quickly. Many of the Protestant ministers and evangelists who had backed efforts to purify their churches of Darwinian influences enlisted in the new push against teaching evolution in public schools. William Bell Riley stood second only to Bryan in inciting the national crusade. As pastor of an enormous Baptist church in downtown Minneapolis, Riley had fought for biblical orthodoxy within the Northern Baptist Convention and, in 1919, organized the interdenominational World's Christian Fundamentals Association (a precursor of the current National Association of Evangelicals) to coordinate the war against modernism throughout the Protestant church. By the fall of 1922, following Bryan's lead, Riley began speaking nationally against evolutionary teaching in public schools and threw the full weight of his Association behind the cause.

Even as others jumped on the bandwagon, Bryan remained the chief driver of the crusade to outlaw evolutionary teaching. It had all the trappings of a national political campaign, with Bryan giving hundreds of stump speeches in dozens of states on the topic over a three-year period, including invited addresses to nine different state legislatures. Although no region of the country was exempt from its impact, anti-evolutionism found its strongest support in the South and Midwest. Yet even Bryan could not seed a storm without clouds in the sky. Undoubtedly the spread of compulsory public secondary education provided a necessary condition for the particular form that anti-evolutionism took in the 1920s. Prior to that time, most American teenagers did not attend high school and many communities did not provide public education beyond the eighth grade. The expansion of public secondary education carried evolutionary teaching to an increasing number of students, and did so by force of law at taxpayer expense. This expansion coincided with the anti-evolution crusade. Thus Bryan could ask, as he did to the West Virginia legislature in 1923, "What right have the evolutionists—a relatively small percentage of the population—to teach *at public expense* a so-called scientific interpretation of the Bible when orthodox Christians are not permitted to teach an orthodox interpretation of the Bible?"[5] Two years later, the same Tennessee legisla-

---

5. William Jennings Bryan, *Speech to Legislature*, in ORTHODOX CHRISTIANITY VERSUS MODERNISM, 46 (William Jennings Bryan ed., 1923) (emphasis in original).

ture that passed the nation's first law against teaching evolution also funded the state's first comprehensive system of public high schools.

At the time, most American states had part-time legislatures that only met in general session during the first few months of odd-numbered years. Kentucky was an exception, but when its anti-evolution bill died early in 1922, Bryan and his followers had to wait until 1923 for their next shot a lawmaking. The legislatures in six southern and border states (including Tennessee) actively debated anti-evolution laws during the spring of 1923, but only two lesser measures passed. Sobered by their failures in 1923, anti-evolutionists focused their attention on building grassroots support in Tennessee and a few other promising states in advance of the 1925 legislative sessions. Victories in those states could lead to later successes elsewhere, they reasoned. Bryan, Riley, and other prominent national anti-evolution leaders spoke in Tennessee on multiple occasions during 1924. As a result of their efforts, teaching evolution became a major issue there during the 1924 elections, with many legislative candidates vowing to support "Bryan and the Bible."

The groundwork paid off handsomely. Shortly after the Tennessee legislature convened in January, 1925, Representative John W. Butler, a farmer-legislator and Primitive Baptist lay leader from rural East Tennessee, introduced an anti-evolution bill of his own composition into the Tennessee House of Representatives. After it sailed through the House in a matter of days with little opposition, the proposal became the focus of intense public discussion. Newspaper editorialists, educators, and liberal clerics in Tennessee and elsewhere tended to denounce it while evangelicals and fundamentalists throughout the country generally embraced it. During the ensuing Senate floor debate over the bill, lawmakers on both sides dwelt more on issues of religious freedom than science education. Proponents argued that public schools should not force students to learn theories that undermine their religious beliefs. Opponents countered that no one's religion should set the standards for what is taught in public schools. In the end, the bill passed the Senate by a comfortable margin and was signed into law by Governor Austin Peay in March, 1925. The new law provided as follows:

TENNESSEE ANTI–EVOLUTION STATUTE (1925)

AN ACT prohibiting the teaching of the Evolution Theory in all the Universities, Normals and all other public schools of Tennessee, which are supported in whole or in part by the public school funds of the State, and to provide penalties for the violations thereof.

Sec. 1.   Be it enacted by the General Assembly of the State of Tennessee, That it shall be unlawful for any teacher in any of the Universities, Normals and all other public schools of the State which are supported in whole or in part by the public school funds of the State, to teach any theory that denies the story of the Divine Creation of man as taught in the Bible, and to teach instead that man has descended from a lower order of animals.

Sec. 2. Be it further enacted, That any teacher found guilty of the violation of this Act, Shall be guilty of a misdemeanor and upon conviction, shall be fined not less than One Hundred $(100.00) Dollars nor more than Five Hundred ($500.00) Dollars for each offense.

NOTES AND QUESTIONS

1. Tennessee was not the first American state to pass an anti-evolution statute. Responding the Bryan's initial call to arms in 1922, the Oklahoma state Baptist General Session threw its support behind legislation to ban the teaching of evolution in public schools. The following year, junior legislators pledged to support this position took the lead in attaching an anti-evolution floor amendment to a bill providing state funds for public-school textbooks. The amendment provided "that no copyright shall be purchased, nor textbook adopted that teaches the 'Materialistic Conception of History' (i.e.) the Darwin Theory of Creation verses the Bible Account of Creation." Bryan hailed the measure as the first victory in his campaign against evolutionary teaching. Was it a real or symbolic victory? Oklahoma's textbook restriction remained law only until 1925, when the underlying program providing states funds for textbooks was repealed. Textbook content would remain one focal point for legal battles over evolutionary teaching into the twenty-first century, however. Why do textbooks so often become a flashpoint for controversy? Is attention to textbook content an effective legal strategy for supporters and opponents of evolutionary teaching? Partisans on various sides of this issue typically view textbooks as an "under the radar" means to shape classroom instruction without imposing direct and potentially unpopular restrictions on teachers.

2. By 1922, Bryan had moved from Nebraska to Miami and was rumored to be considering a run for the U.S. Senate from Florida in 1926. When the Florida legislature convened in 1923, he called for it to outlaw "the teaching in public schools or colleges, atheism, agnosticism, or the teaching as true of Darwinism or any other evolutionary hypothesis that links man in blood relation with any form of animal life below man." He added, however, "I do not think there should be any penalty attached to the bill. We are not dealing with a criminal class and a mere declaration of the state's policy is sufficient." The Florida legislature promptly responded by passing a concurrent resolution declaring that it was "improper and subversive to the best interests of the people" for any public-school teacher "to teach or permit to be taught Atheism, or Agnosticism, or to teach as true Darwinism or any other hypothesis that links man in blood relation to any form of lower life." How does this resolution respond to Bryan's call? It does not actually outlaw the teaching of evolution. What impact would its passage likely have on public-school teachers? Could parents or school administrators use it to limit the content of public-school instruction? Bryan believed that by simply making it illegal to teach evolution in tax-supported schools without imposing a criminal penalty, parents and taxpayers could stop those schools from teaching evolution

without creating sympathy for teachers who refused to comply. He wanted dissenting teachers to appear as ungrateful scofflaws rather than as principled martyrs.

3.   The Florida resolution declared it improper only to teach Darwinism "as true." In addressing this issue, Bryan had advised Florida lawmakers that teaching Darwinism "as a hypothesis can be considered as giving information as to views held, which is very different from teaching it as a fact." Does seeking to bar only teaching Darwinism as true rather than teaching it at all represent a sincere policy position or a public-relations strategy? Distinctions about whether Darwinism is taught "as only a theory," "not as a fact," "as true," or "as science" will reemerge throughout the legal battles over evolutionary instruction in American public school.

4.   The Tennessee statute and Florida resolution addressed solely the teaching of human evolution, not the evolution of other organic species. This reflected Bryan's particular concern with the social impact of people believing that humans evolved through a Darwinian process rather than being specially created by God. On strictly religious grounds, many early twentieth century Christian leaders expressed far greater opposition to the theory of human evolution than to Darwinism generally. They typically gave several reasons for this. At a literal level, the Genesis account contains a detailed account of human creation by God whereas it only speaks generally about the divine creation of other animals and depicts the land producing plants. At a theological level, the Bible repeatedly affirms that humans are special because they were created in God's image; the Christian doctrine of original sin relies on the temptation and fall of Adam and Eve as the first humans; and the New Testament refers to Christ as "the second Adam" whose crucifixion redeemed his followers from Adam's fall. How much do religious concerns underlay the opposition to teaching human evolution? These religious concerns were reflected in the Tennessee and Oklahoma statutes depicting Darwinism as opposed to the Biblical account of creation and the Florida resolution equating the teaching of Darwinism to the teaching of atheism and agnosticism.

II.   TESTING THE TENNESSEE LAW IN COURT

Bryan rejoiced upon hearing that Tennessee had outlawed teaching the theory of human evolution. "Other states North and South will follow the example of Tennessee," he predicted.[6] Fearing that result, opponents of the law set about to derail it. Leading this charge, the American Civil Liberties Union (ACLU) issued a press release in New York City offering to defend any Tennessee school teacher willing to challenge the validity of the new statute in state court. Its leaders saw the law as a clear violation of free speech, academic freedom, and the separation of church and state: three principles standing at the core of the ACLU's civil-liberties agenda but which, at the time, received scant legal protection against acts done by

---

6.   Letter from William Jennings Bryan to Austin Peay (Mar. 24, 1925), *in* William Jennings Bryan Papers, Library of Congress, Washington, D.C.

state governments. John Scopes, a 24–year–old science teacher in the small East Tennessee town of Dayton, promptly accepted the ACLU's offer.

Like so many quintessentially American events, the trial itself began as a publicity stunt. Inspired by the ACLU offer to supply distinguished counsel to defend any local teacher willing to challenge the highly controversial new statute, Dayton civil leaders saw a chance to gain attention for their ambitious young community. A show trial featuring prominent New York attorneys should draw crowds to Dayton, they reasoned, and perhaps economic development opportunities. Scopes became their willing defendant at the urging of local school officials even though, strictly speaking, he was not a biology teacher. The young teacher was neither jailed nor ostracized. Quite to the contrary, in the month before his trial, Scopes was feted at a formal dinner in New York City; embraced by the presidents of Harvard, Columbia, and Stanford Universities; received at the Supreme Court in Washington; and awarded a scholarship for graduate study at the University of Chicago. When it became clear that the ACLU (in apparent collaboration with local officials and aided by the American Association for the Advancement of Science) was seeking to discredit Tennessee's new anti-evolution statute through the Scopes trial, Bryan volunteered to assist the prosecution. He hoped to use the coming event to publicize the need for such restrictions. If the civic leaders of Dayton wanted a show trial, Bryan would help give them one.

Bryan's pending appearance in Dayton drew in Clarence Darrow. By the 1920s, Darrow stood out as the most famous criminal-defense lawyer in America. As a young Chicago attorney during the politically unstable 1890s, he gained widespread attention as an impassioned defender of labor organizers and militant leftists. Darrow's notoriety grew as he spoke out against religious influences in public life, particularly biblically inspired legal restrictions on personal freedom. His opposition to religious lawmaking stemmed from his belief that revealed religion, especially Christianity, divided people into warring sects, caused them to be judgmental, and was an irrational basis for action in an modern scientific age. In speeches and popular books, Darrow sought to expose biblical literalism as both irrational and harmful. In its stead, he offered rational science—particularly a vaguely Lamarckian form of evolutuionism—as a better basis for ethics and human values. This set the stage for a classic confrontation between Bryan and Darrow. Both men were affable enough—indeed they had been friends since 1896, when Darrow (as a Democratic candidate for Congress) supported Bryan's first presidential campaign—but their world views clashed. When Bryan offered to prosecute Scopes, Darrow volunteered to defend him. The 67–year–old litigator immediately became the brightest light in an already luminous defense team assembled by the ACLU to challenge Tennessee's anti-evolution law.

The prospect of these two renowned orators—Bryan and Darrow—actually litigating the matter of evolutionary science versus biblical religion turned the trial into a media sensation then and the stuff of legend thereafter. News of the trial dominated the headlines during the weeks leading up to it and pushed nearly everything else off American front pages throughout the eight-day event. Two hundred reporters covered the story in Dayton, including some from Europe. Thousands of miles of telegraph wires were hung to transmit every word spoken in court, and pioneering live radio broadcasts carried the oratory to the listening public. Newsreel cameras recorded the encounter, with the film flown directly to major American cities for projection in movie houses. Telegraphs transmitted more words to Britain about the Scopes trial than had ever before been sent over trans-Atlantic cables about any single American event. At the time, people commonly called it the Tennessee Monkey Trial. A trained chimp performed on the courthouse lawn as a carnival-like atmosphere descended on Dayton. Editorial cartoonists in the United States and Europe drew countless variations on the theme of Bryan acting like an ape or monkeys denying any kinship to him.

The courtroom arguments and speeches by both sides addressed the nation rather than the jurors (who missed most of the oratory anyway because it had so little to do with the facts of the case that it was delivered with the jury excused). The defense divided its arguments among its three principal attorneys. The prominent New York attorney Arthur Garfield Hays raised the standard ACLU arguments that Tennessee's anti-evolution statute violated the individual rights of teachers. Bryan's former Assistant Secretary of State, Dudley Field Malone, a liberal Catholic, argued that the scientific theory of evolution did not conflict with a modernist interpretation of Genesis. Darrow, for his part, concentrated on debunking fundamentalist reliance on revealed scripture as a source of knowledge about nature suitable for setting education standards. Their common goal, as Hays stated at the time, was to make it "possible that laws of this kind will hereafter meet the opposition of an aroused public opinion."[7]

The prosecution countered with seven lawyers led by Attorney General and future U.S. senator Tom Stewart plus Bryan and his son, William Jennings Jr., a former U.S. Attorney for Los Angeles. In court, they focused on proving that Scopes violated the law and objected to any attempt to litigate the merits of that statute. The public, acting through elected legislators, should control the content of public education, they maintained. The elder Bryan, who had not practiced law for three decades, stayed uncharacteristically quiet in court, and saved his oratory for lecturing the assembled press and public outside the courtroom about the vices of teaching evolution and the virtues of majority rule.

Before the actual trial began, the parties wrangled for three days over a pre-trial motion offered by the defense to strike the statute as unconstitutional. Although these arguments occasionally soared into dramatic pleas from the defense for individual liberty and from the prosecution for legislative control over public education, they rarely touched on the

---

7. Arthur Garfield Hays, *Strategy of the Scopes Defense*, THE NATION, Aug. 5, 1925, at 158.

scientific or religious status of evolution theory. Strictly following Tennessee precedent, the trial judge denied the motion. Such issues were reserved for the state supreme court to resolve on appeal, he ruled.

The prosecution then presented uncontested testimony by students and school officials that Scopes had taught evolution. Following the prosecution's brief presentation, the defense attempted to offer the testimony of a dozen nationally recognized evolutionary scientists and modernist theologians, all prepared to defend the theory of evolution as valid science that could be taught without public harm. The prosecution immediately objected to such testimony as irrelevant to the issue of whether Scopes broke the law. The anti-evolution statute was not on trial, prosecutors argued, only the defendant. After three more days of debate, the judge sided with the prosecution. The trial appeared to have ended without ever directly addressing the supposed conflict between evolutionary science and biblical Christianity.

Frustrated by his failure to discredit the anti-evolution law through the testimony of scientists and theologians, Darrow sought the same result by inviting Bryan to take the witness stand and face questions about it. Although he could have declined, Bryan accepted Darrow's challenge. Up to this point, lead prosecutor Tom Stewart had masterfully limited the proceedings and, with help from a friendly judge, confined his wily opponents. But Stewart could not control his impetuous co-counsel, especially because the judge seemed eager to hear Bryan defend the faith.

Thinking the trial all but over, except for the much awaited closing oratory, and hearing that cracks had appeared in the ceiling below the overcrowded, second-floor courtroom, the judge had moved the day's session outside, onto the courthouse lawn. The crowd swelled as word of the encounter spread. From the 500 persons that evacuated the courtroom, the number rose to an estimated 3000 people spread over the lawn—nearly twice the town's normal population. Darrow posed the well-worn questions of the village skeptic: Did Jonah live inside a whale for three days? How could Joshua lengthen the day by having the sun (rather than the earth) stand still? Where did Cain get his wife? In a narrow sense, as Stewart persistently complained, Darrow's questions had nothing to do with the case because they never inquired about human evolution. In a broad sense, as Hays repeatedly countered, they had everything to do with it because they challenged biblical literalism. Best of all for Darrow, no good answers existed to them. Bryan could either affirm his belief in seemingly irrational biblical accounts, and thus suggest that his opposition to teaching about evolution rested on religious rather than scientific or social grounds, or concede that the Bible required interpretation. He tried both tacks at various times without appreciable success. To Bryan's growing frustration, Darrow never asked about the theory of evolution itself—probably because he knew that Bryan would deliver a stump speech in response.

Darrow raised only two issues involving the supposed conflict between science and scripture, and in both cases Bryan sought to reconcile the them. In a modest concession to Copernican astronomy, Bryan suggested that God extended the day for Joshua by stopping the earth rather than the sun—an occurrence that would defy the laws of Newtonian physics, Darwin noted. Similarly, in line with established evangelical theology, Bryan affirmed his understanding that the days of creation in Genesis represented geologic ages or periods. The earth could be 600,000,000 years old, Bryan asserted. Though he had not ventured far beyond the bounds of biblical literalism, the defense made the most of it. "Bryan had conceded that he interpreted the Bible," Hays gloated. "He must have agreed that others have the same right."[8] Of course the reporters loved it. Forget Scopes and his inevitable conviction by a jury that had heard but two hours of testimony during the week-long trial (and none of Bryan's testimony), the lead story became Bryan's public humiliation. A next-day editorial in the usually staid *New York Times* commented about Bryan, "It has long been known to many that he was only a voice calling from a poorly furnished brain-room. But how almost absolutely unfurnished it was the public didn't know till he was forced to make an inventory."[9]

Although partisans on both sides claimed the advantage, at the time, most neutral observers viewed the trial as a draw, and few saw it as decisive. America's adversarial legal system tends to drive parties apart rather than to reconcile them. That certainly resulted in this case. Despite Bryan's stumbling on the witness stand (which his supporters attributed to his notorious interrogator's wiles), both sides effectively communicated their message from Dayton—maybe not well enough to win converts, but at least sufficiently to energize those already predisposed toward their viewpoint. Due largely to the media's portrayal of Darrow's effective cross-examination of Bryan, later made even more cutting in the popular 1955 play and 1960 movie about the trial, *Inherit the Wind*, millions of Americans thereafter ridiculed religious opposition to the theory of evolution. Yet the widespread coverage give Bryan's impassioned objections to that theory made anti-evolutionism all but an article of faith among American fundamentalists. When Bryan died a week later in Dayton, they acquired a martyr to this cause. On appeal, although the state supreme court reversed Scopes's conviction on a technicality and thus ended the lawsuit, it affirmed the anti-evolution statute in the following opinion:

SCOPES v. STATE

Supreme Court of Tennessee
154 Tenn. 105 (1927)

GREEN, C. J.: [John] Scopes was convicted of a violation of chapter 27 of the Acts of 1925, for that he did teach in the public schools of Rhea county a certain theory that denied the story of the divine creation of man, as

8. ARTHUR GARFIELD HAYS, LET FREEDOM RING 77 (1928).
9. *Ended at Last*, NEW YORK TIMES, July 22, 1925, at 18.

taught in the Bible, and did teach instead thereof that man had descended from a lower order of animals. After a verdict of guilty by the jury, the trial judge imposed a fine of $100, and Scopes brought the case to this court by an appeal in the nature of a writ of error. . . .

Chapter 27 of the Acts of 1925, known as the Tennessee Anti–Evolution Act is set out in the margin.[10] While the act was not drafted with as much care as could have been desired, nevertheless there seems to be no great difficulty in determining its meaning. It is entitled:

> An act prohibiting the teaching of the evolution theory in all the Universities, normals and all other public schools in Tennessee, which are supported in whole or in part by the public school funds of the state, and to provide penalties for the violations thereof.

Evolution, like prohibition, is a broad term. In recent bickering, however, evolution has been understood to mean the theory which holds that man has developed from some pre-existing lower type. This is the popular significance of evolution, just as the popular significance of prohibition is prohibition of the traffic in intoxicating liquors. It was in that sense that evolution was used in this act. It is in this sense that the word will be used in this opinion, unless the context otherwise indicates. It is only to the theory of the evolution of man from a lower type that the act before us was intended to apply, and much of the discussion we have heard is beside this case. The words of a statute, if in common use, are to be taken in their natural and ordinary sense. O'Neil v. State, 115 Tenn. 427; State ex rel. v. Turnpike Co., 2 Sneed (34 Tenn.) 90.

Thus defining evolution, this act's title clearly indicates the purpose of the statute to be the prohibition of teaching in the schools of the state that man has developed or descended from some lower type or order of animals. . . . So interpretated, the statute does not seem to be uncertain in its meaning nor incapable of enforcement for such a reason, notwithstanding the argument to the contrary. The indictment herein follows the language of the statute. The statute being sufficiently definite in its terms, such an indictment is good. State v. Odam, 2 Lea (70 Tenn.) 220; Villines v. State, 96 Tenn. 141; Griffin v. State, 109 Tenn. 17. The assignments of error, which challenge the sufficiency of the indictment and the uncertainty of the act, are accordingly overruled.

It is contended that the statute violates section 8 of article 1 of the Tennessee Constitution, and section 1 of the Fourteenth Amendment of

---

10. "An act prohibiting the teaching of the evolution theory in all the Universities, normals and other public schools of Tennessee, which are supported in whole or in part by the public school funds of the state, and to provide penalties for the violations thereof. Section 1. Be it enacted by the General Assembly of the state of Tennessee, that it shall be unlawful for any teacher in any of the Universities, normals and all other public schools of the state which are supported in whole or in part by the public school funds of the state, to teach any theory that denies the story of the divine creation of man as taught in the Bible and to teach instead that man has descended from a lower order of animals. Sec. 2. Be it further enacted, that any teacher found guilty of the violation of this act, shall be guilty of a misdemeanor and upon conviction shall be fined not less than one hundred ($100.00) dollars nor more than five hundred ($500.00) dollars for each offense. Sec. 3. Be it further enacted, that this act take effect from and after its passage, the public welfare requiring it."

the Constitution of the United States—the law of the land clause of the state Constitution, and the due process of law clause of the federal Constitution, which are practically equivalent in meaning.

We think there is little merit in this contention. The plaintiff in error was a teacher in the public schools of Rhea County. He was an employee of the state of Tennessee or of a municipal agency of the state. He was under contract with the state to work in an institution of the state. He had no right or privilege to serve the state except upon such terms as the state prescribed. His liberty, his privilege, his immunity to teach and proclaim the theory of evolution, elsewhere than in the service of the state, was in no wise touched by this law.

The statute before us is not an exercise of the police power of the state undertaking to regulate the conduct and contracts of individuals in their dealings with each other. On the other hand, it is an act of the state as a corporation, a proprietor, an employer. It is a declaration of a master as to the character of work the master's servant shall, or rather shall not, perform. In dealing with its own employees engaged upon its own work, the state is not hampered by the limitations of section 8 of article 1 of the Tennessee Constitution, nor of the Fourteenth Amendment to the Constitution of the United States.

In People v. Crane, 214 N. Y. 154, the validity of a statute of that state, providing that citizens only should be employed upon public works was sustained. In the course of opinion (page 175) it was said:

> The statute is nothing more, in effect, than a resolve by an employer as to the character of his employees. An individual employer would communicate the resolve to his subordinates by written instructions or by word of mouth. The state, an incorporeal master, speaking through the Legislature, communicates the resolve to its agents by enacting a statute. Either the private employer or the state can revoke the resolve at will. Entire liberty of action in these respects is essential unless the state is to be deprived of a right which has heretofore been deemed a constituent element of the relationship of master and servant, namely, the right of the master to say who his servants shall (and therefore shall not) be.

A case involving the same statute reached the Supreme Court of the United States, and the integrity of the statute was sustained by that tribunal. Heim v. McCall, 239 U. S. 175. The Supreme Court referred to People v. Crane, supra, and approvingly quoted a portion of the language of Barrett, Chief Judge, that we have set out above.

At the same term of the Supreme Court of the United States an Arizona statute, prohibiting individuals and corporations with more than five workers from employing less than 80 per cent. thereof of qualified electors or native-born citizens of the United States was held invalid. Truax v. Raich, 239 U. S. 33.

These two cases from the Supreme Court make plain the differing tests to be applied to a statute regulating the state's own affairs and a statute regulating the affairs of private individuals and corporations.

A leading case is Atkin v. Kansas, 191 U. S. 207. The court there considered and upheld a Kansas statute making it a criminal offense for a contractor for a public work to permit or require an employee to perform labor upon that work in excess of eight hours each day. In that case it was laid down:

> ... For, whatever may have been the motives controlling the enactment of the statute in question, we can imagine no possible ground to dispute the power of the state to declare that no one undertaking work for it or for one of its municipal agencies, should permit or require an employee on such work to labor in excess of eight hours each day, and to inflict punishment upon those who are embraced by such regulations and yet disregard them.

> It cannot be deemed a part of the liberty of any contractor that he be allowed to do public work in any mode he may choose to adopt, without regard to the wishes of the state. On the contrary, it belongs to the state, as the guardian and trustee for its people, and having control of its affairs, to prescribe the conditions upon which it will permit public work to be done on its behalf, or on behalf of its municipalities. No court has authority to review its action in that respect. Regulations on this subject suggest only considerations of public policy. And with such considerations the courts have no concern.

In Ellis v. United States, 206 U. S. 246, Atkins v. Kansas was followed, and an act of Congress sustained which prohibited, under penalty of fine or imprisonment, except in case of extraordinary emergency, the requiring or permitting laborers or mechanics employed upon any of the public works of the United States or of the District of Columbia to work more than eight hours each day.

These cases make it obvious that the state or government, as an incident to its power to authorize and enforce contracts for public services, "may require that they shall be carried out only in a way consistent with its views of public policy, and may punish a departure from that way." Ellis v. United States, supra.

To the same effect is Waugh v. Board of Trustees, 237 U. S. 589, in which a Mississippi statute was sanctioned that prohibited the existence of Greek letter fraternities and similar societies in the state's educational institutions, and deprived members of such societies of the right to receive or compete for diplomas, class honors, etc.

This court has indicated a like view in Leeper v. State, 103 Tenn. 500, in which the constitutionality of chapter 205 of the Acts of 1899, known as the Uniform Text Book Law, was sustained. In the opinion in that case Judge Wilkes observed:

If the authority to regulate and control schools is legislative, then it [is] must have an unrestricted right to prescribe methods, and the courts cannot interfere with it unless some scheme is devised which is contrary to other provisions of the Constitution....

In Marshall & Bruce Co. v. City of Nashville, 109 Tenn. 495, the charter of the city of Nashville required that all contracts for goods and supplies furnished the city, amounting to over $50, must be let out at competitive bidding to the lowest responsible bidder. In the face of such a charter provision, an ordinance of the city, which provided that all city printing should bear the union label, was held unauthorized—necessarily so. The lowest bidder, provided he was responsible, was entitled to such a contract, whether he employed union labor, and was empowered to affix the union label to his work or not. Other things said in that case were not necessary to the decision.

Traux v. Raich, supra, Meyer v. Nebraska, 262 U. S. 390, Pierce v. Society of Sisters of the Holy Names of Jesus and Mary, 268 U. S. 510, and other decisions of the Supreme Court of the United States, pressed upon us by counsel for the plaintiff in error, deal with statutes affecting individuals, corporations, and private institutions, and we do not regard these cases as in point.

Since the state may prescribe the character and the hours of labor of the employees on its works, just as freely may it say what kind of work shall be performed in its service, what shall be taught in its schools, so far at least as section 8 of article 1 of the Tennessee Constitution, and the Fourteenth Amendment to the Constitution of the United States, are concerned.

But it is urged that chapter 27 of the Acts of 1925 conflicts with section 12 of article 11, the educational clause, and section 3 of article 1, the religious clause, of the Tennessee Constitution. It is to be doubted if the plaintiff in error, before us only as the state's employee, is sufficiently protected by these constitutional provisions to justify him in raising such questions. Nevertheless, as the state appears to concede that these objections are properly here made, the court will consider them.

The relevant portion of section 12 of article 11 of the Constitution is in these words:

... It shall be the duty of the General Assembly in all future periods of this government, to cherish literature and science.

The argument is that the theory of the descent of man from a lower order of animals is now established by the preponderance of scientific thought and that the prohibition of the teaching of such theory is a violation of the legislative duty to cherish science.

While this clause of the Constitution has been mentioned in several of our cases, these references have been casual, and no act of the Legislature has ever been held inoperative by reason of such provision. In one of the opinions in Green v. Allen, 5 Humph. (24 Tenn.) 170, the provision was said to be directory. Although this court is loath to say that any language of the Constitution is merely directory (State v Burrow, 119 Tenn. 376; Webb v. Carter, 129 Tenn. 182), we are driven to the conclusion that this particular admonition must be so treated. It is too vague to be enforced by any court. To cherish science means to nourish, to encourage, to foster science.

In no case can the court directly compel the Legislature to perform its duty. In a plain case the court can prevent the Legislature from transgressing its duty under the Constitution by declaring ineffective such a legislative act. The case, however, must be plain, and the legislative act is always given the benefit of any doubt.

If a bequest were made to a private trustee with the avails of which he should cherish science, and there was nothing more, such a bequest would be void for uncertainty. Green v. Allen, 5 Humph. (24 Tenn.) 170, Ewell v. Sneed, 136 Tenn. 602, and cases cited. It could not be enforced as a charitable use in the absence of prerogative power in this respect which the courts of Tennessee do not possess. A bequest in such terms would be so indefinite that our courts could not direct a proper application of the trust fund nor prevent its misapplication. The object of such a trust could not be ascertained.

If the courts of Tennessee are without power to direct the administration of such a trust by an individual, how can they supervise the administration of such a trust by the Legislature? It is a matter of far more delicacy to undertake the restriction of a coordinate branch of government to the terms of a trust imposed by the Constitution than to confine an individual trustee to the terms of the instrument under which he functions. If language be so indefinite as to preclude judicial restraint of an individual, such language could not possibly excuse judicial restraint of the General Assembly.

If the Legislature thinks that, by reason of popular prejudice, the cause of education and the study of science generally will be promoted by forbidding the teaching of evolution in the schools of the state, we can conceive of no ground to justify the court's interference. The courts cannot sit in judgment on such acts of the Legislature or its agents and determine whether or not the omission or addition of a particular course of study tends "to cherish science."

The last serious criticism made of the act is that it contravenes the provision of section 3 of article 1 of the Constitution, "that no preference shall ever be given, by law, to any religious establishment or mode of worship."

The language quoted is a part of our Bill of Rights, was contained in the first Constitution of the state adopted in 1796, and has been brought down into the present Constitution.

At the time of the adoption of our first Constitution, this government had recently been established and the recollection of previous conditions was fresh. England and Scotland maintained state churches as did some of the Colonies, and it was intended by this clause of the Constitution to prevent any such undertaking in Tennessee.

We are not able to see how the prohibition of teaching the theory that man has descended from a lower order of animals gives preference to any religious establishment or mode of worship. So far as we know, there is no religious establishment or organized body that has in its creed or confession of faith any article denying or affirming such a theory. So far as we know, the denial or affirmation of such a theory does not enter into any recognized mode of worship. Since this cause has been pending in this court, we have been favored, in addition to briefs of counsel and various amici curiae, with a multitude of resolutions, addresses, and communications from scientific bodies, religious factions, and individuals giving us the benefit of their views upon the theory of evolution. Examination of these contributions indicates that Protestants, Catholics, and Jews are divided among themselves in their beliefs, and that there is no unanimity among the members of any religious establishment as to this subject. Belief or unbelief in the theory of evolution is no more a characteristic of any religious establishment or mode of worship than is belief or unbelief in the wisdom of the prohibition laws. It would appear that members of the same churches quite generally disagree as to these things.

Furthermore, chapter 277 of the Acts of 1925 requires the teaching of nothing. It only forbids the teaching of the evolution of man from a lower order of animals. Chapter 102 of the Acts of 1915 requires that ten verses from the Bible be read each day at the opening of every public school, without comment, and provided the teacher does not read the same verses more than twice during any session. It is also provided in this act that pupils may be excused from the Bible readings upon the written request of their parents.

As the law thus stands, while the theory of evolution of man may not be taught in the schools of the state, nothing contrary to that theory is required to be taught. It could scarcely be said that the statutory scriptural reading just mentioned would amount to teaching of a contrary theory.

Our school authorities are therefore quite free to determine how they shall act in this state of the law. Those in charge of the educational affairs of the state are men and women of discernment and culture. If they believe that the teaching of the science of biology has been so hampered by chapter 27 of the Acts of 1925 as to render such an effort no longer desirable, this course of study may be entirely omitted from the curriculum of our schools. If this be regarded as a misfortune, it must be charged to the Legislature. It should be repeated that the act of 1925 deals with nothing but the evolution of man from a lower order of animals.

It is not necessary now to determine the exact scope of the religious preference clause of the Constitution and other language of that section. The situation does not call for such an attempt. Section 3 of article 1 is binding alike on the Legislature and the school authorities. So far we are clear that the Legislature has not crossed these constitutional limitations. If hereafter the school authorities should go beyond such limits, a case can then be brought to the courts.

Much has been said in argument about the motives of the Legislature in passing this act. But the validity of a statute must be determined by its natural and legal effect, rather than proclaimed motives. Lochner v. New York, 198 U. S. 45; Grainger v. Douglas Park Jockey Club (C. C. A.) 148 F. 513.

Some other questions are made, but in our opinion they do not merit discussion, and the assignments of error raising such questions are overruled.

This record discloses that the jury found the defendant below guilty, but did not assess the fine. The trial judge himself undertook to impose the minimum fine of $100 authorized by the statute. This was error. Under section 14 of article 6 of the Constitution of Tennessee, a fine in excess of $50 must be assessed by a jury. The statute before us does not permit the imposition of a smaller fine than $100.

Since a jury alone can impose the penalty this act requires, and as a matter of course no different penalty can be inflicted, the trial judge exceeded his jurisdiction in levying this fine, and we are without power to correct his error. The judgment must accordingly be reversed. Upchurch v. State, 153 Tenn. 198.

The court is informed that the plaintiff in error is no longer in the service of the state. We see nothing to be gained by prolonging the life of this bizarre case. On the contrary, we think the peace and dignity of the state, which all criminal prosecutions are brought to redress, will be the better conserved by the entry of a nolle prosequi herein. Such a course is suggested to the Attorney General.

Mr. Justice SWIGGART took no part in the decision. He came on this bench upon the death of Mr. Justice HALL, after the argument and submission hereof. COOK, J., concurs.

CHAMBLISS, J. (concurring): While I concur in the conclusions announced by Chief Justice GREEN, and agree, as so ably shown by him, that it is within the power of the Legislature to so prescribe the public school curriculum as to prohibit the teaching of the evolution of man from a lower order of animal life, even though the teaching of some branches of science may be thereby restricted, I am of opinion that the constitutional objections urged do not apply for yet other reasons, and in another view.

Two theories of organic evolution are well recognized, one the theistic, which not only concedes, but maintains, consistently with the Bible story, that "the Lord God formed man of the dust of the earth, and breathed into his nostrils the breath of life, and man became a living soul." This is the theory advanced eloquently by learned counsel for Scopes, and held to by numerous outstanding scientists of the world. The other theory is known as the materialistic, which denies that God created man, that He was the first cause, and seeks in shadowy uncertainties for the origin of life. The act before us, as I view it, prohibits the teaching in public schools of the state of this latter theory, inconsistent, not only with the common belief of mankind of every clime and creed and "religious establishment," even those that reject Christ or Judaism, and look through Buddha or Mohammed to God, but inconsistent also with our Constitution and the fundamental declaration lying back of it, through all of which runs recognition of and appeal to "God," and a life to come. The Declaration of Independence opens with a reference to "the laws of nature and nature's God," and holds this truth "to be self-evident, that all men are created equal, that they are endowed by their Creator," etc., and concludes "with a firm reliance on the protection of Divine Providence." The Articles of Confederation and Perpetual Union read, "And whereas, it hath pleased the Great Governor of the world." And so section 3 of article 1 of the Constitution of this state, which declares that "no preference shall ever be given, by law, to any religious establishment," opens with the declaration "that all men have a natural and indefeasible right to worship Almighty God," while section 2 of article 9 declares that "no person who denies the being of God, or a future state of rewards and punishments, shall hold any office in the civil department of this state." That the Legislature may prohibit the teaching of the future citizens and office holders to the state a theory which denies the Divine Creator will hardly be denied.

Now I find it conceded in an exceptionally able brief for Scopes, devoted exclusively to the question of uncertainty, that "the act might be construed as only aimed at materialists." This is my view of it. As I read it, the act makes no war on evolution, except in so far as the evolution theory conflicts with the recognition of the divine in creation.

While it is conceded that the language is in some respects ambiguous, analysis of the caption and body of the act as a whole appears to sustain this view. The variance between the caption and the body of the act is significant. The caption refers broadly to "the evolution theory," but it is clear that the act itself, as finally framed and passed, was expressly limited and restricted in its body to the prohibition of the teaching—not of any theory of evolution at all, but of any theory only that denies or controverts "the divine creation of man." While the language used is "any theory that denies the story of the divine creation of man as taught in the Bible," the italicized phraseology may be said to be descriptive only of the essential matter. It may be insisted that these words, when given their proper force, serve to narrow the meaning of the act so as to confine its operation to prohibition against the denial of the Divine Creation of man to the story taught in the Bible as interpreted by those literalists who hold to the instantaneous creation view. In reply, it may be said that, however plausible may be this construction or application of this language, it must be rejected on the very grounds emphasized by learned counsel, who adopt it and then proceed to predicate thereon their argument for the unconstitutionality of the act. The courts may go far to avoid a construction which will destroy the act. This is axiomatic. One may not consistently contend for a construction of language, at all open to construction, which, if applied, will make void the act. Moreover, it would seem that, since "the story as taught in the Bible" of man's creation by God from the dust of the earth is readily susceptible of the construction given it by those known as liberalists, this language is consistent with the conclusion that what the act aims at and effects is the prohibition of the teaching of any such theory only as denies that man was divinely created according to the Bible story, however this story may be interpreted as to details. So long as the story as told in the Bible is so construed as to recognize the divine creation of man, these words have no limiting effect upon the central and essential object of the act as hereinbefore suggested—to restrain the inculcation into the minds of pupils of the public schools of any theory that denies the divine creation of man, and on the contrary traces his origin, in exclusion of the divine, to a lower order of animal life. It is this materialistic teaching which is denounced, and, so construed, the act may clearly be sustained, negative only as it is, first, of the right to teach in the public schools a denial of the existence, recognized by our Constitution, of the Creator of all mankind; and, second, of the right to teach any theory which involves the support or advocacy of either, or any, religious dogma or view. . . .

Now, in this view, it is clear that the constitutional direction to cherish education and science is not disregarded. The teaching of all sciences may have full legitimate sway, with the restriction only that the teaching shall not convey a denial of man's divine origin—God as his Creator. The theories of Drummond, Winchell, Fiske, Hibbens, Millikan, Kenn, Merriam, Angell, Cannon Barnes, and a multitude of others, whose names are invoked in argument and brief, do not deny the story of the divine creation of man as taught in the Bible, evolutionists though they be, but, construing the Scripture for themselves in the light of their learning, accept it as true and their teaching would not come under the ban of this act.

Much that has been said here bears directly upon the contention that section 3, art. 1, of our Constitution is violated, in that a preference is given by law to those "religious establishments which have as one of their tenets or dogmas the instantaneous creation of man." As was said by Chief Justice GREEN, the act gives no preference to any particular religious establishment. The doctrine or tenet of the instantaneous creation of man is not set forth or preferred over other conceptions. It is too well established for argument that "the story of the divine creation of man as taught in the Bible" is accepted—not "denied"—by millions of men and women who do not interpret it as teaching instantaneous creation, who hold with the Psalmist that "a thousand years in thy sight are but as yesterday when it is past," as but a day. It follows that to forbid the teaching of a denial of the biblical account of divine creation does not, expressly or by fair implication, involve acceptance or approval of instantaneous creation, held to by some literalists. One is not prohibited by this act from teaching, either that "days," as used in the book of Genesis, means days of 24 hours, the literalist view, or days of "a thousand years" or more, as held by liberalists, so long as the teaching does not exclude God as the author of human life.

Considering the caption and body of this act as a whole, it is seen to be clearly negative only, not affirmative. It requires nothing to be taught. It prohibits merely. And it prohibits, not the teaching of any theory of evolution, but that theory (of evolution) only that denies, takes issue with, positively disaffirms, the creation of man by God (as the Bible teaches), and that, instead of being so created, he is a product of, springs from, a lower order of animals. No authority is recognized or conferred by the laws of this state for the teaching in the public schools, on the one hand, of the Bible, or any of its doctrines or dogmas, and this act prohibits the teaching on the other hand of any denial thereof. It is purely an act of neutrality. Ceaseless and irreconcilable controversy exists among our citizens and taxpayers, having equal rights, touching matters of religious faith, and it is within the power of the Legislature to declare that the subject shall be excluded from the tax-supported institutions, that the state shall stand neutral, rendering "unto Caesar the things which be Caesar's and unto God the things which be God's," and insuring the completeness of separation of church and state....

In brief, as already indicated, I concur with the majority in the conclusion (1) that this case must be reversed for the error of the judge in fixing the fine; (2) that a nolle prosequi should be entered; and (3) that the act is constitutional as within the power of the Legislature as the employer of its teachers. However, I go further and find the act constitutional for additional reasons, rested upon the view that the act fairly construed is limited to the prohibition of the teaching of any theory of evolution only which denies the divine creation of man, without regard to details of religious belief, or differing interpretations of the story as taught in the Bible. In this view the constitutionality of the act is sustained, but the way is left open for such teaching of the pertinent sciences as is approved by the progressive God recognizing leaders of thought and life.

MCKINNEY, J. (dissenting): An elemental rule of statutory construction, which is well stated by Mr. Justice Sutherland in delivering the opinion of the Supreme Court of the United States in Connally v. General Construction Co., 269 U. S. 385, is as follows:

> That the terms of a penal statute creating a new offense must be sufficiently explicit to inform those who are subject to it what conduct on their part will render them liable to its penalties is a well-recognized requirement, consonant alike with ordinary notions of fair play and the settled rules of law; and a statute which either forbids or requires the doing of an act in terms so vague that men of common intelligence must necessarily guess at its meaning and differ as to its application violates the first essential of due process of law. International Harvester Co. v. Kentucky, 234 U. S. 216, 221; Collins v. Kentucky, 234 U. S. 634, 638.

Applying the foregoing rule to the statute here invoked, I am of the opinion that it is invalid for uncertainty of meaning. I therefore respectfully dissent from the contrary holding of my associates.

NOTES AND QUESTIONS

1. Scopes's defenders argued that the Due Process Clause of the U.S. Constitution and the equivalent clause of the Tennessee constitution barred the state from outlawing evolutionary instruction. They claimed that such a statute violated the protected liberty interests of public-school teachers and students. This argument relied on the 1923 decision in *Meyer v. Nebraska*, in which the U.S. Supreme Court invoked the Due Process Clause to void a Nebraska law that barred anyone from teaching German in a public or private school. Why did the *Scopes* court dismiss this ruling as inapplicable to the Tennessee anti-evolution statute? *Meyer* involved a private-school teacher fined for teaching German at a parochial school. Private-school teachers could still teach evolution under the Tennessee law. Should public-school teachers have a protected liberty interest in what they can teach similar to that enjoyed by private-school teachers under *Meyer*? Should public-school students have a protected liberty interest in receiving evolutionary instruction in biology courses? Courts would face these questions again as the legal controversy over evolutionary teaching unfolded.

2. The *Scopes* court ruled that the Tennessee anti-evolution statute does not give preference to a religious establishment because various religious groups—Protestants, Catholics, and Jews—are internally divided in their views on evolution. None of them, the court explained, treated anti-evolutionism as an article of faith. Further, the court noted that the statute only barred teaching Darwinism and did not mandate teaching creationism, which presumably might rise to the level of an article of faith for some sects. What approach is the court taking to the Establishment Clause? The court did not rule on the unconstitutionality of the state or school district commanding instructors to teach a view of origins that comports to the views of a particular religious group.

3. As noted in the *Scopes* opinion, the Tennessee constitution directs the state legislature "to cherish literature and science." Do you agree with the court that this provision is a mere admonition rather than an enforceable duty? The court goes on to note, "If the Legislature thinks that, by reason of popular prejudice, the cause of education and the study of science generally will be promoted by forbidding the teaching of evolution in the schools of the state, we can conceived of no grounds to justify the court's interference." Can you conceived of such a reason? The court also maintains that the constitutionality of a statute should be judged by its natural and legal effects rather than motive or purpose. Is this reasonable or is it sometimes appropriate for courts to judge the constitutionality of a statute by the stated or proven legislative purpose underlying it?

4. In his opinion for the court, Chief Justice Green concluded that "the statute does not seem to be uncertain in its meaning." According to him, it clearly prohibited teaching in public schools that humans descended from

lower forms of animals. Yet in his concurring opinion, Justice Chambliss maintains that the Tennessee statute only outlaws teaching materialistic theories of human evolution, not theistic one—even though both involve the idea that humans evolved from lower forms of animals. Further, in his dissenting opinion, Justice McKinney asserted that the statute should be "invalid for uncertainty of meaning." Who's right? In part, it depends on whether the two key clauses of the statute, "to teach any theory that denies the story of divine creation as taught in the Bible" and "to teach instead that man has descended from a lower order of animals," are interpreted as so dependant that they merge into a single prohibition against teaching human evolution (as the majority concluded) or as so independent that both must be violated to render a practice illegal (as Justice Chambliss countered).

5.   The Tennessee Supreme Court reversed Scopes's conviction on a technicality in sentencing that was not raised by either party at trial or on appeal. Clarence Darrow and other members of the defense team decrying this ruling as an in improper means by which the state court prevented them from appealing the ruling to the U.S. Supreme Court. In its written opinion, the court all but directed the prosecution to preserve "the peace and dignity of the state" by dismissing the case against Scopes. Was this an appropriate way to end one of the most famous prosecutions in American history? Should the parties have been allowed to carry the case to the U.S. Supreme Court?

III.   POST–*SCOPES* LEGAL DEVELOPMENTS

During the months following Bryan's death after the Scopes trial, dozens of evangelical leaders rushed to pick up the fallen mantle, letting loose a frenzy of uncoordinated and often localized legal activity against evolutionary teaching. Three days after Bryan died, anti-evolution legislation was introduced in Georgia, one of the few states where the legislature remained in regular session for 1925. In 1926, three of the nine state assemblies meeting that year faced such bills, a record number for a legislative off-year. When the bulk of state legislature next convened in the spring of 1927, eighteen different anti-evolution bills appeared in fourteen widely scattered states, an all-time high in both categories.

Supplementing this legislative activity, some state and local educational boards took the initiative in moving against evolutionary teaching. A year before the Scopes trial, the state Board of Education in California had directed teachers to present Darwinism as a theory only while the North Carolina Board had barred state high schools from using biology textbooks that intimate an origin of the human race other than that contained in the Bible. A few months after the Scopes trial, the Texas Textbook Commission, acting at the insistence of Governor Miriam Ferguson, ordered the deletion of evolution from all public school texts. The Louisiana Superintendent of Education took similar steps the following year. Scattered local restrictions against evolutionary teaching also cropped up across America during the late twenties. Despite these administrative successes, legislative relief remained the primary legal objective for anti-evolution crusaders during the first few years after the Scopes trial.

Only one of the bills introduced into state legislatures in the late 1920s became law. This occurred in Mississippi, where local evangelist and Bryan-pretender T. T. Martin led the charge. A fervent tent revivalist with a national ministry, Martin had railed against evolutionary teaching for nearly a decade, called the curious at Dayton to repentance from a street booth during the *Scopes* trial, and formed the Bible Crusaders of America to continue the fight against evolution after Bryan's death. Capturing the tone of his appeal, Martin's leading tract likened evolutionary teachers to German soldiers who were accused of poisoning French children during the First World War. "Ramming poison down the throats of our children is nothing compared to damning their souls with the teaching of evolution," Martin proclaimed.[11] Now he set his sights on his home state legislature, and he would not be denied.

Lobbying efforts by Martin centered on arousing and demonstrating popular support for the measure. He conducted a series of revival meetings and public rallies in and around the state capital during the 1926 legislative session. He organized petition drives across the state and submitted thousands of signatures in support of passing an anti-evolution law. His supporters pack the legislative galleries during floor deliberations on the bill and loudly urged its passage. Finally, personally addressing a joint legislative session, he challenged lawmakers, "It is claimed that the law will bring on Mississippi the ridicule and abuse from the North that has been heaped on Tennessee. Shall the legislature of Mississippi barter the faith of the children of Mississippi in God's word and the Savior for the fulsome praise of a paganized press?"[12] Without any organized opposition to the measure, the bill easily passed both houses of the state legislature and was signed into law by the governor despite receiving adverse committee reports in both chambers.

Arkansas soon followed neighboring Mississippi in enacting an anti-evolution statute. There, after the state legislature narrowly defeated an anti-evolution bill in 1928, the editors of two state church journals, Ben M. Bogard of the *Baptist and Commoner* and J.S. Compere of the *Baptist Advance*, jointly launched a campaign to enact a statute by popular initiative virtually identical to the Mississippi law. With the help of Bogard's Missionary Baptist State Convention and Compere's state Southern Baptist Convention, a petition drive succeeded in placing the measure on the November 1928 ballot as Initiative Act No. 1.

Opponents of the initiative pointed to the scorn heaped on Tennessee during the Scopes trial and urged voters to reject limits on science education. The *Arkansas Gazette*, the state's largest newspaper, editorialized, "To vindicate the Arkansas of the Twentieth century before the

---

11. T.T. MARTIN, HELL AND THE HIGH SCHOOL: CHRIST OR EVOLUTION, WHICH? 9 (1929).

12. T.T. Martin quoted in EDWARD J. LARSON, TRIAL AND ERROR: THE AMERICAN CONTROVERSY OVER CREATION AND EVOLUTION 77 (3d. ed. 2003).

nation every man and woman who loves his state and loves intellectual and educational freedom should vote against this ill-conceived measure."[13] An opposition newspaper advertisement signed by scores of prominent state residents put it even more bluntly, pleading, "Save our state from ridicule."[14]

Under the banner "The Bible or Atheism, Which?," proponents countered with advertisements stating, "If you agree with atheism vote against Act No. 1. If you agree with the Bible vote for Act No. 1." The ads went on to explain, "The bill does not prohibit free speech, it does not seek to help the church. It simply forbids the state attacking the church by having evolution taught in the schools at taxpayer's expense. Should concerned church members be forced to pay taxes to support teachers to teach evolution which will undermine the faith of their children?" Addressing the opposition's main theme, the ads closed with the rhetorical question, "The *Gazette* and Russian Bolsheviks laughed at Tennessee. True, and that sort will laugh at Arkansas. Who cares?"[15] Apparently not Arkansas voters. They passed the initiative measure by a 2 to 1 margin. Both statutes follow:

MISSISSIPPI ANTI–EVOLUTION STATUTE (1926)

AN ACT to prohibit in any university, college, normal, public school or other educational institution in the state of Mississippi, that is supported, in whole or in part, from public funds, the teaching that man descended, or ascended, from a lower order of animals, and providing a penalty for violation thereof. Schools state supported not to teach that man ascended or descended from the lower order of animals.

Sec. 1.   Be it enacted by the Legislature of the State of Mississippi, That it shall be unlawful for any teacher or other instructor in any university, college, normal, public school or other institution of the state which is supported in whole or in part from public funds derived by state or local taxation to teach that mankind ascended or descended from a lower order of animals and also it shall be unlawful for any teacher, text-book commission or other authority exercising the power to select text books for above mentioned educational institutions to adopt or use in any such institution a text book that teaches the doctrine that mankind ascended or descended from the lower order of animals.

Sec. 2.   Be it further enacted that any teacher or other instructor or text book commissioner who is found guilty of violation of this act by teaching, using, or adopting any such text books in any such educational institution shall be guilty of a misdemeanor and upon conviction be fined not exceeding $500.00; and upon conviction shall vacate the position thus held

---

13.   *If You Would Serve Arkansas with Your Ballot*, ARKANSAS GAZETTE, Nov. 2, 1928, at 9.

14.   *Against Act No. 1*, ARKANSAS GAZETTE, Nov. 4, 1928, at 9.

15.   *The Bible or Atheism, Which?*, ARKANSAS GAZETTE, Nov. 4, 1928, at 12.

in any educational institution of the character above mentioned or any commission of which he may then be a member.

ARKANSAS ANTI–EVOLUTION INITIATIVE STATUTE (1929)

AN ACT to Prohibit in Any University, Normal, Public School, College, or Other Educational Institution in the State of Arkansas That is Supported in Whole or in Part, From Public Funds, the Teaching that Man Descended or Ascended from a Lower Order of Animals and Providing a Penalty For Violation Thereof.

Be It Enacted by the People of the State of Arkansas:

Sec. 1. That it shall be unlawful for any teacher or other instructor in any University, College, Normal, Public School, or other institution of the State, which is supported in whole or in part from public funds derived by State and local taxation to teach the theory or Doctrine that mankind ascended or descended from a lower order of animals and also it shall be unlawful for any teacher, textbook commission, or other authority exercising the power to select textbooks for above mentioned educational institutions to adopt or use in any such institution a textbook that teaches the doctrine or theory that mankind descended or ascended from a lower order of animals.

Sec. 2. Be it further enacted that any teacher or other instructor or textbook commissioner who is found guilty of violation of this Act by teaching the theory or doctrine mentioned in Section 1 hereof, or by using, or adopting any such textbooks in any such educational institution shall be guilty of a misdemeanor and upon conviction shall be fined not exceeding five hundred dollars ($500.00); and upon conviction shall vacate the position thus held in any educational institutions of the character above mentioned or any commission of which he may be a member.

Notes and Questions

1. The Mississippi and Arkansas anti-evolution statutes differed from the Tennessee law in several respects. What differences can you spot? They did not mention the Bible or divine account of creation. They also extended the reach of the criminal sanction beyond public-school teachers to include persons who with select textbooks for public-school use. Do these changes reflect different policy positions or do they respond to legal and political concerns? If you were a proponent of anti-evolution laws after the experience of the Scopes trial, what other changes in the statute would you consider?

2. The Mississippi and Arkansas statutes, like the Tennessee law, covered state universities, colleges, and normal schools. "Normal school" was the name then given an institution that trained teachers. Although there is no evidence that these laws were ever formally enforced in institutions of higher education, individual state university and college instructors reported feeling

restrained by them. Since its passage in 1925, some professors and students at the University of Tennessee have lampooned and protested their state's anti-evolution law at Darwin Day events held on campus each year to mark the anniversary of Darwin's birth. What impact would such laws actually have at public universities and colleges? Because of the voluntary nature of college attendance and the maturity of college students, the augment that objecting students should not be forced to receive instruction in evolution was never as compelling when applied to college students as to high school students.

3.   Although anti-evolution bills were introduced into Northern, Midwestern, and Western state legislatures during the 1920s, virtually all of them languished in committee without being reported for floor consideration. The futility of these efforts was shown in 1927 when the Rhode Island legislature referred its anti-evolution bill to the Committee on Fish and Game, where it died without a hearing. What explains regional differences in the enactment of anti-evolution laws during the 1920s? Some historians point out that Protestant fundamentalism was stronger in the South than elsewhere at the time and that, due to the recent legacy of the Civil War and Reconstruction, the region was somewhat cut off from new ideas. After 1925, the wide and largely critical publicity given to the Tennessee Monkey Trial may have stigmatized anti-evolutionism as a Southern phenomenon, and thereby made it less attractive elsewhere.

CHAPTER 2

EXTENDING THE ESTABLISHMENT CLAUSE TO THE STATES

■ ■ ■

I. RELIGIOUS INSTRUCTION IN PUBLIC EDUCATION

The First Amendment to the U.S. Constitution begins by guaranteeing that "congress shall make no laws respecting an establishment of religion, or prohibiting the free exercise thereof." Over the past half century, the legal controversies surrounding the teaching of evolution and creation in public schools have focused on the interpretation of these two clauses in Constitution, with the Establishment Clause becoming a bulwark for evolutionary teaching, and the Free Exercise Clause invoked for teaching creationism. That neither clause figured prominently earlier bespeaks a changing interpretation of the Constitution. The change was twofold.

On its face, the United State Constitution does not say much about state (as opposed to federal) restrictions on individual liberty beyond the broad Fourteenth Amendment bar against states depriving "any person of life, liberty, or property, without due process of law." Earlier amendments, including the First, had focused on protecting individuals from excessive national power rather than from excessive state power. Even with respect to the Due Process Clause, added to the Constitution as part of the Fourteenth Amendment in connection with ending slavery in the 1860s, progressives of the 1920s worried mainly about conservative federal judges using it to strike down state economic regulations designed to protect workers, such as by minimum-wage and maximum-hour laws. Such regulations, some conservatives maintained, limited the economic freedom of workers to take low paying jobs or to work long hours. This placed the ACLU in an awkward position when it sought to use the same clause to prevent Tennessee from imposing conditions on Scopes's employment. Taking a broad view of the matter, the progressive *New Republic* magazine asked in 1925, "Why should the Civil Liberties Union have consented to charge the State of Tennessee with disobeying the Constitution in order legally to exonerate Mr. Scopes? They should have participated in the case, if at all, for the purpose of fastening the responsibility for vindicating Mr. Scopes, not on Supreme Court of the United States, but on the legislature and people of Tennessee."[16] Sensitivity to this issue influenced the way in which Scopes's counsel invoked the Due Process Clause at trial—always stressing that it barred patently unreasonable state laws rather than those that violated any specific individual right, even freedom of speech or establishment of religion, lest it provide authority for courts to strike statutes that purportedly limited economic freedom.

As a result, during the anti-evolution crusade in the 1920s, neither courts nor counsel raised the legal argument that state anti-evolution statutes violate the federal Establishment Clause. The clause traditionally barred only a national state church, like the Anglican Church in England. The influential nineteenth-century Supreme Court Justice Joseph Story explained, "The real object of the amendment was ... to exclude all rivalry among Christian sects, and to prevent any national ecclesiastical establishment, which should give to an hierarchy the exclusive patronage of the national government."[17] Since the federal government never established a state church, the Supreme Court rarely dealt with the clause until the *Everson* case questioned the constitutionality of providing public transportation for parochial school students in 1947, and it did so then only by interpreting the clause to preclude aiding religion generally rather than simply establishing a particular denomination. Even more ominous for the anti-evolution statutes, the *Everson* decision, written by Justice Hugo Black, extended this newly recognized constitutional "wall of separation" between religion and government to cover state action. Under *Everson*, the Establishment Clause applied every bit as much to state governments and local school districts as to Congress and the national government.

Further, by the 1940s, federal courts had stopped using the Fourteenth Amendment to strike progressive state economic regulations and instead begun using it to void repressive state social and political legislation. The process began the same year as the Scopes trial, when the Supreme Court first ruled that the "liberty" protected from state infringement by the Due Process Clause incorporated the First Amendment right of free speech. It took more than twenty years before the High Court added the Establishment Clause to the list of individual liberties protected against state action by the Due Process Clause. Once it did, the Court quickly began purging well-entrenched religious practices and influences from state-supported schools. Justice Black had championed the complete incorporation of the federal Bill of Rights into the Fourteenth Amendment since his appointment to the Supreme Court during the height of New Deal disputes over the constitutionality of federal economic legislation, and later he took the lead in applying the Establishment Clause to public education. In 1948, he wrote the initial Supreme Court decision barring religious instruction in public schools. That decision, which follows, laid

---

16. *Conduct of the Scopes Trial*, 43 NEW REPUBLIC 332, 332 (1925).

17. 3 JOSEPH STORY, COMMENTARIES ON THE CONSTITUTION OF THE UNITED STATES 728 (1833).

the foundation for later challenges to the constitutionality of state and local restrictions on teaching evolution:

McCOLLUM v. BOARD OF EDUCATION

Supreme Court of the United States
333 U.S. 203 (1948)

MR. JUSTICE BLACK delivered the opinion of the Court: This case relates to the power of a state to utilize its tax-supported public school system in aid of religious instruction insofar as that power may be restricted by the First and Fourteenth Amendments to the Federal Constitution.

The appellant, Vashti McCollum, began this action for mandamus against the Champaign Board of Education in the Circuit Court of Champaign County, Illinois. Her asserted interest was that of a resident and taxpayer of Champaign and of a parent whose child was then enrolled in the Champaign public schools. Illinois has a compulsory education law which, with exceptions, requires parents to send their children, aged seven to sixteen, to its tax-supported public schools where the children are to remain in attendance during the hours when the schools are regularly in session. Parents who violate this law commit a misdemeanor punishable by fine unless the children attend private or parochial schools which meet educational standards fixed by the State. District boards of education are given general supervisory powers over the use of the public school buildings within the school districts. Ill.Rev.Stat. ch. 122, 123, 301 (1943).

Appellant's petition for mandamus alleged that religious teachers, employed by private religious groups, were permitted to come weekly into the school buildings during the regular hours set apart for secular teaching, and then and there for a period of thirty minutes substitute their religious teaching for the secular education provided under the compulsory education law. The petitioner charged that this joint public-school religious-group program violated the First and Fourteenth Amendments to the United States Constitution. The prayer of her petition was that the Board of Education be ordered to "adopt and enforce rules and regulations prohibiting all instruction in and teaching of all religious education in all public schools in Champaign District Number 71, ... and in all public school houses and buildings in said district when occupied by public schools.". ...

Although there are disputes between the parties as to various inferences that may or may not properly be drawn from the evidence concerning the religious program, the following facts are shown by the record without dispute. In 1940 interested members of the Jewish, Roman Catholic, and a few of the Protestant faiths formed a voluntary association called the Champaign Council on Religious Education. They obtained permission from the Board of Education to offer classes in religious instruction to public school pupils in grades four to nine inclusive. Classes were made up of pupils whose parents signed printed cards requesting that their children be permitted to attend; they were held weekly, thirty minutes for the lower grades, forty-five minutes for the higher. The council employed the religious teachers at no expense to the school authorities, but the instructors were subject to the approval and supervision of the superintendent of schools. The classes were taught in three separate religious groups by Protestant teachers, Catholic priests, and a Jewish rabbi, although for the past several years there have apparently been no classes instructed in the Jewish religion. Classes were conducted in the regular classrooms of the school building. Students who did not choose to take the religious instruction were not released from public school duties; they were required to leave their classrooms and go to some other place in the school building for pursuit of their secular studies. On the other hand, students who were released from secular study for the religious instructions were required to be present at the religious classes. Reports of their presence or absence were to be made to their secular teachers.

The foregoing facts, without reference to others that appear in the record, show the use of tax-supported property for religious instruction and the close cooperation between the school authorities and the religious council in promoting religious education. The operation of the state's compulsory education system thus assists and is integrated with the program of religious instruction carried on by separate religious sects. Pupils compelled by law to go to school for secular education are released in part from their legal duty upon the condition that they attend the religious classes. This is beyond all question a utilization of the tax-established and tax-supported public school system to aid religious groups to spread their faith. And it falls squarely under the ban of the First Amendment (made applicable to the States by the Fourteenth) as we interpreted it in Everson v. Board of Education, 330 U.S. 1. There we said: "Neither a state nor the Federal Government can set up a church. Neither can pass laws which aid one religion, aid all religions, or prefer one religion over another. Neither can force or influence a person to go to or to remain away from church against his will or force him to profess a belief or disbelief in any religion. No person can be punished for entertaining or professing religious beliefs or disbeliefs, for church attendance or nonattendance. No tax in any amount, large or small, can be levied to support any religious activities or institutions, whatever they may be called, or whatever form they may adopt to teach or practice religion. Neither a state nor the Federal Government can, openly or secretly, participate in the affairs of any religious organizations or groups, and vice versa. In the words of Jefferson, the clause against establishment of religion by law was intended to erect 'a wall of separation between Church and State.'" Id., at pages 15, 16 of 330 U.S. . . .

To hold that a state cannot consistently with the First and Fourteenth Amendments utilize its public school system to aid any or all religious faiths or sects in the dissemination of their doctrines and ideals does not, as counsel urge, manifest a governmental hostility to religion or religious teachings. A manifestation of such hostility would be at war with our national tradition as embodied in the First Amendment's guaranty of the free exercise of religion. For the First Amendment rests upon the premise that both religion and government can best work to achieve their lofty aims if each is left free from the other within its respective sphere. Or, as we said in the Everson case, the First Amendment had erected a wall between Church and State which must be kept high and impregnable. . . .

Reversed and remanded.

MR. JUSTICE FRANKFURTER delivered the following opinion, in which MR. JUSTICE JACKSON, MR. JUSTICE RUTLEDGE and MR. JUSTICE BURTON join: . . . The modern public school derived from a philosophy of freedom reflected in the First Amendment. It is appropriate to recall that the Remonstrance of James Madison, an event basic in the history of religious liberty, was called forth by a proposal which involved support to religious education. See Mr. Justice Rutledge's opinion in the Everson case supra, 330 U.S. at pages 36, 37. As the momentum for popular education increased and in turn evoked strong claims for State support of religious education, contests not unlike that which in Virginia had produced Madison's Remonstrance appeared in various form in other States. New York and Massachusetts provide famous chapters in the history that established disassociation of religious teaching from State-maintained schools. In New York, the rise of the common schools led, despite fierce sectarian opposition, to the barring of tax founds to church schools, and later to any school in which sectarian doctrine was taught. In Massachusetts, largely through the efforts of Horace Mann, all sectarian teachings were barred from the common school to save it from being rent by denominational conflict. The upshot of these controversies, often long and fierce, is fairly summarized by saying that long before the Fourteenth Amendment subjected the States to new limitations, the prohibition of furtherance by the State of religious instruction became the guiding principle, in law and feeling, of the American people. In sustaining Stephen Girard's will, this Court referred to the inevitable conflicts engendered by matters ''connected with religious policy'' and particularly ''in a country composed of such a variety of religious sects as our country.'' Vidal et al. v. Girard's Executors, 2 How. 127, 198. That was more than one hundred years ago.

Separation in the field of education, then, was not imposed upon unwilling States by force of superior law. In this respect the Fourteenth Amendment merely reflected a principle then dominant in our national life. To the extent that the Constitution thus made it binding upon the States, the basis of the restriction is the whole experience of our people. Zealous watchfulness against fusion of secular and religious activities by Government itself, through any of its instruments but especially through its educational agencies, was the democratic response of the American community to the particular needs of a young and growing nation, unique in the composition of its people. A totally different situation elsewhere, as illustrated for instance by the English provisions for religious education in State-maintained schools, only serves to illustrate that free societies are not cast in one mold. See the Education Act of 1944, 7 and 8 Geo. VI, c. 31. Different institutions evolve from different historic circumstances.

It is pertinent to remind that the establishment of this principle of separation in the field of education was not due to any decline in the religious beliefs of the people. Horace Mann was a devout Christian, and the deep religious feeling of James Madison is stamped upon the Remonstrance. The secular public school did not imply indifference to the basic role of religion in the life of the people, nor rejection of religious education as a means of fostering it. The claims of religion were not minimized by refusing to make the public schools agencies for their assertion. The nonsectarian or secular public school was the means of reconciling freedom in general with religious freedom. The sharp confinement of the public schools to secular education was a recognition of the need of a democratic society to educate its children, insofar as the State undertook to do so, in an atmosphere free from pressures in a realm in which pressures are most resisted and where conflicts are most easily and most bitterly engendered. Designed to serve as perhaps the most powerful agency for promoting cohesion among a heterogeneous democratic people, the public school must keep scrupulously free from entanglement in the strife of sects. The preservation of the community from divisive conflicts, of Government from irreconcilable pressures by religious groups, of religion from censorship and coercion however subtly exercised, requires strict confinement of the State to instruction other than religious, leaving to the individual's church and home, indoctrination in the faith of his choice. . . .

Separation means separation, not something less. Jefferson's metaphor in describing the relation between Church and State speaks of a "wall of separation," not of a fine line easily overstepped. The public school is at once the symbol of our democracy and the most pervasive means for promoting our common destiny. In no activity of the State is it more vital to keep out divisive forces than in its schools, to avoid confusing, not to say fusing, what the Constitution sought to keep strictly apart. . . . It is the Court's duty to enforce this principle in its full integrity. We renew our conviction that "we have staked the very existence of our country on the faith that complete separation between the state and religion is best for the state and best for religion." Everson v. Board of Education, 330 U.S. at page 59. If nowhere else, in the relation between Church and State, "good fences make good neighbors."

MR. JUSTICE JACKSON, concurring: While we may and should end such formal and explicit instruction as the Champaign plan and can at all times prohibit teaching of creed and catechism and ceremonial and can forbid forthright proselyting in the schools, I think it remain to be demonstrated whether it is possible, even if desirable, to comply with such demands as plaintiff's completely to isolate and cast out of secular education all that some people may reasonably regard as religious instruction. Perhaps subjects such as mathematics, physics or chemistry are, or can be, completely secularized. But it would not seem practical to teach either practice or appreciation of the arts if we are to forbid exposure of youth to any religious influences. Music without sacred music, architecture minus the cathedral, or painting without the scriptural themes would be eccentric and incomplete, even from a secular point of view. Yet the inspirational appeal of religion in these guises is often stronger than in forthright sermons. Even such a "science" as biology raises the issue between evolution and creation as an explanation of our presence on this planet. Certainly a course in English literature that omitted the Bible and other powerful uses of our mother tongue for religious ends would be pretty barren. And I should suppose it is a proper, if not an indispensable, part of preparation for a worldly life to know the roles that religion and religions have played in the tragic story of mankind. The fact is that, for good or for ill, nearly everything in our culture worth transmitting, everything which gives meaning to life, is saturated with religious influences, derived from paganism, Judaism, Christianity—both Catholic and Protestant—and other faiths accepted by a large part of the world's peoples. One can hardly respect a system of education that would leave the student wholly ignorant of the currents of religious thought that move the world society for a part in which he is being prepared. . . .

The task of separating the secular from the religious in education is one of magnitude, intricacy and delicacy. To lay down a sweeping constitutional doctrine as demanded by complainant and apparently approved by the Court, applicable alike to all school boards of the nation, "to immediately adopt and enforce rules and regulations prohibiting all instruction in and teaching to religious education in all public schools," is to decree a uniform, rigid and, if we are consistent, an unchanging standard for countless school boards representing and serving highly localized groups which not only differ from each other but which themselves from time to time change attitudes. It seems to me that to do so is to allow zeal for our own ideas of what is good in public instruction to induce us to accept the role of a super board of education for every school district in the nation.

It is idle to pretend that this task is one for which we can find in the Constitution one word to help us as judges to decide where the secular ends and the sectarian begins in education. Nor can we find guidance in any other legal source. It is a matter on which we can find no law but our own prepossessions. If with no surer legal guidance we are to take up and decide every variation of this controversy, raised by persons not subject to penalty or tax but who are dissatisfied with the way schools are dealing with the problem, we are likely to have much business of the sort. And, more importantly, we are likely to make the legal "wall of separation between church and state" as winding as the famous serpentine wall designed by Mr. Jefferson for the University he founded.

MR. JUSTICE REED, dissenting: . . . Well-recognized and long-established practice support the validity of the Illinois statute here in question. That statute, as construed in this case, is comparable to those in many states. . . . Cases running into the scores have been in the state courts of last resort that involved religion and the schools. Except where the exercises with religious significance partook of the ceremonial practice of sects or groups, their constitutionality has been generally upheld. Illinois itself promptly struck down as violative of its own constitution required exercises partaking of a religious ceremony. People ex rel. Ring v. Board of Education, 245 Ill. 334. In that case compulsory religious exercises-a reading from the King James Bible, the Lord's Prayer and the singing of hymns-were forbidden as "worship services." In this case, the Supreme Court of Illinois pointed out that in the Ring case, the activities in the school were ceremonial and compulsory; in this, voluntary and educational. 396 Ill. 14, 20, 21 . . . .

With the general statements in the opinions concerning the constitutional requirement that the nation and the states, by virtue of the First and Fourteenth Amendments, may "make no law respecting an establishment of religion," I am in agreement. But . . . I cannot agree with the Court's conclusion that when pupils compelled by law to go to school for secular education are released from school so as to attend the religious classes, churches are unconstitutionally aided. Whatever may be the wisdom of the arrangement as to the use of the school buildings made with The Champaign Council of Religious Education, it is clear to me that past practice shows such cooperation between the schools and a non-ecclesiastical body is not forbidden by the First Amendment. . . . The prohibition of enactments respecting the establishment of religion do not bar every friendly gesture between church and state. It is not an absolute prohibition against every conceivable situation where the two may work together any more than the other provisions of the First Amendment— free speech, free press—are absolutes. If abuses occur such as the use of the instruction hour for sectarian purposes, I have no doubt, in view of the Ring case, that Illinois will promptly correct them. If they are of a kind that tend to the establishment of a church or interfere with the free exercise of religion, this Court is open for a review of any erroneous decision. This Court cannot be too cautious in upsetting practices embedded in our society by many years of experience. A state is entitled to have great leeway in its legislation when dealing with the important social problems of its population. A definite violation of legislative limits must be established. The Constitution should not be stretched to forbid national customs in the way courts act to reach arrangements to avoid federal taxation. Devotion to the great principle of religious liberty should not lead us into a rigid interpretation of the constitutional guarantee that conflicts with accepted habits of our people. This is an instance where, for me, the history of past practices is determinative of the meaning of a constitutional clause not a decorous introduction to the study of its text. The judgment should be affirmed.

NOTES AND QUESTIONS

1. In 1947, after debating for decades the merits of selectively or completely incorporating the individuals liberties protected from federal encroachment under the Bill of Rights into those protected from state action under the Due

Process Clause of the Fourteenth Amendment, the U.S. Supreme Court added the Establishment Clause to the list of incorporated rights in *Everson v. Board of Education*, 330 U.S. 1 (1947). A taxpayer named Arch Everson brought the case to protest a New Jersey law authorizing local school districts to reimburse parents for the cost of transporting their children to and from public or private schools, including parochial ones. After losing in state court, Everson appeal to the U.S. Supreme Court claiming that the practice indirectly aided religious schools in violation of the Establishment Clause. In a sweeping declaration quoted in *McCollum*, Justice Black wrote for the majority, "Neither a state nor the Federal Government can set up a church. Neither can pass laws which aid one religion, aid all religions, or prefer one religion over another." Id. at 15. Despite these words and their landmark importance in extending the Establishment Clause to the states, the majority found that state subsidies for bussing students to all schools—public, private, and parochial—did not violate it. Four justices dissented on the grounds that the decision did not go far enough. In an opinion joined by Justices Burton, Frankfurter, and Jackson, Justice Rutledge wrote, "Here parents pay money to send their children to parochial schools and funds raised by taxation are used to reimburse them. This not only helps the children to get to school and the parents to send them. It aids them in a substantial way to get the very thing which they are sent to the particular school to secure, namely, religious training and teaching." *Id.*, at 45 (Rutledge, J., dissenting). This ruling set the stage for *McCollum* a year later. Can you distinguish between the permissible indirect aid at issue in *Everson* and the impermissible direct aid at issue in *McCollum*? Both decisions remain valid. In crafting and reviewing subsequent governmental programs involving religion in education, legislators and judges have attempted to walk the fine line created by these two decisions.

2.   In *McCollum*, four dissenting justices from *Everson* joined Justice Black and three other justices from the *Everson* majority to overturn a local Illinois program providing religious instruction by private teachers in public schools. Similar programs had long existed in public schools throughout the country as an alternative to providing religious instruction by public-school teachers. By making the religious instruction optional and using private teachers not paid with public funds, school officials hoped to immunize it from legal or constitutional attack. This 1948 decision marked the first use of the Establishment Clause to bar a state or local statute or practice and sparked a nationwide uproar from people who believed that government should foster religion in an even-handed, non-discriminatory manner. In his dissenting opinion, Justice Reed spoke for many Americans when he wrote, "The prohibition of enactments respecting the establishment of religion do not bar every friendly gesture between church and state. It is not an absolute prohibition against every conceivable situation where the two may work together any more than the other provisions of the First Amendment—free speech, free press—are absolutes." He also stressed that the Court should not lightly overturn programs long accepted by the public in many states. How would you answer Justice Read's comments? The public debate over constitutional limits to religion in public education sparked by *McCollum* remains as lively today as it was in 1948.

3. In both *Everson* and *McCollum*, the majority cited the "wall of separation" metaphor from President Thomas Jefferson's 1802 letter to the Danbury Baptists. In that letter, Jefferson wrote:

> Believing with you that religion is a matter which lies solely between Man & his God, that he owes account to none other for his faith or his worship, that the legitimate powers of government reach actions only, & not opinions, I contemplate with sovereign reverence that act of the whole American people which declared that their legislature should "make no law respecting an establishment of religion, or prohibiting the free exercise thereof," thus building a wall of separation between Church & State.

Jefferson, however, did not participate in drafting either the Constitution or the First Amendment. Why should his words, written as President to a small group of interested individuals thirteen years after the Amendment's ratification, carry weight in its interpretation? Constitutional scholars have debated this question ever since Justice Black invoked Jefferson's metaphor to interpret the Establishment Clause.

4. In his concurring opinion, Justice Jackson observed that, in teaching many subjects, instructors cannot or should not exclude discussion of religious influences. Courses in art, music, or literature would be eccentric and incomplete without including religious themes, he noted, "yet the inspirational appeal of religion in these guises is often stronger than in forthright sermons," which *McCollum* clearly excluded from the classroom. In a sentence anticipating much of the future debate over teaching evolution and creation, he added, "Even such a 'science' as biology raises the issue between evolution and creation as an explanation of our presence on this planet." The justice goes on to predict that the difficulty in drawing a line between permissible and impermissible instruction will create a wall of separation "as winding as the famous serpentine wall designed by Mr. Jefferson for the University he founded." In explaining this line, commentators typically summarize the rule as being that public-schools students may receive instruction about religion but not religious instruction. When applied to individual close cases, however, does this rule neatly resolve them or simply reframe them?

II. ANTI–EVOLUTION LAWS AS RELIGIOUS INSTRUCTION

Following the Second World War, in which both allied and axis powers relied on scientists to develop new weapons culminating in America's development of the atomic bombs that sealed Japan's defeat, science assumed an increasingly prominent place in the American public education. During the 1950s, Cold War fears that the United States had fallen behind the Soviet Union in science led the Congress to pass the National Defense Education Act, which pumped money into science literacy programs and encouraged the National Science Foundation to finance the development of state-of-the-art science textbooks. Free from market considerations, a team of scientists and educators working under the auspices of the Biological Sciences Curriculum Study (BSCS) produced a series of new high-school biology texts that stressed evolutionary concepts. Commercial publishers rushed to keep pace. Despite scattered protests by conservative Christians, school districts throughout the country adopted the BSCS textbooks—even in the three southern states with anti-evolution laws. No prosecutions resulted, but the new books caused some teachers to question the old statutes. A few of these teachers took their questions to court by filing civil actions challenging the constitutionality of state laws against teaching evolution.

Two of these lawsuits played decisive roles in overturning the old anti-evolution statutes. One began in Arkansas shortly after the Little Rock public schools adopted new textbooks in 1965. That suit challenged the constitutionality of the Arkansas anti-evolution law, which state voters had adopted by popular referendum in the wake of the Scopes trial but which local prosecutors had never enforced. The state teachers' organization instituted this action, and a young biology instructor named Susan Epperson served as the nominal plaintiff. The Arkansas Attorney General personally argued the state's case at trial, vainly attempting to present the statute as reasonable by questioning the validity of the theory of human evolution. Rejecting this defense and limiting the issue to the freedom of teachers to instruct students about various theories of origins, early in 1966, the trial judge overturned the statute on federal constitutional grounds. In Tennessee a year later, Gary L. Scott threatened to challenge his state's anti-evolution law after losing his temporary teaching post for reportedly telling students that the Bible was "a bunch of fairy tales." His case generated headlines because it arose just as the Tennessee legislature wrestled with bills to repeal the law. Proponents of repeal compared Scott to Scopes as fellow victims of the statute. Indeed, the media referred to Scott's suit as "Scopes II," and John Scopes, who recently had reemerged from obscurity after publishing his memoirs, spoke out in support of both Epperson and Scott.

After passing the Tennessee House of Representative in April 1967, the repeal legislation fell one vote short of passage in the state Senate. Opponents of the law then used Scott's threatened lawsuit to pressure legislature to act. The national ACLU offered its assistance to Scott, as did noted defense attorney William M. Kunstler—a latter-day Clarence Darrow. Sixty Tennessee teachers and the National Science Teachers' Association joined as co-plaintiffs when Scott filed his challenge to the anti-evolution statute in federal court on May 15, 1967. "Nobody is asking any legislator to sacrifice any personal religious convictions by taking this law off the books," the state's leading newspaper commented in its lead editorial that day. "Repeal simply means ... that Tennessee would be saved the ordeal of another trial in which a proud state is required to make a monkey of itself in a court of law."[18] The Senate capitulated the next day. With network news cameras recording the action, it voted

---

18. *Anti–Evolution Law Brings Shame on State*, NASHVILLE TENNESSEAN, May 15, 1976, at 8.

without debate to repeal the 42–year old statute that had spawned the Scopes trial.

Two weeks later, the legal issue sprang to life anew when the Arkansas Supreme Court reversed the trial judge's ruling in the *Epperson* case. The court did not hear oral arguments in the case or issue a formal written opinion. It simply upheld the Scopes-era law. Over four decades after losing the Scopes case, the ACLU finally had a decision that it could appeal to the United States Supreme Court. Both the initial Arkansas Supreme Court and ensuing U.S. Supreme Court rulings follow:

STATE v. EPPERSON

Supreme Court of Arkansas
242 Ark. 922 (1967)

PER CURIAM: Upon the principal issue, that of constitutionality, the court holds that Initiated Measure No. 1 of 1928, Ark.Stat.Ann. § 80–1627 and § 80–1628 (Repl.1960), is a valid exercise of the state's power to specify the curriculum in its public schools. The court expresses no opinion on the question whether the Act prohibits any explanation of the theory of evolution or merely prohibits teaching that the theory is true; the answer not being necessary to a decision in the case, and the issue not having been raised.

BROWN, J., dissents.

WARD, J.: I agree with the first sentence in the majority opinion. To my mind, the rest of the opinion beclouds the clear announcement made in the first sentence.

EPPERSON v. ARKANSAS

Supreme Court of the United States
393 U.S. 97 (1968)

MR. JUSTICE FORTAS delivered the opinion of the Court:

I.

This appeal challenges the constitutionality of the 'anti-evolution' statute which the State of Arkansas adopted in 1928 to prohibit the teaching in its public schools and universities of the theory that man evolved from other species of life. The statute was a product of the upsurge of "fundamentalist" religious fervor of the twenties. The Arkansas statute was an adaption of the famous Tennessee "monkey law" which that State adopted in 1925. The constitutionality of the Tennessee law was upheld by the Tennessee Supreme Court in the celebrated Scopes case in 1927.

The Arkansas law makes it unlawful for a teacher in any state-supported school or university "to teach the theory or doctrine that mankind ascended or descended from a lower order of animals," or "to adopt or use in any such institution a textbook that teaches'' this theory. Violation is a misdemeanor and subjects the violator to dismissal from his position.

The present case concerns the teaching of biology in a high school in Little Rock. According to the testimony, until the events here in litigation, the official textbook furnished for the high school biology course did not have a section on the Darwinian Theory. Then, for the academic year 1965–1966, the school administration, on recommendation of the teachers of biology in the school system, adopted and prescribed a textbook which contained a chapter setting forth "the theory about the origin . . . of man from a lower form of animal."

Susan Epperson, a young woman who graduated from Arkansas' school system and then obtained her master's degree in zoology at the University of Illinois, was employed by the Little Rock school system in the fall of 1964 to teach 10th grade biology at Central High School. At the start of the next academic year, 1965, she was confronted by the new textbook (which one surmises from the record was not unwelcome to her). She faced at least a literal dilemma because she was supposed to use the new textbook for classroom instruction and presumably to teach the statutorily condemned chapter; but to do so would be a criminal offense and subject her to dismissal.

She instituted the present action in the Chancery Court of the State, seeking a declaration that the Arkansas statute is void and enjoining the State and the defendant officials of the Little Rock school system from dismissing her for violation of the statute's provisions. H. H. Blanchard, a parent of children attending the public schools, intervened in support of the action.

The Chancery Court, in an opinion by Chancellor Murray O. Reed, held that the statute violated the Fourteenth Amendment to the United States Constitution. The court noted that this Amendment encompasses the prohibitions upon state interference with freedom of speech and thought which are contained in the First Amendment. Accordingly, it held that the challenged statute is unconstitutional because, in violation of the First Amendment, it "tends to hinder the quest for knowledge, restrict the freedom to learn, and restrain the freedom to teach." In this perspective, the Act, it held, was an unconstitutional and void restraint upon the freedom of speech guaranteed by the Constitution.

On appeal, the Supreme Court of Arkansas reversed. . . . It sustained the statute as an exercise of the State's power to specify the curriculum in public schools. It did not address itself to the competing constitutional considerations.

Appeal was duly prosecuted to this Court under 28 U.S.C. s 1257(2). Only Arkansas and Mississippi have such "anti-evolution" or "monkey" laws on their books. There is no record of any prosecutions in Arkansas under its statute. It is possible that the statute is presently more of a curiosity than a vital fact of life in these States.[19] Nevertheless, the present case was brought, the appeal as of right is properly here, and it is our duty to decide the issues presented.

II.

At the outset, it is urged upon us that the challenged statute is vague and uncertain and therefore within the condemnation of the Due Process Clause of the Fourteenth Amendment. The contention that the Act is vague and uncertain is supported by language in the brief opinion of Arkansas' Supreme Court. That court, perhaps reflecting the discomfort which the statute's quixotic prohibition necessarily engenders in the modern mind,[20] stated that it "expressed no opinion" as to whether the Act prohibits "explanation" of the theory of evolution or merely forbids "teaching that the theory is true." Regardless of this uncertainty, the court held that the statute is constitutional.

On the other hand, counsel for the State, in oral argument in this Court, candidly stated that, despite the State Supreme Court's equivocation, Arkansas would interpret the statute "to mean that to make a student aware of the theory . . . just to teach that there was such a theory" would be grounds for dismissal and for prosecution under the statute; and he said "that the Supreme Court of Arkansas' opinion should be interpreted in that manner." He said: "If Mrs. Epperson would tell her students that 'Here is Darwin's theory, that man ascended or descended from a lower form of being,' then I think she would be under this statute liable for prosecution."

In any event, we do not rest our decision upon the asserted vagueness of the statute. On either interpretation of its language, Arkansas' statute cannot stand. It is of no moment whether the law is deemed to prohibit mention of Darwin's theory, or to forbid any or all of the infinite varieties of communication embraced within the term "teaching." Under either interpretation, the law must be stricken because of its conflict with the constitutional prohibition of state laws respecting an establishment of religion or prohibiting the free exercise thereof. The overriding fact is that Arkansas' law selects from the body of knowledge a particular segment which it proscribes for the sole reason that it is deemed to conflict with a particular religious doctrine; that is, with a particular interpretation of the Book of Genesis by a particular religious group.

---

19. Clarence Darrow, who was counsel for the defense in the Scopes trial, in his biography published in 1932, somewhat sardonically pointed out that States with anti-evolution laws did not insist upon the fundamentalist theory in all respects. He said: "I understand that the States of Tennessee and Mississippi both continue to teach that the earth is round and that the revolution on its axis brings the day and night, in spite of all opposition." The Story of My Life 247 (1932).

20. R. Hofstadter & W. Metzger, in The Development of Academic Freedom in the United States 324 (1955), refer to some of Darwin's opponents as "exhibiting a kind of phylogenetic snobbery (which led them) to think that Darwin had libeled the (human) race by discovering simian rather than seraphic ancestors."

III.

The antecedents of today's decision are many and unmistakable. They are rooted in the foundation soil of our Nation. They are fundamental to freedom.

Government in our democracy, state and national, must be neutral in matters of religious theory, doctrine, and practice. It may not be hostile to any religion or to the advocacy of noreligion; and it may not aid, foster, or promote one religion or religious theory against another or even against the militant opposite. The First Amendment mandates governmental neutrality between religion and religion, and between religion and nonreligion.

As early as 1872, this Court said: "The law knows no heresy, and is committed to the support of no dogma, the establishment of no sect." Watson v. Jones, 13 Wall. 679, 728. This has been the interpretation of the great First Amendment which this Court has applied in the many and subtle problems which the ferment of our national life has presented for decision within the Amendment's broad command.

Judicial interposition in the operation of the public school system of the Nation raises problems requiring care and restraint. Our courts, however, have not failed to apply the First Amendment's mandate in our educational system where essential to safeguard the fundamental values of freedom of speech and inquiry and of belief. By and large, public education in our Nation is committed to the control of state and local authorities. Courts do not and cannot intervene in the resolution of conflicts which arise in the daily operation of school systems and which do not directly and sharply implicate basic constitutional values. On the other hand, "(t)he vigilant protection of constitutional freedoms is nowhere more vital than in the community of American schools," Shelton v. Tucker, 364 U.S. 479, 487 (1960). As this Court said in Keyishian v. Board of Regents, the First Amendment 'does not tolerate laws that cast a pall of orthodoxy over the classroom.' 385 U.S. 589, 603 (1967).

The earliest cases in this Court on the subject of the impact of constitutional guarantees upon the classroom were decided before the Court expressly applied the specific prohibitions of the First Amendment to the States. But as early as 1923, the Court did not hesitate to condemn under the Due Process Clause "arbitrary" restrictions upon the freedom of teachers to teach and of students to learn. In that year, the Court, in an opinion by Justice McReynolds, held unconstitutional an Act of the State of Nebraska making it a crime to teach any subject in any language other than English to pupils who had not passed the eighth grade. The State's purpose in enacting the law was to promote civic cohesiveness by encouraging the learning of English and to combat the "baneful effect" of permitting foreigners to near and educate their children in the language of the parents' native land. The Court recognized these purposes, and it acknowledged the State's power to prescribe the school curriculum, but it held that these were not adequate to support the restriction upon the liberty of teacher and pupil. The challenged statute it held, unconstitutionally interfered with the right of the individual, guaranteed by the Due Process Clause, to engage in any of the common occupations of life and to acquire useful knowledge. Meyer v. Nebraska, 262 U.S. 390 (1923). See also Bartels v. Iowa, 262 U.S. 404 (1923).

For purposes of the present case, we need not re-enter the difficult terrain which the Court, in 1923, traversed without apparent misgivings. We need not take advantage of the broad premise which the Court's decision in Meyer furnishes, nor need we explore the implications of that decision in terms of the justiciability of the multitude of controversies that beset our campuses today. Today's problem is capable of resolution in the narrower terms of the First Amendment's prohibition of laws respecting an establishment of religion or prohibiting the free exercise thereof.

There is and can be no doubt that the First Amendment does not permit the State to require that teaching and learning must be tailored to the principles or prohibitions of any religious sect or dogma. In Everson v. Board of Education, this Court, in upholding a state law to provide free bus service to school children, including those attending parochial schools, said: "Neither (a State nor the Federal Government) can pass laws which aid one religion, aid all religions, or prefer one religion over another." 330 U.S. 1, 15 (1947).

At the following Term of Court, in People of State of Ill. ex rel. McCollum v. Board of Education, 333 U.S. 203 (1948), the Court held that Illinois could not release pupils from class to attend classes of instruction in the school buildings in the religion of their choice. This, it said, would involve the State in using tax-supported property for religious purposes, thereby breaching the "wall of separation" which, according to Jefferson, the First Amendment was intended to erect between church and state. Id., at 211. See also Engel v. Vitale, 370 U.S. 421, 428 (1962); Abington School District v. Schempp, 374 U.S. 203 (1963). While study of religions and of the Bible from a literary and historic viewpoint, presented objectively as part of a secular program of education, need not collide with the First Amendment's prohibition, the State may not adopt programs or practices in its public schools or colleges which 'aid or oppose' any religion. Id., at 225. This prohibition is absolute. It forbids alike the preference of a religious doctrine or the prohibition of theory which is deemed antagonistic to a particular dogma. As Mr. Justice Clark stated in Joseph Burstyn, Inc. v. Wilson, "the state has no legitimate interest in protecting any or all religions from views distasteful to them...." 343 U.S. 495, 505 (1952). The test was stated as follows in Abington School District v. Schempp, supra, 374 U.S. at 222: "(W)hat are the purpose and the primary effect of the enactment? If either is the advancement or inhibition of religion then the enactment exceeds the scope of legislative power as circumscribed by the Constitution."

These precedents inevitably determine the result in the present case. The State's undoubted right to prescribe the curriculum for its public schools does not carry with it the right to prohibit, on pain of criminal penalty, the teaching of a scientific theory or doctrine where that prohibition is based upon reasons that violate the First Amendment. It is much too late to argue that the State may impose upon the teachers in its schools any conditions that it chooses, however restrictive they may be of constitutional guarantees. Keyishian v. Board of Regents, 385 U.S. 589, 605–606 (1967).

In the present case, there can be no doubt that Arkansas has sought to prevent its teachers from discussing the theory of evolution because it is contrary to the belief of some that the Book of Genesis must be the exclusive source of doctrine as to the origin of man. No suggestion has been made that Arkansas' law may be justified by considerations of state policy other than the religious views of some of its citizens. It is clear that fundamentalist sectarian conviction was and is the law's reason for existence.[21] Its antecedent, Tennessee's "monkey law," candidly stated its purpose: to make it unlawful "to teach any theory that denies the story of the Divine Creation of man as taught in the Bible, and to teach instead that man has descended from a lower order of animals." Perhaps the sensational publicity attendant upon the Scopes trial induced Arkansas to adopt less explicit language. It eliminated Tennessee's reference to "the story of the Divine Creation of man" as taught in the Bible, but there is no doubt that the motivation for the law was the same: to suppress the teaching of a theory which, it was thought, "denied" the divine creation of man.

Arkansas' law cannot be defended as an act of religious neutrality. Arkansas did not seek to excise from the curricula of its schools and universities all discussion of the origin of man. The law's effort was confined to an attempt to blot out a particular theory because of its supposed conflict with the Biblical account, literally read. Plainly, the law is contrary to the mandate of the First, and in violation of the Fourteenth, Amendment to the Constitution.

The judgment of the Supreme Court of Arkansas is reversed.

Mr. Justice Black concurring: It is plain that a state law prohibiting all teaching of human development or biology is constitutionally quite different from a law that compels a teacher to teach as true only one theory of a

---

21. The following advertisement is typical of the public appeal which was used in the campaign to secure adoption of the statute: "THE BIBLE OR ATHEISM, WHICH? All atheists favor evolution. If you agree with atheism vote against Act No. 1. If you agree with the Bible vote for Act No. 1 . . . . Shall conscientious church members be forced to pay taxes to support teachers to teach evolution which will undermine the faith of their children? The Gazette said Russian Bolshevists laughed at Tennessee. True, and that sort will laugh at Arkansas. Who cares? Vote FOR ACT NO. 1." The Arkansas Gazette, Little Rock, Nov. 4, 1928, p. 12, cols. 4–5. Letters from the public expressed the fear that teaching of evolution would be "subversive of Christianity," id., Oct. 24, 1928, p. 7, col. 2; see also id., Nov. 4, 1928, p. 19, col. 4; and that it would cause school children "to disrespect the Bible," id., Oct. 27, 1928, p. 15, col. 5. One letter read: "The cosmogony taught by (evolution) runs contrary to that of Moses and Jesus, and as such is nothing, if anything at all, but atheism. . . . Now let the mothers and fathers of our state that are trying to raise their children in the Christian faith arise in their might and vote for this anti-evolution bill that will take it out of our tax supported schools. When they have saved the children, they have saved the state." Id., at cols. 4–5.

given doctrine. It would be difficult to make a First Amendment case out of a state law eliminating the subject of higher mathematics, or astronomy, or biology from its curriculum. And, for all the Supreme Court of Arkansas has said, this particular Act may prohibit that and nothing else. This Court, however, treats the Arkansas Act as though it made it a misdemeanor to teach or to use a book that teaches that evolution is true. But it is not for this Court to arrogate to itself the power to determine the scope of Arkansas statutes. Since the highest court of Arkansas has deliberately refused to give its statute that meaning, we should not presume to do so.

It seems to me that in this situation the statute is too vague for us to strike it down on any ground but that: vagueness. Under this statute as construed by the Arkansas Supreme Court, a teacher cannot know whether he is forbidden to mention Darwin's theory, at all or only free to discuss it as long as he refrains from contending that it is true. It is an established rule that a statute which leaves an ordinary man so doubtful about its meaning that he cannot know when he has violated it denies him the first essential of due process. See, e.g., Connally v. General Construction Co., 269 U.S. 385, 391 (1926). Holding the statute too vague to enforce would not only follow long-standing constitutional precedents but it would avoid having this Court take unto itself the duty of a State's highest court to interpret and mark the boundaries of the State's laws. And, more important, it would not place this Court in the unenviable position of violating the principle of leaving the States absolutely free to choose their own curriculums for their own schools so long as their action does not palpably conflict with a clear constitutional command.

The Court, not content to strike down this Arkansas Act on the unchallengeable ground of its plain vagueness, chooses rather to invalidate it as a violation of the Establishment of Religion Clause of the First Amendment. I would not decide this case on such a sweeping ground for the following reasons, among others.

1. In the first place I find it difficult to agree with the Court's statement that "there can be no doubt that Arkansas has sought to prevent its teachers from discussing the theory of evolution because it is contrary to the belief of some that the Book of Genesis must be the exclusive source of doctrine as to the origin of man." It may be instead that the people's motive was merely that it would be best to remove this controversial subject from its schools; there is no reason I can imagine why a State is without power to withdraw from its curriculum any subject deemed too emotional and controversial for its public schools. And this Court has consistently held that it is not for us to invalidate a statute because of our views that the "motives" behind its passage were improper; it is simply too difficult to determine what those motives were. See, e.g., United States v. O'Brien, 391 U.S. 367, 382–383 (1968).

2. A second question that arises for me is whether this Court's decision forbidding a State to exclude the subject of evolution from its

schools infringes the religious freedom of those who consider evolution an anti-religious doctrine. If the theory is considered anti-religious, as the Court indicates, how can the State be bound by the Federal Constitution to permit its teachers to advocate such an "anti-religious" doctrine to schoolchildren? The very cases cited by the Court as supporting its conclusion that the State must be neutral, not favoring one religious or anti-religious view over another. The Darwinian theory is said to challenge the Bible's story of creation; so too have some of those who believe in the Bible, along with many others, challenged the Darwinian theory. Since there is no indication that the literal Biblical doctrine of the origin of man is included in the curriculum of Arkansas schools, does not the removal of the subject of evolution leave the State in a neutral position toward these supposedly competing religious and anti-religious doctrines? Unless this Court is prepared simply to write off as pure nonsense the views of those who consider evolution an anti-religious doctrine, then this issue presents problems under the Establishment Clause far more troublesome than are discussed in the Court's opinion.

3. I am also not ready to hold that a person hired to teach school children takes with him into the classroom a constitutional right to teach sociological, economic, political, or religious subjects that the school's managers do not want discussed. This Court has said that the rights of free speech "while fundamental in our democratic society, still do not mean that everyone with opinions or beliefs to express may address a group at any public place and at any time." Cox v. State of Louisiana, 379 U.S. 536, 554; Cox v. State of Louisiana, 379 U.S. 559, 574. I question whether it is absolutely certain, as the Court's opinion indicates, that "academic freedom" permits a teacher to breach his contractual agreement to teach only the subjects designated by the school authorities who hired him.

Certainly the Darwinian theory, precisely like the Genesis story of the creation of man, is not above challenge. In fact the Darwinian theory has not merely been criticized by religionists but by scientists, and perhaps no scientist would be willing to take an oath and swear that everything announced in the Darwinian theory is unquestionably true. The Court, it seems to me, makes a serious mistake in bypassing the plain, unconstitutional vagueness of this statute in order to reach out and decide this troublesome, to me, First Amendment question. However wise this Court may be or may become hereafter, it is doubtful that, sitting in Washington, it can successfully supervise and censor the curriculum of every public school in every hamlet and city in the United States. I doubt that our wisdom is so nearly infallible.

I would either strike down the Arkansas Act as too vague to enforce, or remand to the State Supreme Court for clarification of its holding and opinion.

MR. JUSTICE HARLAN, concurring: ... I concur in so much of the Court's opinion as holds that the Arkansas statute constitutes an "establishment of religion" forbidden to the States by the Fourteenth Amendment. I do not understand, however, why the Court finds it necessary to explore at length appellants' contentions that the statute is unconstitutionally vague and that it interferes with free speech, only to conclude that these issues need not be decided in this case. In the process of not deciding them, the Court obscures its otherwise straightforward holding, and opens its opinion to possible implications from which I am constrained to disassociate myself.

MR. JUSTICE STEWART, concurring in the result: The States are most assuredly free "to choose their own curriculums for their own schools." A State is entirely free, for example, to decide that the only foreign language to be taught in its public school system shall be Spanish. But would a State be constitutionally free to punish a teacher for letting his students know that other languages are also spoken in the world? I think not.

It is one thing for a State to determine that "the subject of higher mathematics, or astronomy, or biology" shall or shall not be included in its public school curriculum. It is quite another thing for a State to make it a criminal offense for a public school teacher so much as to mention the very existence of an entire system of respected human thought. That kind of criminal law, I think, would clearly impinge upon the guarantees of free communication contained in the First Amendment, and made applicable to the States by the Fourteenth.

The Arkansas Supreme Court has said that the statute before us may or may not be just such a law. The result, as Mr. Justice BLACK points out, is that "a teacher cannot know whether he is forbidden to mention Darwin's theory at all." Since I believe that no State could constitutionally forbid a teacher 'to mention Darwin's theory at all,' and since Arkansas may, or may not, have done just that, I conclude that the statute before us is so vague as to be invalid under the Fourteenth Amendment. See Cramp v. Board of Pub. Instruction, 368 U.S. 278.

NOTES AND QUESTIONS

1. In the unsigned Arkansas Supreme Court decision in *Epperson*, the justices assert, "The court expresses no opinion on the question of whether the Act prohibits any explanation of the theory of evolution or merely prohibits teaching that the theory is true." How is the former construction of the statute possible given the language of the statute, which declares it unlawful for any public school teacher "to teach the theory or Doctrine that mankind ascended or descended from a lower order of animals?" Why would the court raise this issue simply then to say that the answer is not necessary to the decision? It was suggested at the time that at least one justice insisted that he could only uphold the statute on the grounds that it allowed teaching about Darwinism as a scientific theory.

2. *Epperson* stands out as one of the few U.S. Supreme Court decisions to strike down a statute under the Establishment Clause solely for having a religious purpose. At the time, the court was moving toward a tri-part test for

Establishment Clause violations. As the Court subsequently explained, "First, the statute must have a secular legislative purpose; second, its principal or primary effect must be one that neither advances nor inhibits religion; finally, the statute must not foster an excessive government entanglement with religion." *Lemon v. Kurtzman*, 403 U.S. 602, 613–14 (1971). A challenged statute must satisfy all three prongs of the test. The second and third prongs typically proved the most problematic because having *any* secular purpose, even a secondary one, satisfied the first prong. The *Epperson* court found that Arkansas voters passed their anti-evolution initiative solely for religious reasons. In support of its finding, the Court cites several pro-initiative advertisements or letters to the editor and the language of Tennessee's anti-evolution statute. Justice Black, who was serving as an elected Alabama senator when voters in nearby Arkansas passed the antievolution law and understood southern politics, rejected this finding. He observed in his concurring opinion, "It may be instead that the people's motive was merely that it would be best to remove this controversial subject from its schools." Do you agree with the majority or with Justice Black? Even if Justice Black is correct, should it still violate the test's purpose prong to remove a subject because it is controversial if the sole source of the controversy is religious? It is interesting to note that, despite finding that the Arkansas anti-evolution statute was enacted solely for religious reasons, the Court did not find that its principal or primary effect was to advance religion. It may be because, as the Court noted, "There is no record of any prosecutions in Arkansas under its statute." From this observation, the Court may have reasoned that the statute never had any effect.

3.   In his concurring opinion, Justice Black also raised the argument that, if most Arkansas voters believe teaching Darwinism inhibits religion, then it might violate the Establishment Clause to teach it. Is this a valid argument? Similar reasoning frequently appears in anti-evolutionist literature. It was implicit in William Jennings Bryan's plea that public schools should remain neutral on the religiously sensitive question of origins by not teaching ether evolution or creation. In contrast, the majority opinion in *Epperson* stressed that the Arkansas anti-evolution statute cannot be defended on neutrality grounds because it *only* removed evolution, not creation, from the curricula. Would it be constitutional for a state to remove all discussion of human origins from public-school biology classes? Surveys of actual teaching practices find that many teachers and schools districts follow this approach. Justice Black noted in his concurring opinion that state and local school officials (rather than teachers) should have ultimate authority in determining what subjects are taught in public schools. In his concurrence, Justice Potter Stewart counters that it would violate the First Amendment's Free Speech Clause for a state to bar public-school teachers from mentioning the existence of an entire system of respected human thought, such as Darwinism.

III.   *EPPERSON'S* IMMEDIATE IMPACT

Repeal of the Tennessee anti-evolution statute in 1967 followed by the *Epperson* decision overturning the Arkansas statute in 1968 left only the Mississippi anti-evolution statute still standing. The legal drive against it began late in 1969, when Mrs. Arthur G. Smith of Jackson filed suit in state court complaining that the law both improperly denied her school-age daughter's freedom to learn and violated the Establishment Clause of the federal Constitution. Smith's suit was hampered by the lack of state declaratory judgment procedures, forcing her to seek an injunction against enforcement rather than a declaration of unconstitutionality. The state moved before trial for a dismissal, claiming that the absence of any actual or threatened enforcement precluded an injunction. By as much as admitting that no one enforced the statute, the state conceded the substance of the law to save the form. Further, by interpreting the Mississippi anti-evolution statute to bar only teaching Darwinism as fact, the state claimed that its law differed from the voided Arkansas statute, even though the two measures contained nearly identical language. With the state's pre-trial motion pending in state court, a declaratory judgment suit against the Mississippi law was filed in federal district court but the federal judge deferred action until the state courts reached a final decision.

The state's dismissal motion remained undecided when the legislature turned its attention to the issue. Soon after the 1970 Mississippi House of Representatives convened, a Jackson legislator introduced the first anti-evolution repealer offered in Mississippi since the 1920s. Guided by a friendly Judiciary Committee Chair, the measure raced through committee and appeared before the full House on January 21st. The committee chair opened the floor debate by describing the old statute as "a restriction on man's mind, thoughts, and beliefs which the state should not abrogate to itself." But his call for repeal met entrenched resistance. Denouncing Darwin as an atheist who "wanted to give you a reason why we were here," a rural lawmaker sounded Bryan's cry for educational neutrality. "Since it is against the law to teach religion, it should be against the law to teach atheism." Another opponent of repeal added in a plea going beyond neutrality to religious establishment, "Let's hold the line as a Christian state. This is another attempt to chip away at religion."[22]

At least in the Mississippi legislature, little had apparently changed since 1926. The 42 to 70 vote against the repealer nearly mirrored the 1926 vote for the statute. Yet by 1969, the Mississippi legislature, much like the Tennessee legislature two years earlier, acted in the shadow of the federal courts. In Tennessee, this shadow spurred Senate action. But the Mississippi legislature was fed up with the federal courts. Even as the House debated repeal, the Jackson public schools were closed pending court-ordered racial desegregation. Similar federal-court decrees wrenched public education systems throughout the state, leading the 1970 state legislature to enact several constitutionally suspicious laws supporting white-only private schools. Reflecting this mood, one legislator stubbornly declared during the anti-evolution debate, "If this law is to be repealed, let it be done by a federal judge—not by this legislature." So the issue

---

22. Charles M. Hills, Jr., *Ban Against Teaching Evolution Upheld*, JACKSON CLARION-LEDGER, Jan. 22, 1970, at 1 (quotes).

remained in the courts. Two weeks later, the state trial court hearing Smith's challenge displayed similar defiance to federal constitutional law by granting the pre-trial motion to dismiss the case. The issue then rose to the Mississippi Supreme Court on appeal, leading to the following opinion:

SMITH v. STATE

Supreme Court of Mississippi
242 So.2d 692 (Miss. 1970)

INZER, JUSTICE: . . . Mrs. Arthur G. Smith, individually and as next friend of her minor daughter, Frances Owen Smith, brought suit in the Chancery Court of the First Judicial District of Hinds County seeking an injunction to enjoin the State of Mississippi and the State Board of Education from enforcing Sections 6798 and 6799. The trial court sustained a general demurrer to amended bill of complaint and entered a decree dismissing the bill of complaint. Hence this appeal.

The bill of complaint as amended alleged that [1] Frances Owen Smith is now and has been enrolled in the public schools of this state and [2] because of the enactment by the legislature of Sections 6798 and 6799, the meaning of which is to absolutely prohibit the teaching of any theory or doctrine of descent or ascent of man from a lower order of animals, that she and other children in the public school systems of this state are being deprived of the full, proper and scientific education because numerous teachers, who have been charged with scientific education of the minor have refused and failed to teach the portions of scientific curricula devoted to the theory that man and other species of animals have evolved from simpler animal forms. The bill of complaint also alleged that this refusal or failure has been fostered by the prohibition and penalties of these statutes. That Frances Owen Smith seeks to obtain a higher education with particular reference to scientific studies and because of these statutes she has been and is now being deprived of the opportunity to gain a basic educational foundation from which she can receive the necessary technical, scientific training required to engage in the profession or business which depends upon scientific knowledge of anthropology and related subjects. It is also charged that she is being further damaged because of these statutes for the reason that she cannot compete with other high school students from other parts of the United States for admission to colleges and universities requiring admission examinations containing scientific questions.

The bill of complaint further charged that the statutes violate the prohibition of the First Amendment of the Constitution of the United States prohibiting laws with respect to the establishment of religion or prohibiting the free exercise thereof. It is alleged that the purpose and intent of these statutes is to establish a religious doctrine in the school systems of the State of Mississippi by prohibiting the teaching as a theory or fact any scientific hypothesis believed to be contrary to the literal interpretation of the Book of Genesis and the Judeo–Christian religious doctrine. In support of this allegation there is attached as exhibits to the amended bill of complaint numerous newspaper reports as to what transpired in the legislature at the time the legislature was considering the passage of these laws....

The ... question to be decided is whether the statutes in question are in violation of the First Amendment of the Constitution of the United States made applicable to the states through the Fourteenth Amendment. In determining this question we are constrained to follow the decisions of the Supreme Court of the United States wherein that Court has construed similar statutes involving the First Amendment to the Constitution of the United States. In the recent case of Epperson v. Arkansas, 393 U.S. 97 (1968), the Supreme Court of the United States held that the Arkansas statutes forbidding the teaching of evolution in public schools and colleges and universities supported in whole or part by public funds were contrary to the freedom of religion mandate of the First Amendment and in violation of the Fourteenth Amendment.... The Court after citing and discussing several antecedent cases in support of its conclusion said:

> While study of religions and of the Bible from a literary and historic viewpoint, presented objectively as part of a secular program of education, need not collide with the First Amendment's prohibition, the State may not adopt programs or practices in its public schools or colleges which "aid or oppose" any religion. Id., at 225. This prohibition is absolute. It forbids alike the preference of a religious doctrine or the prohibition of theory which is deemed antagonistic to a particular dogma. As Mr. Justice Clark stated in Joseph Burstyn, Inc. v. Wilson, "the state has no legitimate interest in protecting any or all religions from views distasteful to them...." 343 U.S. 495, 505 (1952). The test was stated as follows in Abington School District v. Schempp, 374 U.S. at 222: "(W)hat are the purpose and the primary effect of the enactment? If either is the advancement or inhibition of religion then the enactment exceeds the scope of legislative power as circumscribed by the Constitution."

These precedents inevitably determine the result in the present case. The State's undoubted right to prescribe the curriculum for its public schools does not carry with it the right to prohibit, on pain of criminal penalty, the teaching of a scientific theory of doctrine where that prohibition is based upon reasons that violate the First Amendment. It is much too late to argue that the State may impose upon the teachers in its schools any conditions that it chooses, however, restrictive they may be of constitutional guarantees. Keyishian v. Board of Regents, 385 U.S. 589, 605–606 (1967).

Apparently the court had no difficulty in determining that the purpose of the Arkansas statute was to prevent its teachers from teaching the theory of evolution because it is contrary to the belief of some that the Book of Genesis must be the exclusive source of the doctrine as to the origin of man. The court said:

Its antecedent, Tennessee's "monkey law," candidly stated its purpose: to make it unlawful "to teach any theory that denies the store of the Divine Creation of man as taught in the Bible, and to teach instead that man has descended from a lower order of animals." Perhaps the sensational publicity attendant upon the Scopes (Scopes v. State, 154 Tenn. 105) trial induced Arkansas to adopt less explicit language. It eliminated Tennessee's reference to "the story of the Divine Creation of man" as taught in the Bible, but there is no doubt that the motivation for the law was the same: to suppress the teaching of a theory which, it was thought, "denied" the divine creation of man. (393 U.S. at 109).

There can be little doubt, if any, that the court would make the same finding relative to our statute.

In spite of what the Supreme Court said in Epperson, supra, appellees argue that we should uphold the challenged statutes because of the difference in the language in our statute and the Arkansas statute. The only difference insofar as the teaching of evolution is concerned, is that our statute makes the violation to teach that mankind ascended or descended from a lower form of animal. While the Arkansas law made it a violation to teach "the theory or doctrine: that mankind ascended or descended from a lower form of animals." We are unable to see any material difference in the meaning of the two statutes. We are also unable to agree with the learned chancellor that our statute makes it a violation to teach evolution as a fact, and that our statute can be construed to mean that it is permissible to teach it as a theory. However, it is immaterial under the holding of the Supreme Court of the United States whether it can be so construed.

Finally appellees argue that our statute should be upheld because our state laws are such as to make us neutral between religion and religion and between religion and non-religion as required by the First Amendment. It is contended that Section 6216–11, Mississippi Code 1942 Annotated (Supp.1968), which states:

> Doctrinal sectarian or denominational teaching forbidden.—No doctrinal, sectarian or denominated teaching shall be permitted in public schools of this state. It shall be the duty of the county superintendents of education and the superintendents of municipal separate school districts to enforce the provisions of this section.

in effect prohibits the indoctrination of the students that mankind was spontaneously created by God. Appellees say, "Thus, we have complete neutrality. The students may not be indoctrinated either with the idea that mankind evolved from a lower species of animal, nor may they be indoctrinated by the idea that man was created by the spontaneous act of God." It is difficult to believe that appellees are serious in this contention. Whatever Section 6216–11 does mean, it certainly does not mean that the teaching that mankind was spontaneously created by God is prohibited by this statute. We do not have, and should not have, any statute which would prohibit the teaching of the Bible in our public schools. In fact, our Constitution prohibits the enactment of a law prohibiting the use of the Bible in the public schools of this State. Article 3, Section 18, Mississippi Constitution (1890). The use of the Bible in our schools must, of course, be a proper use.

The decisions of the Supreme Court of the United States which interpret the Constitution of the United States are binding upon us and we have no choice other than to follow such decisions. It is clear to us from what was said in Epperson, supra, that the Supreme Court of the United States has for all practical purposes already held that our anti-evolution statutes are unconstitutional. Therefore, we are constrained to hold that Sections 6798 and 6799 are unconstitutional, thus void and of no effect . . .

NOTES AND QUESTIONS

1. In *Scopes*, the Tennessee Supreme Court declined to judge the constitutionality of its state anti-evolution statute based on legislative purpose. Only effect mattered. After *Epperson*, however, the Mississippi Supreme Court in *Smith* invalidated its state anti-evolution statute based on a finding that the legislative acted with a wrongful religious purpose. According to the court, what was that wrongful motive? The opinion was silent about the law's effect and cryptic about its purpose.

2. The *Smith* court, like the *Epperson* Court, expressly rejected the argument that anti-evolution laws could be a constitutional means to promote classroom neutrality on the religiously-charged topic of human origins. The two courts used different reasoning, however. Except perhaps for Hugo Black, the U.S. Supreme Court justices deciding *Epperson* apparently assumed that religious creationism was not (or at least constitutionally should not be) being taught in public school biology classes but nevertheless ruled that deleting topic of human evolution from the curriculum for religious reasons would still violated the Establishment Clause. When it came to what Justice Stewart depicted as "an entire system of respected human thought," neutrality through avoidance simply was not a constitutional option. In contrast, the Mississippi Supreme Court justices deciding *Smith* seemed to assume that religious creationism was being taught in public schools and that therefore deleting Darwinism would not achieve neutrality. "We do not have, and should not have, any statute which would prohibit the use of the Bible in public schools in this State," the court declared. Do these two opinions reflect different regional perspectives on what was happening in public schools during the 1960s? Various studies show that in some regions, such as the South and rural Midwest, public schools continued to offer religious instruction and school prayer long after the U.S. Supreme Court ruled those once-widespread practices unconstitutional.

3. If you were an Arkansas or Mississippi creationist, how would you respond to a court order striking down your state's anti-evolution statutes? As suggested by the opinion in *Smith*, it led some creationists in those states and elsewhere to increase their demands both for also teaching creationism and

for including evidence and arguments against evolution in biology classes. In this sense, *Epperson* and *Smith* did not end the legal controversy over creation and evolution; they simply altered it.

CHAPTER 3

EXPERIMENTING WITH ACCOMMODATION

∎ ∎ ∎

I. RAISING THE RIGHTS OF CREATIONIST STUDENTS

One month before the *Smith* court issued its decision striking down the last of the old anti-evolution statutes, a Houston mother filed suit on behalf of her school-age daughter, Rita Wright, to enjoin the local public schools from teaching evolution. Wright alleged that teaching Darwinism unconstitutionally inhibited the free exercise of her creationist religion while establishing a religion of secularism. These charges touched a raw nerve during the early 1970s, as the case wound its way through the courts. The suit also represented a new tactic for creationists. After years of being on the defensive in court, *Wright* marked the first time creationists instituted a judicial action. Following a decade of legal triumph for evolutionary teaching, creationists began fighting back in court.

Even though the 1977 American Humanist Association statement signed by scores of leading scientists, educators, and liberal religious leaders claimed that evolution is accepted into humanity's general body of knowledge by scientists and other reasonable persons who have familiarized themselves with the evidence, public opinion surveys during the period consistently found at least as many Americans believed in divine creation as in any form of evolution. Most of these surveys were amateur local polls conducted by creationists to boost their cause, but a 1979 survey by the respected Gallup polling organization confirmed these results by finding that nearly half of the adults in the U.S. believed the biblical account that God created Adam and Eve to start the human race.

After obtaining similar results three years later, pollster George Gallup announced, "Debate over the origins of man is as alive today as it was at the time of the famous Scopes trial in 1925, with the public now about evenly divided between those who believe in the biblical account of creation and those who believe either in a strict interpretation of evolution or in an evolutionary process involving God." Looking only at the responses from the South, where creationists scored their greatest political victories during the period, the Gallup survey suggested that about half accepted Biblical creationism, one third believed in theistic evolution, and only about one in twenty adults accepted materialistic evolution.[23] Such widespread faith in special creation certainly could discourage teaching the opposite theory without qualification in public schools.

The *Wright* case, which languished in Houston federal courts from 1970 to 1972 while the lead plaintiff unsuccessfully struggled to retain an attorney, showed the limits on relief available to creationists through the judicial process. The case began when Wright, joined by fellow-minded students, challenged the constitutionality of teaching the theory of evolution as a fact in public schools without reference to other theories that purported to explain the origin of the human species. According to the complaint, such teaching represented a direct attack on creationist religious beliefs in violation of the Free Exercise Clause and lent official support to a religious secularism in violation of the Establishment Clause.

The case never got to trial. Without looking beyond the base allegation, Judge Woodrow Seals issued the following opinion, which dismissed the complaint for failing to state a claim upon which relief could be granted:

WRIGHT v. HOUSTON IND. SCHOOL DIST.

United States District Court for the Southern District of Texas
366 F.Supp. 1208 (S.D. Tex. 1972)

SEALS, DISTRICT JUDGE: Plaintiffs—students of the Houston Independent School District—here seek to enjoin the District and the State Board of Education from teaching the theory of evolution as part of the District's academic curriculum and from adopting textbooks which present that theory without critical analysis and to the exclusion of other theories regarding the origins of man. Plaintiffs base their claim for relief upon the provisions of 42 U.S.C. § 1983. Jurisdiction is invoked pursuant to 28 U.S.C. § 1343. The case is presently before the Court on Defendants' motion to dismiss for failure to state a claim.

Plaintiffs' principal contention is that the teaching of the theory of evolution in the Houston Independent School District inhibits Plaintiffs in the free exercise of their religion and constitutes an "establishment of religion," in contravention of the First Amendment to the United States Constitution. The theory of evolution is, according to Plaintiffs, presented by Defendants without critical analysis and without reference to other theories which purport to explain the origin of the human species. The "other theory" whose case Plaintiffs here champion is the explanation derived from the Bible, the basis of which is that man was created by God. In Plaintiffs' view, the theory of evolution is so inimical to the Creation account that its presentation as part of the academic curriculum should be

---

23. George Gallup, *Public Evenly Divided Between Evolutionists, Creationists* 1–2 (1982) (Los Angeles Times Syndicate press release). According to the survey, although the percentages of persons affirming biblical creationism were lower in other region than in the South, that figure did not fall below 40% for any region of the country.

deemed a direct attack upon Plaintiffs' religious beliefs by an organ of government. The State, by implicitly rejecting a central tenet of Plaintiffs' religion, is holding that religion up to contempt, scorn, and ridicule, and is thus acting to discourage, if not to restrain, Plaintiffs in the free exercise of their religion.

Plaintiffs also argue a constitutional deprivation in terms of the Establishment Clause of the First Amendment. Plaintiffs maintain that, by restricting the study of human origins to an uncritical examination of the theory of evolution, Defendants are lending official support to a "religion of secularism."[24] Under the guise of scientific theory, Plaintiffs submit that Defendants are engaged in the propagation of a doctrine that is fundamentally religious in nature, and thus, are "establishing" a particular religion in contravention of the First Amendment.

Plaintiffs contend that Defendants' teaching of the theory of evolution violates the doctrine of neutrality which the Supreme Court has held must be State policy in matters of religion. The principle of neutrality was most recently affirmed by the Court in Epperson v. Arkansas, 393 U.S. 97 (1968). In that case, the Court struck down an Arkansas statute which prohibited any teacher in a state school from teaching the theory of evolution. . . .

Plaintiffs have thus attempted to draw an analogy between the Arkansas prohibition and the teaching of the theory of evolution in the Houston Independent School District. From that position, Plaintiffs would suggest an appropriately analogous remedy: an injunction against the teaching of the theory of evolution. But Plaintiffs have wholly failed to establish the analogy.

In the first place, Arkansas chose to promote a particular view regarding human origins by means of legislative enactment. It was clear to the Supreme Court ". . . that fundamentalist sectarian conviction was and is the law's reason for existence." Id., at 108. Defendants, however, are not acting pursuant either to State law or school district regulation. Plaintiffs have not alleged that there exists even a school district policy regarding the theory of evolution. All that can be said is that certain textbooks selected by school officials present what Plaintiffs deem a biased view in support of the theory. This Court has been cited to no case in which so nebulous an intrusion upon the principle of religious neutrality has been condemned by the Supreme Court.

Neither have Plaintiffs alleged that Defendants attempt to discourage the free discussion of the subject of human origins. There has no suggestion that Plaintiffs, or any other students, have been denied the opportunity to challenge their teachers' presentation of the Darwinian theory.

---

24. In School District of Abington Township v. Schempp, 374 U.S. 203 (1963), the Supreme Court held that the State may not establish a "religion of secularism" in the sense of affirmatively opposing or showing hostility to religion and thus preferring those who believe in no religion over those who do believe.

Arkansas, on the other hand, prohibited any discussion of the subject of evolution.

In short, whereas Arkansas labelled as a criminal offense the mere reference to an entire body of scientific opinion, neither the State of Texas nor the Houston Independent School District has given legislative expression to any view of the subject of evolution. The State, at most, has a general policy of approving textbooks which present the theory of evolution in a favorable light. No position regarding human origins is even indirectly proscribed by State or District. Furthermore, Plaintiffs have failed even to assert the suppression of opposing ideas. Clearly, Defendants' "policy" (or lack thereof) regarding the theory of evolution is far removed from Arkansas' blanket censorship.

Plaintiffs' case depends in large measure upon their demonstrating a connection between "religion," as employed in the First Amendment, and Defendants' approach to the subject of evolution. The Court is convinced that the connection is too tenuous a thread on which to base a First Amendment complaint.

In Cornwell v. State Board of Education, 314 F.Supp. 340 (D.Md., 1969), aff'd, 428 F.2d 471 (C.A. 4, 1970), a group of Baltimore children and their parents sought to enjoin the enforcement of a bylaw, adopted by the State Board of Education, requiring "the local school system to provide a comprehensive program of family life and sex education in every elementary and secondary school for all students." Among other contentions, the Plaintiffs asserted that the sex education program constituted an establishment of religion and that its implementation denied to them the free exercise of their religious beliefs: Reminding Plaintiffs that the First Amendment does not say that in all respects there must be a separation of church and state, the District Court applied the test devised by the Supreme Court in School District of Abington Township v. Schempp, 374 U.S. 203 (1963), for determining the validity of a legislative provision under the Establishment Clause of the First Amendment:

> "[W]hat are the purpose and the primary effect of the enactment? If either is the advancement or inhibition of religion then the enactment exceeds the scope of legislative power as circumscribed by the Constitution." Schempp, supra, at 222.

The *Cornwell* court was convinced that the

> "... purpose and primary effect of the bylaw here is not to establish any particular religious dogma or precept, and that the bylaw does not directly or substantially involve the state in religious exercises or in the favoring of religion or any particular religion." Cornwell, supra, at 344.

In the case at bar, the offending material is peripheral to the matter of religion. Science and religion necessarily deal with many of the same questions, and they may frequently provide conflicting answers. But, as the Supreme Court wrote twenty years ago, it is not the business of government to suppress real or imagined attacks upon a particular religious doctrine. Burstyn v. Wilson, 343 U.S. 495, 505 (1952). Teachers of science in the public schools should not be expected to avoid the discussion of every scientific issue on which some religion claims expertise.

Avoidance of any reference to the subject of human origins is, indeed, a decidedly totalitarian approach to the problem presented here. Book-burning is always dangerous, but never more dangerous than when practiced on behalf of young and impressionable minds. How is the teacher to respond to the inquiry of a high school biology student regarding the theory of evolution? Is he to be told that the subject is taboo, that the teacher is not permitted to speak of it, that he mustn't ask such questions?

Plaintiffs, however, would propose another approach that, at first glance, seems reasonable and fair: "equal time" for all theories regarding human origins.[25] If the beliefs of fundamentalism were the sole alternative to the Darwinian theory, such a remedy might at least be feasible. But virtually every religion known to man holds its own peculiar view of human origins. Within the scientific community itself, there is much debate over the details of the theory of evolution. This Court is hardly qualified to select from among the available theories those which merit attention in a public school biology class. Nor have Plaintiffs suggested to the Court what standards might be applied in making such a selection.

Plaintiffs' case must ultimately fail, then, because the proposed solutions are more onerous than the problem they purport to alleviate. For this Court to require the District to keep silent on the subject of evolution is to do that which the Supreme Court has declared the Arkansas legislature is powerless to do. To insist upon the presentation of all theories of human origins is, on the other hand, to prescribe a remedy that is impractical, unworkable and ineffective.

The State Board of Education, as one of the Defendants in this action, has suggested that Plaintiffs may be assisted by taking advantage of the provisions of § 21.104 of the Texas Education Code, V.T.C.A., which permits any child to be exempted, without penalty, from receiving instruction in certain areas of physiology and hygiene, upon the presentation of a signed statement from his parent or guardian that the material conflicts with the family's religious beliefs.[26] Defendants maintain that § 21.104 is

---

25. If this approach were applied in other areas, teachers might be obliged to provide equal time for an exposition of the Mormon belief in the inequality of the races, and for indoctrination in the Christian Science view of health and disease.

26. § 21.104 reads as follows:"All textbooks on physiology and hygiene purchased in the future for use in the public schools of this State shall include at least one chapter on the effects of alcohol and narcotics. Although physiology and hygiene must be taught in all public schools, any child may be exempted, without penalty, from receiving instruction therein if his parent or guardian presents to the school principal a signed statement that the teaching of disease, its symptoms, development and treatment, and the viewing of pictures or motion pictures on such subjects conflict with the religious teachings of a well-established church or denomination to which the parent or guardian and the child belong."

broad enough to encompass Plaintiffs' objections to the teaching of the theory of evolution.

Plaintiffs assert, however, that reliance on § 21.104 is misplaced, because the requirement of a signed statement compels a student "to profess a belief" in a religion, contrary to the Supreme Court's decision in Torcaso v. Watkins, 367 U.S. 488 (1961). Torcaso, however, dealt with a provision of the Maryland Constitution which required declaration of a belief in the existence of God as a qualification for holding public office.... Plaintiffs in the case at bar are attempting to have it both ways. On the one hand, they argue that they are forced to submit to teachings which deeply offend their religious beliefs. And yet they reject the option of leaving the classroom during the presentation of the offending material, contending that their exit under such circumstances is equivalent to the coerced expression of religious belief. For that matter, the mere filing of the present civil action puts Plaintiffs on record as holding certain religious views. But the fundamental difference between the compulsion of a test oath and ... that underlying § 21.104 is simply too great to ignore.

The Court thus finds that, under the facts pleaded, each of Plaintiffs' contentions regarding the teaching of the theory of evolution in the Houston public schools—that it inhibits Plaintiffs in the free exercise of their religion and that it constitutes an establishment of religion—fails to state a claim upon which relief can be granted.... Accordingly, Defendants' motion to dismiss for failure to state a claim is granted and this cause of action is hereby dismissed.

NOTES AND QUESTIONS

1. Judge Seals dismissed the plaintiffs' complaint for failing to state a claim upon which relief could be granted. Why did it fail to state such a claim? Dismissal on this severe procedural ground occurs only when the complaint itself demonstrates no possible basis for a judicial remedy under any conceivable facts. The plaintiffs' unusual allegations only made this dismissal more telling. The controlling court rule provided "that the more extreme or even far-fetched is the asserted theory of liability, the more important it is that the conceptual legal theories be explored and assessed in the light of actual facts, not a pleader's suppositions." Yet the judge found the plaintiffs' allegations too far-fetched to survive even this least restrictive standard. It was not that the judge doubted the motive behind the case. Indeed, he described the principal protagonist, Rita Wright's mother, as "an obviously sincere and concerned parent." But he totally rejected her cause.

2. In his opinion, Judge Seals depicted plaintiffs' proposed solutions as "more onerous than the problem they purport to alleviate." What were those solutions? The judge rejected as "decidedly totalitarian" the solution of barring all instruction in human origins. "Science and religion necessarily deal with many of the same questions, and they may frequently provide conflicting answers," he reasoned. "Teachers of science in the public schools should not be expected to avoid the discussion of every scientific issue in which some religions claim expertise." Judge Seals came down just as hard

against required " 'equal time' for all theories regarding human origins" on the grounds that there were too many such theories. "This Court is hardly qualified to select from among the available theories those which merit attention in a public school biology class," he wrote. What about the school district's proposed solution of letting creationist students opt out of classes presenting Darwinism? Plaintiffs claimed that it would expose the exempted students to undue peer pressure.

3. Can you distinguish between the plaintiffs' Establishment Clause claims and their Free Exercise Clause claims? Does the exclusive teaching of Darwinism as the biological explanation for the origin of species, including humans, establish a religion of secularism? Does such teaching represent a direct attack on the plaintiffs' religious beliefs by an organ of government? Is it for the judge to determine, as he does here, that "the offending material is peripheral to the matter of religion"?

4. In a brief, unsigned opinion issued in 1973, a federal appellate court affirmed the Judge Seals' decision on all points. When the U.S. Supreme Court refused to review this ruling in 1974, Wright and her fellow plaintiffs were left without a direct judicial remedy. The first appeal by creationists to the courts was an utter failure. At every level, the judiciary refused even to permit a trial on the merits of creationist arguments for restricting evolutionary teaching.

II. EARLY CREATIONIST LAWMAKING

As the *Wright* decision suggested, building a credible scientific challenge against a century-long tradition of evolutionary research in biology took time, and some creationists would not wait. Confident of popular support for their cause, they reopened a legislative front in their battle to qualify evolutionary teaching. During the 1970s, dozens of bills appeared in state legislatures across America to require the classroom presentation of creationist religious concepts as a foil to evolutionary teaching. Their proponents apparently recognized the judicial restrictions against banning evolutionary teaching altogether but typically did not fully appreciate either the established limits on religious instruction or emerging claims of scientific creationism. Once again, Tennessee provided the first breakthrough.

The Tennessee Genesis Bill was introduced into the state Senate on March 26, 1973, by a bipartisan collation of five senators. All five were members of the 1967 legislature that repealed the old anti-evolution statute but none of them had voted for repeal. Now they struck back. The legislation required that all public-school textbooks presenting a theory of human origin identify the concept as a theory rather than as a scientific fact. The bill also mandated that texts presenting any such theory give equal space to other theories including, but not limited to, the Genesis account in the Bible. The measure neither banned evolutionary teaching nor specifically promoted scientific creationism, rather it aimed at defending creationist religious beliefs by qualifying the treatment of evolution in textbooks.

The idea for the bill came from Russell Artist, a biology professor at a small, church-affiliated Tennessee college. As a member of the Creation Research Society, a national association of scientifically and technologically trained creationists, Artist co-authored the 1970 creationist textbook, *Biology: A Search for Order in Complexity*. After failing to get the text approved by the State Textbook Commission for use in Tennessee public schools, Artist sought and offered the book as a model of balanced treatment. "What's the matter with evolutionists that they can't stand a scrutiny by honest scientists? We're not telling them to teach it—let them teach it all they want," Artist declared. "Now is that being prejudiced? No, it's simply asking that we should have the same amount of time to present our creation point of view."[27] Wrapped in such notions of fairness, the Genesis Bill swept through the Tennessee Senate barely three weeks after its introduction with only one dissenting vote. Even the eight remaining senators who voted to repeal the old anti-evolution statute now voted to give equal time to the Genesis account. Clearly, the new approach had broad appeal.

The only drama during the Senate action came from the unusual presence of network-news cameras. Although the Genesis Bill obviously had local popular support, senators feared that the network reporters were there to subject them to the same sort of public ridicule that had been associated with the Scopes trial. To avoid national television coverage reinforcing the Scopes stereotype, the Senate acted without floor debate. In a flash, lawmakers approved friendly amendments specifying that alternative theories of origins receive equal emphasis rather than equal space in state textbooks and then passed the bill without comment.

The Tennessee House of Representatives brought the bill up for floor action a week after receiving it. This time the television cameras got some footage as House members vigorously debated and amended the bill for over an hour. "The plain facts of the situation are that these people who want to teach a theory like Darwinism and can't prove it want to say 'Let us teach the children what we want them to know and the hell with everything else,'" a key proponent proclaimed. "I think they want to brainwash our children." Perhaps reflecting its broad popular support, even House critics of the measure avoided directly denouncing it during the floor debate and instead raised questions that were unlikely to offend creationist constituents. For the most part, they attacked the proposal for requiring the presentation of all explanations of human origins, including the Genesis account, as mere theories. Calling it "a sacrilege to my religion," the leading opponent of the measure proclaimed, "I believe the Biblical account is fact, not theory." Belying the sincerity of this claim, however, that lawmaker had voted to repeal the anti-evolution statute in 1967. The allegation hit home, however, and the House amended the bill to exempt "the Holy Bible" from carrying the disclaimer required for textbooks—and thereby all but assured that it would be declared unconsti-

---

27. Russell Artist, quoted in Tom Gillem, *Prof's Textbook Campaign Led to Genesis Bill*, NASHVILLE TENNESSEEAN, Apr. 30, 1973, at 1.

tutional for favoring a particular religious view. House critics also charged that the legislation would crowd textbooks with hundreds of strange and weird theories about creation. One opponent, who had also voted to repeal the anti-evolution law in 1967, now went so far as to profess that the bill mandated teaching creation theories propounded by "draft evaders who fled this country during its hour of need to engage in a marijuana smoking party." In response, the floor manager for the measure assured House members that the bill only required teaching the Genesis account along with evolution. To be safe, however, House members added an amendment barring the teaching of occult or satanic beliefs of human origins—which further served to undermine the measure's constitutionality. These House amendments carried through the popular intent behind the bill of defending the Genesis account from dogmatic evolutionary teaching. Testifying to its popularity, the Speaker of the House reported receiving about 500 letters for the proposal and only one against it. Riding the crest of such popular support, the Genesis Bill passed the House by a margin of 69 to 16.[28] After the Senate concurred in the House amendments, the bill automatically became law a week later when the governor declined either to sign or veto the popular measure.

Judicial challenges to the Tennessee creationism law quickly appeared. University of Tennessee law professor Frederic S. Le Clercq began plotting a federal court attack almost immediately and soon asked support from the National Association of Biology Teachers (NABT). That organization agreed and, with Le Clercq serving as counsel, filed suit against the law in federal district court on behalf of itself and three local members, Joseph Daniel, Arthur Jones, and Larry Wilder. Alleging that the law violated the prohibition against the establishment of religion, freedom of speech and freedom of the press, the plaintiffs sought to have the statute declared unconstitutional. Before the state answered the *Daniel* complaint, another national organization with a long history of involvement in this issue, the Americans United for Separation of Church and State, joined by three of its local member including Harold Steele, challenged the statute in state court. Claiming that the law was intended to aid particular religious points of view, the *Steele* complaint attacked the law for violating both state and federal constitutional prohibitions against the establishment of religion. When the *Daniel* trial court granted the state's motion to defer further action pending the resolution of the state court action, the plaintiffs appealed for relief to the Sixth Circuit U.S. Court of Appeals.

While the state trial court struggled to unravel the issue by considering legal arguments for and against the Genesis Act, the federal appellate court decided the statute's fate. Without hearing any substantive arguments, the *Daniel* appellate court declared the Genesis Act to be patently unconstitutional. After the attorney general declined to appeal this deci-

---

28. The House floor debate, including quotes, is from John Haile, *Genesis Bill Wins House Passage*, NASHVILLE TENNESSEAN, Apr. 27, 1973, at 1; John Pope, *House Amends Proposal on Creation of Man*, NASHVILLE BANNER, Apr. 27, 1973, at 16; and *House Alters Some Senate Theories on Creation*, MEMPHIS COMMERCIAL-APPEAL, Apr. 27, 1973, at 3.

sion, the Tennessee Supreme Court issued a brief concurring opinion in *Steele*. The statute and both court decisions follow:

1973 TENNESSEE GENESIS ACT (1973)

Be it enacted by the General Assembly of the State of Tennessee:

Sec. 1.   Tennessee Code Annotated, Section 49–2008, is amended by adding the following paragraph: Any biology textbook used for teaching in the public schools, which expresses an opinion of, or relates to a theory about origins or creation of man and his world shall be prohibited from being used as a textbook in such system unless it specifically states that it is a theory as to the origin and creation of man and his world and is not represented to be scientific fact. Any textbook so used in the public education system which expresses an opinion or relates to a theory or theories shall give in the same text book and under the same subject commensurate attention to, and an equal amount of emphasis on, the origins and creation of man and his world as the same is recorded in other theories, including, but not limited to, the Genesis account in the Bible. The provisions of this Act shall not apply to use of any textbook now legally in use, until the beginning of the school year of 1975–1976; provided, however, that the textbook requirements stated above shall in no way diminish the duty of the state textbook commission to prepare a list of approved standard editions of textbooks for use in the public schools of the state as provided in this section. Each local school board may use textbooks or supplementary material as approved by the State Board of Education to carry out the provisions of this section. The teaching of all occult or satanical beliefs of human origin is expressly excluded from this act.

Sec. 2.   Provided however that the Holy Bible shall not be defined as a textbook, but is hereby declared to be a reference work, and shall not be required to carry the disclaimer above provided for textbooks.

Sec. 3.   The provisions of this Act are hereby declared to be severable; and if any of its sections, provisions, clauses, or parts be held unconstitutional or void, then the remainder of this Act shall continue in full force and effect, it being the legislative intent now hereby declared that this Act would have been adopted even if such unconstitutional or void matter had not been included herein.

DANIEL v. WATERS

United States Court of Appeals for the Sixth Circuit
515 F.2d 485 (6th Cir. 1975)

EDWARDS, CIRCUIT JUDGE: We are confronted in this appeal by a 1973 version of the legislative effort to suppress the theory of evolution which produced the famous Scopes "monkey trial" of 1925. See Scopes v. State, 154 Tenn. 105 (1927). In this instance the Tennessee Legislature has sought to avoid direct suppression of speech and has eschewed direct criminal sanctions. But the purpose of establishing the Biblical version of the creation of man over the Darwinian theory of the evolution of man is as clear in the 1973 statute as it was in the statute of 1925.

Plaintiffs are teachers of biology in Tennessee public schools, some of whom are also parents of public school students, plus the National Association of Biology Teachers. The defendants are members of the Tennessee state board which is charged with the responsibility of selecting public school textbooks. Jurisdiction is invoked under 28 U.S.C. sec. 1343(3) (1970).

The statute at issue [is] Chapter 377 of the 1973 Public Acts of Tennessee.... The First Amendment to the Constitution of the United States says in applicable part:

> Congress shall make no law respecting an establishment of religion, or prohibiting the free exercise thereof; ...

The Fourteenth Amendment to the Constitution of the United States says in applicable part:

> No State shall make or enforce any law which shall abridge the privileges or immunities of citizens of the United States; nor shall any State deprive any person of life, liberty, or property, without due process of law; nor deny to any person within its jurisdiction the equal protection of the laws.

We have previously indicated that the statute complained of does not directly forbid the teaching of evolution. It does, however, prohibit the selection of any textbook which teaches evolution unless it also contains a disclaimer stating that such doctrine is "a theory as to the origin and creation of man and his world and is not represented to be scientific fact." And the same statute expressly requires the inclusion of the Genesis version of creation (if any version at all is taught) while permitting that version alone to be printed without the above disclaimer. (Section 2 of the statute quoted above says: "Provided, however, that the Holy Bible shall not be defined as a textbook, but is hereby declared to be a reference work, and shall not be required to carry the disclaimer above provided for textbooks.") Furthermore, "the teaching of all occult or satanical beliefs of human origin is expressly excluded from this act," presumably meaning that religious beliefs deemed "occult" or "satanical" need not be printed in biology texts along with the other theories.

We believe that in several respects the statute under consideration is unconstitutional on its face, [and] that no state court interpretation of it can save it....

First, the statute requires that any textbook which expresses an opinion about the origin of man "shall be prohibited from being used" unless the book specifically states that the opinion is "a theory" and "is not represented to be scientific fact." The statute also requires that the Biblical account of creation (and other theories of creation) be printed at the same time, with commensurate attention and equal emphasis. As to all such theories, except only the Genesis theory, the textbook must print the disclaimer quoted above. But the proviso in Section 2 would allow the printing of the Biblical account of creation as set forth in Genesis without any such disclaimer. The result of this legislation is a clearly defined preferential position for the Biblical version of creation as opposed to any account of the development of man based on scientific research and reasoning. For a state to seek to enforce such a preference by law is to seek to accomplish the very establishment of religion which the First Amendment to the Constitution of the United States squarely forbids.

We believe the provisions of the Tennessee statute are obviously in violation of the First Amendment prohibition on any law "respecting the establishment of religion" as that phrase has been authoritatively interpreted in Epperson v. Arkansas, 393 U.S. 97 (1968), and Lemon v. Kurtzman, 403 U.S. 602 (1971).

In Epperson the Supreme Court said:

> In any event, we do not rest our decision upon the asserted vagueness of the statute. On either interpretation of its language, Arkansas' statute cannot stand. It is of no moment whether the law is deemed to prohibit mention of Darwin's theory, or to forbid any or all of the infinite varieties of communication embraced within the term "teaching." Under either interpretation, the law must be stricken because of its conflict with the constitutional prohibition of state laws respecting an establishment of religion or prohibiting the free exercise thereof. The overriding fact is that Arkansas' law selects from the body of knowledge a particular segment which it proscribes for the sole reason that it is deemed to conflict with a particular religious doctrine; that is, with a particular interpretation of the Book of Genesis by a particular religious group.

The antecedents of today's decision are many and unmistakable. They are rooted in the foundation soil of our Nation. They are fundamental to freedom.

> Government in our democracy, state and national, must be neutral in matters of religious theory, doctrine, and practice. It may not be hostile to any religion or to the advocacy of no-religion; and it may not aid, foster, or promote one religion or religious theory against another or even against the militant opposite. The First Amendment mandates governmental neutrality between religion and religion, and between religion and nonreligion.

> As early as 1872, this Court said: "The law knows no heresy, and is committed to the support of no dogma, the establishment of no sect." Watson v. Jones, 13 Wall. 679, 728 (80 U.S. 679.) This has been the interpretation of the great First Amendment which this Court has applied in the many and subtle problems which the ferment of our national life has presented for decision within the Amendment's broad command.

Judicial interposition in the operation of the public school system of the Nation raises problems requiring care and restraint. Our courts, however, have not failed to apply the First Amendment's mandate in our educational system where essential to safeguard the fundamental values of freedom of speech and inquiry and of belief. By and large, public education in our Nation is committed to the control of state and local authorities. Courts do not and cannot intervene in the resolution of conflicts which arise in the daily operation of school systems and which do not directly and sharply implicate basic constitutional values. On the other hand, "(t)he vigilant protection of constitutional freedoms is nowhere more vital than in the community of American schools," Shelton v. Tucker, 364 U.S. 479, 487 (1960). As this Court said in Keyishian v. Board of Regents, the First Amendment "does not tolerate laws that cast a pall of orthodoxy over the classroom." 385 U.S. 589, 603 (1967).

There is and can be no doubt that the First Amendment does not permit the State to require that teaching and learning must be tailored to the principles or prohibitions of any religious sect or dogma. In Everson v. Board of Education, this Court, in upholding a state law to provide free bus service to school children, including those attending parochial schools, said: "Neither (a State nor the Federal Government) can pass laws which aid one religion, aid all religions, or prefer one religion over another." 330 U.S. 1, 15 (1947).

At the following Term of Court, in McCollum v. Board of Education, 333 U.S. 203 (1948), the Court held that Illinois could not release pupils from class to attend classes of instruction in the school buildings in the religion of their choice. This, it said, would involve the State in using tax-supported property for religious purposes, thereby breaching the "wall of separation" which, according to Jefferson, the First Amendment was intended to erect between church and state. Id., at 211. See also Engel v. Vitale, 370 U.S. 421, 428 (1962); Abington School District v. Schempp, 374 U.S. 203 (1963). While study of religions and of the Bible from a literary and historic viewpoint, presented objectively as part of a secular program of education, need not collide with the First Amendment's prohibition, the State may not adopt programs or practices in its public schools or colleges which "aid or oppose" any religion. Id., at 225. This prohibition is absolute. It forbids alike the preference of a religious doctrine or the prohibition of theory which is deemed antagonistic to a particular dogma. As Mr. Justice Clark stated in Joseph Burstyn, Inc. v. Wilson, "the state has no legitimate interest in protecting any or all religions from views distasteful to them...." 343 U.S. 495, 505 (1952). The test was stated as follows in Abington School District v. Schempp, supra, (374 U.S.) at 222: "(W)hat are the purpose and the primary effect of the enactment? If either is the advancement or inhibition of religion then the enactment exceeds the scope of legislative power as circumscribed by the Constitution."...

In Lemon Chief Justice Burger said:

In the absence of precisely stated constitutional prohibitions, we must draw lines with reference to the three main evils against which the Establishment Clause was intended to afford protection: "sponsorship, financial support, and active involvement of the sovereign in religious activity." Walz v. Tax Commission, 397 U.S. 664, 668 (1970).

Every analysis in this area must begin with consideration of the cumulative criteria developed by the Court over many years. Three such tests may be gleaned from our cases. First, the statute must have a secular legislative purpose; second, its principal or primary effect must be one that neither advances nor inhibits religion, Board of Education v. Allen, 392 U.S. 236, 243 (1968); finally, the statute must not foster "an excessive government entanglement with religion." Walz, supra, (397 U.S.) at 674.

Lemon v. Kurtzman, 403 U.S. 602, 612–13 (1971).

While the requirement of preferential treatment of the Bible clearly offends the Establishment Clause of the First Amendment, the exclusion at the end of Section 1 of the statute would inextricably involve the State Textbook Commission in the most difficult and hotly disputed of theological arguments in direct conflict with Chief Justice Burger's third standard. Throughout human history the God of some men has frequently been regarded as the Devil incarnate by men of other religious persuasions. It would be utterly impossible for the Tennessee Textbook Commission to determine which religious theories were "occult" or "satanical" without seeking to resolve the theological arguments which have embroiled and frustrated theologians through the ages.

The requirement that some religious concepts of creation, adhered to presumably by some Tennessee citizens, be excluded on such grounds in favor of the Bible of the Jews and the Christians represents still another method of preferential treatment of particular faiths by state law and, of course, is forbidden by the Establishment Clause of the First Amendment.

We deem the two constitutional violations described above to be patent and obvious on the face of the statute and impossible for any state interpretation to cure. Under these circumstances, we find no need to determine whether the terms "occult" and "satanical" are, as claimed by appellants, also void for vagueness under the Due Process Clause of the Fourteenth Amendment. Nor for the same reason do we feel it is necessary or desirable to pass on appellants' claims that the statute as drawn represents violation of the Freedom of Speech and Press Clauses of the First Amendment. . . .

Celebrezze, Circuit Judge (dissenting) [on procedural grounds. Opinion omitted.]

STEELE v. WATERS

Supreme Court of Tennessee
527 S.W.2d 72 (Tenn. 1975)

PER CURIAM: Hugh Waters, Chairman of the Textbook Commission of the State of Tennessee, and others, have appealed from the decree of the Chancery Court of Davidson County, Tennessee declaring unconstitutional the second and third paragraphs of Chapter 377 of the Public Acts of 1973 as being violative of the First Amendment to the United States Constitution and Article 1, Section 3, of the Constitution of Tennessee, and permanently enjoining the enforcement and execution of the statute.

During the pendency of the appeal, the United States Court of Appeals for the Sixth Circuit rendered an opinion in an action brought by Daniel (Arthur W. Jones, Larry Ray Wilder, and the National Association of Biology Teachers) v. Waters (Textbook Commission of the State of Tennessee and other officials of the State), 515 F.2d 485, to challenge the constitutionality of Chapter 377 of the Public Acts of 1973. In the opinion, the Sixth Circuit Court of Appeals concluded that the Act in issue was "unconstitutional on its face." Specifically, the Court held:

(1) ... (T)he provisions of the Tennessee statute are obviously in violation of the first Amendment prohibition on any law "respecting the establishment of religion" as that phrase has been authoritatively interpreted in Epperson v. Arkansas, 393 U.S. 97 (1968), and Lemon v. Kurtzman, 403 U.S. 602 (1971);

(2) ... (T)he exclusion at the end of Section 1 of the statute would inextricably involve the State Textbook Commission in the most difficult and hotly disputed Chief Justice Burger's third standard (set out in Lemon v. Kurtzman, 403 U.S. 602, 612–613 (1971)). Throughout human history the God of some men has frequently been regarded as the Devil incarnate by men of other religious persuasions. It would be utterly impossible for the Textbook Commission to determine which religious theories were "occult" or "satanical" without seeking to resolve the theologians through the ages.

The requirement that some religious concepts of creation, adhered to presumably by some Tennessee citizens, be excluded on such grounds in favor of the Bible of the Jews and the Christians represents still another method of preferential treatment of particular faiths by state law and, of course, is forbidden by the establishment Clause of the First Amendment.

The officials of the State of Tennessee did not seek a review of the holding of the Sixth Circuit Court of Appeals by filing a petition for certiorari in the Supreme Court of the United States.

We concur in the holding of the Sixth Circuit Court of Appeals that Chapter 377 of the Public Acts of 1973 violates the First Amendment to the United States Constitution, and further hold that for the same reasons, the Act violates Article 1, Section 3, of the Constitution of the State of Tennessee as held by the Chancellor. Accordingly, the decree of the Chancery Court of Davidson County is affirmed. Costs are adjudged against the appellants.

NOTES AND QUESTIONS

1.   Unlike Tennessee's 1925 anti-evolution statute, the state's 1973 Genesis Act targeted textbooks rather than teachers. What are the advantages for those seeking restrictions on Darwinian instruction of imposing legal mandates on the content of textbooks rather than limits on what a teacher can say in class? On the one hand, to the extent that textbooks guide what instructors teach and students learn, they effectively shape curricular content without seeming to limit the freedom or discretion of individual teachers. On the other hand, textbooks provide an easy target for supporters of evolutionary instruction, who can challenge the constitutionality of using a textbook that promotes a religious viewpoint.

2.   Without the benefit of a trial, the appellate court in *Daniel* declared the Genesis Act to be "patently unconstitutional." This ruling represented as dramatic a repudiation of creationist legal claims as the dismissal of plaintiffs' complaint in *Wright* for failing to state a cause of action. The district court in *Daniel* had not considered the Act's merits. For the appellate court to overturn it at this point rather than to direct the district court to proceed with a trial required a finding that the statute was unconstitutional on its face and no further fact finding could save it. Typically, this procedure is reserved for direct violations of established constitutional principles. What were those established principles in this case? The *Daniel* court singled out two provisions in the Act as clear-cut violations of the Establishment Clause. First, exempting the Genesis account from carrying a disclaimer wrongly gave a "preferential position for the Biblical view of creation as opposed to any account of the development of man based on scientific research and reasoning." Second, expressly excluding occult or satanic theories of origins from coverage under the Act improperly embroiled the state in identifying and censoring particular religious or anti-religious views. Do you see other potential constitutional problems with the Act? Would a trial have been required to resolve those issues?

3.   The two provisions of the Genesis Act ruled by the court to be patently unconstitutional on their face—exempting only the biblical account from carrying a disclaimer and excluding occult theories the Act's protections— were not in the original bill as passed by the Senate. The House added them as amendments in response to critics. Sometimes lawmakers opposed to a popular bill offer seeming friendly amendments designed to render it unconstitutional. This strategy is sometimes called "loving a bill to death." Why might legislators vote for a bill that they think is unconstitutional or amend a bill to make it unconstitutional?

4.   In *Steele*, the Tennessee Supreme Court declared the Genesis Act to be unconstitutional after the federal appeal court had done so. What did that second ruling add? Is it significant that the state supreme court declared the

Act to violate the Tennessee Constitution as well as the U.S. Constitution? In adopting the federal court's rationale for striking the Act, the state court quoted only the portion of the federal-court opinion condemning the Act for disfavoring allegedly occult theories and did not mention the portion censuring it for favoring the biblical account.

* * * * *

Shortly after Tennessee enacted its Genesis Act, a similar proposal failed to pass in neighboring Kentucky. At the time, some Bluegrass State legislators said that they wanted to see how the courts ruled on the Genesis Act before proceeding. In 1976, following the *Daniel* decision, Kentucky lawmakers crafted a more modest creation-teaching bill that sailed through both chambers with almost no legislative debate or public comment. The Senate placed the measure on the consent calendar for noncontroversial legislation and approved it on a vote of 32 to 3. The House added its overwhelming approval during a hectic afternoon meeting devoted to clearing away a backlog of popular bills. The measure became law on March 30, 1967. By neither imposing restrictions on either students or teachers nor challenging the scientific status of evolution, this statute, which follows, has escaped the legal and political controversies that had dogged all previous anti-evolution laws:

KENTUCKY CREATION TEACHING ACT (1976)

Be it enacted by the General Assembly of the Commonwealth of Kentucky:

Sec. 1.   A new Section of KRS Chapter 158 is created to read as follows:

(1) In any public school instruction concerning the theories of the creation of man and the earth, and which involves the theory thereon commonly known as evolution, any teacher so desiring may include as a portion of such instruction the theory of creation as presented in the Bible, and may accordingly read such passages in the Bible as are deemed necessary for instruction on the theory of creation, thereby affording students a choice as to which such theory to accept.

(2) For those students receiving such instruction, and who accept the Bible theory of creation, credit shall be permitted on any examination in which adherence to such theory is propounded, provided the response is correct according to the instruction received.

(3) No teacher in a public school may stress any particular denominational religious belief.

(4) This section is not to be construed as being adverse to any decision which has been rendered by any court of competent jurisdiction.

NOTES AND QUESTIONS

1.   Section (1) of the Kentucky Creation–Teaching Act authorizes teachers to balance Darwinian science with religious creationism in public-school courses.

It does not require them to do so. On its face, does the Act violate the Establishment Clause by authorizing religious instruction in a manner prohibited by *McCollum* or does it merely allow teachers to inform students about religious concepts as permitted under *McCollum*? The Act has not been challenged in court. It cannot immunize otherwise unconstitutional activity by teachers but it could encourage teachers to exercise fully their right to teach about religious concepts of creation.

2. Section (2) of the Act grants creationist students the right to receive credit for learning biblical concepts of creation as taught in their classes. Credit cannot be given to students who do not accept the Bible theory of creation. What is the purpose of making this statutory distinction? It could serve to reward creationist students with course credit. Alternatively, it could protect non-creationist students from having to learn the Bible in public schools.

* * * * *

As Kentucky legislators were passing their notably uncontroversial Creation–Teaching Act, a different approach toward accommodating creationist beliefs ran amuck across the Ohio River in the Indiana suburbs of Louisville, Kentucky. It began innocently enough in 1973, when the Indiana Textbook Commission adopted the same creationist text that had earlier created a storm in Tennessee, *Biology: A Search for Order in Complexity*, as one of seven biology textbooks approved for use by Indiana public schools. Since all of the other texts presented a traditional evolutionary perspective, the Commission claimed that the creationist alternative served as a valid means to inculcate in the students an open and questioning mind on the science of origins. But what seemed a fair accommodation at the state level and in the five local school districts adopting *A Search for Order* along with one of the other approved texts created a constitutional controversy in 1976, when the West Clark Community Schools adopted it as the only biology text approved for local use.

After the Commission rejected ensuing demands to withdraw approval for the creationist text, the Indiana ACLU filed suit in 1974 against both the Commission and the West Clark schools on behalf of a local student named Jon Hendren and others. In a notable recognition of the principle of religious accommodation, the ACLU's complaint differentiated sharply between the local decision to use only the creationist textbook and the Commission approval for that text along with several evolutionary books. Both acts allegedly violated a state law against sectarian textbooks but only the local action was challenged as unconstitutional.

Pursuant to normal state administrative-law procedures, the complaint was then referred to the Commission for a hearing. At the hearing, the ACLU presented a string of Indiana biologists and theologians who uniformly described the textbook as a sectarian presentation of fundamentalist Christian beliefs. Despite this testimony, the Commission reaffirmed its earlier decision. "What the school board of Clark County has done is not the Commission's fault," one steadfast commissioner stated in support of the original compromise. "We solely adopted the book, and what the actions of the school board have done is something outside the matter of this hearing."[29] Frustrated, the ACLU returned to court alleging that the Commission action violated both state law and the Establishment Clause leading to the following trial court decision:

HENDREN v. CAMPBELL

Superior Court #5 for Marion County, Indiana
1977 WL 372669 (Ind. Sup. Ct. 1977)

MICHAEL T. DUGAN, II, J: Before the Court is a Verified Petition for Review (Amended Complaint) filed on March 23, 1977 on behalf of a ninth grade student, Jon Hendren, his father and another parent of a student in the West Clark Community School Corporation. The defendants are members of the Indiana Textbook Commission.

The Textbook Commission is responsible for the adoption of textbooks to be used in the public schools of Indiana. In the general area of biology the Commission adopted seven books, including the one at issue. From that list local school boards may then adopted texts to be used for a period of five years. Five school systems co-adopted this text with another text. Two systems, West Clark Community Schools and South Ripley Community Schools adopted only *A Search for Order in Complexity*.

In all of these systems the text is in current use in the first year of the five year cycle.

On March 18, 1977 the Textbook Commission pursuant to an order of the Court convened a hearing on the use of this text. The Commission issued findings of fact on that date denying the request of the plaintiffs that the text be withdrawn.

This petition is brought under the Indiana Administrative Adjudication Act IC 1971, 4–22–1–2 et seq. in a judicial review of the action of the Textbook Commission.... The Court is ... asked to view the Commission's findings and the text in light of the Establishment Clause of the First and Fourteenth Amendments of the Constitution of the United States....

REVIEW OF THE COMMISSION HEARINGS
TESTIMONY AND EXHIBITS

At the hearing of the Commission, the Plaintiffs called ten witnesses, among them being biologists and theologians. The Attorney General called one witness, one of the authors of the text. All of the Plaintiff's witnesses complained that the book was "sectarian" in viewpoint. One witness, Dr. Jon R. Hendix, was also a member of the State Science Advisory Committee that wrote guidelines for science instruction for the State of Indiana.

---

29. Bill Mundy in Transcription of Tapes and Notes Taken at a Hearing Before the Textbook Adoption Commission 9 contained in Hendren v. Campbell, No. S577–0138 (Marion Co. Ind. Super. Ct. No. 5 court file).

Dr. Hendix testified that the book was outside of state guidelines. The witness had recommended disapproval of the book.

The witness for the Attorney General, Dr. Larry G. Butler, was one of the authors of the book. Dr. Butler felt the book was "in accord" with his own Christian perspective. A witness for the plaintiff, Donald L. Nead, observed that the main-line Protestant denominations, including Presbyterians, Methodist, United Church of Christ, Christian Church (Disciples of Christ), and certain elements of the Lutheran and American Baptist Convention had not considered the theological basis of the book viable for many years.

The Plaintiff also introduced nine exhibits including the book, Teachers Guide, and various letters and booklets from the publisher. In terms of the purpose of the textbook, a letter from Henry M. Morris, Ph.D., Director of the Institute for Creation Research relates:

> The Institute for Creation Research in the research division of the Christian Heritage College, and all of the students in the College are given 90 class hours of instruction in creationism, so that they are all well-equipped to be leaders in the creationist movement in the future.

In another exhibit, Dr. Tim F. LaHaye, President of Christian Heritage College, discusses "the ministry of the Institute for Creation Research ...," it is a ... "unique missionary organization ...," "... it has a remarkable evangelistic and spiritual outreach." In a distribution brochure, including the text at issue, the publisher states:

> We are seeking to inform the public about the latest findings regarding special creation, but we also desire to publish and distribute material which will educate the reader concerning scriptural evidence and religious thought, and which will help build up the body of Christ.

Dr. Morris, in an article entitled "Creation in the Christian School," relates:

> Although a considerable part of ICR's activity is aimed at the restoration of creationism in the nation's public schools and state universities, we realize this is difficult to accomplish and is a long-range goal rather than one quickly attainable.
>
> In the public schools, for example, we urge that creationism be taught as an alternative to evolutionism not on a religious basis, but strictly on a scientific basis.
>
> In a private Christian school, however, this neutral approach is neither necessary or desirable. Although students in such schools should be taught about evolution, the curriculum should stress throughout that creation is the only Biblical position and the only realistic scientific position as well.

EXAMINATION OF THE TEXTBOOK AND TEACHER'S GUIDE

The textbook *A Search for Order in Complexity*, of some 595 pages, and the Teachers Guide, of some 96 pages, were published in 1974 in revised editions by the Zondervan Publishing House. Distribution and promotion was thereafter done through the Institute for Creation Research. The text itself includes some 29 chapters with corresponding teacher's guide with suggested answers to questions for students in the text. The text in its preface indicates:

> There are essentially only two philosophic viewpoints of origins among modern biologists—the doctrine of evolution and the doctrine of special creation. Proponents of the former postulate the gradual appearance of the various forms of life and of life itself by natural processes over vast ages of time. Exponents of the latter assume the essentially instantaneous origin of life and of the major kinds of living organisms by special creative acts utilized directly by the Creator Himself.

The text asserts that the two viewpoints "cannot really be harmonized . . . since they represent diametrically opposite viewpoints of origins."

The index to the text seems, on its face, to support the assertion that the text attempts to present both viewpoints for consideration by the thoughtful student. . . . In fact, the text consistently presents creationism in a positive light and evolution in a negative posture. . . . [A]t pages xxii and xxiii of the preface, the editor states:

> Evidences usually presented in support of evolution as a model of origins are accurately presented and considered. At the same time, it is explicit throughout the text that the most reasonable explanation for the actual facts of biology as they are known scientifically is that of biblical creationism.
>
> We hope this approach will be attractive first of all to the many private schools directed by those seeking to maintain an educational philosophy and methodology consistent with traditional Christian perspectives. We trust it will also be of interest and use in public school systems by teachers desiring to develop a genuine scientific attitude in their students rather than an artificially induced evolutionary worldview.

Most of the chapters in the text itself deal with non-controversial elements of biological science such as insects, chemical principles, algae, one-celled organisms, and so on. The book is, replete, however, with references to biblical topics, the "wonderful findings of God's creation," and "divine creation" as being the only correct viewpoint to be considered. Throughout the text, while both viewpoints are mentioned, biblical creation is consistently presented as the only correct "scientific" view. Two entire chapters, in fact are devoted to lengthy discussions of the fallacies and weaknesses of the evolution viewpoint. Chapter 21 "weakness of Geologic Evidence" goes into great detail disputing evolutionary theories as to fossils and geologic evidence. It explains fossils ". . . . by the fact that most fossil material was laid down by the flood in Noah's time." Chapter 24, "Problems for Evolutionists" devotes some eight pages to arguments refuting evolution theory. There are no chapters or passages in the text which deal critically with biblical creationism.

Also persuasive as to the avowed purpose of the book is the Teachers Guide. This publication, designed for teachers in using the text, summarizes the text, offers suggestions for use and enrichment and provides answers to questions found at the end of textbook chapters. These questions are designed to test the student as to his understanding and study of each chapter. A review of some of the questions and corresponding "correct" answers is instructive:

Question 10, page 163, text: "To what extent was Alexander Fleming's discovery based on chance, and to what extent on training?"

Answer, page 39, Teachers Guide: "It was 'chance' (under the direction of God's providence) which allowed the penicillin spores to get into the culture dishes of bacteria . . ."

Question 8, page 77, text: "Why does an old human skeleton of low type sometimes receive more attention than an old human skeleton of the same type as living men?"

Answer, page 77, Teacher's Guide: "Some persons believe that evolution has been amply demonstrated to be true. When a skeleton of low type is found, they jump to the conclusion that it is ancestral to modern man. Such persons forget that they are using their assumption of evolution as proof of evolution."

Question 7, page 459, text: "How does the doctrine of evolution by natural selection explain the development of altruism, or doesn't it?"

Answer, page 79, Teacher's Guide: "If the doctrine of evolution were true, it would favor heartless ruffians such as bandits and weeds. An altruistic person would be less 'fit' to survive. On the other hand, where a majority of a group of people recognize God, they appreciate and favor the altruistic person." . . .

Question 8, page 471, text: "What do hydra, the opossum and the jack pine teach about development of complexity?"

Answer, page 81. Teacher's Guide: "A complex animal or plant does not, because of its complexity, have an advantage in the struggle for existence. Complexity must have been conferred by the Creator rather than by natural conditions such as we observe today."

APPLICATION OF STATUTORY AND CONSTITUTIONAL STANDARDS

Numerous cases in the history of the United States have dealt with issues of the 1st Amendment to the Constitution. The United States Supreme Court has frequently determined that the authors of the Constitution did not merely prohibit the establishment of a state church or a state religion. In fact a sense of neutrality has been a goal of the Courts as it relates to the state and religion. . . .

Three tests have been offered by the Supreme Court to measure whether the action of the state has stepped beyond the prohibition of the First Amendment. These tests are designed to prevent "sponsorship," financial support, and active involvement of the sovereign in religious activity." These tests are:

1. The statute must have a secular legislative purpose.

2. The principal or primary effect must be one that neither advances nor inhibits religion.

3. The statute must not foster an excessive governmental entanglement with religion.

... [W]e face a textbook which, on its face, appears to present a balanced view of evolution and Biblical Creation. The record and the text itself do not support this assertion of fairness. Since the *Scopes* controversy over fifty years ago, the courts of this county have faced repeated attempts by groups of every conceivable persuasion to impose particular standards, whether religious or ethical, on the populace as a whole. We may note that with each new decision of the courts religious proponents have attempted to modify or tailor their approach to active lobbying in state legislatures and agencies. Softening positions and amending language, these groups have, time and again, forced the courts to reassert and redefine the prohibitions of the First Amendment. Despite new and continued attempts by such groups, however, the courts are bound to determine, if possible, the purpose of the approach.

Clearly, the purpose of *A Search for Order in Complexity* is the promotion and inclusion of fundamentalist Christian doctrine in the public schools. The publishers, themselves, admit that this text is designed to find its way into the public schools to stress Biblical Creationism. The court takes no position as to the validity of either evolution or Biblical Creationism. That is not the issue. The question is whether a text obviously designed to present only the view of Biblical Creationism in a favorable light is constitutionally acceptable in the public schools of Indiana. Two hundred years of constitutional government demand that the answer be no. The asserted object of the text to present a balanced or neutral argument is a sham that breaches that "wall of separation" between church and state voiced by Thomas Jefferson. Any doubts of the text's fairness is dispelled by the demand for "correct" Christian answers demanded by the Teacher's Guide. The prospect of biology teachers and students alike, forced to answer and respond to continued demand for "correct" fundamentalist Christian doctrines, has no place in the public schools. The attempt to present Biblical Creationism as the only accepted scientific theory, while novel, does not rehabilitate the constitutional violation.

After consideration of the text and the evidence at the agency hearing, the action of the Indiana State Textbook Commission is untenable.... The textbook *A Search for Order in Complexity*, as used in the public schools, violates I.C.1971 20–10–19–11, Article 1, Section 4 of the Constitution of the State of Indiana, and the First Amendment of the Constitution of the United States.

IT IS THEREFORE ORDERED AND ADJUDGED that the findings of the Indiana State Textbook Commission are reversed, and the commission is ordered to make findings not inconsistent with this decision after rehearing.

NOTES AND QUESTIONS

1. In *Hendren*, Judge Dugan characterized as "novel" the attempt made by the challenged textbook to present Genesis as containing a scientifically viable account of creation. Although not new in creationist circles, it did represent a new legal strategy for creationists. Earlier anti-evolution laws and lawsuits had sought to defend biblical concepts on religious and social grounds. Although William Jennings Bryan and other early anti-evolutionists questioned the scientific basis for Darwinism, they never offered Genesis as a scientific alternative. The situation changed radically by the 1970s. *A Search for Order in Complexity* was written by members of the Creation Research Society (CRS), an organization of creationists trained in science or engineering dedicated to finding evidence in nature to support a literal reading of the Bible, such as geological evidence of catastrophic water action in the Grand Canyon supportive of their belief that the Noachian flood shaped the earth's features and paleontological evidence of humans living amid dinosaurs in accord with the Genesis account of God creating all land animals on the same day with the first humans then naming all the different kinds. This body of evidence and purportedly rational inferences from it became known as scientific creationism or, more commonly, "creation-science." As noted in Judge Dugan's opinion, Virginia Tech engineering professor Henry M. Morris stood at the center of this burgeoning creation-science movement. A CRS leader and devout Southern Baptist apologist, Morris co-authored *A Search for Order in Complexity* and co-founded the Institute of Creation Research (ICR), which distributed it. Originally motivated by a desire to give reasons for Christians to believe the Bible in a scientific age, Morris subsequently concluded that scientific evidence of creation (stripped of its biblical ties) should be a valid topic for public-school biology courses. Why shouldn't all scientific evidence be acceptable in public schools regardless of its source? In *Hendren*, Judge Dugan concluded that any textbook designed to promote the biblical account of creation violated the Establishment Clause even if it featured scientific sounding evidence. The issue would not go away with one state-court decision, however, and grew to dominant the creation-evolution legal debate during the 1980s.

2. The *Hendren* opinion cited testimony offered by the plaintiffs suggesting that virtually all mainline Protestant denominations, whose members at the time constituted over half of all American Protestants, rejected both a literal interpretation of the Genesis account of creation and the basic tenets of creation-science. Indeed, by the mid-twentieth century, many mainline Christians had incorporated evolutionary concepts of human and organic progress into their basic theological outlook and viewed God as creating through evolution. By teaching creation-science in public schools, some argued, the

government was entangling itself in an inter-denominational squabble in violation of the Establishment Clause. In any event, theological disputes among Christians over the interpretation of Genesis all but assured that political and legal battles over the teaching of Darwinism and creation-science in public schools would continue into the late-twentieth century.

III. EXPANDING CREATIONIST PUSHBACK

Creationists persisted in seeking judicial relief during the 1970s and into the early 1980s. For example, two such cases were filed in the federal district court for Washington, D.C., during the period. In 1972, William T. Willoughby, the religion editor of the conservative *Washington Star–News*, filed suit against the National Science Foundation for funding the Darwinist BSCS textbooks. Two years later, Dale Crowley of the conservative National Foundation for Fairness in Education instituted a similar action against Darwinist educational exhibits at the Smithsonian Institution. Both complaints alleged that government support for one-sided evolutionary presentations unconstitutionally inhibited the free exercise of creationist religions and established a religion of secular humanism. Each action sought either to stop the offending activity or to secure equal support for creationist presentations. Neither case made it to trial. The federal district court in Washington handed down pretrial judgments against both plaintiffs. The federal appellate court for the District of Columbia affirmed these decisions, with a published opinion only in the *Crowley* case.

As these cases worked their way through the courts in Washington, D.C., creationists were having more success elsewhere. Working from their modest east Texas home, Mel and Norma Gabler had been battling their state's Board of Education over textbook content since the 1950s, beginning with allegations that American history textbooks suppressed and distorted conservative political ideas. By the 1960s, the Gablers had added Darwinism to their growing list of targets and, in 1970, secured a formal Board ruling that textbooks should present evolution as a theory. This ruling potentially had national impact because Texas purchased textbooks at the state level. Any publisher wishing to compete for this large market needed to follow the Board's directives. Not satisfied with this concession, the Gablers pressed the Board either to provide equal space for creationism in biology textbooks or to delete all evolutionary dogma from such texts. In mid–1974, the Board adopted a compromise resolution acceptable to the Gablers. "Textbooks that treat the theory of evolution should identify it as only one of several explanations of the origins of humankind and avoid limiting young people in their search for meanings of their human existence," the Board ruled. "Textbooks presented for adoption which treat the subject of evolution substantially in explaining the historical origins of man shall be edited, if necessary, to clarify that the treatment is theoretical rather than factually verifiable. Furthermore, each textbook must carry a statement on an introductory page that any material on evolution included in the book is clearly presented as theory rather than verified."[30] Applying this new regulation, the Board than rejected all three versions of the BSCS texts.

Also beginning in the 1960s and driven by similar convictions, two southern California suburban homemakers, Nell Segraves and Jean Sumrall, acting on behalf of their school-aged children, petitioned their state's Board of Education for relief for the allegedly dogmatic way that evolution was being presented in local public schools. The Creation Research Society assisted Segraves and Sumrall in preparing this petition. California creationists drew first blood in 1963 when the elected state Superintendent of Public Instruction Max Rafferty, a conservative Republican educator and politician, responded to the petition by ordering that textbooks identify evolution as a theory. He based this order on a vague state Department of Justice opinion concluding that public schools could not constitutionally prescribe irreligious teaching. Segraves and other California creationists were far from satisfied. With Rafferty's active encouragement, they continued agitating throughout the decade for the state Board of Education to mandate the addition of creationism to the public school biology curriculum, leading to the incorporation into the Board's 1969 *Science Framework for California Public Schools* the affirmation, "Some of the scientific data, (e.g., the regular absence of transitional forms) may be best explained by a creation theory, while other data (e.g., transmutation of species) substantiates a process of evolution."[31] This document gave California creationists grounds to call for teaching evidence and arguments from nature for a creation, or "creation-science." In 1972, however, when the time first arrived for approving biology textbooks under the 1969 *Framework*, the Board was deluged with protests from scientists and scientific organizations opposed to including creationism in the texts. Instead of including creationism in the new texts, the Board adopted a policy requiring that "dogmatism be changed to conditional statements where speculation is offered as explanation for origins." In this respect, the policy statement added, "Science should emphasize 'how' and not 'ultimate cause' for origins." The resulting textual changes were modest and generally acceptable to protesting scientists. In response to further creationist demands, the California board voted in 1973 to include creationism in social-science textbooks, but revoked this too before ever applying it. The creationist affirmations were formally dropped from the Board's *Science Framework* in 1974, leaving the 1972 anti-dogmatism policy as the only relic of the stormy California creationism controversy.

By the mid–1970s, Nell Segraves's son Kelly had three children of his own. Very much his mother's son, Segraves objected to the evolutionary teaching that his children received in class. After failing to persuade the

---

30. TEX. EDUC. CODE ANN., Tit. 19, § 81.63. (West 1975).

31. *Science Framework for California Public Schools Kindergarten—Grades One Through Twelve*, quoted in John A. Moore, *Creationism in California, in* SCIENCE AND ITS PUBLIC 196 (Gerald Holton and William A. Blanpied eds., 1976).

state Board of Education to restore restrictions on Darwinian instruction to its *Science Framework*, in 1979, Segraves filed suit on behalf of his children against the allegedly dogmatic way that evolution was actually presented in California public schools. After a prominent conservative Republican member of Congress from San Diego, William Dannemeyer, joined the suit as an added plaintiff, state and national media began taking notice. Segraves's complaint feigned a broad attack on evolutionary teaching replete with demands for giving equal time to creation-science but Segraves executed a planned retreat at trial. Describing the only issue as religious freedom, Segraves's attorney demanded in his opening statement only that "they must stop posing the theory that man and all life on earth developed from a common ancestor, as a fact, in the schools of this State." Putting this issue in its best light, he pleaded that "at the very least, we might expect that the government not affirmatively tell my clients' children in the public school that their beliefs are wrong."

With national broadcast and print reporters covering the trial and newspapers billing it as "Scopes II" or "a reverse Scopes," Segraves's moderated demands for schools to accommodate his son's religious beliefs struck a responsive chord with Irving Perluss, the progressive-minded trial judge hearing the case. When the state moved for the customary dismissal on the grounds that science teaching cannot infringe on religious freedom because science is neutral on religious matter, Perluss expressed skepticism and bid the trial proceed. Segraves's new approach forced the state to drop its plan to discredit creation-science through the testimony of over a dozen leading scientists and scholars. Instead, the parties fought for days over whether or not the wording of state-approved textbooks and teaching guidelines unduly infringed on religious freedom. In the end, the judge was most impressed by the 1972 anti-dogmatism policy and testimony from a Board member that the policy still applied. Both the 1980 federal circuit court opinion in *Crowley* and Judge Perluss's 1981 bench ruling in *Segraves* follow:

CROWLEY v. SMITHSONIAN INSTITUTION

United States Court of Appeals for the District of Columbia Circuit
636 F.2d 738 (D.C. Cir. 1980)

OBERDORFER, J.: Appellants are an individual and two organizations, the National Foundation for Fairness in Education and National Bible Knowledge, Inc. They refer to their conception of the origin of life as "scientific creationism." They assert that by marshalling and interpreting data in a scientific way, they can support the proposition that human and other forms of life were brought into existence in completed form, all at one time, by a Creator. They conscientiously disagree with the theory of evolution which postulates that all plant, animal, and human life "have arisen from a single source which itself came from an inorganic form."

Appellees are the Smithsonian Institution and two Smithsonian employees. Using federal funds, appellees planned (for 1979) and conducted (in 1978) two exhibitions containing references to evolution at the Smithsonian's Museum of Natural History (Museum). The exhibit presented at the Museum in 1978 was entitled "The Emergence of Man." The one planned for (and presumably completed in) 1979, contemplated using specimens from the Museum's collection to dramatize the diversity of life on Earth, the adaptation of plant and animal life to their environments, and the way in which organisms change over time in response to environmental and other influences.

Appellants sued in the United States District Court for the District of Columbia for a declaratory judgment that the Smithsonian's charter (20 U.S.C. § 41 et seq.) did not authorize the use of federal funds for such exhibits and that, if the charter did authorize such use of federal funds, the charter and the expenditures violated the First Amendment's prohibition against the establishment of religion and inhibited appellants' free exercise of their religion. Appellants urged that by explaining and advocating the theory of evolution, appellees unconstitutionally supported the religion of Secular Humanism. Appellants sought an injunction prohibiting the exhibits and federal funding of them or, in the alternative, an order requiring appellees to commit equal funds to explain creation along the lines of the Biblical account in Genesis.

Appellees moved in the District Court for dismissal or, in the alternative, for summary judgment.... Applying, then, the well-established test as it is stated in Tilton v. Richardson, 403 U.S. 672, 678 (1971), the District Court concluded that (1) appellees' "presentation of evolutionary theory has the solid secular purpose of 'increasing and diffusing knowledge among men'" and that appellees do not "oppose or show hostility to religion" and do not "create a religion of secularism;" 426 F.Supp. at 727, (2) the exhibits neither advance a religious theory nor inhibit appellants in theirs; (3) neither the Smithsonian enabling legislation nor the exhibits involve excessive entanglement with religion; and (4) the appellants' free exercise of their religion is not actionably impaired merely because, should they visit the Smithsonian, they may be confronted with exhibits which are distasteful to their religion.... Satisfied that there were no material facts in dispute and that the trial court correctly decided the legal issues, we affirm.

I.

... There has been no dispute about the physical elements of the exhibits in question. The exhibit planned for 1979 was to emphasize specimens from the Museum's collection depicting adaptations of plants and animals to their environment by such devices as camouflage, the overproduction of offspring and other defense mechanisms. It was to include an introductory display of a variety of specimens such as trays of bird eggs, mammal skulls, and jars of amphibians. There were also to be displays on genetics, natural selection, and one showing differentiation of populations.

The 1978 exhibit, the "Emergence of Man," is described in an accompanying pamphlet as "the story of how, when and where modern human beings evolved from homonid ancestors who lived millions of years ago." This exhibit, consisting of data from the natural world, illustrated the physical similarities and differences between man and what were reported to be geneological ancestors.

The concept of evolution was referred to in these exhibits. They did not, however, express implicitly or explicitly "that the evolutionary theory of the origin of man and of all plants and animal life is 'the only credible theory of the origin of life.' " Affidavit of Porter M. Kier, Director of the National Museum of Natural History, App. at p. 46. The exhibits did not mention religion in general or Secular Humanism in particular. Neither by their terms nor by implication did the exhibits disparage religion or any religious tenet.

Appellants' opposition to the summary judgment motion was essentially a challenge to the concept of evolution. It questioned whether that concept is any more susceptible to scientific proof than appellants' concept of the supernatural origins of life, and characterized this issue as one of material fact. In support of their contentions, they offered the affidavit, among others, of Dr. Richard B. Bliss, Director of Curriculum Development for the Institute of Creation Research of San Diego, California. Dr. Bliss' affidavit characterized evolution as "a nonobservable and alleged phenomenon which can neither be proven nor verified by the scientific method.... [E]volution of life from primal matter is impossible to observe...." App. at 37. Since the evolution theory cannot be tested by the scientific method, according to Dr. Bliss' opinion, it is not a true science, but is a "faith position." In addition, Dr. Bliss' affidavit stated, from personal observation of the exhibits in question, but without specification, that they contained "false and misleading statements concerning evolution" and that the exhibits are indoctrinating the public in the faith of evolution. App. at page 39. Finally, Dr. Bliss asserted that, in his opinion, evolution itself is a religion and that many evolutionists so acknowledge and "promote" it as such. App. at p. 39.

II.

Assuming, arguendo, that, as asserted in Dr. Bliss' affidavit, the evolution theory cannot be proved "scientifically" in the laboratory and in that sense rests ultimately on "faith," such fact is not material because it would not establish as a matter of law that the exhibits in question establish any religion such as Secular Humanism.

The fact that religions involve acceptance of some tenets on faith without scientific proof obviously does not mean that all beliefs and all theories which rest in whole or in part on faith are therefore elements of a religion as that term is used in the First Amendment. For example, appellees suggest that the theory of relativity defies absolute laboratory proof. Obviously the Constitution would not interdict government development and diffusion of knowledge about relativity even if it were based on some hypotheses which are not susceptible to physically demonstrable proof.

Nor does it follow that government involvement in a subject which is also important to practitioners of a religion becomes, therefore, activity in support of religion. For example, birth control and abortion are topics that involve both religious beliefs and general health and welfare concerns. Many religious leaders have vigorously opposed government support of the teaching and practice of birth control and government support, or even toleration, of abortion. Controversy, including litigation, about these subjects has been prolific and spirited. No court, however, has finally held that government advocacy of or opposition to either birth control or abortion violates the establishment clause of the first amendment. Indeed, the Supreme Court recently and summarily rejected an argument that the limiting of medicaid funds for abortions violated the establishment clause "because it incorporates into law the doctrines of the Roman Catholic Church...." Harris v. McRae, 448 U.S. 297, 319 (1980). The Court reasoned that:

> Although neither a State nor the Federal Government can constitutionally "pass laws which aid one religion, aid all religions, or prefer one religion over another," Everson v. Board of Education, 330 U.S. 1, 15, it does not follow that a statute violates the Establishment Clause because it "happens to coincide or harmonize with the tenets of some or all religions." McGowan v. Maryland, 366 U.S. 420.

Id. So here, we cannot conclude that the exhibits in question are impermissible because their message may coincide or harmonize with a tenet of Secular Humanism or may be repugnant to creationism.

Our resolution of appellants' establishment claim as a matter of law disposes of their procedural contention that the District Court erroneously resolved a material issue of fact short of trial. The dispute about whether the evolution theory was based on scientific proof or on faith is immaterial to the question of whether the Smithsonian exhibits supported establishment of Secular Humanism as a religion. The fact that appellants were able to identify one religious group that espoused evolution as one of its tenets is immaterial. Accordingly, we are satisfied that the District Court did not leave unresolved any material issues of fact.

III.

Although the foregoing discussion furnishes an adequate basis for decision, we briefly address the trial court's disposition of appellants' substantive contentions.... Courts should be particularly sensitive to claims by groups that government is involved in their religion either by interfering with it, or by supporting a competing theology. The Supreme Court has mandated "government neutrality between religion and religion, and between religion and non-religion." Epperson v. Arkansas, 393 U.S. 97, 104 (1968). Government, including its judicial branch, is cautioned not "to require that teaching and learning must be tailored to the principles or prohibitions of any religious sect or dogma." Id. at 106; see also Everson v. Board of Education, 330 U.S. 1, 15–16 (1947). The constitution either by operation of the first amendment or the fourteenth, protects a citizen's right to receive information and to "acquire useful knowledge." See, e.g., ... Meyer v. Nebraska, 262 U.S. 390, 399 (1923); Bartels v. Iowa, 262 U.S. 404 (1923).

Application of the Supreme Court's caution to this case necessarily requires a balance between appellants' freedom to practice and propagate their religious beliefs in creation without suffering government competition or interferences and appellees' right to disseminate, and the public's right to receive, knowledge from government, through schools and other institutions such as the Smithsonian. This balance was long ago struck in favor of diffusion of knowledge based on responsible scientific foundations, and against special constitutional protection of religious believers from the competition generated by such knowledge diffusion....[32]

SEGRAVES v. CALIFORNIA

Superior Court for Sacramento County, California
No. 278,978 (Cal. Super. Ct. March 6, 1981)

Oral Opinion of the Court

Irving H. Perluss, J.: Now, we are concerned with the constitutional guarantee, and I think it's worthwhile just to repeat it again, although all of us have heard it and read it many, many times during the course of this case. It is set forth in the First Amendment, "Congress shall make no law respecting an establishment of religion or prohibiting the free exercise thereof." And some people may say, "Well, that is directed toward the Congress, how does the State of California get involved with this?" Well, the Supreme Court of the United States has held that both clauses are incorporated in the Fourteenth Amendment, which applies to the states, and accordingly the guarantees also apply to state action.

Now, often there is tension between the clauses and at the beginning of that case as we read the pleadings, we really thought that perhaps that was going to be the situation here. And, for example, it could be argued that the use of federal funds to provide chaplains for the Armed Forces might violate the Establishment Clause, and yet the Supreme Court has said a lonely soldier stationed at some far away out point could complain that a government which did not provide for pastoral guidance was

---

32. Appellants have, at various stages of this litigation, contended that the exhibits at the Museum have interfered with the free exercise of their religion. This claim has not been pressed vigorously on appeal and we find it to be without merit. In any event, there is no allegation that such financial support has any "coercive effect" upon appellants' "practice of ... religion." Harris v. McRae, supra, 448 U.S. at 320, quoting with approval, Abington School District v. Schempp, 374 U.S. 203, 223 (1963). Appellants allege no effect on their ability freely to exercise their religion or teach it to their children. See Wisconsin v. Yoder, 406 U.S. 205 (1972); Sherbert v. Verner, 374 U.S. 398 (1963). Finally, appellants are under no compulsion to go to the Museum. If they choose to do so, they are free to avoid the exhibits which they find offensive and may focus on the other exhibits of which there are many. Compare e.g., West Virginia State Board of Education v. Barnette, 319 U.S. 624 (1943) with Hamilton v. Regents, 293 U.S. 245(1934).

prohibiting his free exercise of religion. This is a classic case of the tensions, the confrontation, if you will, between the Establishment Clause on the one side and the free exercise clause on the other.

We thought, as I said, that this was that kind of case because of the Pleadings, and this problem arises where free exercise is threatened so that accommodation is necessary, but the accommodation of—itself may violate the Establishment Clause. Let me give you some examples of that. Release time for religious instruction presents such a problem. An accommodation in which religious instruction was given in the public schools that was held to be an unconstitutional and forbidden accommodation was when the children had religious instruction in the public schools. That was forbidden by the constitution, but on the other hand, the Supreme Court of the United States has held that the release time program which—in which children were allowed to leave the public school in order to receive religious instruction elsewhere was a permissible accommodation.

The play between establishment on the one hand, in terms of accommodation, and free exercise on the other. Now, fortunately—I say, "fortunately," because I'm the fellow that has to make the decision—the issues have been narrowed here to the point where we are not faced with such a dilemma, and thus there is no contention here that evolution should not be taught in the public schools. I think you've heard me say on several occasions that if there were, it would be rejected as an impermissible accommodation, for that battle was fought and resolved by the Supreme Court of the United States in Epperson v. Arkansas.

Now, moreover, the Plaintiffs have disclaimed any interest in an accommodation which would require the teaching of special creation in the public schools. And I might say in—and of course, this is what they call "dicta," this is not part of the decision in this case, but this is my view—that it was appropriate that they do so, for I have no doubt, whatever, that such a accommodation would be held to be violated with the Establishment Clause, and forbidden. I think this is so, as a matter of law. It was basically held to be such in the opinion of the California Attorney General in 53 Attorney General Opinions 262. And, of course, it was held in the decision of Daniels v. Waters in the Sixth Circuit, which was referred to during the course of our trial.

Now, the issues, simply stated, accordingly, is whether or not the free exercise of religion by Mr. Segraves and his children was thwarted by the instruction in [evolutionary] science that children had received in school, and if so, has there been sufficient accommodation for their views?

I must say, first of all, there can be absolutely no doubt of the sincerity of the Segraves family. I'm particularly impressed with the young man who has been seated here during this trial listening to all these dull proceedings. He's an outstanding young man. And the Court also has been truly impressed with the outstanding people who have made contributions and are making contributions to our public schools, people who have appeared here as witnesses, just tremendous people.

And, further, the Court is prepared to find that the State Board of Education has acted throughout in good faith, just as the Court finds the Plaintiffs herein have acted throughout in good faith. The Court, in addition, is prepared to find and does find that the science framework, as written, and if qualified by the [anti-discrimination] policy of the Board exemplified by Exhibit N,[33] does provide sufficient accommodation for the views of Plaintiff. This is so, in my judgment, even if . . . there is some problem about whether that was ever officially adopted as a policy by the Board because the fact is now that by virtue of the statement of the representative of the Board, more than one, not only the Attorney General but the representatives of the Board, that is current Board policy and shall remain as current Board policy until a Board changes it. So, I think we have to assume that this is so. In effect, it is stipulated and agreed that this is Board policy, but this is not, of course, the end of the story.

. . . It seems to me that what has happened here has developed from a lack of communication from the Board to the school to the classroom teacher. I think it is the emphasis, the emphasis on tolerance and understanding that should be communicated as a fundamental policy of the State Board of Education. This is true not only in science, but it's true throughout the entire public school system.

. . . The child who is a Jehovah's Witness should not be made to feel guilty because he cannot salute the flag. The student who is a Seventh Day Adventist should not be scorned because he cannot participate in his school car wash because it is held on a Saturday, his Sabbath. The Jewish child who cannot participate in Easter and Christmas celebrations should not be made to feel rejected. And, parenthetically, I—I must add that it seems to the Court, also, that persons seeking tolerance and understanding must practice it, also. Only in this way; can all of us enjoy the religious liberty which is our fundamental right.

[Plaintiffs' Counsel] has already quoted from the concurring opinion of Justice Stewart in Sherbert v. Verner [374 U.S. 398 (1963)]. I think it's worth repeating because those are resounding and beautiful words where he said, "I am convinced that no liberty is more essential to the continued vitality of the free society which our constitution guarantees than is the religious liberty protected by the Free Exercise Clause explicit in the First Amendment and embedded in the Fourteenth." I think Justice Stewart has spoken well.

In the final analysis, ladies and gentlemen, counsel, all that Plaintiffs seek, in the Court's view, presently is contained in Board policy. It appears, however, that this Board policy may not have been communicated to all who should know of it, and who should be guided by that policy. As this is a Court of equity, it seems to the Court that an appropriate remedy may be fashioned.

---

33. [As described by the Court, California's so-called anti-discrimination policy "provides that in a discussion of origins in science texts and classes (a) dogmatism be changed to conditional statements where speculation is offered as explanation for origins and (b) that science emphasizes 'how' and not 'ultimate cause' for origins."]

It will be the order of the Court that there shall be disseminated to all the publishers, institutions, school districts, schools, and persons regularly receiving the science framework a copy of the Board policy set forth in Exhibit N. By this, the Court means, insofar as possible, the policy shall be sent to those who have received the framework in the past. It shall be included in the framework disseminated in the future. It follows that if there are violations of this policy when disseminated it becomes a matter of concern for students and parents to adjust with their local teachers, their local schools, and their local school boards.

Now, the Court has said on several occasions during the trial that it would be presumptuous if it sought to write the content of a framework or of any of these other publications which have been presented to the Court. Although, of course, we are concerned with qualification and accommodation, I was so impressed with the words of Dr. Mayer that I asked the reporter to transcribe them for me, and I would like to read them again to you:

Mr. Mayer said, "There is, in the realm of knowledge, a structure we—we speak of it as epistemology, we learn different things in different ways. This doesn't mean that any of this is wrong. For example, when you look at a mountain and a poet says, 'it's purple mountain majesty.' If a mineralogist looks at a mountain and says, 'it's composed of copper,' same mountain, he's not in error. A geologist may say, 'why, that's a plastic dyke.' Well, so it maybe, and he's not in error. Where the problem begins to be confusing is when we begin of mingle epistemological systems and try to make the poet and the mineralogist and the geologist all look at that mountain the same way. Now, when you begin to think of textbooks that talk about belief, now to me belief is not a scientific word. One knows, one accumulates data, one has a comprehension of, one understands, one does a lot of things; but to me belief always, in my situation, has been something I associate with my theology. [I] would not like to see my theology and my science get mixed. I have never dealt with a scientific process where somebody says, 'I believe.' I have dealt with theological processes where one believes. In short, I think at that point you begin to mix epistemologies, and that's confusing."

And then I said to him, "But I see, as I comprehend this case, we are talking about the very kind of disclaimer that you have just told us about, that at the beginning of a science textbook should there not be a statement—because not everyone is a scientist and knows all the background of scientists—but shouldn't there be a statement saying, 'this does not deal with theology?'"

Dr. Mayer, "Absolutely. I would—I would say there should be a clear explanation that perhaps should run through the entire textbook establishing within the student's mind what it is he's dealing with. He is dealing with science. We are not making pretence to teach him music, art, poetry, theology, or any other discipline. Science does these things, and outside of that realm, science is not only moot, but might even be harmful."

Court, "And, moreover, science is not dogmatic in that it is open ended and there is an absence of preset conclusions?"

The witness, "Yes, sir."

I commend this, to the State Board of Education, as a beautiful and pertinent statement of what science is all about, as a layman. . . .

Justice Stewart also said in the concurring opinion in the Sherbert case, and these are the words that I felt were most pertinent to our case where he said, "And I think that the guarantee of religious liberty embodied in the free exercise clause affirmatively requires government to create an atmosphere of hospitality and accommodation to individual belief or disbelief. In short, I think our Constitution commands the positive protection by government of religious freedom, not only for a minority, however, small, not only for the majority, however large, but for each of us." I don't think any of us could really quarrel with that. . . .

Written Findings of Fact and Conclusions of Law

. . . The Court having heard the testimony and having examined the proofs offered by the respective parties, and the cause having been submitted for decision, and the Court being fully advised in the premises makes its findings of fact as follows:

Findings of Fact

It is true that:

1. Plaintiffs are sincere in their religious beliefs and in their conviction that plaintiff Kasey Segraves has been denied his right to free exercise of his religion guaranteed to them and to him by the First and Fourteenth Amendments to the Constitution of the United States and Article I, Section 4 of the California Constitution.

2. Defendant State Board of Education has acted in good faith and has taken no action which would deny plaintiffs herein and particularly plaintiff Kasey Segraves their or his rights to free exercise of their religion guaranteed to them and him by the First and Fourteenth Amendments to the Constitution of the United States and Article 1, Section 4 of the California Constitution.

3. To the contrary, defendant State Board of Education has had for a number of years and currently has a policy exemplified by defendant's Exhibit N which provides that in a discussion of origins in science texts and classes (a) dogmatism be changed to conditional statements where speculation is offered as explanation for origins and (b) that science emphasizes "how" and not "ultimate cause" for origins.[34]

---

34. [Having originally adopted its so-called anti-dogmatism policy in 1972, the California Board of Education revised it in 1989. The policy currently reads:

4. The policy of defendant State Board of Education, as set forth in paragraph 3 herein, however, may not have been communicated to all who should know of it, and who must be guided by that policy. From the foregoing facts, the Court concludes:

Conclusions of Law

1. The policy of defendant State Board of Education, as set forth in paragraph 3 herein, is an appropriate accommodation which permits plaintiffs to freely exercise their religion as guaranteed by the First and Fourteenth Amendments to the Constitution of the United States and Article 1, Section 4 of the California Constitution.

2. If such policy were not disseminated to all publishers, school districts, schools (and science teachers in the schools) and all other persons regularly receiving the Science Framework, an appropriate accommodation would not be made as guaranteed by the First and Fourteenth Amendments to the Constitution of the United States and Article 1, Section 4 of the California Constitution.

3. To assure plaintiffs and all others concerned that their rights to free exercise of their religion will not be infringed, the Court will require defendant State Board of Education to disseminate to all publishers, school districts, schools (and science teachers in the schools) and all other persons regularly receiving the Science Framework a copy of the policy of the State Board of Education (defendant's Exhibit N), including all those who have received the Science Framework in the past, and such policy statement shall be included in future Science Framework.

4. Each side shall bear their own costs of suit and attorneys' fees.

NOTES AND QUESTIONS

1. The *Crowley* decision speaks of striking a balance between plaintiffs' freedom to practice and propagate their religious beliefs without suffering governmental competition or interference and the Smithsonian Institution's right to disseminate (and the public's right to receive) knowledge. Perhaps reflecting the cultural significance accorded science, the court concluded, "This balance was long ago struck in favor of diffusion of knowledge based on

---

The domain of the natural sciences is the natural world. Science is limited by its tools—observable facts and testable hypotheses.

Discussions of any scientific fact, hypothesis, or theory related to the origins of the universe, the earth, and life (the *how*) are appropriate to the science curriculum. Discussions of divine creation, ultimate purposes, or ultimate causes (the *why*) are appropriate to the history—social science and English—language arts curricula.

Nothing in science or in any other field of knowledge shall be taught dogmatically. Dogma is a system of beliefs that is not subject to scientific test and refutation. Compelling belief is inconsistent with the goal of education; the goal is to encourage understanding.

To be fully informed citizens, students do not have to accept everything that is taught in the natural science curriculum, but they do have to understand the major strands of scientific thought, including its methods, facts, hypotheses, theories, and laws. . . .

Cal. State. Bd. Educ., *State Board of Education Policy on the Teaching of Natural Sciences, in* SCIENCE FRAMEWORK FOR CALIFORNIA PUBLIC SCHOOLS ix, ix (Cal. State Bd. Educ., 2004).]

responsible scientific foundations, and against special constitutional protection of religious believers from the competition generated by such knowledge diffusion." Does this balance tip toward diffusion only (or especially) in cases involving scientific knowledge? What if the case instead involved an exhibition at the Smithsonian's art museum of paintings that the plaintiffs reasonably considered both offensive and prejudicial to their religious beliefs—would the balance still tip as heavily toward diffusion? In *Crowley* and *Willoughby*, the court's rulings effectively precluded a courtroom trial for religious challenges to Darwinist exhibits, textbooks, and (by implication) teaching. Trials are for deciding factual disputes but religious creationism loses under any facts so long as the courts automatically deferred to scientific opinion over religious belief in questions involving science instruction. Creationists' better hope lay in lowering the scientific status of evolution or raising the scientific status of creationism and then basing their legal claims on this anti-evolutionary science. As noted above, *Hendren* suggested the limits of this approach but creationists would keep trying to exploit it.

2.   The *Crowley* court dealt with the argument (long popular among creationists) that the theory of human evolution is not "true science" because the evolution of humans from a preexisting species was not observed and is not now testable. In this sense, as argued in the cited affidavit of ICR Director Richard Bliss, the theory that species evolved from preexisting ones is as much a "faith position" as creation-science. At least as applied to distinctly different kinds of current or past animals and plants, neither "theory" can now be observed, proved, or fully tested. If the evolutionary "faith position" supports a religion of secular humanism or undermines some theistic religions, creationists argued, then it should be as unconstitutional to teach Darwinism in public schools as it is to teach creation-science. How did the *Crowley* court deal with this common creationist argument? The court noted that not all ideas resting wholly or partly on faith are religious even if some religions claim them as central tenets. What then differentiates the supposedly scientific theory of evolution from the supposedly religious theory of creation-science? Some argue that the former theory has been tested successfully by the scientific method while the later theory has not. Others add that evolutionary scientists derived their theories from natural observations and laboratory experiments while creation-scientists derived their theories on faith from the Bible and then sought evidence from nature to support them. Ultimately, many simply defer to scientists or prevailing scientific opinion in deciding what is and what is not science. Look for this question and various answers to it in later cases.

3.   Arguing by analogy to address the plaintiffs' charge that the Establishment and Free Exercise Clauses bar government from supporting activities that either favor or disfavor particular religions, the *Crowley* court noted that the government may fund researching, teaching, and using birth control and abortion even though many Americans have sincere religious objections to birth control and abortion. This analogy may fit cases like *Crowley* and *Willoughby* involving museum exhibits and funding for writing textbooks, but not cases involving Darwinian teaching in public schools? Surely it would violate the Constitution for the government to force citizens to use birth control or obtain an abortion contrary to their religious beliefs. Under

compulsory school attendance laws, are public-school students more like museum visitors or persons forced to use birth control? Given his reasoning in *Segraves*, how would Judge Perluss likely answer this question? Judge Perluss expressly rejected either requiring public schools to teach creationism or barring them from teaching Darwinism but he clearly concluded that the Free Exercise Clause mandated that public schools offer some accommodation for the sincere religious beliefs of creationist students. Does California's 1972 anti-discrimination policy go far enough? Judge Perluss thought so. Would the policy's current language satisfy him? In his exchange with defense witness Mayer on the anti-discrimination policy, Judge Perluss cast it in terms of the so-called non-overlapping magisterial approach to science and religion later popularized by paleontologist and popular science writer Stephen Jay Gould. This approach holds that science and religion represent different ways of knowing, with the former better suited to answer questions of how and the latter better suited to address questions of why. The legendary Italian astronomer Galileo Galilei famously captured this viewpoint in his 1615 *Letter to Madame Christine of Lorraine, Grand Duchess of Tuscany* in which he wrote that the Bible teaches "us how to go to Heaven, and not how the heavens go."

4.   Both sides claimed victory following the decision in *Segraves*. The court-ordered letter from the State Board of Education distributing the anti-discrimination policy stated that the court "upheld the validity of the State Board's 1978 Science Framework against a legal action" by creationists. The letter went on to state that equal time should not be given to creationism. Meanwhile, in a letter to his supporters, Segraves emphasized the court-mandated anti-dogmatism policy and announced plans to apply "the court injunction to state approved textbooks for science." He stressed that, according to the court, the Free Exercise Clause requires that science teaching accommodate religious beliefs regardless of the scientific validity of those beliefs.

CHAPTER 4

THE RISE AND FALL OF BALANCED TREATMENT

▪ ▪ ▪

I. CREATION–SCIENCE LEGISLATION

In 1980, creation-science leader Henry M. Morris boasted that the 1970s had been the decade of creation and predicted that the term would apply even more to the 1980s. That same year, Republican presidential nominee Ronald Reagan blessed both prongs of the creationist offensive by describing evolution as only a theory and endorsing public-school instruction in creationism wherever evolution is taught. By then, the creation-evolution controversy was back in the courts, with creationists trying both to qualify evolutionary teaching and to secure a place for creationist concepts while evolutionists sought to oust creationism from the science classroom once and for all. The *Epperson* decision left these three issues unresolved. That decision simply ruled that a state could not prevent its teachers from discussing the theory of evolution—it did not address either restrictions on the nature of such discussion or the constitutionality of teaching creationism. Some partisans on both sides leaped at these openings with a religious fervor.

Shortly after the *Hendren* decision Wendell Bird, an evangelical Christian Yale Law School student, took time out from his studies to devise a legal strategy for the creationist movement. He was motivated by personal experience. Because of his high-school biology instruction, Bird later wrote, I "came to believe in 'theistic evolution,' because [I] did not realize that the Bible taught anything different or that any scientists held any other viewpoint."[35] Once set straight, he longed to protect other students from a similar fate by securing a place for creationism in the classroom. In January 1978 he published his legal strategy as a long student note in the *Yale Law Journal* and won a school prize for his efforts.

Starting from the proposition that several religious denominations affirm divine creation as a cardinal tenet of faith, Bird revived the well-

---

35. Wendell R. Bird, *Evolution in Public Schools and Creation in Students' Homes*, *in* DECADE OF CREATION 119 (Henry M. Morris & Donald H. Rohrer eds., 1981).

worn argument that teaching only evolution violated the free exercise of such religions by compelling public-school students from those denominations to receive instruction in heretical views or to forgo biology training. By appealing to three reasons given in earlier Supreme Court decisions interpreting the Free Exercise Clause to exempt Amish children from compulsory attendance at high school and Jehovah's Witnesses from classroom flag ceremonies, Bird argued that evolutionary teaching unconstitutionally undermined creationist beliefs, infringed on religious principles of separation from unholy doctrines, and compelled responses by students contrary to their personal beliefs. Applying the constitutional principle that the government may not restrict individual rights more than necessary in achieving its objectives, Bird then proposed that when furthering the goal of biology instruction, schools should neutralize their curriculum by teaching both creationism and Darwinism.

Using past creationist defeats to support this conclusion, Bird read *Daniel* and *Hendren* as prohibiting only the teaching of religious creationism and *Epperson* as overturning religiously motivated restrictions aimed solely at evolutionary teaching. "Incorporation of scientific creationism to neutralize public school instruction in the origin of the universe and life would not have the primary effect of advancing some religions," Bird asserted. Primarily citing the work of Morris and his associates at the Institute for Creation Research (ICR), Bird maintained that a model of creationism and critique of evolution "could be constructed from scientific discussion of empirical evidence divorced from theological reasoning and terminology."[36] This, then, was the cornerstone of Bird's argument— creation-science was science, not religion, and teaching it did not violate the Establishment Clause, while not teaching it violated the free-exercise rights of creationist students. Addressing the precedent that he could not distinguish, Bird dismissed *Wright* and *Willoughby* for not recognizing the coercion against religious freedom caused by evolutionary instruction.

Bird's legal analysis relied on a series of factual assumptions. These included the centrality of creationism to widely held religious beliefs, the insupportable burden placed on those beliefs by evolutionary teaching, the appropriateness of parallels drawn from constitutional protections for the Amish and Jehovah's Witnesses, the suitability of protecting creationist students from evolutionary ideas by balancing those ideas with creationist alternatives, and, most critically, the non-religious basis of creation-science. Although these assumptions may appear self-evident to an avid creationist like Bird, others could question them. To fellow believers, however, Bird offered a legal theory that, when combined with Morris's scientific theories, provided a hope for a meaningful victory. Better than simply presenting evolution as a theory, exempting creationist students from attendance, or even banning all instruction in origins, schools would teach creationism as science. By offering this hope, Bird and Morris

---

36. Wendell R. Bird, *Freedom of Religion and Science Instruction in Public Schools*, 83 YALE L.J. 515, 556, 561 (1978).

together influenced the course of creationist legal efforts more than any individuals since Bryan sounded the original call for anti-evolution laws.

After finishing law school, Bird joined Morris at ICR, serving as a legal adviser and, for a time, as staff attorney. One of his first tasks was to update the ICR model balanced-treatment resolution. This resolution, first written by Morris in the early 1970s, was designed for adoption by school boards wishing to include creation-science in the curriculum.

Bird's new resolution began by summarizing the key points of his student note to provide an express constitutional justification for the measure. In a strident litany of creationist affirmations, this summary hammered home the dialectic that creationism was as scientific as Darwinism and Darwinism was as religious as creationism. Reaching a crescendo, the resolution affirmed that, although teaching only evolution violated religious freedom, the presentation of both the theory of evolution and the theory of creation-science would not because it would involve presenting the scientific evidence for each theory rather than any religious doctrine. Based on these affirmative findings, the resolution then directed schools to give balanced treatment to both theories in classroom lectures, textbooks, library materials, and other educational programs. As if wishing it could make it so, the resolution concluded by requiring that the treatment of both theories "must be limited to scientific evidence and must not include religious doctrine."[37]

The Institute for Creation Research distributed this draft resolution by the thousands to supporters throughout the country in 1979. Each copy carried the disclaimer, "Please note that this is a suggested *resolution*, to be adopted by boards of education, not *legislation* proposed for enactment as law. ICR has always taken the position that the route of education and persuasion on this issue is more fruitful in the long run than that of coercion."[38] As a scion of anti-evolutionism, however, the creation-science movement fed into an older cause and its work product was regularly appropriated by anti-evolutionists long accustomed to coercing reform by legal means. Paul Ellwanger, a private citizen who had battled evolutionary teaching in his own state of South Carolina for years, almost immediately transformed Bird's resolution into model legislation for introduction into his home state legislature and for distribution to fellow believers throughout the country. Although the measure failed in South Carolina, similar bills surfaced in eight state legislatures during 1980 and fourteen such assemblies in 1981. Ellwanger sent one copy of his proposal to the Rev. A. A. Blount in suburban North Little Rock, Arkansas. Early in 1981, when a local biology teacher was challenged for teaching creationism, Blount remembered the bill and passed it on to his state senator, James L. Holsted, who introduced it into the Arkansas Senate later that year.

---

37. Wendell R. Bird, *No. 71, Resolution for Balanced Presentation of Evolution and Scientific Creationism*, ICR IMPACT SERIES, May 1979, at iii.

38. Id., at i.

The Bird–Ellwanger–Holsted balanced-treatment bill sailed through the Arkansas legislature. Only days before adjourning for the year, the state Senate took up and passed it in less than an hour. Using a procedure reserved for non-controversial bills, the Senate leadership scheduled the measure for a vote without either a prior committee hearing or any advance public notice. When fifteen minutes of floor debate disclosed no active opposition, the bill was put to vote and passed by a margin of 22 to 2. The state House of Representatives followed suit three days later. After a ten-minute, pro-forma committee hearing earlier in the day, cheering House members passed the bill by a margin of 69 to 18. In the press of last-minute business, efforts to amend or to debate the bill on the House floor were ruled out of order. Arkansas Governor Frank White signed the bill into law less than a week after it was first taken up by the legislature. Given the speed of its passage during a hectic part of the session, probably few lawmakers fully understood the bill. Even the Governor admitted having not read it before adding his signature.

While the Arkansas legislature enacted its balanced-treatment statute rapidly and with virtually no dissent, lawmakers in neighboring Louisiana were approaching the issue somewhat more cautiously. Disturbed by evolutionary teaching in his local public schools, Senator Bill Keith of Shreveport had introduced a home-brewed creation-teaching bill into the state Senate in 1980, but it died without a vote. Hearing about the effort, Ellwanger then sent a copy of his model legislation to Keith along with ICR literature and tactical advice about stressing scientific rather than religious objections to teaching evolution. Adopting Ellwanger's approach as his own, Keith introduced a balanced-treatment bill into the Louisiana Senate on the opening day of the 1981 session.

Following a series of public hearings, the Senate Education Committee amended Keith's new bill so that it merely allowed balanced treatment for teaching creation-science as a local option. The committee also dropped Bird's creationist findings of fact, the list of inferences from the two theories, and the bar against referring to religious doctrine. Balanced treatment was defined to mean simply that instruction needed to provide insight into both theories rather than equivalent treatment. A further committee amendment authorized local schools to develop creation-science teaching skills and resources with the aid of seven Louisiana creationists to be named by the governor. These changes transformed Keith's balanced-treatment mandate into a compromise measure somewhat similar to the non-controversial Kentucky law permitting teachers to temper evolutionary teaching with creationist concepts. On this basis, the measure passed the Senate with little comment or dissent.

The state House of Representatives soon upset the Senate compromise and brought Louisiana into the creationism legal controversy for the first time. After a lengthy public hearing, the House Education Committee restored the mandate for balanced treatment to the bill while leaving the other Senate amendments intact. The committee then added provisions requiring teachers to present both evolution and creation as unproven theories and prohibiting public schools and universities from discriminating against creationist teachers. This approach found favor in the full House. Defeating a series of amendments designed to weaken the measure, it approved the committee's handiwork by a margin of 71 to 19. The Senate promptly concurred in the House amendments and sent the bill to the Governor David C. Treen who, after expressing some doubts about the measure, reluctantly signed it. Both statutes follow:

ARKANSAS BALANCED–TREATMENT ACT (1981)

AN ACT to Require Balanced Treatment of Creation–Science and Evolution–Science in Public Schools; to Protect Academic Freedom By Providing Student Choice; to Ensure Freedom of Religious Exercise; to Guarantee Freedom of Belief and Speech; to Prevent Establishment of Religion; to Prohibit Religious Instruction Concerning Origins; to Bar Discrimination on the Basis of Creationists or Evolutionist Belief; to Provide Definitions and Clarifications; to Declare the Legislative Purpose and Legislative Findings of Fact; to Provide for Severability of Provisions; to Provide for Repeal of Contrary Laws; and to Set Forth an Effective Date.

Be It Enacted by the General Assembly of the State of Arkansas:

Sec. 1.   Requirement for Balanced Treatment. Public Schools within this State shall give balanced treatment to creation-science and to evolution-science. Balanced treatment to these two models shall be given in classroom lectures taken as a whole for each course, in textbook materials taken as a whole for each course, in library materials taken as a whole for the sciences and taken as a whole for the humanities, and in other educational programs in public schools, to the extent that such lectures, textbooks, library materials, or educational programs deal in any way with the subject of the origin of man, life, the earth, or the universe.

Sec. 2.   Prohibition against Religious Instruction. Treatment of either evolution-science or creation-science shall be limited to scientific evidence for each model and inferences from those scientific evidences, and must not include any religious instruction or references to religious writings.

Sec. 3.   Requirement for Nondiscrimination. Public schools within this State, or their personnel, shall not discriminate, by reducing a grade of a student or by singling out and making public criticism, against any student who demonstrates a satisfactory understanding of both evolution-science and creation-science and who accepts or rejects either model in whole or part.

Sec. 4.   Definitions. As used in this Act:

(a) "Creation-science" means the scientific evidences for creation and inferences from those scientific evidences. Creation-science includes the scientific evidences and related inferences that indicate: (1) Sudden creation of the universe, energy, and life from nothing; (2) The insufficiency of mutation and natural selection in bringing about development of all living kinds from a single organism; (3) Changes only within fixed limits of originally created kinds of plants and animals; (4) Separate ancestry for man and apes; (5) Explanation of the earth's geology by catastrophism, including the occurrence of a worldwide flood; and (6) A relatively recent inception of the earth and living kinds.

(b) "Evolution-science" means the scientific evidences for evolution and inferences from those scientific evidences. Evolution-science includes the scientific evidences and related inferences that indicate: (1) Emergence by naturalistic processes of the universe from disordered matter and emergence of life from nonlife; (2) The sufficiency of mutation and natural selection in bringing about development of present living kinds from simple earlier kinds; (3) Emergence by mutation and natural selection of present living kinds from simple earlier kinds; (4) Emergence of man from a common ancestor with apes; (5) Explanation of the earth's geology and the evolutionary sequence by uniformitarianism; and (6) An inception several billion years ago of the earth and somewhat later of life.

(c) "Public schools" mean public secondary and elementary schools.

Sec. 5. Clarification. This Act does not require or permit instruction in any religious doctrine or materials. This Act does not require any instruction in the subject of origins, but simply requires instruction in both scientific models (of evolution-science and creation-science) if public schools choose to teach either. This Act does not require each individual textbook or library book to give balanced treatment to the models of evolution-science and creation-science; it does not require any school books to be discarded. This Act does not require each individual classroom lecture in a course to give such balanced treatment, but simply requires the lectures as a whole to give balanced treatment; it permits some lectures to present evolution-science and other lectures to present creation-science.

Sec. 6. Legislative Declaration of Purpose. This Legislature enacts this Act for public schools with the purpose of protecting academic freedom for students' differing values and beliefs; ensuring neutrality toward students' diverse religious convictions; ensuring freedom of religious exercise for students and their parents; guaranteeing freedom of belief and speech for students; preventing establishment of Theologically Liberal, Humanist, Nontheist, or Atheist religions; preventing discrimination against students on the basis of their personal beliefs concerning creation and evolution; and assisting students in their search for truth. This Legislature does not have the purpose of causing instruction in religious concepts or making an establishment of religion.

Sec. 7. Legislative Findings of Fact. This Legislature finds that:

(a) The subject of the origin of the universe, earth, life, and man is treated within many public school courses, such as biology, life science, anthropology, sociology, and often also in physics, chemistry, world history, philosophy, and social studies.

(b) Only evolution-science is presented to students in virtually all of those courses that discuss the subject of origins. Public schools generally censor creation-science and evidence contrary to evolution.

(c) Evolution-science is not an unquestionable fact of science, because evolution cannot be experimentally observed, fully verified, or logically falsified, and because evolution-science is not accepted by some scientists.

(d) Evolution-science is contrary to the religious convictions or moral values or philosophical beliefs of many students and parents, including individuals of many different religious faiths and with diverse moral values and philosophical beliefs.

(e) Public school presentation of only evolution-science without any alternative model of origins abridges the United States Constitution's protections of freedom of religious exercise and of freedom of belief and speech for students and parents, because it undermines their religious convictions and moral or philosophical values, compels their unconscionable professions of belief, and hinders religious training and moral training by parents.

(f) Public school presentation of only evolution-science furthermore abridges the Constitution's prohibition against establishment of religion, because it produces hostility toward many Theistic religions and brings preference to Theological Liberalism, Humanism, Non-theistic religions, and Atheism, in that these religious faiths general include a religious belief in evolution.

(g) Public school instruction in only evolution-science also violates the principle of academic freedom, because it denies students a choice between scientific models and instead indoctrinates them in evolution-science alone.

(h) Presentation of only one model rather than alternative scientific models of origins is not required by any compelling interest of the State, and exemption of such students from a course or class presenting only evolution-science does not provide an adequate remedy because of teacher influence and student pressure to remain in that course or class. (i) Attendance of those students who are at public schools is compelled by law, and school taxes from their parents and other citizens are mandated by law.

(j) Creation-science is an alternative scientific model of origins and can be presented from a strictly scientific standpoint without any religious doctrine just as evolution-science can, because there are scientists who conclude that scientific data best support creation-science and because scientific evidences and inferences have been presented for creation-science.

(k) Public school presentation of both evolution-science and creation-science would not violate the Constitution's prohibition against establishment of religion, because it would involve presentation of the scientific evidences and related inferences for each model rather than any religious instruction.

(1) Most citizens, whatever their religious beliefs about origins, favor balanced treatment in public schools of alternative scientific models of origins for better guiding students in their search for knowledge, and they favor a neutral approach toward subjects affecting the religious and moral and philosophical convictions of students.

Sec. 8.   Short Title. This Act shall be known as the "Balanced Treatment for Creation–Science and Evolution–Science Act."

1981 LOUISIANA BALANCED–TREATMENT ACT (1981)

An Act to amend Part III of Chapter I of Title 17 of the Louisiana Revised Statutes of 1950 by adding thereto a new Sub–Part, to be designated as Sub–Part D–2 thereof, comprised of Sections 286.1 through 286.7, both inclusive, relative to balanced treatment of creation-science and evolution-science in public schools, to require such balanced treatment, to bar discrimination on the basis of creationist or evolutionist belief, to provide definitions and clarifications, to declare the legislative purpose, to provide relative to inservice teacher training and materials acquisition, to provide relative to curriculum development, and otherwise to provide with respect thereto.

Be it enacted by the Legislature of Louisiana:

§ 286.1.   Short Title: This Subpart shall be known as the "Balanced Treatment for Creation–Science and Evolution–Science Act."

§ 286.2.   Purpose: This Subpart is enacted for the purposes of protecting academic freedom.

§ 286.3.   Definitions: As used in this Subpart, unless otherwise clearly indicated, these terms have the following meanings:

(1) "Balanced treatment" means providing whatever information and instruction in both creation and evolution models the classroom teacher determines is necessary and appropriate to provide insight into both theories in view of the textbooks and other instructional materials available for use in his classroom.

(2) "Creation-science" means the scientific evidences for creation and inferences from those scientific evidences.

(3) "Evolution-science" means the scientific evidences for evolution and inferences from those scientific evidences.

(4) "Public schools" mean public secondary and elementary schools.

§ 286.4.   Authorization for balanced treatment; requirement for nondiscrimination:

A.   Commencing with the 1982–1983 school year, public schools within this state shall give balanced treatment to creation-science and to evolution-science. Balanced treatment of these two models shall be given in classroom lectures taken as a whole for each course, in textbook materials taken as a whole for each course, in library materials taken as a whole for the sciences and taken as a whole for the humanities, and in other educational programs in public schools, to the extent that such lectures, textbooks, library materials, or educational programs deal in any way with the subject of the origin of man, life, the earth, or the universe. When creation or evolution is taught, each shall be taught as a theory, rather than as proven scientific fact.

B.   Public schools within this state and their personnel shall not discriminate by reducing a grade of a student or by singling out and publicly criticizing any student who demonstrates a satisfactory understanding of both evolution-science or creation-science and who accepts or rejects either model in whole or part.

C.   No teacher in public elementary or secondary school or instructor in any state-supported university in Louisiana, who chooses to be a creation-scientist or to teach scientific data which points to creationism shall, for that reason, be discriminated against in any way by any school board, college board, or administrator.

§ 286.5.   Clarifications: This Subpart does not require any instruction in the subject of origins but simply permits instruction in both scientific models (of evolution-science and creation-science) if public schools choose to teach either. This Subpart does not require each individual textbook or library book to give balanced treatment to the models of evolution-science and creation-science; it does not require any school books to be discarded. This Subpart does not require each individual classroom lecture in a course to give such balanced treatment but simply permits the lectures as a whole to give balanced treatment; it permits some lectures to present evolution-science and other lectures to present creation-science.

§ 286.6   Funding of inservice training and materials acquisition: Any public school that elects to present any model of origins shall use existing teacher inservice training funds to prepare teachers of public school courses presenting any model of origins to give balanced treatment to the creation-science model and the evolution-science model. Existing library acquisition funds shall be used to purchase nonreligious library books as are necessary to give balanced treatment to the creation-science model and the evolution-science model.

§ 286.7.   Curriculum Development:

A.   Each city and parish school board shall develop and provide to each public school classroom teacher in the system a curriculum guide on presentation of creation-science.

B.   The governor shall designate seven creation-scientists who shall provide resource services in the development of curriculum guides to any city or parish school board upon request. Each such creation-scientist shall be designated from among the full-time faculty members teaching in any college and university in Louisiana. These creation-scientists shall serve at the pleasure of the governor and without compensation.

NOTES AND QUESTIONS

1.   Is it troublesome that the Arkansas Balanced–Treatment Act contained express legislative findings of fact when, in fact, the legislature never conducted any fact-finding hearings or investigation and did not discuss any of the findings on the floor before passing the measure? These findings included a mix of scientific, legal, and social-scientific facts, ranging from finding that public schools generally censor evidence contrary to evolution to finding that most citizens favor balanced treatment in public schools for alternative models of origins. Did the legislature find these facts by simply decreeing them as found? What is their legal significance? In the next opinion, observe how the court treated them.

2.   The definition of creation-science in the Arkansas Balanced–Treatment Act featured several elements that are grounded more in the Bible's particular account of creation other than in the general concept of creation ex nihilo. For example, including the idea of "fixed limits of originally created kinds of plants and animals" (rather than the traditional creationist concept of the immutability of species) springs from first chapter of Genesis, which state in conventional English translations that God created the various kinds of plants and animals, not each species. Assuming that a "kind" is broader than a "species," this interpretation of creation allows for considerable evolution within each kind of plant and animal to produce the current array of species. Using this understanding of Genesis, some biblical literalists assert that God could have created a single finch-like kind of bird that subsequently evolved into all the various known species of finch rather than each finch species or perhaps even created a single bird-like kind of animal that evolved into all the known bird species. Creationists accept this limited form of evolution, which they sometimes call "micro-evolution," to explain how all the various kinds of animals could have fit in Noah's ark and thus been saved from the worldwide deluge that is depicted in Genesis as having destroyed all life on earth outside the ark. Similarly, including "a worldwide flood" and the "relatively recent inception of the earth" into the very definition of "creation-science" has less to do with the concept of creation than with the specific account of creation in Genesis. Given the prior Supreme Court decisions against religious instruction in public schools, why did the sponsors include these elements in the definition of "creation-science"?

3.   The definition of evolution-science in the Arkansas Balanced–Treatment Act is also problematic. For example, its states that evolution-science includes the emergence of life from non-life and the sufficiency of mutation and natural selection to bring about the current kinds of life from simple early kinds. Classical Darwinism deals with the evolution of organic species from prior organic species, not the evolution of life from non-life. Further, neither traditional Darwinism nor modern neo-Darwinian synthesis relies on mutation and natural selection as the exclusive means and mechanism of evolution. Rejecting the sufficiency of inborn mutations to feed the evolutionary process, for example, Darwin depicted acquired characteristics as a significant source

of variation within species and many modern evolutionists look to gene-flows across species as one among many causes of variation. Further, Darwinists have long supplement the theory of natural selection with such concepts as sexual selection and genetic drift to account for the propagation of varieties and formation of new species.

4. The Arkansas Act prohibits religious instruction in public schools. If a court determined that creation-science was primarily a religious doctrine, would the Act prohibit teaching creation-science?

5. What are the main differences between the Arkansas and Louisiana Balanced–Treatment Acts? Among these differences, the Louisiana statute did not contain either legislative findings of fact or the explicit definitions of "creation-science" and "evolution-science" that featured so prominently in the Arkansas law. The Louisiana statute also provided for the development of curriculum in creation-science. What concerns might account for these differences in what began as virtually identical bills?

II. BALANCED TREATMENT GETS ITS DAY IN COURT

Before the Arkansas governor signed his state's Balanced Treatment Act into law and before Louisiana legislators even passed their statute, the ACLU had vowed to challenge both measures, if enacted, in federal court. Marshalling its considerable resources for a battle royal against creation-science following enactment of the two statutes, the ACLU moved first against the more vulnerable Arkansas law. In doing so, the ACLU generated the most dramatic creation-evolution courtroom confrontation since the Scopes trial. Dozens of scientists, theologians, and scholars assembled in Little Rock, Arkansas, to testify at the two-week-long bench trial. Seventy-five news media organizations from across the country and as far away as London registered with the court to cover the proceedings. A team of nine New York attorneys for the ACLU and three local lawyers pressed the case against the embattled Arkansas attorney general's office.

As a facial challenge to the statute brought under the Establishment Clause, the case was tried to a judge rather than a jury. "Our strategy from the beginning of the case through the trial was to avoid challenging the scientific merits of the creationists claims," lead ACLU counsel Jack D. Novik later explained. "It was our position, not that creationism was bad science, but that it was not science at all. Rather, we argued, it was religious apologetics, and a particular religious view at that."[39] One of the attorneys assisting Novik added, "Since the seminal case interpreting the Establishment Clause of the First Amendment (*Everson v. Board of Education*), it has been the law that, to survive constitutional challenge, legislation must have a secular purpose and have a 'primary effect' that neither advances nor inhibits religion."[40] Accordingly, the Little Rock trial

---

39. Jack D. Novik, *Litigating the Religion of Creation Science*, 42 FED'N AM. SOC'Y EXPERIMENTAL BIOLOGY PROC. 42 (1983).

40. Mark E. Herlihy, *Trying Creationism: Scientific Disputes and Legal Strategies, in* CREATIONISM, SCIENCE, AND THE LAW: THE ARKANSAS CASE 135 (Marcel C. La Follette ed., 1983).

focused more on the religious purpose and effect of the Arkansas statute than on the relate merits of Darwinism and creation-science.

In line with its legal strategy of focusing the case on religion, the ACLU assembled a remarkable collection of state religious leaders to bring the suit. Highlighting the deep rift between mainline and conservative Christians in Arkansas over the law, these plaintiffs were led off by the Rev. Bill McLean, principal official of the United Presbyterian Church in Arkansas, and included the bishops of the United Methodist, Episcopal, Roman Catholic, African Methodist Episcopal churches in the state as well as seven prominent local ministers. A variety of national Jewish groups and professional teachers' associations joined as organizational plaintiffs. Their complaint was filed in May, 1981, with the federal district court at Little Rock, and the matter proceeded to trial in December before U.S. District Judge William R. Overton, a 42–year–old jurist then in his second year on the bench.

Concentrating their assault on the Establishment Clause questions, the ACLU gathered an impressive array of leading experts to testify that the Arkansas statute had a purely religious purpose and effect. "Consistent with this approach," one of the plaintiff's lawyers explained, "the expert testimony at the trial was intended to offer the trial judge an understanding of the history and social context of the 'creation-science' movement, of the consideration and conclusions of the scientific and philosophical communities regarding the status of 'creation-science' as science, of the relationship of the 'two-model approach' enshrined in the Act and the history and theology of Christian Fundamentalism, and of the impact of Act 590 on the educational system within Arkansas."[41]

The plaintiffs' ten expert witnesses were divided into two teams. "The ACLU first presented expert witnesses from their 'religious team,' " reported one of those witnesses, Cornell University sociologist Dorothy Nelkin. "These witnesses argued that, historically, philosophically, and sociologically, creationism is a religious movement of fundamentalists who base their beliefs on the inerrancy of the Bible and that creation science is no more than religious apologetics." Nelkin went on, "The ACLU then presented its 'scientific team': a geneticist, a paleontologist, a geologist, and a biophysicist. They documented the absence of scientific evidence for the creationist beliefs" and the affirmative case for evolution.[42] "Here then is the significance of science in the case," ACLU attorney Jack Novik explained. "For if, as we contended, creationism was not science at all, then whatever else the Arkansas legislature thought it was doing, meaningful science education could not provide a legitimate secular purpose for enacting the creationism statute without teaching religious doctrine."[43] For the first time, expert testimony on the creation-evolution controversy had made it into court.

---

41. *Id.,* at 98–99.

42. DOROTHY NELKIN, THE CREATION CONTROVERSY: SCIENCE OR SCRIPTURE IN THE SCHOOLS 140–41 (1982).

43. Novik, *supra* note 39, at 40.

According to plaintiffs' counsel this use of expert witnesses had two purposes. First, it allowed the judge to rely on experts rather than having to determine any scientific facts for himself. Second, it reinforced the plaintiffs' claim that scientists and educators, rather than legislators and voters, should determine the content of science education. At the very least, this approach asked the judge to use expert testimony in determining whether creation-science was primarily a religious doctrine. Pushed further, it flowed into the plaintiffs' alternative pleas for academic freedom. In violation of the so-called "Constitutional doctrine of academic freedom," the plaintiffs argued, "the Arkansas legislature has overridden the professional judgment of teachers, scientists and educators, that 'creation-science' lacks recognized educational value, thereby giving this subject matter a most peculiar and privileged place in the curriculum."[44]

Struggling to deflect this assault, Arkansas Attorney General Steve Clark, who rejected the offer of Wendell Bird to direct the defense, adopted the basic line of argument presented in Bird's law-journal article but did so (creationist would later complain) with visible lack of conviction. This argument centered on defending creation-science as a scientific, non-religious theory of origins constitutionally worthy of equal treatment with evolution. "Rather than advancing religion, Act 590 advances both scientific inquiry and academic freedom," Clark's trial brief asserted. "Scientific inquiry is advanced by providing students with an alternative scientific theory to evolution-science. The proof will show that many competent scientists believe that the scientific data on origins best supports creation-science. Act 590 has the primary effect of furthering academic freedom in that a controversial scientific theory should not be squelched or censored based on one small segment of society's political, philosophical, or religious opposition to the theory."[45] The state here rested its defense squarely on showing that competent scientists accepted creationism as good science.

For the state, the difficulty lay in finding recognized scientists who could testify on behalf of creation-science without being discredited for their religious presuppositions. Obviously Henry Morris and his colleagues at ICR were out of the question because they readily admitted a religious purpose and effect for their activities. In the end, the best that the state produced were scientists who questioned evolution without necessarily accepting creation-science or creationists whose science was influenced by their religious beliefs. Fitting the first mold, British astrophysicist Chandra N. Wickramasinghe testified that the mathematical probability of chance chemical combinations producing life from non-life was essentially nil, but then totally rejected the basic tenets of creation-science and added his own views that life was seeded on earth by comets. In the second mold, creationist chemist Donald Chittich refused to acknowledge whether he could ever accept any scientific result at odds with a literal reading of

---

44. *Plaintiffs' Outline of Legal Issues and Proof, in* CREATIONISM, supra note 40, at 28.

45. Brief for Defendant at 17, McLean v. Arkansas Bd. of Educ., 529 F.Supp. 1255 (E.D. Ark. 1982).

Scripture. In an effort to bolster his case, Clark advanced the argument that creationist instruction served the constitutionally valid purpose of neutralizing evolutionary teaching and presented evidence of the overwhelming public support for balancing the two views. Judge Overton's ruling follows, along with an official opinion of the Texas Attorney General interpreting and applying the *McLean* decision to related issues less than two years later:

McLEAN v. ARKANSAS BD. OF EDUC.

United States District Court for the Eastern District of Arkansas
529 F.Supp. 1255 (E.D. Ark. 1982)

OVERTON, DISTRICT JUDGE: On March 19, 1981, the Governor of Arkansas signed into law Act 590 of 1981, entitled the "Balanced Treatment for Creation–Science and Evolution–Science Act." The Act is codified as Ark.Stat.Ann. § 80–1663, et seq. (1981 Supp.). Its essential mandate is stated in its first sentence: "Public schools within this State shall give balanced treatment to creation-science and to evolution-science." On May 27, 1981, this suit was filed challenging the constitutional validity of Act 590 on three distinct grounds.

This Court's jurisdiction arises under 28 U.S.C. §§ 1331, 1343(3) and 1343(4). The power to issue declaratory judgments is expressed in 28 U.S.C. §§ 2201 and 2202.

First, it is contended that Act 590 constitutes an establishment of religion prohibited by the First Amendment to the Constitution, which is made applicable to the states by the Fourteenth Amendment. Second, the plaintiffs argue the Act violates a right to academic freedom which they say is guaranteed to students and teachers by the Free Speech Clause of the First Amendment. Third, plaintiffs allege the Act is impermissibly vague and thereby violates the Due Process Clause of the Fourteenth Amendment.

The individual plaintiffs include the resident Arkansas Bishops of the United Methodist, Episcopal, Roman Catholic and African Methodist Episcopal Churches, the principal official of the Presbyterian Churches in Arkansas, other United Methodist, Southern Baptist and Presbyterian clergy, as well as several persons who sue as parents and next friends of minor children attending Arkansas public schools. One plaintiff is a high school biology teacher. All are also Arkansas taxpayers. Among the organizational plaintiffs are the American Jewish Congress, the Union of American Hebrew Congregations, the American Jewish Committee, the Arkansas Education Association, the National Association of Biology Teachers and the National Coalition for Public Education and Religious Liberty, all of which sue on behalf of members living in Arkansas....

The defendants include the Arkansas Board of Education and its members, the Director of the Department of Education, and the State Textbooks and Instructional Materials Selecting Committee. The Pulaski County Special School District and its Directors and Superintendent were voluntarily dismissed by the plaintiffs at the pre-trial conference held October 1, 1981.

The trial commenced December 7, 1981, and continued through December 17, 1981. This Memorandum Opinion constitutes the Court's findings of fact and conclusions of law. Further orders and judgment will be in conformity with this opinion.

I.

There is no controversy over the legal standards under which the Establishment Clause portion of this case must be judged. The Supreme Court has on a number of occasions expounded on the meaning of the clause, and the pronouncements are clear. Often the issue has arisen in the context of public education, as it has here. In Everson v. Board of Education, 330 U.S. 1, 15–16 (1947), Justice Black stated:

> The "establishment of religion" clause of the First Amendment means at least this: Neither a state nor the Federal Government can set up a church. Neither can pass laws which aid one religion, aid all religions, or prefer one religion over another. Neither can force nor influence a person to go to or to remain away from church against his will or force him to profess a belief or disbelief in any religion. No person can be punished for entertaining or professing religious beliefs or disbeliefs, for church-attendance or non-attendance. No tax, large or small, can be levied to support any religious activities or institutions, whatever they may be called, or whatever form they may adopt to teach or practice religion. Neither a state nor the Federal Government can, openly or secretly, participate in the affairs of any religious organizations or groups and vice versa. In the words of Jefferson, the clause . . . was intended to erect "a wall of separation between church and State."

The Establishment Clause thus enshrines two central values: voluntarism and pluralism. And it is in the area of the public schools that these values must be guarded most vigilantly.

> Designed to serve as perhaps the most powerful agency for promoting cohesion among a heterogeneous democratic people, the public school must keep scrupulously free from entanglement in the strife of sects. The preservation of the community from divisive conflicts, of Government from irreconcilable pressures by religious groups, of religion from censorship and coercion however subtly exercised, requires strict confinement of the State to instruction other than religious, leaving to the individual's church and home, indoctrination in the faith of his choice.

McCollum v. Board of Education, 333 U.S. 203, 216–217 (1948) (Opinion of Frankfurter, J., joined by Jackson, Burton and Rutledge, JJ.).

The specific formulation of the establishment prohibition has been refined over the years, but its meaning has not varied from the principles articulated by Justice Black in Everson. In Abington School District v.

Schempp, 374 U.S. 203, 222 (1963), Justice Clark stated that "to withstand the strictures of the Establishment Clause there must be a secular legislative purpose and a primary effect that neither advances nor inhibits religion." The Court found it quite clear that the First Amendment does not permit a state to require the daily reading of the Bible in public schools, for "(s)urely the place of the Bible as an instrument of religion cannot be gainsaid." Id. at 224. Similarly, in Engel v. Vitale, 370 U.S. 421 (1962), the Court held that the First Amendment prohibited the New York Board of Regents from requiring the daily recitation of a certain prayer in the schools. With characteristic succinctness, Justice Black wrote, "Under (the First) Amendment's prohibition against governmental establishment of religion, as reinforced by the provisions of the Fourteenth Amendment, government in this country, be it state or federal, is without power to prescribe by law any particular form of prayer which is to be used as an official prayer in carrying on any program of governmentally sponsored religious activity." Id. at 430. Black also identified the objective at which the Establishment Clause was aimed: "Its first and most immediate purpose rested on the belief that a union of government and religion tends to destroy government and to degrade religion." Id. at 431.

Most recently, the Supreme Court has held that the clause prohibits a state from requiring the posting of the Ten Commandments in public school classrooms for the same reasons that officially imposed daily Bible reading is prohibited. Stone v. Graham, 449 U.S. 39 (1980). The opinion in Stone relies on the most recent formulation of the Establishment Clause test, that of Lemon v. Kurtzman, 403 U.S. 602 (1971):

> First, the statute must have a secular legislative purpose; second, its principal or primary effect must be one that neither advances nor inhibits religion ...; finally, the statute must not foster "an excessive government entanglement with religion."

Stone v. Graham, 449 U.S. at 40.

It is under this three part test that the evidence in this case must be judged. Failure on any of these grounds is fatal to the enactment.

II.

The religious movement known as Fundamentalism began in nineteenth century America as part of evangelical Protestantism's response to social changes, new religious thought and Darwinism. Fundamentalists viewed these developments as attacks on the Bible and as responsible for a decline in traditional values.

The various manifestations of Fundamentalism have had a number of common characteristics,[46] but a central premise has always been a literal

---

46. The authorities differ as to generalizations which may be made about Fundamentalism. For example, Dr. Geisler testified to the widely held view that there are five beliefs characteristic of all Fundamentalist movements, in addition, of course, to the inerrancy of Scripture: (1) belief in the virgin birth of Christ, (2) belief in the deity of Christ, (3) belief in the substitutional atonement of Christ, (4) belief in the second coming of Christ, and (5) belief in the physical resurrection of all departed souls. Dr. Marsden, however, testified that this generalization, which

interpretation of the Bible and a belief in the inerrancy of the Scriptures. Following World War I, there was again a perceived decline in traditional morality, and Fundamentalism focused on evolution as responsible for the decline. One aspect of their efforts, particularly in the South, was the promotion of statutes prohibiting the teaching of evolution in public schools. In Arkansas, this resulted in the adoption of Initiated Act 1 of 1929.

Between the 1920s and early 1960s, anti-evolutionary sentiment had a subtle but pervasive influence on the teaching of biology in public schools. Generally, textbooks avoided the topic of evolution and did not mention the name of Darwin. Following the launch of the Sputnik satellite by the Soviet Union in 1957, the National Science Foundation funded several programs designed to modernize the teaching of science in the nation's schools. The Biological Sciences Curriculum Study (BSCS), a nonprofit organization, was among those receiving grants for curriculum study and revision. Working with scientists and teachers, BSCS developed a series of biology texts which, although emphasizing different aspects of biology, incorporated the theory of evolution as a major theme. The success of the BSCS effort is shown by the fact that fifty percent of American school children currently use BSCS books directly and the curriculum is incorporated indirectly in virtually all biology texts. (Testimony of Mayer; Nelkin, Px 1)

In the early 1960's, there was again a resurgence of concern among Fundamentalists about the loss of traditional values and a fear of growing secularism in society. The Fundamentalist movement became more active and has steadily grown in numbers and political influence. There is an emphasis among current Fundamentalists on the literal interpretation of the Bible and the Book of Genesis as the sole source of knowledge about origins.

The term "scientific creationism" first gained currency around 1965 following publication of The Genesis Flood in 1961 by Whitcomb and Morris. There is undoubtedly some connection between the appearance of the BSCS texts emphasizing evolutionary thought and efforts by Fundamentalists to attack the theory. (Mayer)

In the 1960s and early 1970s, several Fundamentalist organizations were formed to promote the idea that the Book of Genesis was supported by scientific data. The terms "creation science" and "scientific creationism" have been adopted by these Fundamentalists as descriptive of their study of creation and the origins of man. Perhaps the leading creationist organization is the Institute for Creation Research (ICR), which is affiliated with the Christian Heritage College and supported by the Scott Memorial Baptist Church in San Diego, California. The ICR, through the Creation–Life Publishing Company, is the leading publisher of creation

---

has been common in religious scholarship, is now thought to be historical error. There is no doubt, however, that all Fundamentalists take the Scriptures as inerrant and probably most take them as literally true.

science material. Other creation science organizations include the Creation Science Research Center (CSRC) of San Diego and the Bible Science Association of Minneapolis, Minnesota. In 1963, the Creation Research Society (CRS) was formed from a schism in the American Scientific Affiliation (ASA). It is an organization of literal Fundamentalists[47] who have the equivalent of a master's degree in some recognized area of science. A purpose of the organization is "to reach all people with the vital message of the scientific and historic truth about creation." Nelkin, *The Science Textbook Controversies and the Politics of Equal Time*, 66. Similarly, the CSRC was formed in 1970 from a split in the CRS. Its aim has been "to reach the 63 million children of the United States with the scientific teaching of Biblical creationism." Id. at 69.

Among creationist writers who are recognized as authorities in the field by other creationists are Henry M. Morris, Duane Gish, G. E. Parker, Harold S. Slusher, Richard B. Bliss, John W. Moore, Martin E. Clark, W. L. Wysong, Robert E. Kofahl and Kelly L. Segraves. Morris is Director of ICR, Gish is Associate Director and Segraves is associated with CSRC.

Creationists view evolution as a source of society's ills, and the writings of Morris and Clark are typical expressions of that view.

> Evolution is thus not only anti-Biblical and anti-Christian, but it is utterly unscientific and impossible as well. But it has served effectively as the pseudo-scientific basis of atheism, agnosticism, socialism, fascism, and numerous other false and dangerous philosophies over the past century.

Morris and Clark, *The Bible Has The Answer*, (Px 31 and Pretrial Px 89).

Creationists have adopted the view of Fundamentalists generally that there are only two positions with respect to the origins of the earth and life: belief in the inerrancy of the Genesis story of creation and of a worldwide flood as fact, or belief in what they call evolution. Henry Morris has stated, "It is impossible to devise a legitimate means of harmonizing the Bible with evolution." Morris, "Evolution and the Bible," *ICR Impact Series Number 5* (undated, unpaged), quoted in Mayer, Px 8, at 3. This dualistic approach to the subject of origins permeates the creationist literature.

The creationist organizations consider the introduction of creation science into the public schools part of their ministry. The ICR has

---

47. Applicants for membership in the CRS must subscribe to the following statement of belief: "(1) The Bible is the written Word of God, and because we believe it to be inspired thruout (sic), all of its assertions are historically and scientifically true in all of the original autographs. To the student of nature, this means that the account of origins in Genesis is a factual presentation of simple historical truths. (2) All basic types of living things, including man, were made by direct creative acts of God during Creation Week as described in Genesis. Whatever biological changes have occurred since Creation have accomplished only changes within the original created kinds. (3) The great Flood described in Genesis, commonly referred to as the Noachian Deluge, was an historical event, world-wide in its extent and effect. (4) Finally, we are an organization of Christian men of science, who accept Jesus Christ as our Lord and Savior. The account of the special creation of Adam and Eve as one man and one woman, and their subsequent Fall into sin, is the basis for our belief in the necessity of a Savior for all mankind. Therefore, salvation can come only thru (sic) accepting Jesus Christ as our Savior." (Px 115)

published at least two pamphlets[48] containing suggested methods for convincing school boards, administrators and teachers that creationism should be taught in public schools. The ICR has urged its proponents to encourage school officials to voluntarily add creationism to the curriculum.[49]

Citizens For Fairness In Education is an organization based in Anderson, South Carolina, formed by Paul Ellwanger, a respiratory therapist who is trained in neither law nor science. Mr. Ellwanger is of the opinion that evolution is the forerunner of many social ills, including Nazism, racism and abortion. (Ellwanger Depo. at 32–34). About 1977, Ellwanger collected several proposed legislative acts with the idea of preparing a model state act requiring the teaching of creationism as science in opposition to evolution. One of the proposals he collected was prepared by Wendell Bird, who is now a staff attorney for ICR. From these various proposals, Ellwanger prepared a "model act" which calls for "balanced treatment" of "scientific creationism" and "evolution" in public schools. He circulated the proposed act to various people and organizations around the country.

Mr. Ellwanger's views on the nature of creation science are entitled to some weight since he personally drafted the model act which became Act 590. His evidentiary deposition with exhibits and unnumbered attachments (produced in response to a subpoena duces tecum) speaks to both the intent of the Act and the scientific merits of creation science. Mr. Ellwanger does not believe creation science is a science. In a letter to Pastor Robert E. Hays he states, "While neither evolution nor creation can qualify as a scientific theory, and since it is virtually impossible at this point to educate the whole world that evolution is not a true scientific theory, we have freely used these terms—the evolution theory and the theory of scientific creationism—in the bill's text." (Unnumbered attachment to Ellwanger Depo., at 2.) He further states in a letter to Mr. Tom Bethell, "As we examine evolution (remember, we're not making any scientific claims for creation, but we are challenging evolution's claim to be scientific). . . ." (Unnumbered attachment to Ellwanger Depo. at 1.)

Ellwanger's correspondence on the subject shows an awareness that Act 590 is a religious crusade, coupled with a desire to conceal this fact. In a letter to State Senator Bill Keith of Louisiana, he says, "I view this whole battle as one between God and anti-God forces, though I know there are a large number of evolutionists who believe in God." And further,

---

48. Px 130, Morris, Introducing Scientific Creationism Into the Public Schools (1975), and Bird, "Resolution for Balanced Presentation of Evolution and Scientific Creationism," ICR Impact Series No. 71, App. 14 to Plaintiffs' Pretrial Brief.

49. The creationists often show candor in their proselytization. Henry Morris has stated, "Even if a favorable statute or court decision is obtained, it will probably be declared unconstitutional, especially if the legislation or injunction refers to the Bible account of creation." In the same vein he notes, "The only effective way to get creationism taught properly is to have it taught by teachers who are both willing and able to do it. Since most teachers now are neither willing nor able, they must first be both persuaded and instructed themselves." Px 130, Morris, Introducing Scientific Creationism Into the Public Schools (1975) (unpaged).

"... it behooves Satan to do all he can to thwart our efforts and confuse the issue at every turn." Yet Ellwanger suggests to Senator Keith, "If you have a clear choice between having grassroots leaders of this statewide bill promotion effort to be ministerial or non-ministerial, be sure to opt for the non-ministerial. It does the bill effort no good to have ministers out there in the public forum and the adversary will surely pick at this point ... Ministerial persons can accomplish a tremendous amount of work from behind the scenes, encouraging their congregations to take the organizational and P.R. initiatives. And they can lead their churches in storming Heaven with prayers for help against so tenacious an adversary." (Unnumbered attachment to Ellwanger Depo. at 1.)

Ellwanger shows a remarkable degree of political candor, if not finesse, in a letter to State Senator Joseph Carlucci of Florida:

> 2.   It would be very wise, if not actually essential, that all of us who are engaged in this legislative effort be careful not to present our position and our work in a religious framework. For example, in written communications that might somehow be shared with those other persons whom we may be trying to convince, it would be well to exclude our own personal testimony and/or witness for Christ, but rather, if we are so moved, to give that testimony on a separate attached note. (Unnumbered attachment to Ellwanger Depo. at 1.)

The same tenor is reflected in a letter by Ellwanger to Mary Ann Miller, a member of FLAG (Family, Life, America under God) who lobbied the Arkansas Legislature in favor of Act 590:

> ... we'd like to suggest that you and your co-workers be very cautious about mixing creation-science with creation-religion ... Please urge your co-workers not to allow themselves to get sucked into the 'religion' trap of mixing the two together, for such mixing does incalculable harm to the legislative thrust. It could even bring public opinion to bear adversely upon the higher courts that will eventually have to pass judgment on the constitutionality of this new law. (Ex. 1 to Miller Depo.)

Perhaps most interesting, however, is Mr. Ellwanger's testimony in his deposition as to his strategy for having the model act implemented:

> Q.   You're trying to play on other people's religious motives.

> A.   I'm trying to play on their emotions, love, hate, their likes, dislikes, because I don't know any other way to involve, to get humans to become involved in human endeavors. I see emotions as being a healthy and legitimate means of getting people's feelings into action, and ... I believe that the predominance of population in America that represents the greatest potential for taking some kind of action in this area is a Christian community. I see the Jewish community as far less potential in taking action ... but I've seen a lot of interest among Christians and I feel, why not exploit that to get the bill going if that's what it takes. (Ellwanger Depo. at 146–147.)

Mr. Ellwanger's ultimate purpose is revealed in the closing of his letter to Mr. Tom Bethell: "Perhaps all this is old hat to you, Tom, and if so, I'd appreciate your telling me so and perhaps where you've heard it before—the idea of killing evolution instead of playing these debating games that we've been playing for nigh over a decade already." (Unnumbered attachment to Ellwanger Depo. at 3.)

It was out of this milieu that Act 590 emerged. The Reverend W. A. Blount, a Biblical literalist who is pastor of a church in the Little Rock area and was, in February, 1981, chairman of the Greater Little Rock Evangelical Fellowship, was among those who received a copy of the model act from Ellwanger.[50]

At Reverend Blount's request, the Evangelical Fellowship unanimously adopted a resolution to seek introduction of Ellwanger's act in the Arkansas Legislature. A committee composed of two ministers, Curtis Thomas and W. A. Young, was appointed to implement the resolution. Thomas obtained from Ellwanger a revised copy of the model act which he transmitted to Carl Hunt, a business associate of Senator James L. Holsted, with the request that Hunt prevail upon Holsted to introduce the act.

Holsted, a self-described "born again" Christian Fundamentalist, introduced the act in the Arkansas Senate. He did not consult the State Department of Education, scientists, science educators or the Arkansas Attorney General.[51] The Act was not referred to any Senate committee for hearing and was passed after only a few minutes' discussion on the Senate floor. In the House of Representatives, the bill was referred to the Education Committee which conducted a perfunctory fifteen minute hearing. No scientist testified at the hearing, nor was any representative from the State Department of Education called to testify.

Ellwanger's model act was enacted into law in Arkansas as Act 590 without amendment or modification other than minor typographical changes. The legislative "findings of fact" in Ellwanger's act and Act 590 are identical, although no meaningful fact-finding process was employed by the General Assembly.

Ellwanger's efforts in preparation of the model act and campaign for its adoption in the states were motivated by his opposition to the theory of evolution and his desire to see the Biblical version of creation taught in the public schools. There is no evidence that the pastors, Blount, Thomas, Young or The Greater Little Rock Evangelical Fellowship were motivated by anything other than their religious convictions when proposing its adoption or during their lobbying efforts in its behalf. Senator Holsted's sponsorship and lobbying efforts in behalf of the Act were motivated solely

---

50. The model act had been revised to insert "creation science" in lieu of creationism because Ellwanger had the impression people thought creationism was too religious a term. (Ellwanger Depo. at 79.)

51. The original model act had been introduced in the South Carolina Legislature, but had died without action after the South Carolina Attorney General had opined that the act was unconstitutional.

by his religious beliefs and desire to see the Biblical version of creation taught in the public schools.[52]

The State of Arkansas, like a number of states whose citizens have relatively homogeneous religious beliefs, has a long history of official opposition to evolution which is motivated by adherence to Fundamentalist beliefs in the inerrancy of the Book of Genesis. This history is documented in Justice Fortas' opinion in Epperson v. Arkansas, 393 U.S. 97 (1968), which struck down Initiated Act 1 of 1929, Ark.Stat.Ann. §§ 80–1627–1628, prohibiting the teaching of the theory of evolution. To this same tradition may be attributed Initiated Act 1 of 1930, Ark.Stat. Ann. § 80–1606 (Repl.1980), requiring "the reverent daily reading of a portion of the English Bible" in every public school classroom in the State.

It is true, as defendants argue, that courts should look to legislative statements of a statute's purpose in Establishment Clause cases and accord such pronouncements great deference. See, e.g., Committee for Public Education & Religious Liberty v. Nyquist, 413 U.S. 756, 773 (1973) and McGowan v. Maryland, 366 U.S. 420, 445 (1961). Defendants also correctly state the principle that remarks by the sponsor or author of a bill are not considered controlling in analyzing legislative intent. See, e.g., United States v. Enmons, 410 U.S. 396 (1973) and Chrysler Corp. v. Brown, 441 U.S. 281 (1979).

Courts are not bound, however, by legislative statements of purpose or legislative disclaimers. Stone v. Graham, 449 U.S. 39 (1980); Abington School Dist. v. Schempp, 374 U.S. 203 (1963). In determining the legislative purpose of a statute, courts may consider evidence of the historical context of the Act, Epperson v. Arkansas, 393 U.S. 97 (1968), the specific sequence of events leading up to passage of the Act, departures from normal procedural sequences, substantive departures from the normal, Village of Arlington Heights v. Metropolitan Housing Corp., 429 U.S. 252 (1977), and contemporaneous statements of the legislative sponsor, Fed. Energy Admin. v. Algonquin SNG, Inc., 426 U.S. 548, 564 (1976).

The unusual circumstances surrounding the passage of Act 590, as well as the substantive law of the First Amendment, warrant an inquiry into the stated legislative purposes. The author of the Act had publicly proclaimed the sectarian purpose of the proposal. The Arkansas residents who sought legislative sponsorship of the bill did so for a purely sectarian purpose. These circumstances alone may not be particularly persuasive, but when considered with the publicly announced motives of the legislative sponsor made contemporaneously with the legislative process; the lack of any legislative investigation, debate or consultation with any

---

52. Specifically, Senator Holsted testified that he holds to a literal interpretation of the Bible; that the bill was compatible with his religious beliefs; that the bill does favor the position of literalists; that his religious convictions were a factor in his sponsorship of the bill; and that he stated publicly to the *Arkansas Gazette* (although not on the floor of the Senate) contemporaneously with the legislative debate that the bill does presuppose the existence of a divine creator. There is no doubt that Senator Holsted knew he was sponsoring the teaching of a religious doctrine. His view was that the bill did not violate the First Amendment because, as he saw it, it did not favor one denomination over another.

educators or scientists; the unprecedented intrusion in school curriculum;[53] and official history of the State of Arkansas on the subject, it is obvious that the statement of purposes has little, if any, support in fact. The State failed to produce any evidence which would warrant an inference or conclusion that at any point in the process anyone considered the legitimate educational value of the Act. It was simply and purely an effort to introduce the Biblical version of creation into the public school curricula. The only inference which can be drawn from these circumstances is that the Act was passed with the specific purpose by the General Assembly of advancing religion. The Act therefore fails the first prong of the three-pronged test, that of secular legislative purpose, as articulated in Lemon v. Kurtzman and Stone v. Graham.

III.

If the defendants are correct and the Court is limited to an examination of the language of the Act, the evidence is overwhelming that both the purpose and effect of Act 590 is the advancement of religion in the public schools.

Section 4 of the Act provides:

Definitions. As used in this Act:

(a) "Creation-science" means the scientific evidences for creation and inferences from those scientific evidences. Creation-science includes the scientific evidences and related inferences that indicate: (1) Sudden creation of the universe, energy, and life from nothing; (2) The insufficiency of mutation and natural selection in bringing about development of all living kinds from a single organism; (3) Changes only within fixed limits of originally created kinds of plants and animals; (4) Separate ancestry for man and apes; (5) Explanation of the earth's geology by catastrophism, including the occurrence of a worldwide flood; and (6) A relatively recent inception of the earth and living kinds.

(b) "Evolution-science" means the scientific evidences for evolution and inferences from those scientific evidences. Evolution-science includes the scientific evidences and related inferences that indicate: (1) Emergence by naturalistic processes of the universe from disordered matter and emergence of life from nonlife; (2) The sufficiency of mutation and natural selection in bringing about development of present living kinds from simple earlier kinds; (3) Emergence by mutation and natural selection of present living kinds from simple earlier kinds; (4) Emergence of man from a common ancestor with apes; (5) Explanation of the earth's geology and the evolutionary

---

53. The joint stipulation of facts establishes that the following areas are the only information specifically required by statute to be taught in all Arkansas schools: (1) the effects of alcohol and narcotics on the human body, (2) conservation of national resources, (3) Bird Week, (4) Fire Prevention, and (5) Flag etiquette. Additionally, certain specific courses, such as American history and Arkansas history, must be completed by each student before graduation from high school.

sequence by uniformitarianism; and (6) An inception several billion years ago of the earth and somewhat later of life.

(c) "Public schools" mean public secondary and elementary schools.

The evidence establishes that the definition of "creation science" contained in 4(a) has as its unmentioned reference the first 11 chapters of the Book of Genesis. Among the many creation epics in human history, the account of sudden creation from nothing, or creatio ex nihilo, and subsequent destruction of the world by flood is unique to Genesis. The concepts of 4(a) are the literal Fundamentalists' view of Genesis. Section 4(a) is unquestionably a statement of religion, with the exception of 4(a)(2) which is a negative thrust aimed at what the creationists understand to be the theory of evolution.

Both the concepts and wording of Section 4(a) convey an inescapable religiosity. Section 4(a)(1) describes "sudden creation of the universe, energy and life from nothing." Every theologian who testified, including defense witnesses, expressed the opinion that the statement referred to a supernatural creation which was performed by God.

Defendants argue that: (1) the fact that 4(a) conveys ideas similar to the literal interpretation of Genesis does not make it conclusively a statement of religion; (2) that reference to a creation from nothing is not necessarily a religious concept since the Act only suggests a creator who has power, intelligence and a sense of design and not necessarily the attributes of love, compassion and justice;[54] and (3) that simply teaching about the concept of a creator is not a religious exercise unless the student is required to make a commitment to the concept of a creator.

The evidence fully answers these arguments. The ideas of 4(a)(1) are not merely similar to the literal interpretation of Genesis; they are identical and parallel to no other story of creation.[55]

The argument that creation from nothing in 4(a)(1) does not involve a supernatural deity has no evidentiary or rational support. To the contrary, "creation out of nothing" is a concept unique to Western religions. In traditional Western religious thought, the conception of a creator of the world is a conception of God. Indeed, creation of the world "out of nothing" is the ultimate religious statement because God is the only actor.

---

54. Although defendants must make some effort to cast the concept of creation in non-religious terms, this effort surely causes discomfort to some of the Act's more theologically sophisticated supporters. The concept of a creator God distinct from the God of love and mercy is closely similar to the Marcion and Gnostic heresies, among the deadliest to threaten the early Christian church. These heresies had much to do with development and adoption of the Apostle's Creed as the official creedal statement of the Roman Catholic Church in the West. (Gilkey.)

55. The parallels between Section 4(a) and Genesis are quite specific: (1) "sudden creation from nothing" is taken from Genesis, 1:1–10 (Vawter, Gilkey); (2) destruction of the world by a flood of divine origin is a notion peculiar to Judeo–Christian tradition and is based on Chapters 7 and 8 of Genesis (Vawter); (3) the term "kinds" has no fixed scientific meaning, but appears repeatedly in Genesis (all scientific witnesses); (4) "relatively recent inception" means an age of the earth from 6,000 to 10,000 years and is based on the genealogy of the Old Testament using the rather astronomical ages assigned to the patriarchs (Gilkey and several of defendants' scientific witnesses); (5) separate ancestry of man and ape focuses on the portion of the theory of evolution which Fundamentalists find most offensive, Epperson v. Arkansas, 393 U.S. 97 (1968).

As Dr. Langdon Gilkey noted, the Act refers to one who has the power to bring all the universe into existence from nothing. The only "one" who has this power is God.

The leading creationist writers, Morris and Gish, acknowledge that the idea of creation described in 4(a)(1) is the concept of creation by God and make no pretense to the contrary. The idea of sudden creation from nothing, or creatio ex nihilo, is an inherently religious concept. (Vawter, Gilkey, Geisler, Ayala, Blount, Hicks.)

The argument advanced by defendants' witness, Dr. Norman Geisler, that teaching the existence of God is not religious unless the teaching seeks a commitment, is contrary to common understanding and contradicts settled case law. Stone v. Graham, 449 U.S. 39 (1980); Abington School District v. Schempp, 374 U.S. 203 (1963).

The facts that creation science is inspired by the Book of Genesis and that Section 4(a) is consistent with a literal interpretation of Genesis leave no doubt that a major effect of the Act is the advancement of particular religious beliefs. The legal impact of this conclusion will be discussed further at the conclusion of the Court's evaluation of the scientific merit of creation science.

IV.(A)

The approach to teaching "creation science" and "evolution science" found in Act 590 is identical to the two-model approach espoused by the Institute for Creation Research and is taken almost verbatim from ICR writings. It is an extension of Fundamentalists' view that one must either accept the literal interpretation of Genesis or else believe in the godless system of evolution.

The two model approach of the creationists is simply a contrived dualism[56] which has no scientific factual basis or legitimate educational purpose. It assumes only two explanations for the origins of life and existence of man, plants and animals: It was either the work of a creator or it was not. Application of these two models, according to creationists, and the defendants, dictates that all scientific evidence which fails to support the theory of evolution is necessarily scientific evidence in support of creationism and is, therefore, creation science "evidence" in support of Section 4(a).

---

56. Morris, the Director of ICR and one who first advocated the two model approach, insists that a true Christian cannot compromise with the theory of evolution and that the Genesis version of creation and the theory of evolution are mutually exclusive. Px 31, Morris, Studies in the Bible & Science, 102–103. The two model approach was the subject of Dr. Richard Bliss's doctoral dissertation. (Dx 35). It is presented in Bliss, Origins: Two Models–Evolution, Creation (1978). Moreover, the two model approach merely casts in educationalist language the dualism which appears in all creationist literature-creation (i.e. God) and evolution are presented as two alternative and mutually exclusive theories. See, e.g., Px 75, Morris, Scientific Creationism (1974) (public school edition); Px 59, Fox, Fossils: Hard Facts from the Earth. Particularly illustrative is Px 61, Boardman, et al., Worlds Without End (1971), a CSRC publication: "One group of scientists, known as creationists, believe that God, in a miraculous manner, created all matter and energy ... Scientists who insist that the universe just grew, by accident, from a mass of hot gases without the direction or help of a Creator are known as evolutionists."

IV.(B)

The emphasis on origins as an aspect of the theory of evolution is peculiar to creationist literature. Although the subject of origins of life is within the province of biology, the scientific community does not consider origins of life a part of evolutionary theory. The theory of evolution assumes the existence of life and is directed to an explanation of how life evolved. Evolution does not presuppose the absence of a creator or God and the plain inference conveyed by Section 4 is erroneous.[57]

As a statement of the theory of evolution, Section 4(b) is simply a hodgepodge of limited assertions, many of which are factually inaccurate.

For example, although 4(b)(2) asserts, as a tenet of evolutionary theory, "the sufficiency of mutation and natural selection in bringing about the existence of present living kinds from simple earlier kinds," Drs. Ayala and Gould both stated that biologists know that these two processes do not account for all significant evolutionary change. They testified to such phenomena as recombination, the founder effect, genetic drift and the theory of punctuated equilibrium, which are believed to play important evolutionary roles. Section 4(b) omits any reference to these. Moreover, 4(b) utilizes the term "kinds" which all scientists said is not a word of science and has no fixed meaning. Additionally, the Act presents both evolution and creation science as "package deals." Thus, evidence critical of some aspect of what the creationists define as evolution is taken as support for a theory which includes a worldwide flood and a relatively young earth.[58]

IV.(C)

In addition to the fallacious pedagogy of the two model approach, Section 4(a) lacks legitimate educational value because "creation science" as defined in that section is simply not science. Several witnesses suggested definitions of science. A descriptive definition was said to be that science is what is "accepted by the scientific community" and is "what scientists do." The obvious implication of this description is that, in a free society, knowledge does not require the imprimatur of legislation in order to become science.

More precisely, the essential characteristics of science are:

(1) It is guided by natural law;

(2) It has to be explanatory by reference to natural law;

(3) It is testable against the empirical world;

---

57. The idea that belief in a creator and acceptance of the scientific theory of evolution are mutually exclusive is a false premise and offensive to the religious views of many. (Hicks) Dr. Francisco Ayala, a geneticist of considerable renown and a former Catholic priest who has the equivalent of a Ph.D. in theology, pointed out that many working scientists who subscribed to the theory of evolution are devoutly religious.

58. This is so despite the fact that some of the defense witnesses do not subscribe to the young earth or flood hypotheses. Dr. Geisler stated his belief that the earth is several billion years old. Dr. Wickramasinghe stated that no rational scientist would believe the earth is less than one million years old or that all the world's geology could be explained by a worldwide flood.

(4) Its conclusions are tentative, i.e., are not necessarily the final word; and

(5) It is falsifiable. (Ruse and other science witnesses).

Creation science as described in Section 4(a) fails to meet these essential characteristics. First, the section revolves around 4(a)(1) which asserts a sudden creation "from nothing." Such a concept is not science because it depends upon a supernatural intervention which is not guided by natural law. It is not explanatory by reference to natural law, is not testable and is not falsifiable.[59]

If the unifying idea of supernatural creation by God is removed from Section 4, the remaining parts of the section explain nothing and are meaningless assertions.

Section 4(a)(2), relating to the "insufficiency of mutation and natural selection in bringing about development of all living kinds from a single organism," is an incomplete negative generalization directed at the theory of evolution.

Section 4(a)(3) which describes "changes only within fixed limits of originally created kinds of plants and animals" fails to conform to the essential characteristics of science for several reasons. First, there is no scientific definition of "kinds" and none of the witnesses was able to point to any scientific authority which recognized the term or knew how many "kinds" existed. One defense witness suggested there may be 100 to 10,000 different "kinds". Another believes there were "about 10,000, give or take a few thousand." Second, the assertion appears to be an effort to establish outer limits of changes within species. There is no scientific explanation for these limits which is guided by natural law and the limitations, whatever they are, cannot be explained by natural law.

The statement in 4(a)(4) of "separate ancestry of man and apes" is a bald assertion. It explains nothing and refers to no scientific fact or theory.

Section 4(a)(5) refers to "explanation of the earth's geology by catastrophism, including the occurrence of a worldwide flood." This assertion completely fails as science. The Act is referring to the Noachian flood described in the Book of Genesis. The creationist writers concede that any kind of Genesis Flood depends upon supernatural intervention. A worldwide flood as an explanation of the world's geology is not the product of natural law, nor can its occurrence be explained by natural law.

Section 4(a)(6) equally fails to meet the standards of science. "Relatively recent inception" has no scientific meaning. It can only be given meaning by reference to creationist writings which place the age at between 6,000 and 20,000 years because of the genealogy of the Old

---

59. "We do not know how God created, what processes He used, for God used processes which are not now operating anywhere in the natural universe. This is why we refer to divine creation as Special Creation. We cannot discover by scientific investigation anything about the creative processes used by God." Px 78, Gish, Evolution? The Fossils Say No !, 42 (3d ed. 1979) (emphasis in original).

Testament. See, e.g. Px 78, Gish (6,000 to 10,000); Px 87, Segraves (6,000 to 20,000). Such a reasoning process is not the product of natural law; not explainable by natural law; nor is it tentative.

Creation science, as defined in Section 4(a), not only fails to follow the canons defining scientific theory, it also fails to fit the more general descriptions of "what scientists think" and "what scientists do." The scientific community consists of individuals and groups, nationally and internationally, who work independently in such varied fields as biology, paleontology, geology and astronomy. Their work is published and subject to review and testing by their peers. The journals for publication are both numerous and varied. There is, however, not one recognized scientific journal which has published an article espousing the creation science theory described in Section 4(a). Some of the State's witnesses suggested that the scientific community was "close-minded" on the subject of creationism and that explained the lack of acceptance of the creation science arguments. Yet no witness produced a scientific article for which publication had been refused. Perhaps some members of the scientific community are resistant to new ideas. It is, however, inconceivable that such a loose knit group of independent thinkers in all the varied fields of science could, or would, so effectively censor new scientific thought.

The creationists have difficulty maintaining among their ranks consistency in the claim that creationism is science. The author of Act 590, Ellwanger, said that neither evolution nor creationism was science. He thinks both are religion. Duane Gish recently responded to an article in Discover critical of creationism by stating:

> Stephen Jay Gould states that creationists claim creation is a scientific theory. This is a false accusation. Creationists have repeatedly stated that neither creation nor evolution is a scientific theory (and each is equally religious). Gish, letter to editor of *Discover*, July, 1981, App. 30 to Plaintiffs' Pretrial Brief.

The methodology employed by creationists is another factor which is indicative that their work is not science. A scientific theory must be tentative and always subject to revision or abandonment in light of facts that are inconsistent with, or falsify, the theory. A theory that is by its own terms dogmatic, absolutist and never subject to revision is not a scientific theory.

The creationists' methods do not take data, weigh it against the opposing scientific data, and thereafter reach the conclusions stated in Section 4(a). Instead, they take the literal wording of the Book of Genesis and attempt to find scientific support for it. The method is best explained in the language of Morris in his book (Px 31) *Studies in The Bible and Science* at page 114:

> ... it is ... quite impossible to determine anything about Creation through a study of present processes, because present processes are not creative in character. If man wishes to know anything about Creation (the time of Creation, the duration of Creation, the order of

Creation, the methods of Creation, or anything else) his sole source of true information is that of divine revelation. God was there when it happened. We were not there ... Therefore, we are completely limited to what God has seen fit to tell us, and this information is in His written Word. This is our textbook on the science of Creation!

The Creation Research Society employs the same unscientific approach to the issue of creationism. Its applicants for membership must subscribe to the belief that the Book of Genesis is "historically and scientifically true in all of the original autographs." The Court would never criticize or discredit any person's testimony based on his or her religious beliefs. While anybody is free to approach a scientific inquiry in any fashion they choose, they cannot properly describe the methodology used as scientific, if they start with a conclusion and refuse to change it regardless of the evidence developed during the course of the investigation.

IV.(D)

In efforts to establish "evidence" in support of creation science, the defendants relied upon the same false premise as the two model approach contained in Section 4, i.e., all evidence which criticized evolutionary theory was proof in support of creation science. For example, the defendants established that the mathematical probability of a chance chemical combination resulting in life from non-life is so remote that such an occurrence is almost beyond imagination. Those mathematical facts, the defendants argue, are scientific evidences that life was the product of a creator. While the statistical figures may be impressive evidence against the theory of chance chemical combinations as an explanation of origins, it requires a leap of faith to interpret those figures so as to support a complex doctrine which includes a sudden creation from nothing, a world-wide flood, separate ancestry of man and apes, and a young earth.

The defendants' argument would be more persuasive if, in fact, there were only two theories or ideas about the origins of life and the world. That there are a number of theories was acknowledged by the State's witnesses, Dr. Wickramasinghe and Dr. Geisler. Dr. Wickramasinghe testified at length in support of a theory that life on earth was "seeded" by comets which delivered genetic material and perhaps organisms to the earth's surface from interstellar dust far outside the solar system. The "seeding" theory further hypothesizes that the earth remains under the continuing influence of genetic material from space which continues to affect life. While Wickramasinghe's theory about the origins of life on earth has not received general acceptance within the scientific community, he has, at least, used scientific methodology to produce a theory of origins which meets the essential characteristics of science.

Perhaps Dr. Wickramasinghe was called as a witness because he was generally critical of the theory of evolution and the scientific community, a tactic consistent with the strategy of the defense. Unfortunately for the defense, he demonstrated that the simplistic approach of the two model analysis of the origins of life is false. Furthermore, he corroborated the plaintiffs' witnesses by concluding that "no rational scientist" would believe the earth's geology could be explained by reference to a worldwide flood or that the earth was less than one million years old.

The proof in support of creation science consisted almost entirely of efforts to discredit the theory of evolution through a rehash of data and theories which have been before the scientific community for decades. The arguments asserted by creationists are not based upon new scientific evidence or laboratory data which has been ignored by the scientific community.

Robert Gentry's discovery of radioactive polonium haloes in granite and coalified woods is, perhaps, the most recent scientific work which the creationists use as argument for a "relatively recent inception" of the earth and a "worldwide flood." The existence of polonium haloes in granite and coalified wood is thought to be inconsistent with radiometric dating methods based upon constant radioactive decay rates. Mr. Gentry's findings were published almost ten years ago and have been the subject of some discussion in the scientific community. The discoveries have not, however, led to the formulation of any scientific hypothesis or theory which would explain a relatively recent inception of the earth or a worldwide flood. Gentry's discovery has been treated as a minor mystery which will eventually be explained. It may deserve further investigation, but the National Science Foundation has not deemed it to be of sufficient import to support further funding.

The testimony of Marianne Wilson was persuasive evidence that creation science is not science. Ms. Wilson is in charge of the science curriculum for Pulaski County Special School District, the largest school district in the State of Arkansas. Prior to the passage of Act 590, Larry Fisher, a science teacher in the District, using materials from the ICR, convinced the School Board that it should voluntarily adopt creation science as part of its science curriculum. The District Superintendent assigned Ms. Wilson the job of producing a creation science curriculum guide. Ms. Wilson's testimony about the project was particularly convincing because she obviously approached the assignment with an open mind and no preconceived notions about the subject. She had not heard of creation science until about a year ago and did not know its meaning before she began her research.

Ms. Wilson worked with a committee of science teachers appointed from the District. They reviewed practically all of the creationist literature. Ms. Wilson and the committee members reached the unanimous conclusion that creationism is not science; it is religion. They so reported to the Board. The Board ignored the recommendation and insisted that a curriculum guide be prepared.

In researching the subject, Ms. Wilson sought the assistance of Mr. Fisher who initiated the Board action and asked professors in the science departments of the University of Arkansas at Little Rock and the University of Central Arkansas for reference material and assistance, and attended a workshop conducted at Central Baptist College by Dr. Richard Bliss of the ICR staff. Act 590 became law during the course of her work so she used Section 4(a) as a format for her curriculum guide.

Ms. Wilson found all available creationists' materials unacceptable because they were permeated with religious references and reliance upon religious beliefs.

It is easy to understand why Ms. Wilson and other educators find the creationists' textbook material and teaching guides unacceptable. The materials misstate the theory of evolution in the same fashion as Section 4(b) of the Act, with emphasis on the alternative mutually exclusive nature of creationism and evolution. Students are constantly encouraged to compare and make a choice between the two models, and the material is not presented in an accurate manner.

A typical example is *Origins* (Px 76) by Richard B. Bliss, Director of Curriculum Development of the ICR. The presentation begins with a chart describing "preconceived ideas about origins" which suggests that some people believe that evolution is atheistic. Concepts of evolution, such as "adaptive radiation," are erroneously presented. At page 11, figure 1.6, of the text, a chart purports to illustrate this "very important" part of the evolution model. The chart conveys the idea that such diverse mammals as a whale, bear, bat and monkey all evolved from a shrew through the process of adaptive radiation. Such a suggestion is, of course, a totally erroneous and misleading application of the theory. Even more objectionable, especially when viewed in light of the emphasis on asking the student to elect one of the models, is the chart presentation at page 17, figure 1.6. That chart purports to illustrate the evolutionists' belief that man evolved from bacteria to fish to reptile to mammals and, thereafter, into man. The illustration indicates, however, that the mammal from which man evolved was a rat.

Biology, A Search For Order in Complexity is a high school biology text typical of creationists' materials. The following quotations are illustrative:

> Flowers and roots do not have a mind to have purpose of their own; therefore, this planning must have been done for them by the Creator.—at page 12.

> The exquisite beauty of color and shape in flowers exceeds the skill of poet, artist, and king. Jesus said (from Matthew's gospel), "Consider the lilies of the field, how they grow; they toil not, neither do they spin . . ."—at page 363.

The "public school edition" texts written by creationists simply omit Biblical references but the content and message remain the same. For example, *Evolution–The Fossils Say No !*, contains the following:

> Creation. By creation we mean the bringing into being by a supernatural Creator of the basic kinds of plants and animals by the process of sudden, or fiat, creation.

> We do not know how the Creator created, what processes He used, for He used processes which are not now operating anywhere in the natural universe. This is why we refer to creation as Special Creation. We cannot discover by scientific investigation anything about the creative processes used by the Creator.—page 40

Gish's book also portrays the large majority of evolutionists as "materialistic atheists or agnostics."

Scientific Creationism (Public School Edition) by Morris, is another text reviewed by Ms. Wilson's committee and rejected as unacceptable. The following quotes illustrate the purpose and theme of the text:

> Parents and youth leaders today, and even many scientists and educators, have become concerned about the prevalence and influence of evolutionary philosophy in modern curriculum. Not only is this system inimical to orthodox Christianity and Judaism, but also, as many are convinced, to a healthy society and true science as well.—at page iii.

> The rationalist of course finds the concept of special creation insufferably naive, even "incredible". Such a judgment, however, is warranted only if one categorically dismisses the existence of an omnipotent God.—at page 17.

Without using creationist literature, Ms. Wilson was unable to locate one genuinely scientific article or work which supported Section 4(a). In order to comply with the mandate of the Board she used such materials as an article from *Reader's Digest* about "atomic clocks" which inferentially suggested that the earth was less than 4 1/2 billion years old. She was unable to locate any substantive teaching material for some parts of Section 4 such as the worldwide flood. The curriculum guide which she prepared cannot be taught and has no educational value as science. The defendants did not produce any text or writing in response to this evidence which they claimed was usable in the public school classroom.

The conclusion that creation science has no scientific merit or educational value as science has legal significance in light of the Court's previous conclusion that creation science has, as one major effect, the advancement of religion. The second part of the three-pronged test for establishment reaches only those statutes having as their primary effect the advancement of religion. Secondary effects which advance religion are not constitutionally fatal. Since creation science is not science, the conclusion is inescapable that the only real effect of Act 590 is the advancement of religion. The Act therefore fails both the first and second portions of the test in Lemon v. Kurtzman, 403 U.S. 602 (1971).

IV.(E)

Act 590 mandates "balanced treatment" for creation science and evolution science. The Act prohibits instruction in any religious doctrine or references to religious writings. The Act is self-contradictory and compliance is impossible unless the public schools elect to forego significant portions of subjects such as biology, world history, geology, zoology, botany, psychology, anthropology, sociology, philosophy, physics and chemistry. Presently, the concepts of evolutionary theory as described in 4(b) permeate the public school textbooks. There is no way teachers can teach the Genesis account of creation in a secular manner.

The State Department of Education, through its textbook selection committee, school boards and school administrators will be required to constantly monitor materials to avoid using religious references. The school boards, administrators and teachers face an impossible task. How is the teacher to respond to questions about a creation suddenly and out of nothing? How will a teacher explain the occurrence of a worldwide flood? How will a teacher explain the concept of a relatively recent age of the earth? The answer is obvious because the only source of this information is ultimately contained in the Book of Genesis.

References to the pervasive nature of religious concepts in creation science texts amply demonstrate why State entanglement with religion is inevitable under Act 590. Involvement of the State in screening texts for impermissible religious references will require State officials to make delicate religious judgments. The need to monitor classroom discussion in order to uphold the Act's prohibition against religious instruction will necessarily involve administrators in questions concerning religion. These continuing involvements of State officials in questions and issues of religion create an excessive and prohibited entanglement with religion. Brandon v. Board of Education, 487 F.Supp. 1219, 1230 (N.D.N.Y.), aff'd., 635 F.2d 971 (2nd Cir. 1980).

V.

These conclusions are dispositive of the case and there is no need to reach legal conclusions with respect to the remaining issues. The plaintiffs raised two other issues questioning the constitutionality of the Act and, insofar as the factual findings relevant to these issues are not covered in the preceding discussion, the Court will address these issues. Additionally, the defendants raised two other issues which warrant discussion.

V.(A)

First, plaintiff teachers argue the Act is unconstitutionally vague to the extent that they cannot comply with its mandate of "balanced" treatment without jeopardizing their employment. The argument centers around the lack of a precise definition in the Act for the word "balanced." Several witnesses expressed opinions that the word has such meanings as equal time, equal weight, or equal legitimacy. Although the Act could have been more explicit, "balanced" is a word subject to ordinary understanding. The proof is not convincing that a teacher using a reasonably acceptable understanding of the word and making a good faith effort to comply with the Act will be in jeopardy of termination. Other portions of the Act are arguably vague, such as the "relatively recent" inception of the earth and life. The evidence establishes, however, that relatively recent means from 6,000 to 20,000 years, as commonly understood in creation science literature. The meaning of this phrase, like Section 4(a) generally, is, for purposes of the Establishment Clause, all too clear.

V.(B)

The plaintiffs' other argument revolves around the alleged infringement by the defendants upon the academic freedom of teachers and students. It is contended this unprecedented intrusion in the curriculum by the State prohibits teachers from teaching what they believe should be taught or requires them to teach that which they do not believe is proper. The evidence reflects that traditionally the State Department of Education, local school boards and administration officials exercise little, if any, influence upon the subject matter taught by classroom teachers. Teachers have been given freedom to teach and emphasize those portions of subjects the individual teacher considered important. The limits to this discretion have generally been derived from the approval of textbooks by the State Department and preparation of curriculum guides by the school districts.

Several witnesses testified that academic freedom for the teacher means, in substance, that the individual teacher should be permitted unlimited discretion subject only to the bounds of professional ethics. The Court is not prepared to adopt such a broad view of academic freedom in the public schools.

In any event, if Act 590 is implemented, many teachers will be required to teach material in support of creation science which they do not consider academically sound. Many teachers will simply forego teaching subjects which might trigger the "balanced treatment" aspects of Act 590 even though they think the subjects are important to a proper presentation of a course.

Implementation of Act 590 will have serious and untoward consequences for students, particularly those planning to attend college. Evolution is the cornerstone of modern biology, and many courses in public schools contain subject matter relating to such varied topics as the age of the earth, geology and relationships among living things. Any student who is deprived of instruction as to the prevailing scientific thought on these topics will be denied a significant part of science education. Such a deprivation through the high school level would undoubtedly have an impact upon the quality of education in the State's colleges and universities, especially including the pre-professional and professional programs in the health sciences.

V.(C)

The defendants argue in their brief that evolution is, in effect, a religion, and that by teaching a religion which is contrary to some students' religious views, the State is infringing upon the student's free exercise rights under the First Amendment. Mr. Ellwanger's legislative findings, which were adopted as a finding of fact by the Arkansas Legislature in Act 590, provides:

> Evolution-science is contrary to the religious convictions or moral values or philosophical beliefs of many students and parents, including individuals of many different religious faiths and with diverse moral and philosophical beliefs." Act 590, § 7(d).

The defendants argue that the teaching of evolution alone presents both a free exercise problem and an establishment problem which can only be redressed by giving balanced treatment to creation science, which is admittedly consistent with some religious beliefs. This argument appears to have its genesis in a student note written by Mr. Wendell Bird, "Freedom of Religion and Science Instruction in Public Schools," 87 Yale L.J. 515 (1978). The argument has no legal merit.

If creation science is, in fact, science and not religion, as the defendants claim, it is difficult to see how the teaching of such a science could "neutralize" the religious nature of evolution.

Assuming for the purposes of argument, however, that evolution is a religion or religious tenet, the remedy is to stop the teaching of evolution; not establish another religion in opposition to it. Yet it is clearly established in the case law, and perhaps also in common sense, that evolution is not a religion and that teaching evolution does not violate the Establishment Clause, Epperson v. Arkansas, supra; Willoughby v. Stever, No. 15574–75 (D.D.C. May 18, 1973); aff'd. 504 F.2d 271 (D.C.Cir.1974), cert. denied, 420 U.S. 927 (1975); Wright v. Houston Indep. School Dist., 366 F.Supp. 1208 (S.D.Tex.1972), aff'd. 486 F.2d 137 (5th Cir. 1973), cert. denied 417 U.S. 969 (1974).

V.(D)

The defendants presented Dr. Larry Parker, a specialist in devising curricula for public schools. He testified that the public school's curriculum should reflect the subjects the public wants taught in schools. The witness said that polls indicated a significant majority of the American public thought creation science should be taught if evolution was taught. The point of this testimony was never placed in a legal context. No doubt a sizeable majority of Americans believe in the concept of a Creator or, at least, are not opposed to the concept and see nothing wrong with teaching school children about the idea.

The application and content of First Amendment principles are not determined by public opinion polls or by a majority vote. Whether the proponents of Act 590 constitute the majority or the minority is quite irrelevant under a constitutional system of government. No group, no matter how large or small, may use the organs of government, of which the public schools are the most conspicuous and influential, to foist its religious beliefs on others.

The Court closes this opinion with a thought expressed eloquently by the great Justice Frankfurter:

We renew our conviction that 'we have staked the very existence of our country on the faith that complete separation between the state and religion is best for the state and best for religion.' Everson v. Board of Education, 330 U.S. at 59. If nowhere else, in the relation between Church and State, 'good fences make good neighbors.' McCollum v. Board of Education, 333 U.S. 203, 232 (1948).

An injunction will be entered permanently prohibiting enforcement of Act 590.

1984 TEXAS ATT'Y GEN. OP. JM–134 (MARCH 12, 1984)

Re: Whether certain rules of the State Board of Education concerning the treatment of the subject of evolution in textbooks violate the Establishment Clause of the United States Constitution?

Honorable Oscar H. Mauzy, Chairman
Committee on Jurisprudence
Texas State Senate
P.O. Box 12068, Capitol Station
Austin, Texas 78711

Dear Senator Mauzy:

You have asked whether certain rules of the State Board of Education violate the federal constitutional prohibition against laws "respecting an establishment of religion." U.S. Const. amends. 1, 14. These rules, issued on September 29, 1983, and effective from October 24, 1983, provide:

(a) All adopted textbooks shall meet the following content requirements and limitations:

(1) In accordance with the Texas Education Code § 12.14(c), textbooks shall contain no material of a partisan or sectarian character . . . .

(5) Textbooks that treat the theory of evolution shall identify it as only one of several explanations of the origins of humankind and avoid limiting young people in their search for meanings of their human existence.

(A) Textbooks presented for adoption which treat the subject of evolution substantively in explaining the historical origins of man shall be edited, if necessary, to clarify that the treatment is theoretical rather than factually verifiable. Furthermore, each textbook must carry a statement on an introductory page that any material on evolution included in the book is clearly presented as theory rather than verified.

(B) Textbooks presented for adoption which do not treat evolution substantively as an instructional topic, but make reference to evolution indirectly or by implication, must be modified, if necessary, to ensure that the reference is clearly to a theory and not to a verified fact. These books will not need to carry a statement on the introductory page.

(C) The presentation of the theory of evolution shall be done in a manner which is not detrimental to other theories of origin.

In Epperson v. Arkansas, 393 U.S. 97 (1968), the United States Supreme Court struck down an Arkansas statute that forbade the teaching of evolution. More recently, a federal district court invalidated an Arkansas statute which required public schools to "give balanced treatment to creation-science and to evolution-science." McLean v. Arkansas Board of Education, 529 F.Supp. 1255, 1256 (E.D.Ark.1982). Although the stated purpose of this statute was to provide a "balanced" treatment of the teaching of evolution, the court found it necessary to look behind this stated purpose to consider the historical context of the statute, the specific sequence of events leading up to its passage, and contemporaneous statements of the legislative sponsor. 529 F.Supp. at 1263–64. Examining these circumstances, the court was unable to avoid the conclusion that the statute "was passed with the specific purpose by the General Assembly of advancing religion," and thus failed the first prong of the Supreme Court's test, that of a secular legislative purpose. 529 F.Supp. at 1264.

The rule under consideration here represents a slight modification of a 1974 state board rule which in turn derived from a still earlier version. At hearings conducted before the board in both 1974 and 1983, the board heard testimony from proponents of both evolution and creationism, and it is necessary to consider the kind of controversy which was before the board in both instances. In 1983, the board heard testimony from five groups and 17 individuals. See 8 Tex.Reg., (October 7, 1983), at 3986–87.

Under the federal Constitution, laws suspected of violating the Establishment Clause of the first amendment are subjected to a three-pronged test formulated by the Supreme Court in Lemon v. Kurtzman, 403 U.S. 602 (1971), and later applied in Stone v. Graham, 449 U.S. 39 (1980): Laws must have a secular purpose; they must neither advance nor hinder religion in their primary effect; and they must not foster excessive government entanglement with religion. If a statute, or a rule promulgated pursuant to a statute, violates any of these principles, it must be struck down under the Establishment Clause. See Stone v. Graham, supra. In our opinion, the board's rules on their face fail to satisfy at least the first prong of the Lemon test, in that they fail to demonstrate a secular purpose. Although, like the statute at issue in McLean, see 529 F.Supp. at 1272, the board's rule prohibits any "material of a partisan or sectarian character," we believe that subsequent provisions belie that statement.

The only aspect of "evolution" with which the rule is concerned is that which relates to "the historical origins of man." The rule requires a biology textbook, for example, to carry a disclaimer on its introductory page to the effect that "any material on evolution" included therein is to be regarded as theory rather than as factually verifiable. In the first place, such a disclaimer—which might make sense if applied to all scientific theories—is limited to one aspect—man's origins—of one theory—evolution—of one science—biology. In the context of the controversy between evolutionists and creationists which was before the board at the time of the rules' adoption both in 1974 and 1983, this singling out of one aspect of one theory of one science can be explained only as a response to pressure from creationists.

In the second place, the "theory of evolution," as it is commonly treated in biology texts, is a comprehensive explanation of the development of the various plant and animal species. Only a relatively minor portion is concerned with the "historical origins of man." The latter subject is the primary interest of creationists. See McLean, supra, at 1260. Again, the inference is inescapable from the narrowness of the requirement that a concern for religious sensibilities, rather than a dedication to scientific truth, was the real motivation for the rules.

Finally, the rules require that a textbook identify the theory of evolution "as only one of several explanations" of human origins in order to "avoid limiting young people in their search for meanings of their human existence." Such language is not conducive to an explanation that the purpose of the rule is to insure that impressionable minds will be able to distinguish between scientific theory and dogma. The "meaning of human existence" is not the stuff of science but rather, the province of philosophy and religion. By its injection into the rules language which is clearly outside the scope of science, the board has revealed the non-secular purpose of its rules.

Clearly, the board made an effort, as it has stated, to "insure neutrality in the treatment of subjects upon which beliefs and viewpoints differ dramatically." In our opinion, however, the board, in its desire not to offend any religious group, has injected religious considerations into an area which must be, at least in the public school context, strictly the province of science. As the court said in Wright v. Houston Independent School District, 366 F.Supp. 1208, 1211 (S.D.Tex.1972):

> Science and religion necessarily deal with many of the same questions, and they may frequently provide conflicting answers. But, as the Supreme Court wrote twenty years ago, it is not the business of government to suppress real or imagined attacks upon a particular religious doctrine. Burstyn v. Wilson, 343 U.S. 495, 505 (1952). Teachers of science in the public schools should not be expected to avoid the discussion of every scientific issue on which some religion claims expertise.

If the board feels compelled to legislate in this area, it should, in order to avoid the constitutional prohibition, promulgate a rule which is of general application to all scientific inquiry, which does not single out for its requirement of a disclaimer a single theory of one scientific field, and which does not include language suggesting inquiries which lie totally outside the realm of science. The rules submitted, however, when considered in the context of the circumstances of their adoption, fail to evidence a secular purpose, and hence we believe a court would find that they contravene the first and fourteenth amendments to the United States Constitution.

The rules of the State Board of Education, concerning the subject of evolution, fail to demonstrate a secular purpose and are therefore in contravention of the first and fourteenth amendments to the United States Constitution.

Very truly yours,
Jim Mattox, Attorney General of Texas

NOTES AND QUESTIONS

1. Like *Epperson*, the *McLean* decision turned on the issue of legislative purpose. In both cases, the challenged statute was found to lack a secular purpose. According to *McLean*, what was the Balanced–Treatment Act's fatal non-secular purpose? Legislators inevitably bring their values and beliefs (religious or otherwise) to lawmaking. Few would disqualify a Christian legislator from voting for an anti-abortion bill because she was motivated by her religious beliefs any more than they would disqualify a feminist legislator from voting against the same bill because she was motivated by her feminist beliefs. Applying similar logic to the current case, a Christian legislator might believe that creation-science is valid because of her religious beliefs and then vote for the Balanced Treatment Act because she believes that it advances science education. In contrast, it is arguably more problematic under the Establishment Clause for a Christian legislator to vote for a creation-teaching bill because she wishes to promote belief in the religious doctrine of creation-ism among students compelled by law to attend public schools. Yet the purpose in both cases can be characterized as "religious." Similarly, the 1984 Texas Attorney General's Opinion also relied on the State Board of Education's supposedly non-secular purpose to find that the proposed restrictions on the presentation of evolution in public-school textbooks violated the Establishment Clause. According to the Attorney General, what was the Board's non-secular purpose? Among other findings, his opinion suggested that the Board must have had a non-secular reason for injecting religious matters into science instruction.

2. As noted in the *McLean* decision, promoters of the Arkansas Balanced–Treatment Act urged supporters to distinguish sharply between creation-science and creation-religion, and to only promote the teaching of creation-science. Did the Act itself promote creation-science or creation-religion? The Act's inclusion into the definition of creation-science strictly biblical concepts of creation, such as a worldwide flood, breached this distinction and made the Act more vulnerable to attack as a facial violation of the Establishment Clause. To the extent that the statute mandated teaching biblical concepts as science in public schools, it supported a facial change to the statute as having a primary effect of promoting a particular religious doctrine in public school and entangling the state with religion in mandating and monitoring the teaching of a religious doctrine.

3. To what extent is the two model approach to origins—creation verses evolution—a contrived dualism? Public opinion surveys suggest that up to half of all Americans believe God somehow designed or guides the evolutionary process and thus creates through evolution. Do such theories of theistic evolution neatly fit into a two model approach of origins and, if so, into which model—creation or evolution? As leaders of Methodist, Episcopalian, mainline Presbyterian, or Roman Catholic churches, most of the religious plaintiffs in *Mclean* probably believed in some form of theistic evolution. Does a statute or school-board rule favoring special creation over theistic evolution in public education entangle government with religion in violation of the Establishment Clause? The *McLean* decision does not raise this particular issue but later courts dealing with similar cases would do so.

4. Judge Overton's opinion in *McLean* was notable for setting forth a general and specific definition of science and then applying them to find that Darwinism is science and creation-science is not science. Philosophers of science, including at least one who testified at trial and proposed the definition, subsequently criticized the court's specific definition, which identified the five "essential characteristics" of science: guided by natural law, explained by natural law, tentative, testable, and falsifiable. How can a court decide whether such characteristics are essential to science? The court's general definition "that science is what is 'accepted by the scientific community' and is 'what scientists do,'" has found favor among historians and philosophers of science. Is it appropriate to let scientists define science by the practical norms of their profession? In what ways do the norms or practice of creation-science differ from or comply with the norms or practice of normal science? Should the scientific community's definition of science be critical for determining if teaching creation-science in public schools has a scientific purpose or effect?

5. In what ways did the 1984 Texas Attorney General's Opinion follow from the *McLean* decision? *McLean* voided a state statute mandating balanced treatment for Darwinism and creation-science in public schools. The Texas Attorney General's Opinion dealt with a state School Board rule requiring that textbooks identify Darwinism as being one of several explanations of human origins but without necessarily identifying any alternative explanations. The former statute effectively added religious content to the science curriculum; the latter incorporated a religiously based qualification to it.

6. Following the ruling against the Arkansas Balanced–Treatment Act, creationists publicly denounced Arkansas' 34–year–old Attorney General, Steve Clark, for failing to mount a vigorous defense of the Act and criticized him for socializing with plaintiffs' attorneys and expert witnesses, most of whom came from outside the state. Clark ultimately filed a defamation action against several prominent televangelists for their comments. As Attorney General, Clark had a reputation for lavish entertainment and, in 1990, was convicted of felony theft for using a state credit card for trips and meals at which his family, friends and political contributors were guests. When the Louisiana Balanced–Treatment Act came under fire, the Louisiana Attorney General quickly accepted Wendell Bird's offer to defend the statute and kept his distance from the ensuing litigation.

III. RESOLVING THE CONSTITUTIONALITY OF CREATION–SCIENCE

The *McLean* decision did not necessarily resolve the constitutionality of the Louisiana Balanced–Treatment Act. Many of the more damning features of the Arkansas law were absent from the Louisiana statute, including the creationist findings of fact, the Genesis-like definition for creation-science, and the hasty adoption of the proposal in the exact form supplied by religiously motivated private citizens. These differences obscured both the purpose behind enactment of the Louisiana legislation and the potential effects of its implementation. In the midst of the *McLean* trial and one month before Judge Overton handed down his decision against the Arkansas Balanced–Treatment Act, the ACLU filed suit in New Orleans federal court challenging the constitutionality of the Louisiana statute. The complaint named twenty-six organizational and individual plaintiffs, beginning with local Louisiana educator Donald Aguillard and including such familiar participants as the National Association of Biology Teachers, the National Science Teachers Association, and the American Association for the Advancement of Science. The state deputized Wendell Bird as a special assistant attorney general and gave him overall responsibility for defending the statute. Bird also filed his own suit on behalf of the bill's sponsor, Bill Keith, to compel enforcement of the Balanced–Treatment Act but ultimately this action was dismissed and effectively subsumed within *Aguillard*.[60]

"This case differs vastly from *McLean*," Bird argued in a pre-trial brief submitted in support of the Louisiana law, "because the Balanced Treatment Act is (1) a substantially different statute with (2) an entirely different definition of creation-science and with (3) a markedly different legislative purpose." Elaborating on the new definition of creation-science, the state rejected all the traditional features of the biblical account that figured so prominently in the Arkansas statute, leaving only the broad concept that some organic and inorganic matter initially appeared in complex form rather than every living form evolving by mutation and natural selection from ever simpler ones back to non-living matter. Turning to legislative purpose, the brief pointed to the lengthy deliberations on the measure by both houses to make credible the law's express purpose of protecting academic freedom. To resolve these issues, it demanded a trial on the scientific merits of creation-science and the educational merits of the Louisiana law.[61]

In opposing the Louisiana law, the ACLU relied on the arguments that carried the day in Arkansas. The law "does not have any secular legislative purpose in that creation-science is inherently religious, it is religious apologetics calculated to advance a particular religious belief, it is

---

60. Keith v. Louisiana Department of Education, 553 F.Supp. 295 (M.D.La. 1982).

61. Plaintiffs' Pre–Trial Brief at 2, 5, 48, *Keith*, 553 F.Supp. 295.

not science and it has no educational merit," an ACLU pretrial brief argued. As such, "teaching creation-science in the public schools advances religious beliefs even if attempts are made to eliminate overt references to the Bible, the Creator or other religious concepts." The brief cited *McLean* as determinative authority on both points and suggested that a second trial was unnecessary to void the Louisiana law.[62] After its sweeping victory in Little Rock, the ACLU had nothing further to gain from another trial, while creationists had nothing more to lose.

At first, the *Aguillard* court dodged the core constitutional issues raised by both sides. Acting without a trial in 1982, Judge Adrian Duplantier overturned the statute for reasons wholly unrelated to creationism. According to Duplantier, the Louisiana constitution entrusted total authority over school curriculum matters to the state education board. The legislature wrongly usurped this authority by dictating to the public schools not only that a subject must be taught, but also how it must be taught.[63] No court dealing with the creationism controversy had used this approach to limit legislative authority. *McLean*, for example, maintained that the legislature could control public education so long as it did not abridge constitutional rights in the process. The federal appellate court reviewing the decision referred this novel issue of state constitutional law to the Louisiana Supreme Court. Late in 1983, the state high bench rejected the federal trial court's ruling that the state legislature lacked plenary power of public education in Louisiana. In doing so, however, the state court stressed that its decision did not involve any scientific or religious questions related to creation-science.[64] These questions then returned to the federal court.

Early in 1985, Judge Duplantier tried to dispose of these questions by entering a second pre-trial summary judgment against the Louisiana act, this time on the federal Establishment Clause grounds that the statute lacked a secular purpose.[65] The sponsor of the Louisiana statute, Bill Keith, insisted that this ruling improperly ignored defense arguments about the scientific merits of creation-science and publicly charged the judge with bias. With Bird still at the helm, the state promptly appealed to the Fifth Circuit U.S. Court of Appeals.

A three-judge appellate panel heard Bird's arguments in May, 1985. Those arguments alleged that Duplantier erred in denying a full trial on the scientific and educational merits of creation-science. Federal court rules required that, when deciding motions for summary judgment, courts view disputed facts in a light most favorable to the party resisting the motion and accept uncontroverted affidavits as true. Further, the motion should not be granted where there is a genuine issue as to any material fact. The state had presented the district court with five affidavits from

---

62. Defendants' Pre–Trial Brief at 62–63, *Keith*, 553 F.Supp. 295.

63. Aguillard v. Treen, No. 81–4787, slip op. 6 at (E.D.La. Nov. 22, 1982).

64. Aguillard v. Treen, 440 So.2d 704, 707, n. 6 (La. 1983).

65. Aguillard v. Treen, 634 F.Supp. 426 (E.D. La. 1985).

experts plus a 630–page brief chock-full of scientific references all to the effect that creation-science was a scientific doctrine suitable for teaching in public schools. These affidavits and the state's brief raised genuine issues of material fact requiring a trial, Bird charged.

Countering for the plaintiffs, New York ACLU attorney Allan Blumstein argued that Bird's facts were immaterial. The court voided the statute because it was enacted with a wrongful religious purpose and that remained true even if later affidavits and the state's brief alleged that creation-science had scientific elements. Further, he added, the state's affidavits lacked scientific credibility. Only two of the five came from scientists. One of these was by W. Scot Morrow, an associate professor of chemistry at church-affiliated college in South Carolina. Morrow's short affidavit did not cite any scientific research supporting his assertion that creation-science is scientific, non-religious, and educationally worthwhile. The other was a detailed statement by San Francisco State University biology professor Dean H. Kenyon, a well-known scientist with a long-standing interest in the religious implications of Darwinism. His affidavit focused on scientific evidence *against* current evolutionary theories rather than *for* any particular doctrine of creation, and therefore could be read as supporting the Louisiana law only by accepting Bird's premise that the term creation-science, as used in the statute, meant all non-evolutionary theories of origins. Of the three remaining affidavits, two came from theologians teaching at Bible colleges and one was by a local school administrator. None of the affidavits directly addressed the issue of legislative purpose.

Two panel judges expressed their doubts about the Louisiana law from the bench. "This is a religious effort, that's what it is," Chief Judge John R. Brown asserted. Bird disagreed, claiming that the law only provided for teaching purely scientific evidence for a creation, which need not involve discussing God or a creator. "For a system that's based upon creation, there has to be a creator," Brown shot back. Judge E. Grady Jolly added, "If that's not a law with respect to the establishment of religion, I just can't see it." Jolly expressed particular concern that the state could not find a single current textbook presenting creation-science in a non-religious manner suitable for public-school use.[66] Two months after this exchange, the appellate panel unanimously affirmed Duplantier's ruling.[67]

Undeterred, Louisiana pressed on with its appeal. Orchestrating the state's legal strategy, Bird did not follow the normal course of appealing directly to the U.S. Supreme Court, however, but sought a rehearing *en banc* by the entire fifteen-member Fifth Circuit appellate bench. This represented his best hope. The Supreme Court, in effect led by aging liberal Justice William Brennan, had just decided a series of Establishment Clause cases signaling a tough stand against mixing religion and

---

66. See excerpts from the courtroom argument in John Pope, *Creation Law Trial Is Urged*, TIMES–PICAYUNE/STATES–ITEM, May 9, 1985, at A–37.

67. Aguillard v. Edwards, 765 F.2d 1251 (5th Cir. 1985).

public education. These rulings, issued by a deeply divided Court just days prior to the panel decision in *Aguillard*, struck down a twenty-year-old New York City program providing public remedial education for parochial-school students, a Grand Rapids scheme of offering public-education classes in church schools, and an Alabama statute imposing a moment of silence for student prayer in public schools.

These decisions ran counter to other trends. Repeatedly proclaiming, "I don't believe we should ever have expelled God from the classroom," Ronald Reagan had been elected president five years earlier, promising to appoint federal judges willing to accommodate religion in public education.[68] During the campaign, he embraced official school prayer, voiced support for teaching biblical creationism, and questioned the theory of evolution. His administration had actively intervened before the Supreme Court on the losing side of all three 1985 school-house religion cases, leading one popular news magazine to report, "There is still no Reagan court."[69] But while five years in office had provided Reagan the opportunity to appoint only one of the nine justices on the Supreme Court, he had named six of the fifteen Fifth Circuit appellate-court jurists. Bird appealed to these judges. Indeed, the Louisiana act's sponsor, Bill Keith, opined that God had delayed the lawsuit this long so that more Reagan appointees could join the bench.

Losing litigants can only suggest a rehearing *en banc* by written petition to the full court, and a majority of the judges must agree before such a procedure occurs. The state's petition betrayed Bird's frustration with being denied a trial on the merits of a law that sprang directly from his 1978 law-review article. He had doggedly assembled a massive brief and five affidavits affirming that creation-science was scientific rather than religious and that the Louisiana statute promoted the secular objective of academic freedom. Yet, the petition charged, "The panel and district court *absolutely failed* to view the state's factual allegations (even its uncontroverted affidavits) in the most favorable light—and in actuality failed to consider them at all." To the contrary, it complained, the panel found that creation-science was a religious belief and the law lacked a secular purpose even though these findings directly conflict with the plethora of authority cited by the State and with the uncontroverted (and only) affidavits in the case. After summarizing this authority in the pages allotted for its petition, the state demanded—or at least forcefully requested—a rehearing before the full court.[70] Late in 1985, a bare majority of the court denied Bird's petition without comment over the following dissenting opinion filed by seven of the court's fifteen judges:

AGUILLARD v. EDWARDS

United States Court of Appeals for the Fifth Circuit
778 F.2d 225 (5th Cir. 1985)

---

68. Ronald Reagan, in George J. Church, *Politics from the Pulpit*, Time, Oct. 13, 1983, at 28.

69. Aric Press, *A Reagan Court?*, Newsweek, July 15, 1985, at 69.

70. Suggestion for Rehearing En Banc at 6, 9, *Aguillard*, 765 F.2d 1251.

PER CURIAM: Treating the suggestion for rehearing en banc as a petition for panel rehearing, the petition for panel rehearing is DENIED. The judges in regular active service of this Court having been polled at the request of one of said judges and a majority of said judges not having voted in favor of it (Federal Rules of Appellate Procedure and Local Rule 35), the suggestion for Rehearing En Banc is DENIED.

GEE, CIRCUIT JUDGE, with whom CLARK, CHIEF JUDGE, and REAVLEY, GARWOOD, HIGGINBOTHAM, HILL and JONES, CIRCUIT JUDGES, join dissenting.: Today our full court approves, by declining review en banc, a panel opinion striking down a Louisiana statute as one "respecting an establishment of religion." The panel reasons that by requiring public school teachers to present a balanced view of the current evidence regarding the origins of life and matter (if any view is taught) rather than that favoring one view only and by forbidding them to misrepresent as established fact views on the subject which today remain theories only, the statute promotes religious belief and violates the academic freedom of instructors to teach whatever they like.

The Scopes court upheld William Jennings Bryan's view that states could constitutionally forbid teaching the scientific evidence for the theory of evolution, rejecting that of Clarence Darrow that truth was truth and could always be taught—whether it favored religion or not. By requiring that the whole truth be taught, Louisiana aligned itself with Darrow; striking down that requirement, the panel holding aligns us with Bryan.

I disagree with this holding; and because we endorse it today, I respectfully dissent.

BACKGROUND

In 1981 the Louisiana legislature passed the legislation which is the subject of today's controversy. Sections 17:286.1 through 286.7, Louisiana Revised Statutes. Its full text appears as an appendix to the panel opinion, at 765 F.2d 1251, 1258. The general purport of this law is to provide three things:

1.   That the "subject of origins" of the universe, of life, and of species need not be taught at all in the public schools of Louisiana; but,

2.   That if either "creation-science" (defined as "the scientific evidences for creation and inferences from" them) or "evolution-science" (parallel definition) be taught, balanced treatment be given the other; and,

3.   That, if taught, each be taught as a theory, "rather than as proven scientific fact."

I am as capable as the panel of making an extra-record guess that much, if not most, of the steam which drove this enactment was generated by religious people who were hostile to having the theory of evolution misrepresented to school children as established scientific fact and who wished the door left open to acceptance by these children of the Judeo-

Christian religious doctrine of Divine Creation. If so, however, they did not seek to further their aim by requiring that religious doctrine be taught in public school. Instead, they chose a more modest tactic—one that I am persuaded does not infringe the Constitution.

That was to provide, as my summary of the statute indicates, that neither evolution nor creation be presented as finally established scientific fact and that, when evolution is taught as a theory, the scientific evidence for such competing theories as a "big bang" production of the universe or for the sudden appearance of highly developed forms of life be given equal time (and vice versa). As I noted at the outset, the record contains affidavits—some of them by highly-qualified scientists who there proclaim themselves agnostics and believers in evolution as a theory—which affirm that the above propositions are correct: that evolution is not established fact and that there is strong evidence that life and the universe came about in a different manner, one perhaps less inconsistent with religious doctrine. At the least, these affidavits make a fact issue that those propositions are true. For purposes of reviewing the summary judgment which our panel's opinion affirms, then, the propositions stated must be taken as established: there are two bona fide views.

It follows that the Louisiana statute requires no more than that neither theory about the origins of life and matter be misrepresented as fact, and that if scientific evidence supporting either view of how these things came about be presented in public schools, that supporting the other must be-so that within the reasonable limits of the curriculum, the subject of origins will be discussed in a balanced manner if it is discussed at all. I see nothing illiberal about such a requirement, nor can I imagine that Galileo or Einstein would have found fault with it. Indeed, so far as I am aware even Ms. O'Hair has never asked for more than equal time.

Let it be conceded, for purposes of argument, that many of those who worked to get this legislation passed did so with a religious motive. It well may be that many who advocated Louisiana's Sunday closing Law, recently upheld by us, did so from such a motive. There being evident a credible secular purpose for that law, however, we upheld it. Home Depot, Inc. v. Guste, 773 F.2d 616 (1985). There can be no doubt that the Louisiana Legislature was empowered under the state constitution to enact the law in question, one mandating a particular course of public school instruction; the Louisiana Supreme Court has squarely so held, on certification from us earlier in the course of this appeal. Aguillard v. Treen, 440 So.2d 704 (La.1983).

Despite this, our panel struck the statute down.

THE PANEL OPINION

The panel's reasoning is simple. Lemon v. Kurtzman, 403 U.S. 602 (1971), sets three hurdles before any statute attacked as establishing religion. The panel holds that the Louisiana statute trips over the first, which requires that "the statute must have a secular legislative purpose;. . . ." Lemon, supra, at 612. I cannot agree.

The panel opinion chiefly rests upon such Supreme Court authorities as Lemon (state aid to church schools), Stone v. Graham, 449 U.S. 39 (1980) (posting Ten Commandments in every classroom), and Wallace v. Jaffree, 472 U.S. 38 (1985) (moment of silence for "meditation or voluntary prayer"), as well as on such holdings from our own court as Lubbock Civil Liberties Union v. Lubbock I.S.D., 669 F.2d 1038 (5th Cir.1982) (religious meetings on school property) and Karen B. v. Treen, 653 F.2d 897 (5th Cir.1981) (classroom prayer). Such authorities treat of statutes having a direct and clear religious connection, either by way of granting public assistance to religious schools or by requiring or permitting religious activities in public ones. The statute which concerns us today is quite different: it has no direct religious reference whatever and merely requires that the whole scientific truth be taught on the subject if any is.

In order to invalidate it as "establishing religion," it was therefore necessary for the panel to look beyond the statute's words and beyond legislative statements of secular purpose. To strike the statute down, the panel draws upon its visceral knowledge regarding what must have motivated the legislators. It sifts their hearts and minds, divines their motive for requiring that truth be taught, and strikes down the law that requires it. This approach effectually makes a farce of the judicial exercise of discerning legislative intent. The task is admittedly a most difficult and often impossible one, since legislatures are not known for providing clear guidance to those interpreting their works; but it is a task constitutionally required. To disregard so completely the existing manifestations of intent and impose instead one's personal, subjective ideas as to what must have been the true sentiment of the Louisiana legislature ignores this constitutional restraint on judicial power.

Moreover, even assuming the panel's guess about legislative sentiment is right, the infirmity of its reasoning becomes immediately evident when it is extended from prescribing what is to be taught to the teaching itself. If it is unconstitutional to require secular matter to be taught from a motive to advance religion it must necessarily also be unconstitutional to teach it from such a motive. If so, a public school teacher so indiscreet as to admit to teaching the evidence for creation science from a motive to advance religion is subject to being silenced, while one teaching exactly the same matter without such a motive cannot be interfered with. Like a clock that strikes 13, a rule that produces such a result as this cannot be sound.

I await with interest the application of this new mode of constitutional analysis to other statutes. The bigamy laws, for example, carry tell-tale indicia of having been passed with a motive to favor the Judeo–Christian religious preference for monogamy, singling it out for adoption over the equally workable Moslem view. Perhaps our court, consulting its intuitive knowledge about what motivates legislators, will presently determine that there can be no secular purpose in such a preferment of one model of the marital relationship over another, especially when the effect of doing so is to espouse the religious doctrine of the two larger religious sects in our country over that of the minority of Moslems. But such intriguing possibilities must await another day, and I return to the case in hand.

I should have thought that requiring the truth to be taught on any subject displayed its own secular warrant, one at the heart of the scientific method itself. Put another way, I am surprised to learn that a state cannot forbid the teaching of half-truths in its public schools, whatever its motive for doing so. Today we strike down a statute balanced and fair on its face because of our perception of the reason why it got the votes to pass: one to prevent the closing of children's minds to religious doctrine by misrepresenting it as in conflict with established scientific laws. After today, it does not suffice to teach the truth; one must also teach it with the approved motive. It may be that the Constitution forbids a state to require the teaching of lies in the classrooms of its public schools; perhaps among its emanations or penumbras there can be found means to invalidate such a law, say, as one mandating that students be taught that the earth is flat or that chattel slavery never existed in this country. It comes as news to me, however, that the Constitution forbids a state to require the teaching of truth-any truth, for any purpose, and whatever the effect of teaching it may be. Because this is the holding that we endorse today, I decline to join in that endorsement and respectfully dissent.

JOLLY, CIRCUIT JUDGE, responding to dissent: First, as writer of the panel opinion, I offer my apologies to the majority of this court for aligning it with the forces of darkness and anti-truth. Second, I do not personally align myself with the dissenters in their commitment to the search for eternal truth through state edicts. Third, I commend to the dissenters a serious rereading of the majority opinion that they may recognize the hyperbole of the opinion in which they join. And, finally, I respectfully submit, the panel opinion speaks for itself, modestly and moderately, if one will allow its words to be carefully heard.

NOTES AND QUESTIONS

1. Judge Gee's dissenting opinion began with a striking but curious reference to Clarence Darrow, William Jennings Bryan, and the Scopes Trial. Distancing himself from the creationist Bryan and invoking the agnostic Darrow, Gee claimed that Darrow believed that truth was truth and could be taught in public schools even if it favored religion. No solid historical evidence suggests that Darrow held such a belief. A philosophical relativist, Darrow did not seek truth. Further, he was one the nation's leading exponents of anti-clericalism—devoting extraordinary effort to advocating the removal of religious influences from public life. Perhaps Gee's view of Darrow drew on a historically unsubstantiated quote attributed to Darrow in Bird's law-review article and brief: "Clarence Darrow of Scopes trial fame remarked that it is 'bigotry for public schools to teach only one theory of origins.' " As his source

for this quote, Bird cited an article by religious writer sympathetic to the creationist cause who did not provide any original source for the quote. The Darrow-character in the popular play and movie about the Scopes Trial, *Inherit the Wind,* did make comments similar to the quote—but they were purely fictional. It is unlikely that the real-life Darrow ever said anything of this sort about teaching creationism.

2.   In his dissenting opinion, Judge Gee suggested that (1) public-schools misrepresent the theory of evolution as an established fact, (2) teaching Darwinism in this manner undermines the Judeo–Christian doctrine of creation, and (3) the challenged law would ameliorate this situation. Has he created a straw man? Would it be constitutional for a public school to teaching evolution with the purpose or primary effect of undermining or denying religious doctrine? In answering this question, consider the earlier opinion in *Wright*, in which the court cited with favor a Texas requirement that students with religious objections could opt out of public-school instruction in the theory of evolution. Also consider *Seagraves*, where the court not only hailed a California regulation against teaching any theory of origins dogmatically but ordered that it be widely distributed and suggested that it was required by the Constitution. More generally, the U.S. Supreme Court has repeatedly stated that the Establishment Clause applies to governmental actions that inhibit or hinder religion in the same way as it applies to those that promote or advance religion.

3.   The dissenting opinion condemned as clearly unsound an interpretation of the Establishment Clause that would make it unconstitutional for a public-school teacher to teach creation-science "from a motive to advance religion" but constitutional for her to teach "exactly the same matter without such a motive." Yet this is an arguable interpretation of the first prong of the *Lemon* test, which holds that government actions must have a legitimate secular purpose. Is such an interpretation clearly unsound? Some critics of the *Lemon* test's purpose prong argue that motive should not matter because it is impossible to determine motive. Some critics add that, as a practical matter, it should not matter if a government actor is motivated by a desire to promote religion so long as the resulting action neither has that primary effect nor excessively entangling the government with religion.

* * * * *

Without other legal alternatives for saving the statute, Louisiana next appealed to the U.S. Supreme Court. In the petition requesting Supreme Court review, the state again raised procedural concerns in its bid for a trial on the merits of creation-science. "[T]he decision under review failed to 'take as true' the State's factual assertions in its uncontroverted affidavits," the brief noted, "and instead resolved disputed factual issues by improper judicial notice contrary to the only evidence in the case."[71] Not so, answered the plaintiffs in their reply brief, "the real issue in this case is *not* whether defendant's after-the-fact, created-for-litigation affidavits establish that the doctrine of 'creation-science' has a scientific component to it," but rather if the Balanced–Treatment Act had a fatal religious

---

71.   Jurisdictional Statement at iv-v, Edwards v. Aguillard, 482 U.S. 578 (1987).

purpose.[72] As often happens in litigation, each side framed the issue in terms whereby it could win. If (as the state maintained) the issue was whether creation-science was a scientific concept with educational merit, then the state had raised sufficient factual questions to warrant a trial. If (as the plaintiffs countered) the issues were whether creation-science embodied a religious belief and whether the law was enacted to promote that belief, then the state's facts were largely immaterial and summary disposition of the case was justified. The Supreme Court opted to frame the issue for itself, and scheduled its courtroom showdown on creation-science late in 1987.

The scene was far different from when the creation-evolution controversy first reached the courts in *Scopes*. The sweltering summer heat of Dayton gave way to a cool December day in Washington. The carnival atmosphere of an open-air trial featuring the most famous orators of the era was replaced by the High Bench's august courtroom. The tenor of the arguments reflected the cooler, more dignified physical environment.

Bird opened the oral arguments for the state. "Creation science means the scientific evidence for creation and inferences from those scientific evidences," Bird began. "The teaching of the Bible as part of the implications of the statute would be unconstitutional," he later added. Repeatedly invoking the state's five expert affidavits affirming that creation-science was scientific (as opposed to religious) doctrine, Bird stressed that the statute sanctioned only the teaching of scientific material. According to Bird, creation-science was a technical term that should be resolved as a factual matter. The lower courts simply determined out of thin air that creation-science was religious concept and used this to void the statute for having the unconstitutional religious purpose of promoting that concept. Asking for the Supreme Court to send the case back to the district court for a trial where experts could show that creation-science was scientific, Bird asserted, "The courts did not rely on the record. The courts said what 'creation science' means without looking at the record."[73]

"But couldn't we look at the record, and see if the court was right?" Justice Sandra Day O'Connor asked, as the justices began peppering Bird with questions. No, Bird replied, because the unresolved factual issues about creation-science and legislative purpose required a trial. Under close interrogation from several justices about legislative purpose, Bird noted that lawmakers probably had a variety of reasons for enacting the law, and he conceded that "undoubtedly some legislators had a desire to teach religious doctrine in the classroom." But he maintained that the predominant legislative purpose was to promote "fairness and academic freedom" by including alternative scientific views in the curriculum. Bird faced the toughest questioning from Justice John Paul Stevens, who repeatedly

---

72. Motion to Affirm at 21, 26, *Edwards*, 482 U.S. 578.

73. The transcript of the oral argument is reprinted in MAY IT PLEASE THE COURT: THE MOST SIGNIFICANT ORAL ARGUMENTS MADE BEFORE THE SUPREME COURT SINCE 1955 (Peter H. Irons & Stephanie Guitton eds., 1993). It is summarized in this and the following paragraphs from the author's notes taken during the argument.

asked if creation and evolution represented separate theories that could be balanced in classroom instruction. While Bird maintained that they were distinct and mutually exclusive scientific theories, Justice Stevens argued that a person could view the two as working together in origins, and that therefore the equal-time concept failed to make sense to him.

Following Bird, New York ACLU attorney Jay Topkis argued against the statute. " 'Creation,' this is a term we are all familiar with," Topkis began. He then quoted from a dictionary definition that "creation" meant an "act of creating or fact of being created . . . by divine power or its equivalent." Creation required a creator, Topkis maintained, and creationist teaching therefore involved religious doctrine inappropriate for public schools.

Justice Antonin Scalia, then a new Reagan appointee to the Court, repeatedly interrupted Topkis to question whether creation always must involve a creator, citing both the state's evidence of scientists who described creation-science as non-religious and the example of the ancient Aristotelian scientific theory of a first cause, an unmoved mover. After Topkis conceded that Aristotelianism was not religious, Justice Scalia proclaimed, "Then you could believe in a creation without a creator." When Chief Justice William H. Rehnquist picked up this line of questioning, Topkis simply asserted that creation-science meant "basically the Fundamentalist point of view." Topkis repeatedly lashed out at Bird for concocting non-religious meanings for the term, once comparing his adversary to Tweedledum in Alice's Wonderland. "He wants words to mean what he says they mean. It didn't fool Alice, and I doubt very much it will fool this Court." This prompted the Chief Justice to quip, "Don't overestimate us."

Under questioning by Lewis F. Powell and other moderate justices, Topkis admitted that religion could constitutionally be taught in public schools if done in a neutral fashion for educational reasons. He also conceded to Justice Scalia that a school principal could stop a teacher from teaching factual errors, even if the correction was religiously motivated. The statute failed, according to Topkis, because it mandated teaching a religious doctrine in order to promote religious belief. Dismissing creation-science as Christian apologetics, he asserted that "there is nothing in the legislative history that speaks of a secular purpose." When Justice Stevens asked if the legislators had not spoken of protecting academic freedom, Topkis replied, "Oh sure, we've got to give God equal time."

In addition to hearing these oral arguments, the Supreme Court received sixteen written briefs submitted by organizations or individuals interested in the case. The scientific community's scorn for creation-science was communicated to the Court in briefs submitted either jointly or separately by the National Academy of Sciences, seventeen state academies of science, dozens of professional scientific associations, and an unprecedented array of prominent American scientists, including seventy-two Nobel laureates. Briefs opposing the statute were also filed by the states of New York and Illinois, the mainline National Council of

Churches, and such long-time foes of creationism laws as the National Education Association, People for the American Way, the American Jewish Congress, and American United for Separation of Church and State. Combined, these organizations represented millions of Americans nationwide. Briefs supporting the law came from conservative religious groups, most notably the National Association of Evangelicals and the Concerned Women for America—than a new, half-million-member, grass-roots group headed by Bev LeHaye, the wife of the popular fundamentalist church leader and ICR co-founder Tim LeHaye.

Viewed together, these briefs posed one clear question for the Supreme Court: Was creation-science religion or science? No brief claimed that creation-science was anything other than a religious or scientific concept. Every brief opposing the Louisiana law asserted or plainly assumed that creation-science was solely religious and not scientific. The Nobel laureates' brief perhaps did so most starkly. "This case is crucial to the future of scientific education in this nation," the laureates warned. "Our capacity to cope with problems of food production, health care, and even national defense will be jeopardized if we deliberately strip our citizens of the power to distinguish between phenomena of nature and supernatural article of faith. 'Creation-science' simply has no place in the public-school science classroom."[74] In contrast, every brief supporting the law maintained that creation-science was scientific (or at least as scientific as evolution) and was not religious (or no more so than evolution). For example, the National Association of Evangelicals' brief maintained, "This case is about the arbitrary judicial exclusion of scientific evidence about origins from public school instruction as provided by a state statute."[75] These written arguments mirrored the oral ones presented to the court by Bird and Topkis. The battle lines were neatly drawn.

The Supreme Court announced its decision six months after hearing the case. In its written opinions, the nine-member Court split four ways. Four justices joined Justice William Brennan in the lead opinion striking down the Louisiana Act as violating the Establishment Clause. Two other justices agreed with Justice Brennan's conclusion, but not all his reasoning, and therefore wrote or joined concurring opinions. Two conservative justices, Scalia and Rehnquist, dissented—and would have sent the law back to the district court for a full trial. These various opinions follow:

EDWARDS v. AGUILLARD

Supreme Court of the United States
482 U.S. 578 (1987)

BRENNAN, J., delivered the opinion of the Court: The question for decision is whether Louisiana's "Balanced Treatment for Creation–Science and

---

74. Amicus Curiae Brief of 72 Nobel Laureates, 17 State Academies of Science, and 7 Other Scientific Organizations in Support of Appellees at 4, *Edwards*, 482 U.S. 578.

75. Brief of the Christian Legal Society and National Association of Evangelicals as Amici Curiae Supporting Appellants at 4–5, *Edwards*, 482 U.S. 578.

Evolution–Science in Public School Instruction" Act (Creationism Act), La.Rev.Stat.Ann. §§ 17:286.1–17:286.7 (West 1982), is facially invalid as violative of the Establishment Clause of the First Amendment.

I

The Creationism Act forbids the teaching of the theory of evolution in public schools unless accompanied by instruction in "creation science." § 17:286.4A. No school is required to teach evolution or creation science. If either is taught, however, the other must also be taught. Ibid. The theories of evolution and creation science are statutorily defined as "the scientific evidences for [creation or evolution] and inferences from those scientific evidences." §§ 17.286.3(2) and (3).

Appellees, who include parents of children attending Louisiana public schools, Louisiana teachers, and religious leaders, challenged the constitutionality of the Act in District Court, seeking an injunction and declaratory relief. Appellants, Louisiana officials charged with implementing the Act, defended on the ground that the purpose of the Act is to protect a legitimate secular interest, namely, academic freedom. Appellees attacked the Act as facially invalid because it violated the Establishment Clause and made a motion for summary judgment. The District Court granted the motion. Aguillard v. Treen, 634 F.Supp. 426 (ED La.1985). The court held that there can be no valid secular reason for prohibiting the teaching of evolution, a theory historically opposed by some religious denominations. The court further concluded that "the teaching of 'creation-science' and 'creationism,' as contemplated by the statute, involves teaching 'tailored to the principles' of a particular religious sect or group of sects." Id., at 427 (citing Epperson v. Arkansas, 393 U.S. 97, 106 (1968)). The District Court therefore held that the Creationism Act violated the Establishment Clause either because it prohibited the teaching of evolution or because it required the teaching of creation science with the purpose of advancing a particular religious doctrine.

The Court of Appeals affirmed. 765 F.2d 1251 (CA5 1985). The court observed that the statute's avowed purpose of protecting academic freedom was inconsistent with requiring, upon risk of sanction, the teaching of creation science whenever evolution is taught. Id., at 1257. The court found that the Louisiana Legislature's actual intent was "to discredit evolution by counterbalancing its teaching at every turn with the teaching of creationism, a religious belief." Ibid. Because the Creationism Act was thus a law furthering a particular religious belief, the Court of Appeals held that the Act violated the Establishment Clause. A suggestion for rehearing en banc was denied over a dissent. 778 F.2d 225 (CA5 1985). We noted probable jurisdiction, 476 U.S. 1103 (1986), and now affirm.

II

The Establishment Clause forbids the enactment of any law "respecting an establishment of religion." The Court has applied a three-pronged test to determine whether legislation comports with the Establishment

Clause. First, the legislature must have adopted the law with a secular purpose. Second, the statute's principal or primary effect must be one that neither advances nor inhibits religion. Third, the statute must not result in an excessive entanglement of government with religion. Lemon v. Kurtzman, 403 U.S. 602, 612–613 (1971).[76] State action violates the Establishment Clause if it fails to satisfy any of these prongs.

In this case, the Court must determine whether the Establishment Clause was violated in the special context of the public elementary and secondary school system. States and local school boards are generally afforded considerable discretion in operating public schools. See Bethel School Dist. No. 403 v. Fraser, 478 U.S. 675, 683 (1986); id., at 687 (BRENNAN, J., concurring in judgment); Tinker v. Des Moines Independent Community School Dist., 393 U.S. 503, 507 (1969). "At the same time . . . we have necessarily recognized that the discretion of the States and local school boards in matters of education must be exercised in a manner that comports with the transcendent imperatives of the First Amendment." Board of Education, Island Trees Union Free School Dist. No. 26 v. Pico, 457 U.S. 853, 864 (1982).

The Court has been particularly vigilant in monitoring compliance with the Establishment Clause in elementary and secondary schools. Families entrust public schools with the education of their children, but condition their trust on the understanding that the classroom will not purposely be used to advance religious views that may conflict with the private beliefs of the student and his or her family. Students in such institutions are impressionable and their attendance is involuntary. See, e.g., Grand Rapids School Dist. v. Ball, 473 U.S. 373, 383 (1985); Wallace v. Jaffree, 472 U.S. 38, 60, n. 51 (1985); Meek v. Pittenger, 421 U.S. 349 (1975); Abington School Dist. v. Schempp, 374 U.S. 203, 252–253 (1963) (BRENNAN, J., concurring). The State exerts great authority and coercive power through mandatory attendance requirements, and because of the students' emulation of teachers as role models and the children's susceptibility to peer pressure. See Bethel School Dist. No. 403 v. Fraser, supra, 478 U.S., at 683; Wallace v. Jaffree, supra, 472 U.S., at 81 (O'CONNOR, J., concurring in judgment). Furthermore, "[t]he public school is at once the symbol of our democracy and the most pervasive means for promoting our common destiny. In no activity of the State is it more vital to keep out divisive forces than in its schools. . . ." Illinois ex rel. McCollum v. Board of Education, 333 U.S. 203, 231 (1948) (opinion of Frankfurter, J.).

---

76. The Lemon test has been applied in all cases since its adoption in 1971, except in Marsh v. Chambers, 463 U.S. 783 (1983), where the Court held that the Nebraska Legislature's practice of opening a session with a prayer by a chaplain paid by the State did not violate the Establishment Clause. The Court based its conclusion in that case on the historical acceptance of the practice. Such a historical approach is not useful in determining the proper roles of church and state in public schools, since free public education was virtually nonexistent at the time the Constitution was adopted. See Wallace v. Jaffree, 472 U.S. 38, 80 (1985) (O'CONNOR, J., concurring in judgment) (citing Abington School Dist. v. Schempp, 374 U.S. 203, 238, and n. 7 (1963) (BRENNAN, J., concurring)).

Consequently, the Court has been required often to invalidate statutes which advance religion in public elementary and secondary schools. See, e.g., Grand Rapids School Dist. v. Ball, supra (school district's use of religious school teachers in public schools); Wallace v. Jaffree, supra (Alabama statute authorizing moment of silence for school prayer); Stone v. Graham, 449 U.S. 39 (1980) (posting copy of Ten Commandments on public classroom wall); Epperson v. Arkansas, 393 U.S. 97 (1968) (statute forbidding teaching of evolution); Abington School Dist. v. Schempp, supra (daily reading of Bible); Engel v. Vitale, 370 U.S. 421, 430 (1962) (recitation of "denominationally neutral" prayer).

Therefore, in employing the three-pronged Lemon test, we must do so mindful of the particular concerns that arise in the context of public elementary and secondary schools. We now turn to the evaluation of the Act under the Lemon test.

III

Lemon's first prong focuses on the purpose that animated adoption of the Act. "The purpose prong of the Lemon test asks whether government's actual purpose is to endorse or disapprove of religion." Lynch v. Donnelly, 465 U.S. 668, 690 (1984) (O'CONNOR, J., concurring). A governmental intention to promote religion is clear when the State enacts a law to serve a religious purpose. This intention may be evidenced by promotion of religion in general, see Wallace v. Jaffree, supra, 472 U.S., at 52–53 (Establishment Clause protects individual freedom of conscience "to select any religious faith or none at all"), or by advancement of a particular religious belief, e.g., Stone v. Graham, supra, 449 U.S., at 41 (invalidating requirement to post Ten Commandments, which are "undeniably a sacred text in the Jewish and Christian faiths") (footnote omitted); Epperson v. Arkansas, supra, 393 U.S., at 106 (holding that banning the teaching of evolution in public schools violates the First Amendment since "teaching and learning" must not "be tailored to the principles or prohibitions of any religious sect or dogma"). If the law was enacted for the purpose of endorsing religion, "no consideration of the second or third criteria [of Lemon] is necessary." Wallace v. Jaffree, supra, 472 U.S., at 56. In this case, appellants have identified no clear secular purpose for the Louisiana Act.

True, the Act's stated purpose is to protect academic freedom. La.Rev. Stat.Ann. § 17:286.2 (West 1982). This phrase might, in common parlance, be understood as referring to enhancing the freedom of teachers to teach what they will. The Court of Appeals, however, correctly concluded that the Act was not designed to further that goal.[77] We find no merit in

---

77. The Court of Appeals stated that "[a]cademic freedom embodies the principle that individual instructors are at liberty to teach that which they deem to be appropriate in the exercise of their professional judgment." 765 F.2d, at 1257. But, in the State of Louisiana, courses in public schools are prescribed by the State Board of Education and teachers are not free, absent permission, to teach courses different from what is required. Tr. of Oral Arg. 44–46. "Academic freedom," at least as it is commonly understood, is not a relevant concept in this context. Moreover, as the Court of Appeals explained, the Act "requires, presumably upon risk of sanction

the State's argument that the "legislature may not [have] use[d] the terms 'academic freedom' in the correct legal sense. They might have [had] in mind, instead, a basic concept of fairness; teaching all of the evidence." Tr. of Oral Arg. 60. Even if "academic freedom" is read to mean "teaching all of the evidence" with respect to the origin of human beings, the Act does not further this purpose. The goal of providing a more comprehensive science curriculum is not furthered either by outlawing the teaching of evolution or by requiring the teaching of creation science.

A

While the Court is normally deferential to a State's articulation of a secular purpose, it is required that the statement of such purpose be sincere and not a sham. See Wallace v. Jaffree, 472 U.S., at 64 (POWELL, J., concurring); id., at 75 (O'CONNOR, J., concurring in judgment); Stone v. Graham, supra, 449 U.S., at 41; Abington School Dist. v. Schempp, 374 U.S., at 223–224. As Justice O'CONNOR stated in Wallace: "It is not a trivial matter, however, to require that the legislature manifest a secular purpose and omit all sectarian endorsements from its laws. That requirement is precisely tailored to the Establishment Clause's purpose of assuring that Government not intentionally endorse religion or a religious practice." 472 U.S., at 75 (concurring in judgment).

It is clear from the legislative history that the purpose of the legislative sponsor, Senator Bill Keith, was to narrow the science curriculum. During the legislative hearings, Senator Keith stated: "My preference would be that neither [creationism nor evolution] be taught." 2 App. E–621. Such a ban on teaching does not promote—indeed, it undermines—the provision of a comprehensive scientific education.

It is equally clear that requiring schools to teach creation science with evolution does not advance academic freedom. The Act does not grant teachers a flexibility that they did not already possess to supplant the present science curriculum with the presentation of theories, besides evolution, about the origin of life. Indeed, the Court of Appeals found that no law prohibited Louisiana public school teachers from teaching any scientific theory. 765 F.2d, at 1257. As the president of the Louisiana Science Teachers Association testified, "[a]ny scientific concept that's based on established fact can be included in our curriculum already, and no legislation allowing this is necessary." 2 App. E–616. The Act provides Louisiana school teachers with no new authority. Thus the stated purpose is not furthered by it.

The Alabama statute held unconstitutional in Wallace v. Jaffree, supra, is analogous. In Wallace, the State characterized its new law as one

---

or dismissal for failure to comply, the teaching of creation-science whenever evolution is taught. Although states may prescribe public school curriculum concerning science instruction under ordinary circumstances, the compulsion inherent in the Balanced Treatment Act is, on its face, inconsistent with the idea of academic freedom as it is universally understood." 765 F.2d, at 1257). The Act actually serves to diminish academic freedom by removing the flexibility to teach evolution without also teaching creation science, even if teachers determine that such curriculum results in less effective and comprehensive science instruction.

designed to provide a 1–minute period for meditation. We rejected that stated purpose as insufficient, because a previously adopted Alabama law already provided for such a 1–minute period. Thus, in this case, as in Wallace, "[a]ppellants have not identified any secular purpose that was not fully served by [existing state law] before the enactment of [the statute in question]." 472 U.S., at 59.

Furthermore, the goal of basic "fairness" is hardly furthered by the Act's discriminatory preference for the teaching of creation science and against the teaching of evolution.[78] While requiring that curriculum guides be developed for creation science, the Act says nothing of comparable guides for evolution. La.Rev.Stat.Ann. § 17:286.7A (West 1982). Similarly, resource services are supplied for creation science but not for evolution. § 17:286.7B. Only "creation scientists" can serve on the panel that supplies the resource services. Ibid. The Act forbids school boards to discriminate against anyone who "chooses to be a creation-scientist" or to teach "creationism," but fails to protect those who choose to teach evolution or any other non-creation science theory, or who refuse to teach creation science. § 17:286.4C.

If the Louisiana Legislature's purpose was solely to maximize the comprehensiveness and effectiveness of science instruction, it would have encouraged the teaching of all scientific theories about the origins of humankind.[79] But under the Act's requirements, teachers who were once free to teach any and all facets of this subject are now unable to do so. Moreover, the Act fails even to ensure that creation science will be taught, but instead requires the teaching of this theory only when the theory of evolution is taught. Thus we agree with the Court of Appeals' conclusion that the Act does not serve to protect academic freedom, but has the distinctly different purpose of discrediting "evolution by counterbalancing its teaching at every turn with the teaching of creationism...." 765 F.2d, at 1257.

Moreover, it is astonishing that the dissent, to prove its assertion, relies on a section of the legislation that was eventually deleted by the legislature. Compare § 3702 in 1 App. E–292 (text of section prior to amendment) with La.Rev.Stat.Ann. § 17:286.2 (West 1982). The dissent contends that this deleted section—which was explicitly rejected by the Louisiana Legislature—reveals the legislature's "obviously intended meaning of the statutory terms 'academic freedom.'" Post, at 2601. Quite to the contrary, Boudreaux, the main expert relied on by the sponsor of

78. The Creationism Act's provisions appear among other provisions prescribing the courses of study in Louisiana's public schools. These other provisions, similar to those in other States, prescribe courses of study in such topics as driver training, civics, the Constitution, and free enterprise. None of these other provisions, apart from those associated with the Creationism Act, nominally mandates "equal time" for opposing opinions within a specific area of learning. See, e.g., La.Rev.Stat.Ann. §§ 17:261–17:281 (West 1982 and Supp. 1987).

79. The dissent concludes that the Act's purpose was to protect the academic freedom of students, and not that of teachers. Post, at 2601. Such a view is not at odds with our conclusion that if the Act's purpose was to provide comprehensive scientific education (a concern shared by students and teachers, as well as parents), that purpose was not advanced by the statute's provisions. Supra, at 2579.

the Act, cautioned the legislature that the words "academic freedom" meant "freedom to teach science." 1 App. E–429. His testimony was given at the time the legislature was deciding whether to delete this section of the Act.

B

Stone v. Graham invalidated the State's requirement that the Ten Commandments be posted in public classrooms. "The Ten Commandments are undeniably a sacred text in the Jewish and Christian faiths, and no legislative recitation of a supposed secular purpose can blind us to that fact." 449 U.S., at 41. As a result, the contention that the law was designed to provide instruction on a "fundamental legal code" was "not sufficient to avoid conflict with the First Amendment." Ibid. Similarly Abington School Dist. v. Schempp held unconstitutional a statute "requiring the selection and reading at the opening of the school day of verses from the Holy Bible and the recitation of the Lord's Prayer by the students in unison," despite the proffer of such secular purposes as the "promotion of moral values, the contradiction to the materialistic trends of our times, the perpetuation of our institutions and the teaching of literature." 374 U.S., at 223.

As in Stone and Abington, we need not be blind in this case to the legislature's preeminent religious purpose in enacting this statute. There is a historic and contemporaneous link between the teachings of certain religious denominations and the teaching of evolution. It was this link that concerned the Court in Epperson v. Arkansas, 393 U.S. 97 (1968), which also involved a facial challenge to a statute regulating the teaching of evolution. In that case, the Court reviewed an Arkansas statute that made it unlawful for an instructor to teach evolution or to use a textbook that referred to this scientific theory. Although the Arkansas antievolution law did not explicitly state its predominant religious purpose, the Court could not ignore that "[t]he statute was a product of the upsurge of 'fundamentalist' religious fervor" that has long viewed this particular scientific theory as contradicting the literal interpretation of the Bible. Id., 393 U.S., at 98, 106–107. After reviewing the history of antievolution statutes, the Court determined that "there can be no doubt that the motivation for the [Arkansas] law was the same [as other anti-evolution statutes]: to suppress the teaching of a theory which, it was thought, 'denied' the divine creation of man." Id., at 109. The Court found that there can be no legitimate state interest in protecting particular religions from scientific views "distasteful to them," id., at 107, and concluded "that the First Amendment does not permit the State to require that teaching and learning must be tailored to the principles or prohibitions of any religious sect or dogma," id., at 106.

These same historic and contemporaneous antagonisms between the teachings of certain religious denominations and the teaching of evolution are present in this case. The preeminent purpose of the Louisiana Legislature was clearly to advance the religious viewpoint that a supernatural being created humankind.[80] The term "creation science" was defined as embracing this particular religious doctrine by those responsible for the passage of the Creationism Act. Senator Keith's leading expert on creation science, Edward Boudreaux, testified at the legislative hearings that the theory of creation science included belief in the existence of a supernatural creator. See 1 App. E–421–E–422 (noting that "creation scientists" point to high probability that life was "created by an intelligent mind").[81] Senator Keith also cited testimony from other experts to support the creation-science view that "a creator [was] responsible for the universe and everything in it."[82] 2 App. E–497. The legislative history therefore reveals that the term "creation science," as contemplated by the legislature that adopted this Act, embodies the religious belief that a supernatural creator was responsible for the creation of humankind.

Furthermore, it is not happenstance that the legislature required the teaching of a theory that coincided with this religious view. The legislative history documents that the Act's primary purpose was to change the science curriculum of public schools in order to provide persuasive advantage to a particular religious doctrine that rejects the factual basis of evolution in its entirety. The sponsor of the Creationism Act, Senator Keith, explained during the legislative hearings that his disdain for the theory of evolution resulted from the support that evolution supplied to views contrary to his own religious beliefs. According to Senator Keith, the theory of evolution was consonant with the "cardinal principle[s] of religious humanism, secular humanism, theological liberalism, aetheistism [sic]." 1 App. E312–313; see also 2 App. E499–500. The state senator repeatedly stated that scientific evidence supporting his religious views should be included in the public school curriculum to redress the fact that the theory of evolution incidentally coincided with what he characterized as religious beliefs antithetical to his own.[83] The legislation therefore

---

80. While the belief in the instantaneous creation of humankind by a supernatural creator may require the rejection of every aspect of the theory of evolution, an individual instead may choose to accept some or all of this scientific theory as compatible with his or her spiritual outlook. See Tr. of Oral Arg. 23–29.

81. Boudreaux repeatedly defined creation science in terms of a theory that supports the existence of a supernatural creator. See, e.g., 2 App. E–501–E–502 (equating creation science with a theory pointing "to conditions of a creator"); 1 App. E–153–E–154 ("Creation . . . requires the direct involvement of a supernatural intelligence"). The lead witness at the hearings introducing the original bill, Luther Sunderland, described creation science as postulating "that everything was created by some intelligence or power external to the universe." Id., at E9–10.

82. Senator Keith believed that creation science embodied this view: "One concept is that a creator however you define a creator was responsible for everything that is in this world. The other concept is that it just evolved." Id., at E–280. Besides Senator Keith, several of the most vocal legislators also revealed their religious motives for supporting the bill in the official legislative history. See, e.g., id., at E–441, E–443 (Sen. Saunders noting that bill was amended so that teachers could refer to the Bible and other religious texts to support the creation-science theory); 2 App. E–561–E–562, E–610 (Rep. Jenkins contending that the existence of God was a scientific fact).

83. See, e.g., 1 App. E74–E75 (noting that evolution is contrary to his family's religious beliefs); id., at E313 (contending that evolution advances religions contrary to his own); id., at E357 (stating that evolution is "almost a religion" to science teachers); id., at E418 (arguing that evolution is cornerstone of some religions contrary to his own); 2 App. E763–E764 (author of model bill, from which Act is derived, sent copy of the model bill to Senator Keith and advised

sought to alter the science curriculum to reflect endorsement of a religious view that is antagonistic to the theory of evolution.

In this case, the purpose of the Creationism Act was to restructure the science curriculum to conform with a particular religious viewpoint. Out of many possible science subjects taught in the public schools, the legislature chose to affect the teaching of the one scientific theory that historically has been opposed by certain religious sects. As in Epperson, the legislature passed the Act to give preference to those religious groups which have as one of their tenets the creation of humankind by a divine creator. The "overriding fact" that confronted the Court in Epperson was "that Arkansas' law selects from the body of knowledge a particular segment which it proscribes for the sole reason that it is deemed to conflict with ... a particular interpretation of the Book of Genesis by a particular religious group." 393 U.S., at 103. Similarly, the Creationism Act is designed either to promote the theory of creation science which embodies a particular religious tenet by requiring that creation science be taught whenever evolution is taught or to prohibit the teaching of a scientific theory disfavored by certain religious sects by forbidding the teaching of evolution when creation science is not also taught. The Establishment Clause, however, "forbids alike the preference of a religious doctrine or the prohibition of theory which is deemed antagonistic to a particular dogma." Id., at 106–107. Because the primary purpose of the Creationism Act is to advance a particular religious belief, the Act endorses religion in violation of the First Amendment.

We do not imply that a legislature could never require that scientific critiques of prevailing scientific theories be taught. Indeed, the Court acknowledged in Stone that its decision forbidding the posting of the Ten Commandments did not mean that no use could ever be made of the Ten Commandments, or that the Ten Commandments played an exclusively religious role in the history of Western Civilization. 449 U.S., at 42. In a similar way, teaching a variety of scientific theories about the origins of humankind to schoolchildren might be validly done with the clear secular intent of enhancing the effectiveness of science instruction. But because the primary purpose of the Creationism Act is to endorse a particular religious doctrine, the Act furthers religion in violation of the Establishment Clause.

IV

Appellants contend that genuine issues of material fact remain in dispute, and therefore the District Court erred in granting summary judgment. Federal Rule of Civil Procedure 56(c) provides that summary judgment "shall be rendered forthwith if the pleadings, depositions, answers to interrogatories, and admissions on file, together with the affidavits, if any, show that there is no genuine issue as to any material fact and

---

that "I view this whole battle as one between God and anti-God forces.... if evolution is permitted to continue ... it will continue to be made to appear that a Supreme Being is unnecessary ...").

that the moving party is entitled to a judgment as a matter of law." A court's finding of improper purpose behind a statute is appropriately determined by the statute on its face, its legislative history, or its interpretation by a responsible administrative agency. See, e.g., Wallace v. Jaffree, 472 U.S., at 56–61; Stone v. Graham, 449 U.S., at 41–42; Epperson v. Arkansas, 393 U.S., at 103–109. The plain meaning of the statute's words, enlightened by their context and the contemporaneous legislative history, can control the determination of legislative purpose. See Wallace v. Jaffree, supra, 472 U.S., at 74 (O'CONNOR, J., concurring in judgment); Richards v. United States, 369 U.S. 1, 9 (1962); Jay v. Boyd, 351 U.S. 345, 357 (1956). Moreover, in determining the legislative purpose of a statute, the Court has also considered the historical context of the statute, e.g., Epperson v. Arkansas, supra, and the specific sequence of events leading to passage of the statute, e.g., Arlington Heights v. Metropolitan Housing Dev. Corp., 429 U.S. 252 (1977).

In this case, appellees' motion for summary judgment rested on the plain language of the Creationism Act, the legislative history and historical context of the Act, the specific sequence of events leading to the passage of the Act, the State Board's report on a survey of school superintendents, and the correspondence between the Act's legislative sponsor and its key witnesses. Appellants contend that affidavits made by two scientists, two theologians, and an education administrator raise a genuine issue of material fact and that summary judgment was therefore barred. The affidavits define creation science as "origin through abrupt appearance in complex form" and allege that such a viewpoint constitutes a true scientific theory. See App. to Brief for Appellants A–7 to A–40.

We agree with the lower courts that these affidavits do not raise a genuine issue of material fact. The existence of "uncontroverted affidavits" does not bar summary judgment. Moreover, the post-enactment testimony of outside experts is of little use in determining the Louisiana Legislature's purpose in enacting this statute. The Louisiana Legislature did hear and rely on scientific experts in passing the bill, but none of the persons making the affidavits produced by the appellants participated in or contributed to the enactment of the law or its implementation. The District Court, in its discretion, properly concluded that a Monday-morning "battle of the experts" over possible technical meanings of terms in the statute would not illuminate the contemporaneous purpose of the Louisiana Legislature when it made the law. We therefore conclude that the District Court did not err in finding that appellants failed to raise a genuine issue of material fact, and in granting summary judgment.

V

The Louisiana Creationism Act advances a religious doctrine by requiring either the banishment of the theory of evolution from public school classrooms or the presentation of a religious viewpoint that rejects evolution in its entirety. The Act violates the Establishment Clause of the First Amendment because it seeks to employ the symbolic and financial support of government to achieve a religious purpose. The judgment of the Court of Appeals therefore is affirmed.

JUSTICE POWELL, with whom JUSTICE O'CONNOR joins, concurring: I write separately to note certain aspects of the legislative history, and to emphasize that nothing in the Court's opinion diminishes the traditionally broad discretion accorded state and local school officials in the selection of the public school curriculum.

I

This Court consistently has applied the three-pronged test of Lemon v. Kurtzman, 403 U.S. 602 (1971), to determine whether a particular state action violates the Establishment Clause of the Constitution. See, e.g., Grand Rapids School Dist. v. Ball, 473 U.S. 373, 383 (1985) ("We have particularly relied on Lemon in every case involving the sensitive relationship between government and religion in the education of our children"). The first requirement of the Lemon test is that the challenged statute have a "secular legislative purpose." Lemon v. Kurtzman, supra, 403 U.S., at 612. See Committee for Public Education & Religious Liberty v. Nyquist, 413 U.S. 756, 773 (1973). If no valid secular purpose can be identified, then the statute violates the Establishment Clause.

A

"The starting point in every case involving construction of a statute is the language itself." Blue Chip Stamps v. Manor Drug Stores, 421 U.S. 723, 756 (1975) (POWELL, J., concurring). The Balanced Treatment for Creation–Science and Evolution–Science Act (Act or Balanced Treatment Act), La.Rev.Stat.Ann. § 17:286.1 et seq. (West 1982), provides in part:

> "[P]ublic schools within [the] state shall give balanced treatment to creation-science and to evolution-science. Balanced treatment of these two models shall be given in classroom lectures taken as a whole for each course, in textbook materials taken as a whole for each course, in library materials taken as a whole for the sciences and taken as a whole for the humanities, and in other educational programs in public schools, to the extent that such lectures, textbooks, library materials, or educational programs deal in any way with the subject of the origin of man, life, the earth, or the universe. When creation or evolution is taught, each shall be taught as a theory, rather than as proven scientific fact." § 17:286.4(A).

"Balanced treatment" means "providing whatever information and instruction in both creation and evolution models the classroom teacher determines is necessary and appropriate to provide insight into both theories in view of the textbooks and other instructional materials available for use in his classroom." § 17:286.3(1). "Creation-science" is defined as "the scientific evidences for creation and inferences from those scientific evidences." § 17:286.3(2). "Evolution-science" means "the scientific

evidences for evolution and inferences from those scientific evidences."
§ 17:286.3(3).

Although the Act requires the teaching of the scientific evidences of
both creation and evolution whenever either is taught, it does not define
either term. "A fundamental canon of statutory construction is that,
unless otherwise defined, words will be interpreted as taking their ordinary, contemporary, common meaning." Perrin v. United States, 444 U.S.
37, 42 (1979). The "doctrine or theory of creation" is commonly defined as
"holding that matter, the various forms of life, and the world were created
by a transcendent God out of nothing." Webster's Third New International Dictionary 532 (unabridged 1981). "Evolution" is defined as "the
theory that the various types of animals and plants have their origin in
other preexisting types, the distinguishable differences being due to modifications in successive generations." Id., 463 U.S., at 789. Thus, the
Balanced Treatment Act mandates that public schools present the scientific evidence to support a theory of divine creation whenever they present
the scientific evidence to support the theory of evolution. "[C]oncepts
concerning God or a supreme being of some sort are manifestly religious.... These concepts do not shed that religiosity merely because they
are presented as a philosophy or as a science." Malnak v. Yogi, 440
F.Supp. 1284, 1322 (NJ 1977), aff'd per curiam, 592 F.2d 197 (CA3 1979).
From the face of the statute, a purpose to advance a religious belief is
apparent.

A religious purpose alone is not enough to invalidate an act of a state
legislature. The religious purpose must predominate. See Wallace v. Jaffree, 472 U.S. 38, 56 (1985); id., at 64 (POWELL, J., concurring); Lynch v.
Donnelly, 465 U.S. 668, 681, n. 6 (1984). The Act contains a statement of
purpose: to "protec[t] academic freedom." § 17:286.2. This statement is
puzzling. Of course, the "academic freedom" of teachers to present
information in public schools, and students to receive it, is broad. But it
necessarily is circumscribed by the Establishment Clause. "Academic
freedom" does not encompass the right of a legislature to structure the
public school curriculum in order to advance a particular religious belief.
Epperson v. Arkansas, 393 U.S. 97, 106 (1968). Nevertheless, I read this
statement in the Act as rendering the purpose of the statute at least
ambiguous. Accordingly, I proceed to review the legislative history of the
Act.

B

In June 1980, Senator Bill Keith introduced Senate Bill 956 in the
Louisiana Legislature. The stated purpose of the bill was to "assure
academic freedom by requiring the teaching of the theory of creation ex
nihilo in all public schools where the theory of evolution is taught." 1 App.
E–1. The bill defined the "theory of creation ex nihilo" as "the belief that
the origin of the elements, the galaxy, the solar system, of life, of all the
species of plants and animals, the origin of man, and the origin of all
things and their processes and relationships were created ex nihilo and

fixed by God." Id., at E–1a–E–1b. This theory was referred to by Senator Keith as "scientific creationism." Id., at E–2.

While a Senate committee was studying scientific creationism, Senator Keith introduced a second draft of the bill, requiring balanced treatment of "evolution-science" and "creation-science." Id., at E–108. Although the Keith bill prohibited "instruction in any religious doctrine or materials," id., at E–302, it defined "creation-science" to include

> "the scientific evidences and related inferences that indicate (a) sudden creation of the universe, energy, and life from nothing; (b) the insufficiency of mutation and natural selection in bringing about development of all living kinds from a single organism; (c) changes only within fixed limits or originally created kinds of plants and animals; (d) separate ancestry for man and apes; (e) explanation of the earth's geology by catastrophism, including the occurrence of a worldwide flood; and (f) a relatively recent inception of the earth and living kinds." Id., at E–298–E–299.

Significantly, the model Act on which the Keith bill relied was also the basis for a similar statute in Arkansas. See McLean v. Arkansas Board of Education, 529 F.Supp. 1255 (ED Ark.1982). The District Court in McLean carefully examined this model Act, particularly the section defining creation science, and concluded that "[b]oth [its] concepts and wording ... convey an inescapable religiosity." Id., at 1265. The court found that "[t]he ideas of [this section] are not merely similar to the literal interpretation of Genesis; they are identical and parallel to no other story of creation." Ibid.

The complaint in McLean was filed on May 27, 1981. On May 28, the Louisiana Senate committee amended the Keith bill to delete the illustrative list of scientific evidences. According to the legislator who proposed the amendment, it was "not intended to try to gut [the bill] in any way, or defeat the purpose [for] which Senator Keith introduced [it]," 1 App. E–432, and was not viewed as working "any violence to the bill." Id., at E–438. Instead, the concern was "whether this should be an all inclusive list." Ibid.

The legislature then held hearings on the amended bill that became the Balanced Treatment Act under review. The principal creation scientist to testify in support of the Act was Dr. Edward Boudreaux. He did not elaborate on the nature of creation science except to indicate that the "scientific evidences" of the theory are "the objective information of science [that] point [s] to conditions of a creator." 2 id., at E–501–E–502. He further testified that the recognized creation scientists in the United States, who "numbe[r] something like a thousand [and] who hold doctorate and masters degrees in all areas of science," are affiliated with either or both the Institute for Creation Research and the Creation Research Society. Id., at E–503–E–504. Information on both of these organizations is part of the legislative history, and a review of their goals and activities sheds light on the nature of creation science as it was presented to, and understood by, the Louisiana Legislature.

The Institute for Creation Research is an affiliate of the Christian Heritage College in San Diego, California. The Institute was established to address the "urgent need for our nation to return to belief in a personal, omnipotent Creator, who has a purpose for His creation and to whom all people must eventually give account." 1 id., at E–197. A goal of the Institute is "a revival of belief in special creation as the true explanation of the origin of the world." Therefore, the Institute currently is working on the "development of new methods for teaching scientific creationism in public schools." Id., at E–197–E–199. The Creation Research Society (CRS) is located in Ann Arbor, Michigan. A member must subscribe to the following statement of belief: "The Bible is the written word of God, and because it is inspired throughout, all of its assertions are historically and scientifically true." 2 id., at E–583. To study creation science at the CRS, a member must accept "that the account of origins in Genesis is a factual presentation of simple historical truth."

C

When, as here, "both courts below are unable to discern an arguably valid secular purpose, this Court normally should hesitate to find one." Wallace v. Jaffree, 472 U.S., at 66, (POWELL, J., concurring). My examination of the language and the legislative history of the Balanced Treatment Act confirms that the intent of the Louisiana Legislature was to promote a particular religious belief. The legislative history of the Arkansas statute prohibiting the teaching of evolution examined in Epperson v. Arkansas, 393 U.S. 97 (1968), was strikingly similar to the legislative history of the Balanced Treatment Act. In Epperson, the Court found:

> "It is clear that fundamentalist sectarian conviction was and is the law's reason for existence. Its antecedent, Tennessee's 'monkey law,' candidly stated its purpose: to make it unlawful 'to teach any theory that denies the story of the Divine Creation of man as taught in the Bible, and to teach instead that man has descended from a lower order of animals.' Perhaps the sensational publicity attendant upon the Scopes trial induced Arkansas to adopt less explicit language. It eliminated Tennessee's reference to 'the story of the Divine creation of man' as taught in the Bible, but there is no doubt that the motivation for the law was the same: to suppress the teaching of a theory which, it was thought, 'denied' the divine creation of man." Id., at 107–109 (footnotes omitted).

Here, it is clear that religious belief is the Balanced Treatment Act's "reason for existence." The tenets of creation science parallel the Genesis story of creation, and this is a religious belief. "[N]o legislative recitation of a supposed secular purpose can blind us to that fact." Stone v. Graham, 449 U.S. 39, 41 (1980). Although the Act as finally enacted does not contain explicit reference to its religious purpose, there is no indication in the legislative history that the deletion of "creation ex nihilo" and the four primary tenets of the theory was intended to alter the purpose of teaching creation science. Instead, the statements of purpose of the sources of creation science in the United States make clear that their purpose is to promote a religious belief. I find no persuasive evidence in the legislative history that the legislature's purpose was any different. The fact that the Louisiana Legislature purported to add information to the school curriculum rather than detract from it as in Epperson does not affect my analysis. Both legislatures acted with the unconstitutional purpose of structuring the public school curriculum to make it compatible with a particular religious belief: the "divine creation of man."

That the statute is limited to the scientific evidences supporting the theory does not render its purpose secular. In reaching its conclusion that the Act is unconstitutional, the Court of Appeals "[did] not deny that the underpinnings of creationism may be supported by scientific evidence." 765 F.2d 1251, 1256 (1985). And there is no need to do so. Whatever the academic merit of particular subjects or theories, the Establishment Clause limits the discretion of state officials to pick and choose among them for the purpose of promoting a particular religious belief. The language of the statute and its legislative history convince me that the Louisiana Legislature exercised its discretion for this purpose in this case.

II

Even though I find Louisiana's Balanced Treatment Act unconstitutional, I adhere to the view "that the States and locally elected school boards should have the responsibility for determining the educational policy of the public schools." Board of Education, Island Trees Union Free School Dist. No. 26 v. Pico, 457 U.S. 853, 893 (1982) (POWELL, J., dissenting). A decision respecting the subject matter to be taught in public schools does not violate the Establishment Clause simply because the material to be taught " 'happens to coincide or harmonize with the tenets of some or all religions.' " Harris v. McRae, 448 U.S. 297, 319 (1980) (quoting McGowan v. Maryland, 366 U.S. 420, 442 (1961)). In the context of a challenge under the Establishment Clause, interference with the decisions of these authorities is warranted only when the purpose for their decisions is clearly religious.

The history of the Religion Clauses of the First Amendment has been chronicled by this Court in detail. See, e.g., Everson v. Board of Education, 330 U.S. 1, 8–14 (1947); Engel v. Vitale, 370 U.S. 421, 425–430 (1962); McGowan v. Maryland, supra, 366 U.S., at 437–442. Therefore, only a brief review at this point may be appropriate. The early settlers came to this country from Europe to escape religious persecution that took the form of forced support of state-established churches. The new Americans thus reacted strongly when they perceived the same type of religious intolerance emerging in this country. The reaction in Virginia, the home of many of the Founding Fathers, is instructive. George Mason's draft of the Virginia Declaration of Rights was adopted by the House of Burgesses in 1776. Because of James Madison's influence, the Declaration of Rights embodied the guarantee of free exercise of religion, as opposed to toleration. Eight years later, a provision prohibiting the establishment of religion became a part of Virginia law when James Madison's Memorial and Remonstrance against Religious Assessments, written in response to a proposal that all Virginia citizens be taxed to support the teaching of the Christian religion, spurred the legislature to consider and adopt Thomas Jefferson's Bill for Establishing Religious Freedom. See Committee for Public Education & Religious Liberty v. Nyquist, 413 U.S., at 770, n. 28. Both the guarantees of free exercise and against the establishment of religion were then incorporated into the Federal Bill of Rights by its drafter, James Madison.

While the "meaning and scope of the First Amendment" must be read "in light of its history and the evils it was designed forever to suppress," Everson v. Board of Education, supra, 330 U.S., at 14–15, this Court has also recognized that "this Nation's history has not been one of entirely sanitized separation between Church and State." Committee for Public Education & Religious Liberty v. Nyquist, supra, 413 U.S., at 760. "The fact that the Founding Fathers believed devotedly that there was a God and that the unalienable rights of man were rooted in Him is clearly evidenced in their writings, from the Mayflower Compact to the Constitution itself." Abington School District v. Schempp, 374 U.S. 203, 213 (1963).[84] The Court properly has noted "an unbroken history of official acknowledgment ... of the role of religion in American life." Lynch v. Donnelly, 465 U.S., at 674, and has recognized that these references to "our religious heritage" are constitutionally acceptable. Id., at 677.

As a matter of history, schoolchildren can and should properly be informed of all aspects of this Nation's religious heritage. I would see no constitutional problem if schoolchildren were taught the nature of the Founding Father's religious beliefs and how these beliefs affected the attitudes of the times and the structure of our government. Courses in comparative religion of course are customary and constitutionally appropriate. In fact, since religion permeates our history, a familiarity with the nature of religious beliefs is necessary to understand many historical as well as contemporary events. In addition, it is worth noting that the Establishment Clause does not prohibit per se the educational use of religious documents in public school education. Although this Court has recognized that the Bible is "an instrument of religion," Abington School District v. Schempp, supra, 374 U.S., at 224, it also has made clear that the Bible "may constitutionally be used in an appropriate study of history, civilization, ethics, comparative religion, or the like." Stone v. Graham, 449 U.S., at 42. The book is, in fact, "the world's all-time best seller" with undoubted literary and historic value apart from its religious content. The Establishment Clause is properly understood to prohibit the use of the

---

84. John Adams wrote to Thomas Jefferson: "[T]he Bible is the best book in the world. It contains more of my little philosophy than all the libraries I have seen; and such parts of it as I cannot reconcile to my little philosophy, I postpone for future investigation." Letter of Dec. 25, 1813, 10 Works of John Adams 85 (1856).

Bible and other religious documents in public school education only when the purpose of the use is to advance a particular religious belief.

III

In sum, I find that the language and the legislative history of the Balanced Treatment Act unquestionably demonstrate that its purpose is to advance a particular religious belief. Although the discretion of state and local authorities over public school curricula is broad, "the First Amendment does not permit the State to require that teaching and learning must be tailored to the principles or prohibitions of any religious sect or dogma." Epperson v. Arkansas, 393 U.S., at 106. Accordingly, I concur in the opinion of the Court and its judgment that the Balanced Treatment Act violates the Establishment Clause of the Constitution.

JUSTICE WHITE, concurring in the judgment: As it comes to us, this is not a difficult case. Based on the historical setting and plain language of the Act both courts construed the statutory words "creation science" to refer to a religious belief, which the Act required to be taught if evolution was taught. In other words, the teaching of evolution was conditioned on the teaching of a religious belief. Both courts concluded that the state legislature's primary purpose was to advance religion and that the statute was therefore unconstitutional under the Establishment Clause. . . .

JUSTICE SCALIA, with whom THE CHIEF JUSTICE joins, dissenting: . . .

I

This case arrives here in the following posture: The Louisiana Supreme Court has never been given an opportunity to interpret the Balanced Treatment Act, State officials have never attempted to implement it, and it has never been the subject of a full evidentiary hearing. We can only guess at its meaning. We know that it forbids instruction in either "creation-science" or "evolution-science" without instruction in the other, § 17:286.4A, but the parties are sharply divided over what creation science consists of. Appellants insist that it is a collection of educationally valuable scientific data that has been censored from classrooms by an embarrassed scientific establishment. Appellees insist it is not science at all but thinly veiled religious doctrine. Both interpretations of the intended meaning of that phrase find considerable support in the legislative history.

At least at this stage in the litigation, it is plain to me that we must accept appellants' view of what the statute means. To begin with, the statute itself defines "creation-science" as "the scientific evidences for creation and inferences from those scientific evidences." § 17:286.3(2). If, however, that definition is not thought sufficiently helpful, the means by which the Louisiana Supreme Court will give the term more precise content is quite clear—and again, at this stage in the litigation, favors the appellants' view. "Creation science" is unquestionably a "term of art," see Brief for 72 Nobel Laureates et al. as Amici Curiae 20, and thus, under

Louisiana law, is "to be interpreted according to [its] received meaning and acceptation with the learned in the art, trade or profession to which [it] refer[s]." 12 La.Civ.Code Ann., Art. 15 (West 1952). The only evidence in the record of the "received meaning and acceptation" of "creation science" is found in five affidavits filed by appellants. In those affidavits, two scientists, a philosopher, a theologian, and an educator, all of whom claim extensive knowledge of creation science, swear that it is essentially a collection of scientific data supporting the theory that the physical universe and life within it appeared suddenly and have not changed substantially since appearing. See App. to Juris.Statement A–19 (Kenyon); id., at A–36 (Morrow); id., at A–41 (Miethe). These experts insist that creation science is a strictly scientific concept that can be presented without religious reference. See id., at A–19–A–20, A–35 (Kenyon); id., at A–36–A–38 (Morrow); id., at A–40, A–41, A–43 (Miethe); id., at A–47, A–48 (Most); id., at A–49 (Clinkert). At this point, then, we must assume that the Balanced Treatment Act does not require the presentation of religious doctrine.

Nothing in today's opinion is plainly to the contrary, but what the statute means and what it requires are of rather little concern to the Court. Like the Court of Appeals, 765 F.2d 1251, 1253, 1254 (CA5 1985), the Court finds it necessary to consider only the motives of the legislators who supported the Balanced Treatment Act. After examining the statute, its legislative history, and its historical and social context, the Court holds that the Louisiana Legislature acted without "a secular legislative purpose" and that the Act therefore fails the "purpose" prong of the three-part test set forth in Lemon v. Kurtzman, 403 U.S. 602, 612 (1971). As I explain below, I doubt whether that "purpose" requirement of Lemon is a proper interpretation of the Constitution; but even if it were, I could not agree with the Court's assessment that the requirement was not satisfied here.

This Court has said little about the first component of the Lemon test. Almost invariably, we have effortlessly discovered a secular purpose for measures challenged under the Establishment Clause, typically devoting no more than a sentence or two to the matter. . . . In fact, only once before deciding Lemon, and twice since, have we invalidated a law for lack of a secular purpose. See Wallace v. Jaffree, 472 U.S. 38 (1985); Stone v. Graham, 449 U.S. 39 (1980); Epperson v. Arkansas, 393 U.S. 97 (1968).

Nevertheless, a few principles have emerged from our cases, principles which should, but to an unfortunately large extent do not, guide the Court's application of Lemon today. It is clear, first of all, that regardless of what "legislative purpose" may mean in other contexts, for the purpose of the Lemon test it means the "actual" motives of those responsible for the challenged action. The Court recognizes this, as it has in the past, see, e.g., Witters v. Washington Dept. of Services for Blind, supra, 474 U.S., at 486; Wallace v. Jaffree, supra, 472 U.S., at 56. Thus, if those legislators who supported the Balanced Treatment Act in fact acted with a "sincere" secular purpose, the Act survives the first component of the Lemon test, regardless of whether that purpose is likely to be achieved by the provisions they enacted.

Our cases have also confirmed that when the Lemon Court referred to "a secular ... purpose," 403 U.S., at 612, it meant "a secular purpose." The author of Lemon, writing for the Court, has said that invalidation under the purpose prong is appropriate when "there [is] no question that the statute or activity was motivated wholly by religious considerations." Lynch v. Donnelly, 465 U.S. 668, 680 (1984) (Burger, C.J.); see also id., at 681, n. 6; Wallace v. Jaffree, supra, 472 U.S., at 56 ("[T]he First Amendment requires that a statute must be invalidated if it is entirely motivated by a purpose to advance religion"). In all three cases in which we struck down laws under the Establishment Clause for lack of a secular purpose, we found that the legislature's sole motive was to promote religion. See Wallace v. Jaffree, supra, at 56, 57, 60; Stone v. Graham, supra, 449 U.S., at 41, 43, n. 5; Epperson v. Arkansas, supra, 393 U.S., at 103, 107–108; see also Lynch v. Donnelly, supra, 465 U.S., at 680 (describing Stone and Epperson as cases in which we invalidated laws "motivated wholly by religious considerations"). Thus, the majority's invalidation of the Balanced Treatment Act is defensible only if the record indicates that the Louisiana Legislature had no secular purpose.

It is important to stress that the purpose forbidden by Lemon is the purpose to "advance religion." 403 U.S., at 613; Witters v. Washington Dept. of Services for Blind, supra, 474 U.S., at 486 ("endorse religion"); Wallace v. Jaffree, 472 U.S., at 56 ("advance religion"); ibid. ("endorse ... religion"); Committee for Public Education & Religious Liberty v. Nyquist, supra, 413 U.S., at 788 (" 'advancing' ... religion"); Levitt v. Committee for Public Education & Religious Liberty, supra, 413 U.S., at 481 ("advancing religion"); Walz v. Tax Comm'n of New York City, 397 U.S. 664, 674 (1970) ("establishing, sponsoring, or supporting religion"); Board of Education v. Allen, 392 U.S. 236, 243 (1968) (" 'advancement or inhibition of religion' "). Our cases in no way imply that the Establishment Clause forbids legislators merely to act upon their religious convictions. We surely would not strike down a law providing money to feed the hungry or shelter the homeless if it could be demonstrated that, but for the religious beliefs of the legislators, the funds would not have been approved. Also, political activism by the religiously motivated is part of our heritage. Notwithstanding the majority's implication to the contrary, we do not presume that the sole purpose of a law is to advance religion merely because it was supported strongly by organized religions or by adherents of particular faiths. See Walz v. Tax Comm'n of New York City, supra, 397 U.S., at 670; cf. Harris v. McRae, 448 U.S. 297, 319–320 (1980). To do so would deprive religious men and women of their right to participate in the political process. Today's religious activism may give us the Balanced Treatment Act, but yesterday's resulted in the abolition of slavery, and tomorrow's may bring relief for famine victims.

Similarly, we will not presume that a law's purpose is to advance religion merely because it " 'happens to coincide or harmonize with the tenets of some or all religions,' " Harris v. McRae, supra, at 319, or because it benefits religion, even substantially. We have, for example, turned back Establishment Clause challenges to restrictions on abortion funding, Harris v. McRae, supra, and to Sunday closing laws, McGowan v. Maryland, supra, despite the fact that both "agre[e] with the dictates of [some] Judaeo–Christian religions," id., at 442. "In many instances, the Congress or state legislatures conclude that the general welfare of society, wholly apart from any religious considerations, demands such regulation." Ibid. On many past occasions we have had no difficulty finding a secular purpose for governmental action far more likely to advance religion than the Balanced Treatment Act. See, e.g., Mueller v. Allen, 463 U.S., at 394–395 (tax deduction for expenses of religious education); Wolman v. Walter, 433 U.S., at 236 (plurality opinion) (aid to religious schools); Meek v. Pittenger, 421 U.S., at 363 (same); Committee for Public Education & Religious Liberty v. Nyquist, 413 U.S., at 773 (same); Lemon v. Kurtzman, 403 U.S., at 613 (same); Walz v. Tax Comm'n of New York City, supra, 397 U.S., at 672 (tax exemption for church property); Board of Education v. Allen, supra, 392 U.S., at 243 (textbook loans to students in religious schools). Thus, the fact that creation science coincides with the beliefs of certain religions, a fact upon which the majority relies heavily, does not itself justify invalidation of the Act.

Finally, our cases indicate that even certain kinds of governmental actions undertaken with the specific intention of improving the position of religion do not "advance religion" as that term is used in Lemon. 403 U.S., at 613. Rather, we have said that in at least two circumstances government must act to advance religion, and that in a third it may do so.

First, since we have consistently described the Establishment Clause as forbidding not only state action motivated by the desire to advance religion, but also that intended to "disapprove," "inhibit," or evince "hostility" toward religion, see, e.g., Lynch v. Donnelly, supra, 465 U.S., at 690 (O'CONNOR, J., concurring)); Lynch v. Donnelly, supra, at 673 ("hostility"); Committee for Public Education & Religious Liberty v. Nyquist, supra, 413 U.S., at 788 (" 'inhibi[t]' "); and since we have said that governmental "neutrality" toward religion is the preeminent goal of the First Amendment, see, e.g., Grand Rapids School District v. Ball, 473 U.S., at 382; Roemer v. Maryland Public Works Bd., 426 U.S. 736, 747 (1976) (plurality opinion); Committee for Public Education & Religious Liberty v. Nyquist, supra, 413 U.S., at 792–793; a State which discovers that its employees are inhibiting religion must take steps to prevent them from doing so, even though its purpose would clearly be to advance religion. Cf. Walz v. Tax Comm'n of New York City, supra, 397 U.S., at 673. Thus, if the Louisiana Legislature sincerely believed that the State's science teachers were being hostile to religion, our cases indicate that it could act to eliminate that hostility without running afoul of Lemon's purpose test.

Second, we have held that intentional governmental advancement of religion is sometimes required by the Free Exercise Clause. For example, in Hobbie v. Unemployment Appeals Comm'n of Fla., 480 U.S. 136 (1987); Thomas v. Review Bd., Indiana Employment Security Div., 450 U.S. 707 (1981); Wisconsin v. Yoder, 406 U.S. 205 (1972); and Sherbert v. Verner, 374 U.S. 398 (1963), we held that in some circumstances States must accommodate the beliefs of religious citizens by exempting them from generally applicable regulations. We have not yet come close to reconciling Lemon and our Free Exercise cases, and typically we do not really try. See, e.g., Hobbie v. Unemployment Appeals Comm'n of Fla., supra, 480 U.S., at 144–145; Thomas v. Review Bd., Indiana Employment Security Div., supra, 450 U.S., at 719–720. It is clear, however, that members of the Louisiana Legislature were not impermissibly motivated for purposes of the Lemon test if they believed that approval of the Balanced Treatment Act was required by the Free Exercise Clause.

We have also held that in some circumstances government may act to accommodate religion, even if that action is not required by the First Amendment. See Hobbie v. Unemployment Appeals Comm'n of Fla., supra, 480 U.S., at 144–145. It is well established that "[t]he limits of permissible state accommodation to religion are by no means co-extensive with the noninterference mandated by the Free Exercise Clause." Walz v. Tax Comm'n of New York City, supra, 397 U.S., at 673; see also Gillette v. United States, 401 U.S. 437, 453 (1971). We have implied that voluntary governmental accommodation of religion is not only permissible, but desirable. See, e.g., ibid. Thus, few would contend that Title VII of the Civil Rights Act of 1964, which both forbids religious discrimination by private-sector employers, 78 Stat. 255, 42 U.S.C. § 2000e–2(a)(1), and requires them reasonably to accommodate the religious practices of their employees, § 2000e(j), violates the Establishment Clause, even though its "purpose" is, of course, to advance religion, and even though it is almost certainly not required by the Free Exercise Clause. While we have warned that at some point, accommodation may devolve into "an unlawful fostering of religion," Hobbie v. Unemployment Appeals Comm'n of Fla., supra, 480 U.S., at 145, we have not suggested precisely (or even roughly) where that point might be. It is possible, then, that even if the sole motive of those voting for the Balanced Treatment Act was to advance religion, and its passage was not actually required, or even believed to be required, by either the Free Exercise or Establishment Clauses, the Act would nonetheless survive scrutiny under Lemon's purpose test.

One final observation about the application of that test: Although the Court's opinion gives no hint of it, in the past we have repeatedly affirmed "our reluctance to attribute unconstitutional motives to the States." Mueller v. Allen, supra, 463 U.S., at 394; see also Lynch v. Donnelly, 465 U.S., at 699 (BRENNAN, J., dissenting). We "presume that legislatures act in a constitutional manner." Illinois v. Krull, 480 U.S. 340–351 (1987); see also Clements v. Fashing, 457 U.S. 957, 963 (1982) (plurality opinion); Rostker v. Goldberg, 453 U.S. 57, 64 (1981); McDonald v. Board of Election Comm'rs of Chicago, 394 U.S. 802, 809 (1969). Whenever we are called upon to judge the constitutionality of an act of a state legislature, "we must have 'due regard to the fact that this Court is not exercising a primary judgment but is sitting in judgment upon those who also have taken the oath to observe the Constitution and who have the responsibility for carrying on government.' " Rostker v. Goldberg, supra, 453 U.S., at 64 (quoting Joint Anti–Fascist Refugee Committee v. McGrath, 341 U.S. 123, 164 (1951) (Frankfurter, J., concurring)). This is particularly true, we have said, where the legislature has specifically considered the question of a law's constitutionality. Ibid.

With the foregoing in mind, I now turn to the purposes underlying adoption of the Balanced Treatment Act.

II

A

We have relatively little information upon which to judge the motives of those who supported the Act. About the only direct evidence is the statute itself and transcripts of the seven committee hearings at which it was considered. Unfortunately, several of those hearings were sparsely attended, and the legislators who were present revealed little about their motives. We have no committee reports, no floor debates, no remarks inserted into the legislative history, no statement from the Governor, and no postenactment statements or testimony from the bill's sponsor or any other legislators. Cf. Wallace v. Jaffree, 472 U.S., at 43, 56–57. Nevertheless, there is ample evidence that the majority is wrong in holding that the Balanced Treatment Act is without secular purpose.

At the outset, it is important to note that the Balanced Treatment Act did not fly through the Louisiana Legislature on wings of fundamentalist religious fervor-which would be unlikely, in any event, since only a small minority of the State's citizens belong to fundamentalist religious denominations. See B. Quinn, H. Anderson, M. Bradley, P. Goetting, & P. Shriver, Churches and Church Membership in the United States 16 (1982). The Act had its genesis (so to speak) in legislation introduced by Senator Bill Keith in June 1980. After two hearings before the Senate Committee on Education, Senator Keith asked that his bill be referred to a study commission composed of members of both Houses of the Louisiana Legislature. He expressed hope that the joint committee would give the bill careful consideration and determine whether his arguments were "legitimate." 1 App. E–29–E–30. The committee met twice during the interim, heard testimony (both for and against the bill) from several witnesses, and received staff reports. Senator Keith introduced his bill again when the legislature reconvened. The Senate Committee on Education held two more hearings and approved the bill after substantially amending it (in part over Senator Keith's objection). After approval by the full Senate, the bill was referred to the House Committee on Education. That committee conducted a lengthy hearing, adopted further amendments, and sent the bill on to the full House, where it received favorable consideration. The Senate concurred in the House amendments and on July 20, 1981, the Governor signed the bill into law.

Senator Keith's statements before the various committees that considered the bill hardly reflect the confidence of a man preaching to the converted. He asked his colleagues to "keep an open mind" and not to be "biased" by misleading characterizations of creation science. Id., at E–33. He also urged them to "look at this subject on its merits and not on some preconceived idea." Id., at E–34; see also 2 id., at E–491. Senator Keith's reception was not especially warm. Over his strenuous objection, the Senate Committee on Education voted 5–1 to amend his bill to deprive it of any force; as amended, the bill merely gave teachers permission to balance the teaching of creation science or evolution with the other. 1 id., at E–442–E–461. The House Committee restored the "mandatory" language to the bill by a vote of only 6–5, 2 id., at E–626–E–627, and both the full House (by vote of 52–35), id., at E–700–E–706, and full Senate (23–15), id., at E–735–E–738, had to repel further efforts to gut the bill.

The legislators understood that Senator Keith's bill involved a "unique" subject, 1 id., at E–106 (Rep. M. Thompson), and they were repeatedly made aware of its potential constitutional problems, see, e.g., id., at E–26–E–28 (McGehee); id., at E–38–E–39 (Sen. Keith); id., at E–241–E–242 (Rossman); id., at E–257 (Probst); id., at E–261 (Beck); id., at E–282 (Sen. Keith). Although the Establishment Clause, including its secular purpose requirement, was of substantial concern to the legislators, they eventually voted overwhelmingly in favor of the Balanced Treatment Act: The House approved it 71–19 (with 15 members absent), 2 id., at E–716–E–722; the Senate 26–12 (with all members present), id., at E–741–E–744. The legislators specifically designated the protection of "academic freedom" as the purpose of the Act. La.Rev.Stat.Ann. § 17:286.2 (West 1982). We cannot accurately assess whether this purpose is a "sham," until we first examine the evidence presented to the legislature far more carefully than the Court has done.

Before summarizing the testimony of Senator Keith and his supporters, I wish to make clear that I by no means intend to endorse its accuracy. But my views (and the views of this Court) about creation science and evolution are (or should be) beside the point. Our task is not to judge the debate about teaching the origins of life, but to ascertain what the members of the Louisiana Legislature believed. The vast majority of them voted to approve a bill which explicitly stated a secular purpose; what is crucial is not their wisdom in believing that purpose would be achieved by the bill, but their sincerity in believing it would be.

Most of the testimony in support of Senator Keith's bill came from the Senator himself and from scientists and educators he presented, many of whom enjoyed academic credentials that may have been regarded as quite impressive by members of the Louisiana Legislature. To a substantial extent, their testimony was devoted to lengthy, and, to the layman, seemingly expert scientific expositions on the origin of life. See, e.g., 1 App. E–11–E–18 (Sunderland); id., at E–50–E–60 (Boudreaux); id., at E–86–E–89 (Ward); id., at E–130–E–153 (Boudreaux paper); id., at E–321–E–326 (Boudreaux); id., at E–423–E–428 (Sen. Keith). These scientific lectures touched upon, inter alia, biology, paleontology, genetics, astronomy, astrophysics, probability analysis, and biochemistry. The witnesses repeatedly assured committee members that "hundreds and hundreds" of highly respected, internationally renowned scientists believed in creation science and would support their testimony. See, e.g., id., at E–5 (Sunderland); id., at E–76 (Sen. Keith); id., at E–100–E–101 (Reiboldt); id., at E–327–E–328 (Boudreaux); 2 id., at E–503–E–504 (Boudreaux).

Senator Keith and his witnesses testified essentially as set forth in the following numbered paragraphs:

(1) There are two and only two scientific explanations for the beginning of life-evolution and creation science. 1 id., at E–6 (Sunderland); id., at E–34 (Sen. Keith); id., at E–280 (Sen. Keith); id., at E–417–E–418 (Sen. Keith). Both are bona fide "sciences." Id., at E–6–E–7 (Sunderland); id., at E–12 (Sunderland); id., at E–416 (Sen. Keith); id., at E–427 (Sen. Keith); 2 id., at E–491–E–492 (Sen. Keith); id., at E–497–E–498 (Sen. Keith). Both posit a theory of the origin of life and subject that theory to empirical testing. Evolution posits that life arose out of inanimate chemical compounds and has gradually evolved over millions of years. Creation science posits that all life forms now on earth appeared suddenly and relatively recently and have changed little. Since there are only two possible explanations of the origin of life, any evidence that tends to disprove the theory of evolution necessarily tends to prove the theory of creation science, and vice versa. For example, the abrupt appearance in the fossil record of complex life, and the extreme rarity of transitional life forms in that record, are evidence for creation science. 1 id., at E–7 (Sunderland); id., at E–12–E–18 (Sunderland); id., at E–45–E–60 (Boudreaux); id., at E–67 (Harlow); id., at E–130–E–153 (Boudreaux paper); id., at E–423–E–428 (Sen. Keith).

(2) The body of scientific evidence supporting creation science is as strong as that supporting evolution. In fact, it may be stronger. Id., at E–214 (Young statement); id., at 310 (Sen. Keith); id., at E–416 (Sen. Keith); 2 id., at E–492 (Sen. Keith). The evidence for evolution is far less compelling than we have been led to believe. Evolution is not a scientific "fact," since it cannot actually be observed in a laboratory. Rather, evolution is merely a scientific theory or "guess." 1 id., at E–20–E–21 (Morris); id., at E–85 (Ward); id., at E–100 (Reiboldt); id., at E–328–E–329 (Boudreaux); 2 id., at E–506 (Boudreaux). It is a very bad guess at that. The scientific problems with evolution are so serious that it could accurately be termed a "myth." 1 id., at E–85 (Ward); id., at E–92–E–93 (Kalivoda); id., at E–95–E–97 (Sen. Keith); id., at E–154 (Boudreaux paper); id., at E–329 (Boudreaux); id., at E–453 (Sen. Keith); 2 id., at E–505–E–506 (Boudreaux); id., at E–516 (Young).

(3) Creation science is educationally valuable. Students exposed to it better understand the current state of scientific evidence about the origin

of life. 1 id., at E–19 (Sunderland); id., at E–39 (Sen. Keith); id., at E–79 (Kalivoda); id., at E–308 (Sen. Keith); 2 id., at E–513–E–514 (Morris). Those students even have a better understanding of evolution. 1 id., at E–19 (Sunderland). Creation science can and should be presented to children without any religious content. Id., at E–12 (Sunderland); id., at E–22 (Sanderford); id., at E–35–E–36 (Sen. Keith); id., at E–101 (Reiboldt); id., at E–279–E–280 (Sen. Keith); id., at E–282 (Sen. Keith).

(4) Although creation science is educationally valuable and strictly scientific, it is now being censored from or misrepresented in the public schools. Id., at E–19 (Sunderland); id., at E–21 (Morris); id., at E–34 (Sen. Keith); id., at E–37 (Sen. Keith); id., at E–42 (Sen. Keith); id., at E–92 (Kalivoda); id., at E–97–E–98 (Reiboldt); id., at E–214 (Young statement); id., at E–218 (Young statement); id., at E–280 (Sen. Keith); id., at E–309 (Sen. Keith); 2 id., at E–513 (Morris). Evolution, in turn, is misrepresented as an absolute truth. 1 id., at E–63 (Harlow); id., at E–74 (Sen. Keith); id., at E–81 (Kalivoda); id., at E–214 (Young statement); 2 id., at E–507 (Harlow); id., at E–513 (Morris); id., at E–516 (Young). Teachers have been brainwashed by an entrenched scientific establishment composed almost exclusively of scientists to whom evolution is like a ''religion.'' These scientists discriminate against creation scientists so as to prevent evolution's weaknesses from being exposed. 1 id., at E–61 (Boudreaux); id., at E–63–E–64 (Harlow); id., at E–78–E–79 (Kalivoda); id., at E–80 (Kalivoda); id., at E–95–E–97 (Sen. Keith); id., at E–129 (Boudreaux paper); id., at E–218 (Young statement); id., at E–357 (Sen. Keith); id., at E–430 (Boudreaux).

(5) The censorship of creation science has at least two harmful effects. First, it deprives students of knowledge of one of the two scientific explanations for the origin of life and leads them to believe that evolution is proven fact; thus, their education suffers and they are wrongly taught that science has proved their religious beliefs false. Second, it violates the Establishment Clause. The United States Supreme Court has held that secular humanism is a religion. Id., at E–36 (Sen. Keith) (referring to Torcaso v. Watkins, 367 U.S. 488, 495, n. 11 (1961)); 1 App. E–418 (Sen. Keith); 2 id., at E–499 (Sen. Keith). Belief in evolution is a central tenet of that religion. 1 id., at E–282 (Sen. Keith); id., at E–312–E–313 (Sen. Keith); id., at E–317 (Sen. Keith); id., at E–418 (Sen. Keith); 2 id., at E–499 (Sen. Keith). Thus, by censoring creation science and instructing students that evolution is fact, public school teachers are now advancing religion in violation of the Establishment Clause. 1 id., at E–2–E–4 (Sen. Keith); id., at E–36–E–37, E–39 (Sen. Keith); id., at E–154–E–155 (Boudreaux paper); id., at E–281–E–282 (Sen. Keith); id., at E–313 (Sen. Keith); id., at E–315–E–316 (Sen. Keith); id., at E–317 (Sen. Keith); 2 id., at E–499–E–500 (Sen. Keith).

Senator Keith repeatedly and vehemently denied that his purpose was to advance a particular religious doctrine. At the outset of the first hearing on the legislation, he testified: "We are not going to say today that you should have some kind of religious instructions in our schools.... We are not talking about religion today.... I am not proposing that we take the Bible in each science class and read the first chapter of Genesis." 1 id., at E–35. At a later hearing, Senator Keith stressed: "[T]o ... teach religion and disguise it as creationism ... is not my intent. My intent is to see to it that our textbooks are not censored." Id., at E–280. He made many similar statements throughout the hearings. See, e.g., id., at E–41; id., at E–282; id., at E–310; id., at E–417; see also id., at E–44 (Boudreaux); id., at E–80 (Kalivoda).

We have no way of knowing, of course, how many legislators believed the testimony of Senator Keith and his witnesses. But in the absence of evidence to the contrary,[85] we have to assume that many of them did. Given that assumption, the Court today plainly errs in holding that the Louisiana Legislature passed the Balanced Treatment Act for exclusively religious purposes.

B

Even with nothing more than this legislative history to go on, I think it would be extraordinary to invalidate the Balanced Treatment Act for lack of a valid secular purpose. Striking down a law approved by the democratically elected representatives of the people is no minor matter. "The cardinal principle of statutory construction is to save and not to destroy. We have repeatedly held that as between two possible interpretations of a statute, by one of which it would be unconstitutional and by the other valid, our plain duty is to adopt that which will save the act." NLRB v. Jones & Laughlin Steel Corp., 301 U.S. 1, 30 (1937). So, too, it seems to me, with discerning statutory purpose. Even if the legislative history were

---

85. Although appellees and amici dismiss the testimony of Senator Keith and his witnesses as pure fantasy, they did not bother to submit evidence of that to the District Court, making it difficult for us to agree with them. The State, by contrast, submitted the affidavits of two scientists, a philosopher, a theologian, and an educator, whose academic credentials are rather impressive. See App. to Juris. Statement A–17–A–18 (Kenyon); id., at A–36 (Morrow); id., at A–39–A–40 (Miethe); id., at A–46–A–47 (Most); id., at A–49 (Clinkert). Like Senator Keith and his witnesses, the affiants swear that evolution and creation science are the only two scientific explanations for the origin of life, see id., at A–19–A–20 (Kenyon); id., at A–38 (Morrow); id., at A–41 (Miethe); that creation science is strictly scientific, see id., at A–18 (Kenyon); id., at A–36 (Morrow); id., at A–40–A–41 (Miethe); id., at A–49 (Clinkert); that creation science is simply a collection of scientific data that supports the hypothesis that life appeared on earth suddenly and has changed little, see id., at A–19 (Kenyon); id., at A–36 (Morrow); id., at A–41 (Miethe); that hundreds of respected scientists believe in creation science, see id., at A–20 (Kenyon); that evidence for creation science is as strong as evidence for evolution, see id., at A–21 (Kenyon); id., at A–34–A–35 (Kenyon); id., at A–37–A–38 (Morrow); that creation science is educationally valuable, see id., at A–19 (Kenyon); id., at A–36 (Morrow); id., at A–38–A–39 (Morrow); id., at A–49 (Clinkert); that creation science can be presented without religious content, see id., at A–19 (Kenyon); id., at A–35 (Kenyon); id., at A–36 (Morrow); id., at A–40 (Miethe); id., at A–43–A–44 (Miethe); id., at A–47 (Most); id., at A–49 (Clinkert); and that creation science is now censored from classrooms while evolution is misrepresented as proven fact, see id., at A–20 (Kenyon); id., at A–35 (Kenyon); id., at A–39 (Morrow); id., at A–50 (Clinkert). It is difficult to conclude on the basis of these affidavits-the only substantive evidence in the record-that the laymen serving in the Louisiana Legislature must have disbelieved Senator Keith or his witnesses.

silent or ambiguous about the existence of a secular purpose—and here it is not—the statute should survive Lemon's purpose test. But even more validation than mere legislative history is present here. The Louisiana Legislature explicitly set forth its secular purpose ("protecting academic freedom") in the very text of the Act. La.Rev.Stat. § 17:286.2 (West 1982). We have in the past repeatedly relied upon or deferred to such expressions, see, e.g., Committee for Public Education & Religious Liberty v. Regan, 444 U.S., at 654; Meek v. Pittenger, 421 U.S., at 363; Committee for Public Education & Religious Liberty v. Nyquist, 413 U.S., at 773; Levitt v. Committee for Public Education & Religious Liberty, 413 U.S., at 479–480, n. 7; Tilton v. Richardson, 403 U.S., at 678–679 (plurality opinion); Lemon v. Kurtzman, 403 U.S., at 613; Board of Education v. Allen, 392 U.S., at 243.

The Court seeks to evade the force of this expression of purpose by stubbornly misinterpreting it, and then finding that the provisions of the Act do not advance that misinterpreted purpose, thereby showing it to be a sham. The Court first surmises that "academic freedom" means "enhancing the freedom of teachers to teach what they will,"—even though "academic freedom" in that sense has little scope in the structured elementary and secondary curriculums with which the Act is concerned. Alternatively, the Court suggests that it might mean "maximiz[ing] the comprehensiveness and effectiveness of science instruction,"—though that is an exceedingly strange interpretation of the words, and one that is refuted on the very face of the statute. See § 17:286.5. Had the Court devoted to this central question of the meaning of the legislatively expressed purpose a small fraction of the research into legislative history that produced its quotations of religiously motivated statements by individual legislators, it would have discerned quite readily what "academic freedom" meant: students' freedom from indoctrination. The legislature wanted to ensure that students would be free to decide for themselves how life began, based upon a fair and balanced presentation of the scientific evidence-that is, to protect "the right of each [student] voluntarily to determine what to believe (and what not to believe) free of any coercive pressures from the State." Grand Rapids School District v. Ball, 473 U.S., at 385. The legislature did not care whether the topic of origins was taught; it simply wished to ensure that when the topic was taught, students would receive " 'all of the evidence.' " Tr. of Oral Arg. 60.

As originally introduced, the "purpose" section of the Balanced Treatment Act read: "This Chapter is enacted for the purposes of protecting academic freedom ... of students ... and assisting students in their search for truth." 1 App. E–292. Among the proposed findings of fact contained in the original version of the bill was the following: "Public school instruction in only evolution-science ... violates the principle of academic freedom because it denies students a choice between scientific models and instead indoctrinates them in evolution science alone." Id., at

E–295.[86] Senator Keith unquestionably understood "academic freedom" to mean "freedom from indoctrination." See id., at E–36 (purpose of bill is "to protect academic freedom by providing student choice"); id., at E–283 (purpose of bill is to protect "academic freedom" by giving students a "choice" rather than subjecting them to "indoctrination on origins").

If one adopts the obviously intended meaning of the statutory term "academic freedom," there is no basis whatever for concluding that the purpose they express is a "sham." To the contrary, the Act pursues that purpose plainly and consistently. It requires that, whenever the subject of origins is covered, evolution be "taught as a theory, rather than as proven scientific fact" and that scientific evidence inconsistent with the theory of evolution (viz., "creation science") be taught as well. La.Rev.Stat.Ann. § 17:286.4A (West 1982). Living up to its title of "Balanced Treatment for Creation–Science and Evolution–Science Act," § 17:286.1, it treats the teaching of creation the same way. It does not mandate instruction in creation science, § 17:286.5; forbids teachers to present creation science "as proven scientific fact," § 17:286.4A; and bans the teaching of creation science unless the theory is (to use the Court's terminology) "discredit[ed] '. . . at every turn' " with the teaching of evolution. It surpasses understanding how the Court can see in this a purpose "to restructure the science curriculum to conform with a particular religious viewpoint," "to provide a persuasive advantage to a particular religious doctrine," "to promote the theory of creation science which embodies a particular religious tenet," and "to endorse a particular religious doctrine."

The Act's reference to "creation" is not convincing evidence of religious purpose. The Act defines creation science as "scientific evidenc[e]," § 17:286.3(2), and Senator Keith and his witnesses repeatedly stressed that the subject can and should be presented without religious content. We have no basis on the record to conclude that creation science need be anything other than a collection of scientific data supporting the theory that life abruptly appeared on earth. See n. 4, supra. Creation science, its proponents insist, no more must explain whence life came than evolution must explain whence came the inanimate materials from which it says life evolved. But even if that were not so, to posit a past creator is not to posit the eternal and personal God who is the object of religious veneration. Indeed, it is not even to posit the "unmoved mover" hypothesized by Aristotle and other notably nonfundamentalist philosophers. Senator Keith suggested this when he referred to "a creator however you define a creator." 1 App. E–280.

---

86. The majority finds it "astonishing" that I would cite a portion of Senator Keith's original bill that was later deleted as evidence of the legislature's understanding of the phrase "academic freedom." What is astonishing is the majority's implication that the deletion of that section deprives it of value as a clear indication of what the phrase meant-there and in the other, retained, sections of the bill. The Senate Committee on Education deleted most of the lengthy "purpose" section of the bill (with Senator Keith's consent) because it resembled legislative "findings of fact," which, committee members felt, should generally not be incorporated in legislation. The deletion had absolutely nothing to do with the manner in which the section described "academic freedom." See 1 App. E–314–E–320; id., at E–440–E–442.

The Court cites three provisions of the Act which, it argues, demonstrate a "discriminatory preference for the teaching of creation science" and no interest in "academic freedom." First, the Act prohibits discrimination only against creation scientists and those who teach creation science. § 17:286.4C. Second, the Act requires local school boards to develop and provide to science teachers "a curriculum guide on presentation of creation-science." § 17:286.7A. Finally, the Act requires the Governor to designate seven creation scientists who shall, upon request, assist local school boards in developing the curriculum guides. § 17:286.7B. But none of these provisions casts doubt upon the sincerity of the legislators' articulated purpose of "academic freedom"—unless, of course, one gives that term the obviously erroneous meanings preferred by the Court. The Louisiana legislators had been told repeatedly that creation scientists were scorned by most educators and scientists, who themselves had an almost religious faith in evolution. It is hardly surprising, then, that in seeking to achieve a balanced, "nonindoctrinating" curriculum, the legislators protected from discrimination only those teachers whom they thought were suffering from discrimination. (Also, the legislators were undoubtedly aware of Epperson v. Arkansas, 393 U.S. 97 (1968), and thus could quite reasonably have concluded that discrimination against evolutionists was already prohibited.) The two provisions respecting the development of curriculum guides are also consistent with "academic freedom" as the Louisiana Legislature understood the term. Witnesses had informed the legislators that, because of the hostility of most scientists and educators to creation science, the topic had been censored from or badly misrepresented in elementary and secondary school texts. In light of the unavailability of works on creation science suitable for classroom use (a fact appellees concede, see Brief for Appellees 27, 40) and the existence of ample materials on evolution, it was entirely reasonable for the legislature to conclude that science teachers attempting to implement the Act would need a curriculum guide on creation science, but not on evolution, and that those charged with developing the guide would need an easily accessible group of creation scientists. Thus, the provisions of the Act of so much concern to the Court support the conclusion that the legislature acted to advance "academic freedom."

The legislative history gives ample evidence of the sincerity of the Balanced Treatment Act's articulated purpose. Witness after witness urged the legislators to support the Act so that students would not be "indoctrinated" but would instead be free to decide for themselves, based upon a fair presentation of the scientific evidence, about the origin of life. See, e.g., 1 App. E–18 (Sunderland) ("all that we are advocating" is presenting "scientific data" to students and "letting [them] make up their own mind [s]"); id., at E–19–E–20 (Sunderland) (Students are now being "indoctrinated" in evolution through the use of "censored school books. . . . All that we are asking for is [the] open unbiased education in the classroom . . . your students deserve"); id., at E–21 (Morris) ("A student cannot [make an intelligent decision about the origin of life] unless he is well informed about both [evolution and creation science]"); id., at E–22 (Sanderford) ("We are asking very simply [that] ... creationism [be presented] alongside ... evolution and let people make their own mind[s] up"); id., at E–23 (Young) (the bill would require teachers to live up to their "obligation to present all theories" and thereby enable "students to make judgments themselves"); id., at E–44 (Boudreaux) ("Our intention is truth and as a scientist, I am interested in truth"); id., at E–60–E–61 (Boudreaux) ("[W]e [teachers] are guilty of a lot of brainwashing.... We have a duty to ... [present the] truth" to students "at all levels from gradeschool on through the college level"); id., at E–79 (Kalivoda) ("This [hearing] is being held I think to determine whether children will benefit from freedom of information or if they will be handicapped educationally by having little or no information about creation"); id., at E–80 (Kalivoda) ("I am not interested in teaching religion in schools.... I am interested in the truth and [students] having the opportunity to hear more than one side"); id., at E–98 (Reiboldt) ("The students have a right to know there is an alternate creationist point of view. They have a right to know the scientific evidences which suppor[t] that alternative"); id., at E–218 (Young statement) (passage of the bill will ensure that "communication of scientific ideas and discoveries may be unhindered"); 2 id., at E–514 (Morris) ("[A]re we going to allow [students] to look at evolution, to look at creationism, and to let one or the other stand or fall on its own merits, or will we by failing to pass this bill ... deny students an opportunity to hear another viewpoint?"); id., at E–516–E–517 (Young) ("We want to give the children here in this state an equal opportunity to see both sides of the theories"). Senator Keith expressed similar views. See e.g., 1 id., at E–36; id., at E–41; id., at E–280; id., at E–283.

Legislators other than Senator Keith made only a few statements providing insight into their motives, but those statements cast no doubt upon the sincerity of the Act's articulated purpose. The legislators were concerned primarily about the manner in which the subject of origins was presented in Louisiana schools-specifically, about whether scientifically valuable information was being censored and students misled about evolution. Representatives Cain, Jenkins, and F. Thompson seemed impressed by the scientific evidence presented in support of creation science. See 2 id., at E–530 (Rep. F. Thompson); id., at E–533 (Rep. Cain); id., at E–613 (Rep. Jenkins). At the first study commission hearing, Senator Picard and Representative M. Thompson questioned Senator Keith about Louisiana teachers' treatment of evolution and creation science. See 1 id., at E–71–E–74. At the close of the hearing, Representative M. Thompson told the audience:

"We as members of the committee will also receive from the staff information of what is currently being taught in the Louisiana public schools. We really want to see [it]. I ... have no idea in what manner [biology] is presented and in what manner the creationist theories

[are] excluded in the public school[s]. We want to look at what the status of the situation is." Id., at E–104.

Legislators made other comments suggesting a concern about censorship and misrepresentation of scientific information. See, e.g., id., at E–386 (Sen. McLeod); 2 id., at E–527 (Rep. Jenkins); id., at E–528 (Rep. M. Thompson); id., at E–534 (Rep. Fair).

It is undoubtedly true that what prompted the legislature to direct its attention to the misrepresentation of evolution in the schools (rather than the inaccurate presentation of other topics) was its awareness of the tension between evolution and the religious beliefs of many children. But even appellees concede that a valid secular purpose is not rendered impermissible simply because its pursuit is prompted by concern for religious sensitivities. Tr. of Oral Arg. 43, 56. If a history teacher falsely told her students that the bones of Jesus Christ had been discovered, or a physics teacher that the Shroud of Turin had been conclusively established to be inexplicable on the basis of natural causes, I cannot believe (despite the majority's implication to the contrary) that legislators or school board members would be constitutionally prohibited from taking corrective action, simply because that action was prompted by concern for the religious beliefs of the misinstructed students.

In sum, even if one concedes, for the sake of argument, that a majority of the Louisiana Legislature voted for the Balanced Treatment Act partly in order to foster (rather than merely eliminate discrimination against) Christian fundamentalist beliefs, our cases establish that that alone would not suffice to invalidate the Act, so long as there was a genuine secular purpose as well. We have, moreover, no adequate basis for disbelieving the secular purpose set forth in the Act itself, or for concluding that it is a sham enacted to conceal the legislators' violation of their oaths of office. I am astonished by the Court's unprecedented readiness to reach such a conclusion, which I can only attribute to an intellectual predisposition created by the facts and the legend of Scopes v. State, 154 Tenn. 105 (1927)—an instinctive reaction that any governmentally imposed requirements bearing upon the teaching of evolution must be a manifestation of Christian fundamentalist repression. In this case, however, it seems to me the Court's position is the repressive one. The people of Louisiana, including those who are Christian fundamentalists, are quite entitled, as a secular matter, to have whatever scientific evidence there may be against evolution presented in their schools, just as Mr. Scopes was entitled to present whatever scientific evidence there was for it. Perhaps what the Louisiana Legislature has done is unconstitutional because there is no such evidence, and the scheme they have established will amount to no more than a presentation of the Book of Genesis. But we cannot say that on the evidence before us in this summary judgment context, which includes ample uncontradicted testimony that "creation science" is a body of scientific knowledge rather than revealed belief. Infinitely less can we say (or should we say) that the scientific evidence for evolution is so conclusive that no one could be gullible enough to believe that there is any real scientific evidence to the contrary, so that the legislation's stated purpose must be a lie. Yet that illiberal judgment, that Scopes-in-reverse, is ultimately the basis on which the Court's facile rejection of the Louisiana Legislature's purpose must rest.

Since the existence of secular purpose is so entirely clear, and thus dispositive, I will not go on to discuss the fact that, even if the Louisiana Legislature's purpose were exclusively to advance religion, some of the well-established exceptions to the impermissibility of that purpose might be applicable—the validating intent to eliminate a perceived discrimination against a particular religion, to facilitate its free exercise, or to accommodate it. I am not in any case enamored of those amorphous exceptions, since I think them no more than unpredictable correctives to what is a fundamentally unsound rule. It is surprising, however, that the Court does not address these exceptions, since the context of the legislature's action gives some reason to believe they may be applicable.[87]

Because I believe that the Balanced Treatment Act had a secular purpose, which is all the first component of the Lemon test requires, I would reverse the judgment of the Court of Appeals and remand for further consideration. . . .

NOTES AND QUESTIONS

1. What role did "science" play in *Edwards*? Since the legal controversy over creation and evolution began in the 1920s, science has played an elusive role in it. Early statutes and court rulings dealt with religious objections to Darwinism rather than scientific claims for creationism. Even after the rise of creation-science, courts initially skirted those scientific claims. The *Daniel* court, for example, dispatched the 1973 Tennessee Creationism Statute on the grounds that it gave special treatment to biblical and occult accounts of origins without addressing the scientific claims of creationists. Also largely avoiding core issues of science, *Hendren* barred the public-school use of one particular creation-science textbook, *Biology: A Search for Order in Complexity*, because the book and its teaching manual were replete with explicit biblical references and religious explanations. Similarly, the statute at issue in

---

87. As the majority recognizes, Senator Keith sincerely believed that "secular humanism is a bona fide religion," 1 App. E–36; see also id., at E–418; 2 id., at E–499, and that "evolution is the cornerstone of that religion," 1 id., at E–418; see also id., at E–282; id., at E–312–E–313; id., at E–317; 2 id., at E–499. The Senator even told his colleagues that this Court had "held" that secular humanism was a religion. See 1 id., at E–36, id., at E–418; 2 id., at E–499. (In Torcaso v. Watkins, 367 U.S. 488, 495, n. 11 (1961), we did indeed refer to "Secular Humanism" as a "religio[n].") Senator Keith and his supporters raised the "religion" of secular humanism not, as the majority suggests, to explain the source of their "disdain for the theory of evolution," but to convince the legislature that the State of Louisiana was violating the Establishment Clause because its teachers were misrepresenting evolution as fact and depriving students of the information necessary to question that theory. 1 App. E–2–E–4 (Sen. Keith); id., at E–36–E–37, E–39 (Sen. Keith); id., at E–154–E–155 (Boudreaux paper); id., at E–281–E–282 (Sen. Keith); id., at E–317 (Sen. Keith); 2 id., at E–499–E–500 (Sen. Keith). The Senator repeatedly urged his colleagues to pass his bill to remedy this Establishment Clause violation by ensuring state neutrality in religious matters, see, e.g., 1 id., at E–36; id., at E–39; id., at E–313, surely a permissible purpose under Lemon. Senator Keith's argument may be questionable, but nothing in the statute or its legislative history gives us reason to doubt his sincerity or that of his supporters.

McLean–Arkansas's version of the Balanced-Treatment Act—contained a definition of creation-science clearly lifted from the Genesis account of creation, making it obvious that the statute's essential goal and necessary effect were to present evidence from nature in support of the biblical account. In all of these decisions, the court expelled creation-science from the public-school science curriculum on the basis that it was a religious doctrine without necessarily resolving its scientific merits. Over vigorous dissent, the majority on both the Fifth Circuit Court of Appeals and the Supreme Court effectively did the same in *Edwards*. By definition, those courts decreed, the doctrine of creation is a religious concept and therefore Louisiana violated the Establishment Clause by mandating balanced treatment for it in public-school science courses. "From the face of the statute, a purpose to advance a religious belief is apparent," Justice Brennan wrote for the majority in *Edwards*. In contrast, the dissenting judges on both the Fifth Circuit and Supreme Court wanted a trial on the scientific merits of creation-science to determine if teaching it in public schools would violate the Establishment Clause.

2.   Under the first and second prongs of the *Lemon* test, teaching religious material in public schools only violates the Establishment Clause if the motivating purpose or primary effect of doing so is to advance religion. The Louisiana Balanced–Treatment Act stated that it was "enacted for the purposes of protecting academic freedom." How does the *Edward* Court deal with the factual basis for this claim without a trial on its merits? Noting that the law expressly limits (rather than expands) the freedom of science teachers and constrains (rather than promotes) the effectiveness of science education, the Supreme Court dismissed the law's stated purpose as a sham. In his dissenting opinion, Justice Scalia countered that by "academic freedom" the legislators could have meant "students' freedom from indoctrination" on the issue of how life began. "The legislature did not care whether the topic of origins was taught," he suggested, "it simply wished to ensure that when the topic was taught, students would receive 'all of the evidence.' " If proven at trial, would this represent a valid secular legislative purpose for the statute?

3.   In arguing for a trial, the state relied heavily on the five affidavits from experts that it had submitted to the district court. The affidavits, never formally rebutted by the plaintiffs, provided the basis for the state's assertion that creation-science represented a scientific, non-religious alternative to the theory of evolution suitable for teaching in public schools. Observing that "the post-enactment testimony of outside experts is of little use in determining the Louisiana Legislature's purpose in enacting this statute," the Supreme Court ruled that these affidavits did not raise a genuine issue of material fact requiring a trial. In his dissent, Justice Scalia objected that, as "the only evidence in the record of the 'received meaning and acceptance' of 'creation science'," these uncontroverted affidavits presented a triable factual issue. When the state raised the issue of these affidavits during oral arguments, Justice O'Connor asked, "But couldn't we look at the record, and see if the [trial] court was right [to find the statute facially invalid without a trial]?" It was a rhetorical question that signaled the Court's course. The stature and credibility of the experts who submitted these affidavits may have limited their impact. Only two of the state's five experts were scientists: A junior chemistry professor at a small private college and a senior biology

professor at a state university who had gravitated toward creation-science in mid-life while studying theology and subsequently became embroiled in a widely publicized dispute over his inclusion of creationist concepts in undergraduate courses. When *Edwards* reached the Supreme Court, the National Academy of Sciences, 72 Nobel laureates, and professional associations representing virtually the entire American scientific community submitted friend-of-the-court briefs stating that creation-science was not a scientific concept. Should the Court have considered any of these "post-enactment" materials to determine the statute's essential purpose or principal effect? What weight should be given to expert affidavits submitted at trial versus *amici curiae* briefs from experts submitted to the appellate court? For her part, Justice O'Connor joined the concurring opinion written by Justice Lewis Powell that fleshed out the link between creation-science and the Institute for Creation Research, which he presented as a church-affiliated organization dedicated to Christian evangelism. For these notably pragmatic justices, this connection between ICR and creation-science cinched the constitutional case against the Louisiana statute.

4.   Two decades earlier, in explaining its reasons for striking down Arkansas's anti-evolution law, the Supreme Court in *Epperson* declared, "The law's effort was confined to an attempt to blot out a particular theory because of its supposed conflict with the Biblical account, literally read." This explanation all but invited creationists to offer their own religious or scientific theories of origins for inclusion in public-school science courses. The Supreme Court closed the door on this alternative in *Edward*, but what doors did it leave open? Some creationists would latch on to the Court's comment, "The Act does not grant teachers a flexibility that they did not already possess to supplant the present science curriculum with the presentation of theories, besides evolution, about the origin of life. Indeed, the Court of Appeals found that no law prohibited Louisiana public school teachers from teaching any scientific theory." To believers who see creation-science as scientific, which includes some public-school biology instructors, this passage suggested that individual teachers should be free to teach scientific evidence for creation or intelligent design in nature so long as the state did not mandate it. That issue would become the next battlefield in the ongoing legal controversy over teaching evolution.

CHAPTER 5

CREATIONIST TEXTBOOKS AND TEACHERS

■ ■ ■

I. EVOLUTIONARY TEXTBOOKS UNDER THE FREE EXERCISE CLAUSE

Although opposition to the teaching or truth of Darwinism unites a broad array of theologically and socially conservative or ultra-orthodox Christians, Moslems, and Jews, for many of them it is simply a part of a broad and often highly particularized critique of modernity. Some, like Institute of Creation Research founder Henry Morris, place an evolutionary world view at the heart of a satanic turn in Western civilization that inexorably led to such evils as secular humanism, atheism, agnosticism, communism, socialist, fascism, the sexual revolution, no-fault divorce, a breakdown of family values, and a disregard for human life exemplified for them in a range of activities from the holocaust to legalized abortion. Others, like Christian Reconstructionism leader R. J. Rushdoony, tend to see Darwinism as simply one of many damnable consequences of enlightenment thought that follows from placing human reason over revealed truth as found in scripture. In the context of public education, some anti-evolutionists are mostly concerned about reaching out to convert non-believers to their way of thinking while others are mostly concerned about protecting their own children from deviant ideas. The resulting litigation reflects this complex array of concerns and motivations.

One such case arose during the 1980s in the conservative, Republican, northeastern Tennessee town of Rogersville when a born-again Christian mother, Vicki Frost, objected to the use of a popular series of textbooks to teach critical reading skills to her children in the local public elementary schools. Frost had been meeting with local Christian women to discuss the role of popular books and television programs, like *The Diary of Anne Frank* and *Sesame Street*, in the decline of Christian family values. Then, in August 1983, her daughter Rebecca asked for help in answering questions about mental telepathy from a story, "A Visit from Mars," in the child's elementary-school reader, which was part of the *Basic Reading* series published by Holt, Rinehart and Winston. Frost, who viewed human use of mental telepathy as both a diabolical violation of God's exclusive domain over such powers and a vain attempt to overturn God's division of humanity by language barriers following the idolatrous effort to build the Tower of Babel, immediately feared that her children were being exposed to corrupting influences through the Holt readers. Her fears were confirmed when, on close inspection of the entire series, she found stories that seemed to encourage fantasy, imagination, environmentalism, globalism, humanism, evolutionary thought, and non-traditional roles for women.

Frost took her concerns to Hawkins County school administrators, who initially allowed her children to use alternative readers, and to the community, where some like-minded Christians rallied to her cause. She also contacted Mel Gabler, the long-time critic of Darwinian and anti-American influences in public-school textbooks, who sent her a scathing critique of the Holt readers, which he claimed were loaded with alien ideas and attitudes. In public meetings with school officials, Frost and her local allies now charged that the Holt readers promoted not only Darwinism and evolutionary thinking but also witchcraft and sorcery, feminism, idolatry, gun control, astrology, and Hinduism.

As tensions rose over the readers, Bob Mozart, the leader of a community group called Citizens Organized for Better Schools (COBS), entered the fray with an inflammatory series of letters to the editor of a local newspaper. In these letters, Mozart purported to expose the threat posed by the Holt readers to Christian family and patriotic values. As he presented it, a humanistic world view founded on evolutionism and rooted in secularism stood at the heart of the matter. Allowing dissenters to opt out of using the readers was not enough, Mozart asserted on behalf of COBS, the schools should not use them at all. At least for many Rogersville residents, however, Mozart went too far when he denounced the inclusion of such traditional stories as *Goldilocks* and *The Three Little Pigs* in the Holt readers on the grounds that those stories endorsed the disregard of private-property rights. As the community backlash built, Mozart increasingly inserted himself and COBS at center of the storm. When the national media pick-up the "Goldilocks" dispute late in 1983, Rogersville became a widely discussed battleground in the Reagan Era cultural wars that were then rocking American society.

After COBS not only demanded the removal of the Holt readers from the Hawkins County schools but also the addition of a daily moment of silence, mandatory pledge of allegiance, and a conservative dress code, school board members called Mozart's bluff. With moderate parents rallying to its side, the Board of Education decreed that all students would henceforth be required to use the Holt readers. Any exceptions would unduly burden the schools by disrupting the educational process, it concluded.

With the assistance of lawyers from the national religious advocacy group Concerned Women for America, Mozart, Frost, and some other local parents, students, and taxpayers filed suit in federal court claiming a free-exercise right for religious students to opt out of using the Holt readers.

People for the American Way, a well-funded national organization opposed to excessive religious interference in government, and the Tennessee Commissioner of Education backed the Hawkins County Board of Education in defending the authority of local school officials to determine the curriculum. After the district court initially granted the school district's motion for summary judgment, the Sixth Circuit Court of Appeals reversed and remanded the case for a trial on the merits of the plaintiffs' Free Exercise Clause claims. Following a lengthy trial, the district court held that, while the state had a compelling interest in education, the school district had unconstitutionally burdened the plaintiffs' free-exercise rights by mandating that all students use of the Holt readers. Parents with sincerely held religious objections must be permitted to meet state reading requirements through home schooling even if their children participate in the rest of the public-school curriculum, the district court ordered. The school district then appealed, leading to the following opinion by the Sixth Circuit Court of Appeals:

MOZERT v. HAWKINS CO. BD. OF EDUC.

United States Court of Appeals for the Sixth Circuit
827 F.2d 1058 (6th Cir. 1987)

LIVELY, CHIEF JUDGE: This case arose under the Free Exercise Clause of the First Amendment, made applicable to the states by the Fourteenth Amendment. The district court held that a public school requirement that all students in grades one through eight use a prescribed set of reading textbooks violated the constitutional rights of objecting parents and students. The district court entered an injunction which required the schools to excuse objecting students from participating in reading classes where the textbooks are used and awarded the plaintiff parents more than $50,000 damages.

I.

A.

Early in 1983 the Hawkins County, Tennessee, Board of Education adopted the Holt, Rinehart and Winston basic reading series (the Holt series) for use in grades 1–8 of the public schools of the county. In grades 1–4, reading is not taught as a separate subject at a designated time in the school day. Instead, the teachers in these grades use the reading texts throughout the day in conjunction with other subjects. In grades 5–8, reading is taught as a separate subject at a designated time in each class. However, the schools maintain an integrated curriculum which requires that ideas appearing in the reading programs reoccur in other courses. By statute public schools in Tennessee are required to include "character education" in their curricula. The purpose of this requirement is "to help each student develop positive values and to improve student conduct as students learn to act in harmony with their positive values and learn to become good citizens in their school, community, and society." Tennessee Code Annotated (TCA) 49–6–1007 (1986 Supp.).

Like many school systems, Hawkins County schools teach "critical reading" as opposed to reading exercises that teach only word and sound recognition. "Critical reading" requires the development of higher order cognitive skills that enable students to evaluate the material they read, to contrast the ideas presented, and to understand complex characters that appear in reading material. Plaintiffs do not dispute that critical reading is an essential skill which their children must develop in order to succeed in other subjects and to function as effective participants in modern society. Nor do the defendants dispute the fact that any reading book will do more than teach a child how to read, since reading is instrumental in a child's total development as an educated person.

The plaintiff Vicki Frost is the mother of four children, three of whom were students in Hawkins County public schools in 1983. At the beginning of the 1983–84 school year Mrs. Frost read a story in a daughter's sixth grade reader that involved mental telepathy. Mrs. Frost, who describes herself as a "born again Christian," has a religious objection to any teaching about mental telepathy. Reading further, she found additional themes in the reader to which she had religious objections. After discussing her objections with other parents, Mrs. Frost talked with the principal of Church Hill Middle School and obtained an agreement for an alternative reading program for students whose parents objected to the assigned Holt reader. The students who elected the alternative program left their classrooms during the reading sessions and worked on assignments from an older textbook series in available office or library areas. Other students in two elementary schools were excused from reading the Holt books.

B.

In November 1983 the Hawkins County School Board voted unanimously to eliminate all alternative reading programs and require every student in the public schools to attend classes using the Holt series. Thereafter the plaintiff students refused to read the Holt series or attend reading classes where the series was being used. The children of several of the plaintiffs were suspended for brief periods for this refusal. Most of the plaintiff students were ultimately taught at home, or attended religious schools, or transferred to public schools outside Hawkins County. One student returned to school because his family was unable to afford alternate schooling. Even after the board's order, two students were allowed some accommodation, in that the teacher either excused them from reading the Holt stories, or specifically noted on worksheets that the student was not required to believe the stories.

On December 2, 1983, the plaintiffs, consisting of seven families—14 parents and 17 children—filed this action pursuant to 42 U.S.C. § 1983. In their complaint the plaintiffs asserted that they have sincere religious beliefs which are contrary to the values taught or inculcated by the reading textbooks and that it is a violation of the religious beliefs and convictions of the plaintiff students to be required to read the books and a violation of the religious beliefs of the plaintiff parents to permit their children to read the books. The plaintiffs sought to hold the defendants liable because "forcing the student-plaintiffs to read school books which teach or inculcate values in violation of their religious beliefs and convictions is a clear violation of their rights to the free exercise of religion protected by the First and Fourteenth Amendments to the United States Constitution."

C.

The defendants filed a motion to dismiss or, in the alternative, for summary judgment. The district court granted the defendants' motion for summary judgment, concluding that although passages in the reading textbooks might offend sincere religious beliefs of the plaintiffs, the books appeared neutral on the subject of religion and did not violate the plaintiffs' constitutional rights. Mozert v. Hawkins County Public Schools, 582 F.Supp. 201 (E.D.Tenn.1984). On appeal this court reversed and remanded for further proceedings. Mozert v. Hawkins County Public Schools, 765 F.2d 75 (6th Cir.1985). This court concluded that summary judgment was improper because issues of material fact were present. This conclusion was based largely on the fact that the defendants had filed an answer in which they put in issue, either denying categorically, or for lack of information, many of the allegations of the complaint including the basic issues of the sincerity of the plaintiffs' religious beliefs and the burden that use of the Holt series placed upon those beliefs. In remanding, this court stated, "The court expresses no opinion on the merits of the plaintiffs' claims or those of the defendants as we have considered only the procedural posture of the case under Rule 56, Federal Rules of Civil Procedure." Id. at 79.

II.

A.

Following remand the Commissioner of Education of the State of Tennessee was permitted to intervene as a defendant. At a pretrial hearing the parties made certain stipulations. Counsel for the defendants stipulated that the plaintiffs' religious beliefs are sincere and that certain passages in the reading texts offend those beliefs. However, counsel steadfastly refused to stipulate that the fact that the plaintiffs found the passages offensive made the reading requirement a burden on the plaintiffs' constitutional right to the free exercise of their religion. Similarly, counsel for the plaintiffs stipulated that there was a compelling state interest for the defendants to provide a public education to the children of Hawkins County. However, counsel stipulated only to a narrow definition of the compelling state interest—one that did not involve the exclusive use of a uniform series of textbooks. These stipulations left for trial the issues of whether the plaintiffs could show a burden on their free exercise right, in a constitutional sense, and whether the defendants could show a compelling interest in requiring all students in grades 1–8 of the Hawkins County public schools to use the Holt, Rinehart and Winston basal reading textbooks. These were questions of law to be determined on the basis of evidence produced at trial.

The parties also agreed to a bifurcated trial. The court would conduct a bench trial and if an unconstitutional burden were found and no compelling state interest required judgment for the defendants, a separate jury trial would be held to set damages. The parties subsequently entered a joint waiver of the right to trial by jury, and the district court assessed damages and entered judgment accordingly.

B.

Vicki Frost was the first witness for the plaintiffs and she presented the most complete explanation of the plaintiffs' position. The plaintiffs do not belong to a single church or denomination, but all consider themselves born again Christians. Mrs. Frost testified that the word of God as found in the Christian Bible "is the totality of my beliefs." There was evidence that other members of their churches, and even their pastors, do not agree with their position in this case.

Mrs. Frost testified that she had spent more than 200 hours reviewing the Holt series and had found numerous passages that offended her religious beliefs. She stated that the offending materials fell into seventeen categories which she listed. These ranged from such familiar concerns of fundamentalist Christians as evolution and "secular humanism" to less familiar themes such as "futuristic supernaturalism," pacifism, magic and false views of death.

In her lengthy testimony Mrs. Frost identified passages from stories and poems used in the Holt series that fell into each category. Illustrative is her first category, futuristic supernaturalism, which she defined as teaching "Man As God." Passages that she found offensive described Leonardo da Vinci as the human with a creative mind that "came closest to the divine touch." Similarly, she felt that a passage entitled "Seeing Beneath the Surface" related to an occult theme, by describing the use of imagination as a vehicle for seeing things not discernible through our physical eyes. She interpreted a poem, "Look at Anything," as presenting the idea that by using imagination a child can become part of anything and thus understand it better. Mrs. Frost testified that it is an "occult practice" for children to use imagination beyond the limitation of scriptural authority. She testified that the story that alerted her to the problem with the reading series fell into the category of futuristic supernaturalism. Entitled "A Visit to Mars," the story portrays thought transfer and telepathy in such a way that "it could be considered a scientific concept," according to this witness. This theme appears in the testimony of several witnesses, i.e., the materials objected to "could" be interpreted in a manner repugnant to their religious beliefs.

Mrs. Frost described objectionable passages from other categories in much the same way. Describing evolution as a teaching that there is no God, she identified 24 passages that she considered to have evolution as a theme. She admitted that the textbooks contained a disclaimer that evolution is a theory, not a proven scientific fact. Nevertheless, she felt that references to evolution were so pervasive and presented in such a factual manner as to render the disclaimer meaningless. After describing her objection to passages that encourage children to make moral judgments about whether it is right or wrong to kill animals, the witness stated, "I thought they would be learning to read, to have good English and grammar, and to be able to do other subject work." Asked by plaintiffs' attorney to define her objection to the text books, Mrs. Frost replied:

> Very basically, I object to the Holt, Rhinehart [sic] Winston series as a whole, what the message is as a whole. There are some contents which are objectionable by themselves, but my most withstanding [sic] objection would be to the series as a whole.

Another witness for the plaintiffs was Bob Mozert, father of a middle school and an elementary school student in the Hawkins County system. His testimony echoed that of Vicki Frost in large part, though his answers to questions tended to be much less expansive. He also found objectionable passages in the readers that dealt with magic, role reversal or role elimination, particularly biographical material about women who have been recognized for achievements outside their homes, and emphasis on one world or a planetary society. Both witnesses testified under cross-examination that the plaintiff parents objected to passages that expose their children to other forms of religion and to the feelings, attitudes and values of other students that contradict the plaintiffs' religious views without a statement that the other views are incorrect and that the plaintiffs' views are the correct ones.

C.

The district court held that the plaintiffs' free exercise rights have been burdened because their "religious beliefs compel them to refrain from exposure to the Holt series," and the defendant school board "has effectively required that the student plaintiffs either read the offensive texts or give up their free public education." Mozert v. Hawkins County Public Schools, 647 F.Supp. 1194, 1200 (E.D.Tenn.1986) (emphasis added). In reaching this conclusion the district court analogized the plaintiffs' position to that of a sabbatarian who was denied unemployment compensation benefits for refusing to work on Saturdays, Sherbert v. Verner, 374 U.S. 398 (1963), a Jehovah's Witness who was denied unemployment compensation benefits after quitting a job that required him to work on military tanks, Thomas v. Review Board, 450 U.S. 707 (1981), and a conscientious objector who refused to participate in ROTC training, Spence v. Bailey, 465 F.2d 797 (6th Cir.1972).

The district court went on to find that the state had a compelling interest "in the education of its young," 647 F.Supp. at 1200, but that it had erred in choosing "to further its legitimate and overriding interest in public education by mandating the use of a single basic reading series," id. at 1201, in the face of the plaintiffs' religious objections. The court concluded that the proof at trial demonstrated that the defendants could accommodate the plaintiffs without material and substantial disruption to the educational process by permitting the objecting students to "opt out of the school district's reading program," id. at 1203, and meet the reading requirements by home schooling. Tennessee's school attendance statute requires parents to cause their children between the ages of 7 and 16 to attend either a public or non-public school. "Non-public school" is defined to mean "a church-related school, a private school or a home school." TCA 49–6–3001. Although the statute appears to contemplate that a student will attend one or the other of the three approved types of school, the district court apparently believed that a partial opt-out would be consistent with the statutory scheme.

The court entered an injunction prohibiting the defendants "from requiring the student-plaintiffs to read from the Holt series," and ordering the defendants to excuse the student plaintiffs from their classrooms "[d]uring the normal reading period" and to provide them with suitable space in the library or elsewhere for a study hall. 647 F.Supp. at 1203. The Court also dismissed the individual school board members as defendants on qualified immunity grounds and ordered a hearing on damages against the Hawkins County Board of Education. Id. at 1204. This hearing was held on December 15, 1983, following which the court awarded damages to the plaintiffs in the total amount of $51,531, largely to reimburse the plaintiff families for the costs of sending their children to alternate schools and the costs of pursuing this lawsuit.

III.

A.

The first question to be decided is whether a governmental requirement that a person be exposed to ideas he or she finds objectionable on religious grounds constitutes a burden on the free exercise of that person's religion as forbidden by the First Amendment. This is precisely the way the superintendent of the Hawkins County schools framed the issue in an affidavit filed early in this litigation. In his affidavit the superintendent set forth the school system's interest in a uniformity of reading texts. The affidavit also countered the claims of the plaintiffs that the schools were inculcating values and religious doctrines contrary to their religious beliefs, stating: "Without expressing an opinion as to the plaintiffs' religious beliefs, I am of the opinion that plaintiffs misunderstand the fact that exposure to something does not constitute teaching, indoctrination, opposition or promotion of the things exposed. While it is true that these textbooks expose the student to varying values and religious backgrounds, neither the textbooks nor the teachers teach, indoctrinate, oppose or promote any particular value or religion." That the district court accepted the issue as thus framed is clear from its reference to "exposure to the Holt series."

It is also clear that exposure to objectionable material is what the plaintiffs objected to albeit they emphasize the repeated nature of the exposure. The complaint mentioned only the textbooks that the students were required to read. It did not seek relief from any method of teaching the material and did not mention the teachers' editions. The plaintiffs did not produce a single student or teacher to testify that any student was ever required to affirm his or her belief or disbelief in any idea or practice mentioned in the various stories and passages contained in the Holt series. However, the plaintiffs appeared to assume that materials clearly presented as poetry, fiction and even "make-believe" in the Holt series were presented as facts which the students were required to believe. Nothing in the record supports this assumption.

At numerous places in her testimony Vicki Frost referred to various exercises and suggestions in the teachers' manuals as support for her view that objectionable ideas were being inculcated as truth rather than being offered as examples of the variety of approaches possible to a particular question. However, the students were not required to read the teachers' materials. While these materials suggested various ways of presenting the lessons, including "acting out" and round table discussions, there was no proof that any plaintiff student was ever called upon to say or do anything that required the student to affirm or deny a religious belief or to engage or refrain from engaging in any act either required or forbidden by the student's religious convictions. Mrs. Frost seemed to assume that each teacher used every suggested exercise or teaching tool in the teachers' editions. There was evidence that reading aloud and acting out the themes encountered in school lessons help young people learn. One of the teachers stated that students read some of the stories aloud. Proof that an objecting student was required to participate beyond reading and discussing assigned materials, or was disciplined for disputing assigned materials, might well implicate the Free Exercise Clause because the element of compulsion would then be present. But this was not the case either as pled or proved. The record leaves no doubt that the district court correctly viewed this case as one involving exposure to repugnant ideas and themes as presented by the Holt series.

Vicki Frost testified that an occasional reference to role reversal, pacifism, rebellion against parents, one-world government and other objectionable concepts would be acceptable, but she felt it was the repeated references to such subjects that created the burden. The district court suggested that it was a matter of balance, id. at 1199, apparently believing that a reading series that presented ideas with which the plaintiffs agree in juxtaposition to those with which they disagree would pass constitutional muster. While balanced textbooks are certainly desirable, there would be serious difficulties with trying to cure the omissions in the Holt series, as plaintiffs and their expert witnesses view the texts.

However, the plaintiffs' own testimony casts serious doubt on their claim that a more balanced presentation would satisfy their religious views. Mrs. Frost testified that it would be acceptable for the schools to teach her children about other philosophies and religions, but if the practices of other religions were described in detail, or if the philosophy was "profound" in that it expressed a world view that deeply undermined her religious beliefs, then her children "would have to be instructed to [the] error [of the other philosophy]." It is clear that to the plaintiffs there is but one acceptable view—the Biblical view, as they interpret the Bible. Furthermore, the plaintiffs view every human situation and decision, whether related to personal belief and conduct or to public policy and programs, from a theological or religious perspective. Mrs. Frost testified that many political issues have theological roots and that there would be "no way" certain themes could be presented without violating her religious beliefs. She identified such themes as evolution, false supernaturalism, feminism, telepathy and magic as matters that could not be presented in any way without offending her beliefs. The only way to avoid conflict with the plaintiffs' beliefs in these sensitive areas would be to eliminate all references to the subjects so identified. However, the Supreme Court has clearly held that it violates the Establishment Clause to tailor a public school's curriculum to satisfy the principles or prohibitions of any religion. Epperson v. Arkansas, 393 U.S. 97, 106 (1968).

The testimony of the plaintiffs' expert witness, Dr. Vitz, illustrates the pitfalls of trying to achieve a balance of materials concerning religion in a reading course. He found "markedly little reference to religion, particularly Christianity, and also remarkably little to Judaism" in the Holt series. His solution would be to "beef up" the references to these two dominant religions in the United States. However, an adherent to a less widely professed religion might then object to the slighting of his or her faith. Balance in the treatment of religion lies in the eye of the beholder. Efforts to achieve the particular "balance" desired by any individual or group by the addition or deletion of religious material would lead to a forbidden entanglement of the public schools in religious matters, if done with the purpose or primary effect of advancing or inhibiting religion. Epperson, 393 U.S. at 107; Abington School District v. Schempp, 374 U.S. 203 at 222 (1963)....

E.

At oral argument plaintiffs' counsel identified Grove v. Mead School Dist. No. 354, 753 F.2d 1528 (9th Cir.1985), cert. denied, 474 U.S. 826 (1985), as a decision which strongly supports the plaintiffs' position. In Grove a student and her mother objected to being required to read one book assigned in an English literature class. The student was permitted to read a different book and to leave the classroom during discussion of the book she found offensive; however, she chose to remain during the discussion. The mother brought suit to require the school board to remove the book from the required reading list based on her religious objections to its content. The court of appeals affirmed summary judgment for the school board. In a concurring opinion Judge Canby wrote that plaintiffs' allegation that they believe that "eternal religious consequences" would result to the parents and children from exposure to the offending book "would probably be sufficient to present a free exercise question" if the student had been required to read the book or remain in the classroom while it was being discussed. Id. at 1541–42 (emphasis added). This observation in dicta must be considered in context. The court of appeals in Grove was considering a case where summary judgment had been granted, much as this court considered the present case on the first appeal. Judge Canby did not state that the plaintiff had established a case of burden on the free exercise of religion; he stated only that if she had been required to read the book and remain in class she "probably" would have presented a free exercise question.

While relying on this somewhat speculative observation, the plaintiffs failed to note other positive statements in the same concurring opinion that, while addressing a different issue, are at odds with their theories:

> Were the free exercise clause violated whenever governmental activity is offensive to or at variance with sincerely held religious precepts, virtually no governmental program would be constitutionally possible.

Id. at 1542.

The lesson is clear: governmental actions that merely offend or cast doubt on religious beliefs do not on that account violate free exercise. An actual burden on the profession or exercise of religion is required.

> In short, distinctions must be drawn between those governmental actions that actually interfere with the exercise of religion, and those that merely require or result in exposure to attitudes and outlooks at odds with perspectives prompted by religion.

Id. at 1543. These statements echo similar ones in the majority opinion, e.g.,

> To establish a violation of that clause [Free Exercise], a litigant must show that challenged state action has a coercive effect that operates against a litigant's practice of his or her religion.

Id. at 1533.

IV.

A.

The Supreme Court has recently affirmed that public schools serve the purpose of teaching fundamental values "essential to a democratic society." These values "include tolerance of divergent political and religious views" while taking into account "consideration of the sensibilities of others." Bethel School Dist. No. 403 v. Fraser, 478 U.S. 675 (1986). The Court has noted with apparent approval the view of some educators who see public schools as an "assimilative force" that brings together "diverse and conflicting elements" in our society "on a broad but common ground." Ambach v. Norwick, 441 U.S. 68, 77 (1979), citing works of J. Dewey, N. Edwards and H. Richey. The critical reading approach furthers these goals. Mrs. Frost stated specifically that she objected to stories that develop "a religious tolerance that all religions are merely different roads to God." Stating that the plaintiffs reject this concept, presented as a recipe for an ideal world citizen, Mrs. Frost said, "We cannot be tolerant in that we accept other religious views on an equal basis with ours." While probably not an uncommon view of true believers in any religion, this statement graphically illustrates what is lacking in the plaintiffs' case.

The "tolerance of divergent . . . religious views" referred to by the Supreme Court is a civil tolerance, not a religious one. It does not require a person to accept any other religion as the equal of the one to which that person adheres. It merely requires a recognition that in a pluralistic society we must "live and let live." If the Hawkins County schools had required the plaintiff students either to believe or say they believe that "all religions are merely different roads to God," this would be a different case. No instrument of government can, consistent with the Free Exercise Clause, require such a belief or affirmation. However, there was absolutely no showing that the defendant school board sought to do this; indeed, the school board agreed at oral argument that it could not constitutionally do so. Instead, the record in this case discloses an effort by the school board to offer a reading curriculum designed to acquaint students with a multitude of ideas and concepts, though not in proportions the plaintiffs would like. While many of the passages deal with ethical issues, on the surface at least, they appear to us to contain no religious or anti-religious messages. Because the plaintiffs perceive every teaching that goes beyond the "three Rs" as inculcating religious ideas, they admit that any value-laden reading curriculum that did not affirm the truth of their beliefs would offend their religious convictions.

Although it is not clear that the plaintiffs object to all critical reading, Mrs. Frost did testify that she did not want her children to make critical judgments and exercise choices in areas where the Bible provides the answer. There is no evidence that any child in the Hawkins County schools was required to make such judgments. It was a goal of the school system to encourage this exercise, but nowhere was it shown that it was required. When asked to comment on a reading assignment, a student would be free to give the Biblical interpretation of the material or to interpret it from a different value base. The only conduct compelled by the defendants was reading and discussing the material in the Holt series, and hearing other students' interpretations of those materials. This is the exposure to which the plaintiffs objected. What is absent from this case is the critical element of compulsion to affirm or deny a religious belief or to engage or refrain from engaging in a practice forbidden or required in the exercise of a plaintiff's religion.

B.

In McCollum v. Board of Education, 333 U.S. 203 (1948), the Supreme Court held invalid a practice which permitted weekly religious instruction for consenting pupils in public school classrooms. Those students who did not choose to participate were required to leave their regular classrooms and go to another part of the school building to continue their secular studies. Although McCollum involved the Establishment Clause, the several opinions discussed both religion clauses at some length. In his concurring opinion Justice Jackson emphasized that some compulsion to perform a religiously prohibited ritual or make a religiously prohibited affirmation is essential to a claim of infringement of the free exercise rights of students in public schools. Noting the large number of separate religious bodies existing in the United States, he wrote:

> If we are to eliminate everything that is objectionable to any of these warring sects or inconsistent with any of their doctrines, we will leave public education in shreds. Nothing but educational confusion and a discrediting of the public school system can result from subjecting it to constant law suits.

Id. at 235. The fact that schools might be subjected to constant law suits is certainly not determinative. However, the Supreme Court has cautioned that "[j]udicial interposition in the operation of the public school system of the Nation raises problems requiring care and restraint." Epperson, 393 U.S. at 104. When asked to "interpose," courts must examine the record very carefully to make certain that a constitutional violation has occurred before they order changes in an educational program adopted by duly chosen local authorities.

Quite recently the Supreme Court quoted Justice Douglas, concurring in Sherbert v. Verner, 374 U.S. at 412, as follows:

> [T]he Free Exercise Clause is written in terms of what the government cannot do to the individual, not in terms of what the individual can extract from the government.

Bowen v. Roy, 476 U.S. 693 (1986). Paraphrasing this thought, the Court wrote:

> The Free Exercise Clause affords an individual protection from certain forms of governmental compulsion; it does not afford an individual a right to dictate the conduct of the Government's internal procedures.

Id. Since we have found none of the prohibited forms of governmental compulsion in this case, we conclude that the plaintiffs failed to establish the existence of an unconstitutional burden. Having determined that no burden was shown, we do not reach the issue of the defendants' compelling interest in requiring a uniform reading series or the question, raised by the defendant, of whether awarding damages violated the Establishment Clause.

Judge Boggs concludes that the majority reverses the district court because it found the plaintiffs' claims of First Amendment protection so extreme as obviously to violate the Establishment Clause. This is not the holding of the majority. We do point out that under certain circumstances the plaintiffs, by their own testimony, would only accept accommodations that would violate the Establishment Clause. However, this is not the holding. What we do hold is that the requirement that public school students study a basal reader series chosen by the school authorities does not create an unconstitutional burden under the Free Exercise Clause when the students are not required to affirm or deny a belief or engage or refrain from engaging in a practice prohibited or required by their religion. There was no evidence that the conduct required of the students was forbidden by their religion. Rather, the witnesses testified that reading the Holt series "could" or "might" lead the students to come to conclusions that were contrary to teachings of their and their parents' religious beliefs. This is not sufficient to establish an unconstitutional burden.

Judge Boggs also implies that the majority distorts the record and decides the case on a basis different from that upon which the plaintiffs proceeded. This would be a valid criticism if we were reviewing a judgment on the pleadings. However, as Judge Boggs notes, this case was decided following a full trial. The plaintiffs did not confine themselves to the language of their complaint, but testified expansively with respect to the claims and issues before the court. We have decided the case that was actually tried, as permitted by Rule 15(b), Fed.R.Civ.P.

The judgment of the district court granting injunctive relief and damages is reversed, and the case is remanded with directions to dismiss the complaint. No costs are allowed. The parties will bear their own costs on appeal.

KENNEDY, CIRCUIT JUDGE, concurring; I agree with Chief Judge Lively's analysis and concur in his opinion. However, even if I were to conclude that requiring the use of the Holt series or another similar series constituted a burden on appellees' free exercise rights, I would find the burden justified by a compelling state interest. . . .

In Bethel School Dist. No. 403 v. Fraser, 478 U.S. 675 (1986), the Supreme Court stated: "The role and purpose of the American public school system was well described by two historians, saying 'public education must prepare pupils for citizenship in the Republic.'" Additionally, the Bethel School Court stated that the state through its public schools must "inculcate the habits and manners of civility as values in themselves conducive to happiness and as indispensable to the practice of self-government in the community and the nation." Id. (quoting C. Beard & M. Beard, New Basic History of the United States 228 (1968)). Teaching students about complex and controversial social and moral issues is just as essential for preparing public school students for citizenship and self-government as inculcating in the students the habits and manners of civility.

The evidence at trial demonstrated that mandatory participation in reading classes using the Holt series or some similar readers is essential to accomplish this compelling interest and that this interest could not be achieved any other way. Several witnesses for appellants testified that in order to develop critical reading skills, and therefore achieve appellants' objectives, the students must read and discuss complex, morally and socially difficult issues. Many of these necessarily will be subjects on which appellees believe the Bible states the rule or correct position. Consequently, accommodating appellees' beliefs would unduly interfere with the fulfillment of the appellants' objectives. Cf. United States v. Lee, 455 U.S. 252, 260 (1982). Additionally, mandatory participation in the reading program is the least restrictive means of achieving appellants' objectives. Appellees' objections would arise even if the School Board selected another basal reading textbook series since the students would be required to engage in critical reading and form their own opinions and judgments on many of the same issues. . . .

BOGGS, CIRCUIT JUDGE, concurring: I concur with my colleagues that Hawkins County is not required by the Constitution to allow plaintiffs the latitude they seek in the educational program of these children. However, I reach that result on a somewhat different view of the facts and governing principles here. It seems that the court's opinion rests first on the view that plaintiffs' objection is to any exposure to contrary ideas, and that no one's religious exercise can be burdened simply by compelled exposure. Second, the opinion rests on the view that no burden can exist here because plaintiffs were not compelled to engage in any conduct prohibited by, or refrain from any practice required by, their religious beliefs.

I do not believe these attempted distinctions will survive analysis. If the situation of these children is not a burden on their religious exercise, it must be because of a principle applicable to all religious objectors to public school curricula. Thus, I believe a deeper issue is present here, is implicitly decided in the court's opinion, and should be addressed openly. The school board recognizes no limitation on its power to require any curriculum, no matter how offensive or one-sided, and to expel those who will not study it, so long as it does not violate the Establishment Clause. Our opinion today confirms that right, and I would like to make plain my reasons for taking that position. . . .

II

Returning to the treatment of plaintiffs' free exercise claim, I believe this is a more difficult case than outlined in the court's opinion. I disagree with the first proposition in the court's opinion, that plaintiffs object to any exposure to any contrary idea. I do not believe we can define for plaintiffs their belief as to what is religiously forbidden to be so comprehensive, where both they and the district court have spoken to the contrary. A reasonable reading of plaintiffs' testimony shows they object to the overall effect of the Holt series, not simply to any exposure to any idea opposing theirs. The district court specifically found that the objection was to exposure to the Holt series, not to any single story or idea. 647 F.Supp. at 1199.

Ultimately, I think we must address plaintiffs' claims as they actually impact their lives: it is their belief that they should not take a course of study which, on balance, to them, denigrates and opposes their religion, and which the state is compelling them to take on pain of forfeiting all other benefits of public education.

Their view may seem silly or wrong-headed to some, but it is a sincerely held religious belief. By focussing narrowly on references that make plaintiffs appear so extreme that they could never be accommodated, the court simply leaves resolution of the underlying issues here to another case, when we have plaintiffs with a more sophisticated understanding of our own and Supreme Court precedent, and a more careful and articulate presentation of their own beliefs.

Under the court's assessment of the facts, this is a most uninteresting case. It is not the test case sought, or feared, by either side. The court reviews the record and finds that the plaintiffs actually want a school system that affirmatively teaches the correctness of their religion, and prevents other students from mentioning contrary ideas. If that is indeed the case, then it can be very simply resolved. It would obviously violate the Establishment Clause for any school system to agree with such an extravagant view. . . .

Similarly, plaintiffs may "want" a school system tailored exactly to their religious beliefs (that is why many people choose religious education), but they very well know that that is constitutionally impermissible. They "want" a particular type of accommodation that they have sought in this law suit, and they believe that they are constitutionally entitled to that. Judge Hull, who sat through eight days of trial testimony over these very issues, came to the same conclusion I do, expressed it in the form of a finding, and should not be overturned unless that finding is clearly erroneous. In my reading of the testimony, the judge's finding is not only not clearly erroneous, but it can only be reversed by a failure to recognize a distinction between the ideal education the parents want, and that level of accommodation and education which they believe is constitutionally required and which they "want" here. Thus, I believe we must take plaintiffs' claims as they have stated them—that they desire the accommodation of an opt-out, or alternative reading books, and no more. That is all they have ever asked for in their pleadings, in the arguments at trial and in appellate briefing and argument.

III

I also disagree with the court's view that there can be no burden here because there is no requirement of conduct contrary to religious belief. That view both slights plaintiffs' honest beliefs that studying the full Holt series would be conduct contrary to their religion, and overlooks other Supreme Court Free Exercise cases which view "conduct" that may offend religious exercise at least as broadly as do plaintiffs. . . .

Here, plaintiffs have drawn their line as to what required school activities, what courses of study, do and do not offend their beliefs to the point of prohibition. I would hold that if they are forced over that line, they are "engaging in conduct" forbidden by their religion. The court's excellent summary of its holding on this point, appears to concede that what plaintiffs were doing in school was conduct, but that there "was no evidence that the conduct required of the students was forbidden by their religion." I cannot agree. The plaintiffs provided voluminous testimony of the conflict (in their view) between reading the Holt readers and their religious beliefs, including extensive Scriptural references. The district court found that "plaintiffs' religious beliefs compel them to refrain from exposure to the Holt series." 647 F.Supp. at 1200. I would think it could hardly be clearer that they believe their religion commands, not merely suggests, their course of action. . . .

V

Thus, I believe the plaintiffs' objection is to the Holt series as a whole, and that being forced to study the books is "conduct" contrary to their beliefs. In the absence of a narrower basis that can withstand scrutiny, we must address the hard issues presented by this case: (1) whether compelling this conduct forbidden by plaintiffs' beliefs places a burden on their free exercise of their religion, in the sense of earlier Supreme Court holdings; and (2) whether within the context of the public schools, teaching material which offends a person's religious beliefs, but does not violate the Establishment Clause, can be a burden on free exercise.

Determining whether the school board's action places a substantial burden on the plaintiff's free exercise of their religion requires a determination of the scope of the religious beliefs or practices protected by the Free Exercise Clause. Although the Supreme Court has shied away from attempting to define religion, the past forty years has witnessed an expansion of the court's understanding of religious belief. The concept of religion has shifted from a fairly narrow traditional theism, Davis v. Beason, 133 U.S. 333, 342 (1890); United States v. Macintosh, 283 U.S. 605, 633–34 (1931) (Hughes, C.J., dissenting), overruled, Girouard v. United States, 328 U.S. 61 (1946), to a broader concept providing protection for the views of unorthodox and nontheistic faiths, West Virginia State Board of Education v. Barnette, 319 U.S. 624, 658–59 (1943); Torcaso v. Watkins, 367 U.S. 488, 495 (1961); United States v. Seeger, 380 U.S. 163, 166 (1965); Welsh v. United States, 398 U.S. 333 (1970). This expanded definition has been praised by many commentators, who argue for a definition of religion in the Free Exercise Clause that would protect practices based on an individual's belief system involving matters of ultimate concern, Note, Toward a Constitutional Definition of Religion, 91 Harv.L.Rev. 1056, 1072–75 (1978). Others support an interpretation which would provide protection for all beliefs that are "arguably religious." L. Tribe, American Constitutional Law § 14–6, at 828 (1978). The plaintiffs here have no problem fitting within any of the Court's various definitions of religion, as no one contends that their basic beliefs are not religious.

However, determining that plaintiffs' beliefs are religious does not automatically mean that all practices or observances springing from those beliefs are entitled to the same amount of protection under the Free Exercise Clause. At one point, the Court made a distinction between religious beliefs and actions, indicating that the government could never interfere with belief or opinion, but could always regulate practices. United States v. Reynolds, 98 U.S. (8 Otto) 145, 166 (1878). This distinction did not hold, as the Court has provided protection for such religious conduct as soliciting contributions, Cantwell v. Connecticut, 310 U.S. 296 (1940), and of course, observing one's chosen Sabbath, Sherbert v. Verner, 374 U.S. 398 (1963), or refusing to work on armaments, Thomas v. Review Board, 450 U.S. 707 (1981).

There remains the question of which religious conduct may not be burdened (and thus must be accommodated unless a compelling interest justifies it), by government action. One theory would draw the line between actions that are compelled or dictated by religious belief and those that are merely motivated or influenced by these beliefs. "Not all actions are necessarily required (duties) or forbidden (sins); religion addresses what is 'better' as well as what is 'good.'" M. McConnell, Accommodation of Religion, [1985] S.Ct.Rev. 1, 27 (discussing permissive rather than mandatory accommodation).

The most expansive view of the Free Exercise Clause would be to scrutinize any governmental burden on any activity that is arguably religious and require a balancing test between the government's interest and the burden on the activity. However, the Supreme Court has never gone so far, especially in the context of the public schools. The court has continued to struggle with the questions of which religious actions are protected and how significant the burden on that activity must be in order to trigger the strict scrutiny of the Free Exercise Clause. Wisconsin v. Yoder, 406 U.S. 205 (1972), held that the state's compulsory schooling requirement unduly burdened the free exercise of the religious beliefs of the Old Order Amish. The Court stressed that the Amish mode of life was "essential," "fundamental," and "central" to their religious beliefs and that their religious community would be gravely endangered if not destroyed by the state requirement. Id. at 218–19. While Yoder did not rest on Sherbert v. Verner, 374 U.S. 398 (1963), and was decided before Thomas, its language is considerably less expansive as to the exercise that should not be burdened than are those cases.

For me, the key fact is that the Court has almost never interfered with the prerogative of school boards to set curricula, based on free exercise claims. West Virginia State Board of Education v. Barnette, 319 U.S. 624 (1943), may be the only case, and even there a specific affirmation was required, implicating a non-religious First Amendment basis, as well.

From a common sense view of the word "burden," Sherbert and Thomas are very strong cases for plaintiffs. In any sensible meaning of a burden, the burden in our case is greater than in Thomas or Sherbert. Both of these cases involved workers who wanted unemployment compensation because they gave up jobs based on their religious beliefs. Their actual losses that the Court made good, the actual burden that the Court lifted, was one or two thousand dollars at most. Although this amount of money was certainly important to them, the Court did not give them their jobs back. The Court did not guarantee they would get any future job. It only provided them access to a sum of money equally with those who quit work for other "good cause" reasons.

Here, the burden is many years of education, being required to study books that, in plaintiffs' view, systematically undervalue, contradict and ignore their religion. I trust it is not simply because I am chronologically somewhat closer than my colleagues to the status of the students involved here that I interpret the choice forced upon the plaintiffs here as a "burden."

VI

However, constitutional adjudication, especially for a lower court, is not simply a matter of common sense use of words. We must determine whether the common sense burden on plaintiffs' religious belief is, in the context of a public school curriculum, a constitutional "burden" on their religious beliefs.

I do not support an extension by this court of the principles of Sherbert and Thomas to cover this case, even though there is a much stronger economic compulsion exercised by public schooling than by any unemployment compensation system. I think the constitutional basis for those cases is sufficiently thin that they should not be extended blindly. The exercise there was of a narrow sort, and did not explicitly implicate the purposes or methods of the program itself.

Running a public school system of today's magnitude is quite a different proposition. A constitutional challenge to the content of instruction (as opposed to participation in ritual such as magic chants, or prayers) is a challenge to the notion of a politically-controlled school system. Imposing on school boards the delicate task of satisfying the "compelling interest" test to justify failure to accommodate pupils is a significant step. It is a substantial imposition on the schools to require them to justify each instance of not dealing with students' individual, religiously compelled, objections (as opposed to permitting a local, rough and ready, adjustment), and I do not see that the Supreme Court has authorized us to make such a requirement.

Our interpretation of these key phrases of our Bill of Rights in the school context is certainly complicated by the fact that the drafters of the Bill of Rights never contemplated a school system that would be the most pervasive benefit of citizenship for many, yet which would be very difficult to avoid. See, e.g., Jernigan v. State, 412 So.2d 1242 (Ala.1982), for the criminal conviction of Catholic parents who lived too far from a Catholic school, and thus did not send their child to school.

The average public expenditure for a pupil in Hawkins County is about 20% of the income of the average household there. Even the modest tuition in the religious schools which some plaintiffs attended here amounted to about a doubling of the state and local tax burden of the average resident. Had the Founders recognized the possibility of state intervention of this magnitude, they might have written differently. However, it is difficult for me to see that the words "free exercise of religion," at the adoption of the Bill of Rights, implied a freedom from state teaching, even of offensive material, when some alternative was legally permissible.

Therefore, I reluctantly conclude that under the Supreme Court's decisions as we have them, school boards may set curricula bounded only by the Establishment Clause, as the state contends. Thus, contrary to the analogy plaintiffs suggest, pupils may indeed be expelled if they will not read from the King James Bible, so long as it is only used as literature, and not taught as religious truth. See Abington School Dist. v. Schempp, 374 U.S. 203, 224–25 (1963); Donahoe v. Richards, 38 Me. 379 (1854). Contrary to the position of amicus American Jewish Committee, Jewish students may not assert a burden on their religion if their reading materials overwhelmingly provide a negative view of Jews or factual or historical issues important to Jews, so long as such materials do not assert any propositions as religious truth, or do not otherwise violate the Establishment Clause.

The court's opinion well illustrates the distinction between the goals and values that states may try to impose and those they cannot, by distinguishing between teaching civil toleration of other religions, and teaching religious toleration of other religions. It is an accepted part of public schools to teach the former, and plaintiffs do not quarrel with that. Thus, the state may teach that all religions have the same civil and political rights, and must be dealt with civilly in civil society. The state itself concedes it may not do the latter. It may not teach as truth that the religions of others are just as correct as religions as plaintiffs' own.

It is a more difficult question when, as here, the state presents materials that plaintiffs sincerely believe preach religious toleration of religions by consistent omission of plaintiffs' religion and favorable presentation of opposing views. Our holding requires plaintiffs to put up with what they perceive as an unbalanced public school curriculum, so long as the curriculum does not violate the Establishment Clause. Every other sect or type of religious belief is bound by the same requirement. The rule here is not a rule just for fundamentalist dissenters, for surely the rule cannot be that when the school authorities disagree with non-fundamentalist dissenters, the school loses (See, e.g., Epperson v. Arkansas, 393 U.S. 97 (1968), Spence v. Bailey, 465 F.2d 797 (6th Cir.1972); Edwards v.

Aguillard, 482 U.S. 578 (1987)), and when the school authorities disagree with fundamentalists, the school wins (See, e.g., Mozert; Grove v. Mead School Dist., 753 F.2d 1528 (9th Cir.1985); Wright v. Houston Ind. School District, 366 F.Supp. 1208 (S.D.Tex.1972)). Rather, unless the Supreme Court chooses to extend the principle of Thomas to schools, the democratic principle must prevail.

Schools are very important, and some public schools offend some people deeply. That is one major reason private schools of many denominations—fundamentalist, Lutheran, Jewish—are growing.[88] But a response to that phenomenon is a political decision for the schools to make. I believe that such a significant change in school law and expansion in the religious liberties of pupils and parents should come only from Supreme Court itself, and not simply from our interpretation. It may well be that we would have a better society if children and parents were not put to the hard choice posed by this case. But our mandate is limited to carrying out the commands of the Constitution and the Supreme Court.

I therefore concur in the result and reverse the judgment of the District Court.

NOTES AND QUESTIONS

1. As discussed in previous chapters, in *Wright, Crowley,* and *Willoughby,* conservative Christians had unsuccessfully argued that teaching about or presenting Darwinism in public schools and other institutions established a religion of secularism in violation of the Establishment Clause. Taking a different tact, the plaintiffs in *Mozart* argued that forcing public-school students to study about evolution, humanism, magic, world religions, and certain other topics contrary to their fundamentalist Christian beliefs violated the Free Exercise Clause of the U.S. Constitution. These topics appeared in the Holt series of basic readers used in the critical reading program at the plaintiffs' public school. Ruling for the plaintiffs, the trial court directed the school to permit the objecting students to opt out of the critical reading program. The Sixth Circuit reversed. Writing for a three-judge appellate panel, Chief Judge Pierce Lively, a moderate Republican nominated to the court by President Richard Nixon, found no Free Exercise Clause violation. In the context of public education, he noted, "government actions that merely offend or cast doubt on religious beliefs do not on that account violate free exercise. An actual burden on the profession or exercise of religion is required." Under Judge Lively reasoning, would it violate the Free Exercise Clause to compel students to affirm that evolution was true? In *West Virginia State Board of Education v. Barnette,* 319 U.S. 624 (1943), the Supreme Court held that West Virginia public schools could not compel Seventh–Day Adventist students to pledge allegiance to the flag or government of the United

---

88. See B. Cooper, The Changing Demography of Private Schools, in 16 Education and Urban Society, 429–42 (Sage Publ.1984) (Between 1965 and 1983, enrollment in Lutheran schools grew 35%; in Jewish schools 37%; in non-religious private schools 69% and in all non-Catholic private schools over 130%, National Center for Educational Statistics (1983)); Charles Glenn (Massachusetts Director of Equal Educational Opportunity), Phi Delta Kappan, Feb. 1987, p. 452; U.S. Department of Education, Digest of Education Statistics, pp. 47–48.

States in violation of their sincerely held religious beliefs. In his opinion, Judge Lively noted that the Holt readers contained a disclaimer stating "that evolution is a theory, not a proven scientific fact." Is such a disclaimer constitutional required under the court's holding? Judge Lively stressed that requiring students to read, discuss, and presumably be tested on assigned material could never implicate the Free Exercise Clause because it would not compel any practice or profession of belief in violation of the plaintiffs' religion.

2.   In a long and carefully reasoned concurring opinion, Judge Danny Boggs, a conservative Republican nominated by President Ronald Reagan, argued that mere exposure to the Holt readers *did* violate the plaintiffs' religious beliefs. Nevertheless, he concluded that public schools could not reasonably accommodate the religious beliefs of all their students and therefore they need not accommodate any of them. The only constitutional limits on religious or irreligious instruction in public schools emanate from the Establishment Clause, Judge Boggs reasoned: those schools may not establish a religious view, such as by teaching "as truth that the religions of others are just as correct as religions as plaintiffs' own." Under this view, could public schools teach that the theory of evolution was true or that the biblical account of creation was false? In this respect, Judge Boggs distinguished mandatory recitation of the Pledge of Allegiance in *Barnette* from exposure to Holt readers in *Mozart* by noting that only the former involved compelled affirmations, and thus was problematic under the free-speech as well as the religion clauses. Even if the Free Exercise Clause does not limit the internal operation of public schools, could it still limit their reach? Judge Boggs both noted that "some alternative [to public schooling] was legally permissible" and cited *Wisconsin v. Yoder*, 406 U.S. 205 (1972), which held that states could not compel Amish students to attend school in violation of their religious beliefs.

3.   In a second concurring opinion, Judge Cornelia Kennedy, a progressive Democrat nominated by President Jimmy Carter, struck a middle course. Even if exposure to the Holt readers did burden the plaintiffs' free-exercise rights, she reasoned, that burden would be outweighed by the compelling state interest in teaching critical reading skills. Can students develop critical reading skills without being exposed to material that challenges their religious beliefs? Judge Kennedy suggested that such conflicts were inevitable and must be permitted. Her comments are reminiscent of Justice Potter Stewart observation about anti-evolution laws in *Epperson* that the state could not "make it a criminal offense for a public school teacher so much as to mention the very existence of an entire system of respected human thought." Can students learn modern science without being exposed to the theory of evolution? Under her approach to the case, Judge Kennedy could distinguish *Barnette* by finding no compelling state interest in have students recite the Pledge of Allegiance.

II. CONSIDERING THE CLAIMS OF CREATIONIST TEACHERS

Public-opinion surveys consistently report a wide divergence between the beliefs of American scientists and the American public regarding the origins of species, particularly the human species. Although precise percentages fluctuate over time, among regions, and with the wording of the question, the results reveal a pattern. Virtually all American scientists accept the theory of evolution, with a significant minority of them believing that God guided or designed the processes. The American public roughly divides evenly between creationists and evolutionists, with most of the latter (and all the former) seeing God guiding the process. Not surprisingly, the few available surveys of public-school biology teachers find that they fall somewhere between scientists and the general public on this issue and, perhaps somewhat more surprisingly given the legal barriers to teaching creationism, their beliefs influence their teaching. Again the precise percentages vary, but surveys suggest that between one-in-five to one-in-four public-school biology teachers reject Darwinism and about half of these non-Darwinists present creation-science or Intelligent Design as a valid alternative to the theory of evolution. For example, in 2008 and again in 2011, representative national surveys found that about 13% of American's high-school biology teachers report that they advocate creationism or Intelligent Design in the classroom by spending at least an hour of class time presenting it in a positive light. In these surveys, a similar percentage reports spending at least some time on creationism or Intelligent Design and over half of those responding report not endorsing any theory of origins in class. Only about one quarter of the respondents say that they present evolution as a core, unifying concept in biology.

Legal controversy can result either when parents and students complain about creationist instruction or when administrators prohibit it. Creation-friendly teachers are usually adept at navigating this particular minefield but some insist on taking a public stand in demanding a constitutional right either to teach origins as they see fit or at least to question the Darwinian assertions contained in the assigned textbooks. Indeed, in their willingness to teach an unpopular or unapproved scientific theory, some creationist instructors liken themselves to the evolutionist hero of *Inherit the Wind*, John Scopes. Two such cases were decided by federal appellate courts in the early 1990s, though neither ultimately gained the renown of *Tennessee v. Scopes*.

New Lenox, a growing suburban community 35 miles southwest of downtown Chicago, bills itself as "Home of Proud Americans." In 1987, its quiet demeanor was shaken by complaints from junior-high students and parents, backed by the Illinois ACLU, that a social studies teacher, Ray Webster, was promoting creationism and a Christian world-view in class. The school district's superintendent directed Webster to stick to the prescribed curriculum but he refused. "We should be working for open minds," Webster told the press. "In the Scopes trial, a defense attorney for Scopes himself made basically that same statement." In particular, when the assigned social-science text states that the earth is more than four billion years old, Webster declared, "I would never hesitate to point out to my students that the above statement is misleading and not necessarily true."[89] To Webster, this was a teacher's duty. After the superintendent reiterated his directive against advocating a religious viewpoint in class and ordered the removal pro-Christian material from the class bulletin board, Webster filed suit in federal court claiming a violation of his rights to free speech and equal protection. When the district court summarily dismissed his suit for failing to state a claim upon which relief could be granted, Webster appealed to the Seventh Circuit Court of Appeals, which heard his case in 1990.

Just as Webster's case was being decided, a similar one erupted in a Southern California suburban paradise, San Juan Capistrano, located on the coast in affluent Orange County midway between Los Angeles and San Diego. There, in 1991, an evangelical Christian public-high-school biology teacher named John Peloza received an official reprimand for allegedly preaching to two Jew students. The school's student newspaper, *Paw Prints*, also ran an editorial critical of Peloza's teaching methods, which incorporated creationist critiques of Darwinism. Although signed by a student, Peloza attributed the editorial to the newspaper's faculty advisor, Jim Corbett. Backed by an ad hoc parents group called Citizens for Excellence in Education and a conservative legal defense firm rooting in Christian Reconstructionism, the Rutherford Institute, Peloza filed a $5–million claim with the school district charging that school administrators and the school newspaper had falsely accused him of teaching religion in his science class and debunking the theory of evolution. Peloza maintained that he simply raised scientific problems with evolutionary biology in class and never taught creation-science or religious dogma. "My purpose as a high school biology teacher is to present evidence as it is, and not the politically correct view," he told supporters. "I don't teach dogmatic Darwinism. I don't say, 'Hey kids, you evolved from apes. I can't explain why, but that's the facts.'" He admitted that his views were not represented in the assigned textbook.[90] After the school district rejected his claim, Webster filed suit in federal district court against the school district, seven school-board members, five administrators, and five individual teachers, including Corbett, for violating his constitutional rights under the First and Fourteenth Amendments.

The case did not go well for Peloza. Calling him a "loose cannon" in the classroom, in January 1992, Judge David Williams dismissed Peloza's complaint for failing to state a claim upon which relief could be granted. Two weeks later, school administrators reassigned Peloza in mid-year to teach physical education. Although he had taught biology at Capistrano Valley High School for eight years, Peloza was credentialed to teach physical education and had majored in that subject during college. Then Judge Williams ordered Peloza to pay the school district's $32,603 legal fees and costs. "While granting fees may have a chilling effect on civil rights claims of this matter," the court wrote, "not granting fees may give

---

89. Blair Kamin, *Teacher Sues to Use Creationism*, CHI. TRIB., Mar. 22, 1988, at B–1.

90. Zion Banks and Lily Eng, *Biology Teacher Vows to Keep Up Creation Battle*, L.A. TIMES, Aug. 29, 1991, at C–1.

the appearance of court tolerance of those claims which have not been thoroughly researched and where established case law has already determined the matters before the court."[91] Peloza appealed to Ninth Circuit Court of Appeals, which at first reinstated the lawsuit but then, on its own initiative, reversed course. The appellate court opinions in *Webster* and *Peloza* follow:

WEBSTER v. NEW LENOX SCHOOL DISTRICT #122

United States Court of Appeals for the Seventh Circuit
917 F.2d 1004 (7th Cir. 1990)

RIPPLE, CIRCUIT JUDGE: Ray Webster sought injunctive and declaratory relief based on his claim that the New Lenox School District violated his first and fourteenth amendment rights by prohibiting him from teaching a nonevolutionary theory of creation in the classroom. He appeals the dismissal of his complaint for failure to state a claim. For the following reasons, we affirm the judgment of the district court.

I

The district court dismissed Mr. Webster's suit for failure to state a claim upon which relief can be granted. See Fed.R.Civ.P. 12(b)(6). The grant of a motion to dismiss is, of course, reviewed de novo. It is well settled that, when reviewing the grant of a motion to dismiss, we must assume the truth of all well-pleaded factual allegations and make all possible inferences in favor of the plaintiff. Janowsky v. United States, 913 F.2d 393, 395–96 (7th Cir.1990); Rogers v. United States, 902 F.2d 1268, 1269 (7th Cir.1990)....

Ray Webster teaches social studies at the Oster–Oakview Junior High School in New Lenox, Illinois. In the Spring of 1987, a student in Mr. Webster's social studies class complained that Mr. Webster's teaching methods violated principles of separation between church and state. In addition to the student, both the American Civil Liberties Union and the Americans United for the Separation of Church and State objected to Mr. Webster's teaching practices. Mr. Webster denied the allegations. On July 31, 1987, the New Lenox school board (school board), through its superintendent, advised Mr. Webster by letter that he should restrict his classroom instruction to the curriculum and refrain from advocating a particular religious viewpoint.

Believing the superintendent's letter vague, Mr. Webster asked for further clarification in a letter dated September 4, 1987. In this letter, Mr. Webster also set forth his teaching methods and philosophy. Mr. Webster stated that the discussion of religious issues in his class was only for the purpose of developing an open mind in his students. For example, Mr. Webster explained that he taught nonevolutionary theories of creation to rebut a statement in the social studies textbook indicating that the world

---

91. Peloza v. Capistrano Unified Sch. Dist., No. CV 91–5268–DWW, slip op. at 9 (C.D. Cal. Apr. 14, 1992) (order granting Attorney's Fees and Costs).

is over four billion years old. Therefore, his teaching methods in no way violated the doctrine of separation between church and state. Mr. Webster contended that, at most, he encouraged students to explore alternative viewpoints.

The superintendent responded to Mr. Webster's letter on October 13, 1987. The superintendent reiterated that advocacy of a Christian viewpoint was prohibited, although Mr. Webster could discuss objectively the historical relationship between church and state when such discussions were an appropriate part of the curriculum. Mr. Webster was specifically instructed not to teach creation science, because the teaching of this theory had been held by the federal courts to be religious advocacy.

Mr. Webster brought suit, principally arguing that the school board's prohibitions constituted censorship in violation of the first and fourteenth amendments. In particular, Mr. Webster argued that the school board should permit him to teach a nonevolutionary theory of creation in his social studies class. . . .

II

At the outset, we note that a narrow issue confronts us: Mr. Webster asserts that he has a first amendment right to determine the curriculum content of his junior high school class. He does not, however, contest the general authority of the school board, acting through its executive agent, the superintendent, to set the curriculum.

This case does not present a novel issue. We have already confirmed the right of those authorities charged by state law with curriculum development to require the obedience of subordinate employees, including the classroom teacher. Judge Wood expressed the controlling principle succinctly in Palmer v. Board of Educ., 603 F.2d 1271, 1274 (7th Cir. 1979), cert. denied, 444 U.S. 1026 (1980), when he wrote:

> Parents have a vital interest in what their children are taught. Their representatives have in general prescribed a curriculum. There is a compelling state interest in the choice and adherence to a suitable curriculum for the benefit of our young citizens and society. It cannot be left to individual teachers to teach what they please.

Yet Mr. Webster, in effect, argues that the school board must permit him to teach what he pleases. The first amendment is "not a teacher license for uncontrolled expression at variance with established curricular content." Id. at 1273. See also Clark v. Holmes, 474 F.2d 928 (7th Cir.) (holding that individual teacher has no constitutional prerogative to override the judgment of his superiors as to proper course content), cert. denied, 411 U.S. 972 (1973). Clearly, the school board had the authority and the responsibility to ensure that Mr. Webster did not stray from the established curriculum by injecting religious advocacy into the classroom. "Families entrust public schools with the education of their children, but condition their trust on the understanding that the classroom will not purposely be used to advance religious views that may conflict with the private beliefs of the student and his or her family." Edwards v. Aguillard, 482 U.S. 578, 584 (1987).

A junior high school student's immature stage of intellectual development imposes a heightened responsibility upon the school board to control the curriculum. See Zykan v. Warsaw Community School Corp., 631 F.2d 1300, 1304 (7th Cir.1980). We have noted that secondary school teachers occupy a unique position for influencing secondary school students, thus creating a concomitant power in school authorities to choose the teachers and regulate their pedagogical methods. Id. "The State exerts great authority and coercive power through mandatory attendance requirements, and because of the students' emulation of teachers as role models and the children's susceptibility to peer pressure." Edwards, 482 U.S. at 584.

It is true that the discretion lodged in school boards is not completely unfettered. For example, school boards may not fire teachers for random classroom comments. Zykan, 631 F.2d at 1305. Moreover, school boards may not require instruction in a religiously inspired dogma to the exclusion of other points of view. Epperson v. Arkansas, 393 U.S. 97, 106 (1968). This complaint contains no allegation that school authorities have imposed "a pall of orthodoxy" on the offerings of the entire public school curriculum, Keyishian v. Board of Regents, 385 U.S. 589, 603 (1967), "which might either implicate the state in the propagation of an identifiable religious creed or otherwise impair permanently the student's ability to investigate matters that arise in the natural course of intellectual inquiry." Zykan, 631 F.2d at 1306. Therefore, this case does not present the issue of whether, or under what circumstances, a school board may completely eliminate material from the curriculum. Cf. Zykan, 631 F.2d at 1305–06 (school may not flatly prohibit teachers from mentioning relevant material). Rather, the principle that an individual teacher has no right to ignore the directives of duly appointed education authorities is dispositive of this case. Today, we decide only that, given the allegations of the complaint, the school board has successfully navigated the narrow channel between impairing intellectual inquiry and propagating a religious creed.

Here, the superintendent concluded that the subject matter taught by Mr. Webster created serious establishment clause concerns. Cf. Edwards, 482 U.S. at 583–84 ("The Court has been particularly vigilant in monitoring compliance with the Establishment Clause in elementary and secondary schools."); Epperson, 393 U.S. at 106 (school may not adopt programs that aid or oppose any religion). As the district court noted, the superintendent's letter is directed to this concern. "[E]ducators do not offend the First Amendment . . . so long as their actions are reasonably related to legitimate pedagogical concerns." Hazelwood School Dist. v. Kuhlmeier, 484 U.S. 260, 273 (1988). Given the school board's important pedagogical interest in establishing the curriculum and legitimate concern with possible establishment clause violations, the school board's prohibition on the teaching of creation science to junior high students was appropriate. See Palmer v. Board of Educ., 603 F.2d 1271, 1274 (7th Cir.1979) (school board has "compelling" interest in setting the curriculum). Accordingly, the district court properly dismissed Mr. Webster's complaint.

For the foregoing reasons, the judgment of the district court is affirmed.

PELOZA v. CAPISTRANO UNIFIED SCHOOL DISTRICT

United States Court of Appeals for the Ninth Circuit
37 F.3d 517 (9th Cir. 1994)

PER CURIAM: John E. Peloza is a high school biology teacher. He sued the Capistrano Unified School District and various individuals connected with the school district under 42 U.S.C. § 1983. He alleges in his complaint that the school district requires him to teach "evolutionism" and that evolutionism is a religious belief system. He alleges this requirement violates his rights under the (1) Free Speech Clause of the First Amendment; (2) Establishment Clause of the First Amendment; (3) Due Process Clause of the Fourteenth Amendment; and (4) Equal Protection Clause of the Fourteenth Amendment.[92]

He also alleges the defendants conspired to violate these constitutional rights and attempted by harassment and intimidation to force him to teach evolutionism. He alleges they did this because they have a class-based animus against practicing Christians, a class of which he is a member, in violation of 42 U.S.C. § 1985(3). . . .

The district court dismissed the federal claims for failure to state a claim upon which relief could be granted. Fed.R.Civ.P. 12(b)(6). . . . We affirm. . . .

The following summarizes the allegations of Peloza's complaint:

Peloza is a biology teacher in a public high school, and is employed by the Capistrano Unified School District. He is being forced by the defendants (the school district, its trustees and individual teachers and others) to proselytize his students to a belief in "evolutionism" "under the guise of [its being] a valid scientific theory." Evolutionism is an historical, philosophical and religious belief system, but not a valid scientific theory. Evolutionism is one of "two world views on the subject of the origins of life and of the universe." The other is "creationism" which also is a "religious belief system." "The belief system of evolutionism is based on the assumption that life and the universe evolved randomly and by chance and with no Creator involved in the process. The world view and belief system of creationism is based on the assumption that a Creator created all life and the entire universe." Peloza does not wish "to promote either philosophy or belief system in teaching his biology class." "The general acceptance of . . . evolutionism in academic circles does not qualify it or validate it as a scientific theory." Peloza believes that the defendants seek to dismiss him due to his refusal to teach evolutionism. His first amendment rights have been abridged by interference with his right "to teach

---

92. On appeal, Peloza abandoned his equal protection argument.

his students to differentiate between a philosophical, religious belief system on the one hand and a true scientific theory on the other.''

Peloza further alleges he has been forbidden to discuss religious matters with students the entire time that he is on the school campus even if a conversation is initiated by a student and the discussion is outside of class time.

He also alleges that the defendants have conspired to destroy and damage his professional reputation, career and position as a public school teacher. He has been reprimanded in writing for proselytizing students and teaching religion in the classroom. His inquiries as to whether he is being required to teach evolution as "fact" or "as the only valid scientific theory" have not been answered directly. He has not taught creationism in his classroom. He has been wrongly accused in the school newspaper and in the public press of teaching religion in his science class. He has been harassed by the defendant teachers and has received a formal written reprimand from defendant Thomas R. Anthony, the school principal, wrongly accusing him of proselytizing his students and teaching religion in the classroom, directing him to teach evolution as the only valid scientific theory, and forbidding him from teaching creationism as a valid scientific theory. Anthony further directed him not to discuss religion or attempt to convert students to Christianity while on campus. He has been criticized in a petition signed by faculty members for threatening litigation over the rights of faculty members to speak fully to the news media and each other. . . .

I. The Section 1983 Claim

A. The Establishment Clause

To withstand an Establishment Clause challenge, a state statute, policy or action (1) must have a secular purpose; (2) must, as its primary effect, neither advance nor inhibit religion; and (3) must not foster an excessive government entanglement with religions. Lemon v. Kurtzman, 403 U.S. 602, 612–13 (1971).

Peloza's complaint alleges that the school district has violated the Establishment Clause "by pressuring and requiring him to teach evolutionism, a religious belief system, as a valid scientific theory." Complaint at 19–20. Evolutionism, according to Peloza, "postulates that the 'higher' life forms . . . evolved from the 'lower' life forms . . . and that life itself 'evolved' from non-living matter." Id. at 2. It is therefore "based on the assumption that life and the universe evolved randomly and by chance and with no Creator involved in the process." Id. Peloza claims that evolutionism is not a valid scientific theory because it is based on events which "occurred in the non-observable and non-recreatable past and hence are not subject to scientific observation." Id. at 3. Finally, in his appellate brief he alleges that the school district is requiring him to teach evolutionism not just as a theory, but rather as a fact.

Peloza's complaint is not entirely consistent. In some places he seems to advance the patently frivolous claim that it is unconstitutional for the school district to require him to teach, as a valid scientific theory, that higher life forms evolved from lower ones. At other times he claims the district is forcing him to teach evolution as fact. Although possibly dogmatic or even wrong, such a requirement would not transgress the establishment clause if "evolution" simply means that higher life forms evolved from lower ones.

Peloza uses the words "evolution" and "evolutionism" interchangeably in the complaint. This is not wrong or imprecise for, indeed, they are synonyms. Adding "ism" does not change the meaning nor magically metamorphose "evolution" into a religion. "Evolution" and "evolutionism" define a biological concept: higher life forms evolve from lower ones. The concept has nothing to do with how the universe was created; it has nothing to do with whether or not there is a divine Creator (who did or did not create the universe or did or did not plan evolution as part of a divine scheme).

On a motion to dismiss we are required to read the complaint charitably, to take all well-pleaded facts as true, and to assume that all general allegations embrace whatever specific facts might be necessary to support them. Lujan v. Nat'l Wildlife Federation, 497 U.S. 871, 889 (1990); Abramson v. Brownstein, 897 F.2d 389, 391 (9th Cir.1990).

Charitably read, Peloza's complaint at most makes this claim: the school district's actions establish a state-supported religion of evolutionism, or more generally of "secular humanism." See Complaint at 2–4, 20. According to Peloza's complaint, all persons must adhere to one of two religious belief systems concerning "the origins of life and of the universe:" evolutionism, or creationism. Id. at 2. Thus, the school district, in teaching evolutionism, is establishing a state-supported "religion."

We reject this claim because neither the Supreme Court, nor this circuit, has ever held that evolutionism or secular humanism are "religions" for Establishment Clause purposes. Indeed, both the dictionary definition of religion[93] and the clear weight of the caselaw[94] are to the contrary. The Supreme Court has held unequivocally that while the belief in a divine creator of the universe is a religious belief, the scientific theory that higher forms of life evolved from lower forms is not. Edwards v. Aguillard, 482 U.S. 578 (1987) (holding unconstitutional, under Establish-

---

93. According to Webster's, religion is the "belief in and reverence for a supernatural power accepted as the creator and governor of the universe." Webster's II New Riverside University Dictionary 993 (1988).

94. See Smith v. Board of School Com'rs of Mobile County, 827 F.2d 684, 690–95 (11th Cir.1987) (refusing to adopt district court's holding that "secular humanism" is a religion for Establishment Clause purposes; deciding case on other grounds); United States v. Allen, 760 F.2d 447, 450–51 (2d Cir.1985) (quoting Tribe, American Constitutional Law 827–28 (1978), for the proposition that, while "religion" should be broadly interpreted for Free Exercise Clause purposes, "anything 'arguably non-religious' should not be considered religious in applying the establishment clause").

ment Clause, Louisiana's "Balanced Treatment for Creation–Science and Evolution–Science in Public School Instruction Act").

Peloza would have us accept his definition of "evolution" and "evolutionism" and impose his definition on the school district as its own, a definition that cannot be found in the dictionary, in the Supreme Court cases, or anywhere in the common understanding of the words. Only if we define "evolution" and "evolutionism" as does Peloza as a concept that embraces the belief that the universe came into existence without a Creator might he make out a claim. This we need not do. To say red is green or black is white does not make it so. Nor need we for the purposes of a 12(b)(6) motion accept a made-up definition of "evolution." Nowhere does Peloza point to anything that conceivably suggests that the school district accepts anything other than the common definition of "evolution" and "evolutionism." It simply required him as a biology teacher in the public schools of California to teach "evolution." Peloza nowhere says it required more.

The district court dismissed his claim, stating:

> Since the evolutionist theory is not a religion, to require an instructor to teach this theory is not a violation of the Establishment Clause.... Evolution is a scientific theory based on the gathering and studying of data, and modification of new data. It is an established scientific theory which is used as the basis for many areas of science. As scientific methods advance and become more accurate, the scientific community will revise the accepted theory to a more accurate explanation of life's origins. Plaintiff's assertions that the teaching of evolution would be a violation of the Establishment Clause is unfounded.

Id. at 12–13. We agree.

B.   Free Speech

Peloza alleges the school district ordered him to refrain from discussing his religious beliefs with students during "instructional time," and to tell any students who attempted to initiate such conversations with him to consult their parents or clergy. He claims the school district, in the following official reprimand, defined "instructional time" as any time the students are on campus, including lunch break and the time before, between, and after classes:

> You are hereby directed to refrain from any attempt to convert students to Christianity or initiating conversations about your religious beliefs during instructional time, which the District believes includes any time students are required to be on campus as well as the time students immediately arrive for the purposes of attending school for instruction, lunch time, and the time immediately prior to students' departure after the instructional day.

Complaint at 16. Peloza seeks a declaration that this definition of instructional time is too broad, and that he should be allowed to participate in student-initiated discussions of religious matters when he is not actually teaching class.

The school district's restriction on Peloza's ability to talk with students about religion during the school day is a restriction on his right of free speech. Nevertheless, "the Court has repeatedly emphasized the need for affirming the comprehensive authority of the States and of school officials, consistent with fundamental constitutional safeguards, to prescribe and control conduct in the schools." Tinker v. Des Moines Indep. Community School Dist., 393 U.S. 503, 506–07 (1969). "[T]he interest of the State in avoiding an Establishment Clause violation 'may be [a] compelling' one justifying an abridgment of free speech otherwise protected by the First Amendment. . . ." Lamb's Chapel v. Center Moriches Union Free School Dist., 508 U.S. 384 (1993) (quoting Widmar v. Vincent, 454 U.S. 263, 271 (1981)). This principle applies in this case. The school district's interest in avoiding an Establishment Clause violation trumps Peloza's right to free speech.

While at the high school, whether he is in the classroom or outside of it during contract time, Peloza is not just any ordinary citizen. He is a teacher. He is one of those especially respected persons chosen to teach in the high school's classroom. He is clothed with the mantle of one who imparts knowledge and wisdom. His expressions of opinion are all the more believable because he is a teacher. The likelihood of high school students equating his views with those of the school is substantial. To permit him to discuss his religious beliefs with students during school time on school grounds would violate the Establishment Clause of the First Amendment. Such speech would not have a secular purpose, would have the primary effect of advancing religion, and would entangle the school with religion. In sum, it would flunk all three parts of the test articulated in Lemon v. Kurtzman, 403 U.S. 602 (1971). See Roberts v. Madigan, 921 F.2d 1047, 1056–58 (10th Cir.1990) (teacher could be prohibited from reading Bible during silent reading period, and from stocking two books on Christianity on shelves, because these things could leave students with the impression that Christianity was officially sanctioned), cert. denied, 505 U.S. 1218 (1992).

The district court did not err in dismissing the part of Peloza's section 1983 claim that was predicated on an alleged violation of his right to free speech under the First Amendment.

C. Due Process

Peloza alleges that some of the defendants made defamatory statements to and about him, and that these statements damaged his reputation. He alleges this was state action which violated his right to due process under the Fourteenth Amendment.

To state a claim under 42 U.S.C. § 1983 based on an alleged violation of due process, Peloza must allege a deprivation of a life, liberty or property interest within the meaning of the Fourteenth Amendment's Due

Process Clause. Board of Regents v. Roth, 408 U.S. 564, 571 (1972). The injury Peloza alleges here is to his reputation. An injury to reputation does not deprive Peloza of any interest in life. The district court concluded that it did not deprive him of a liberty or a property interest. Peloza concedes that his interest in his reputation is not a property interest. He argues, however, that the alleged injury to his reputation deprived him of a liberty interest sufficient to state a claim under section 1983 based on a due process violation. We disagree.

In Siegert v. Gilley, 500 U.S. 226 (1991), the Court laid to rest the notion that reputation alone is a sufficient interest to give rise to due process rights. In that case, Siegert, a psychologist working for the federal government, resigned from his job in Washington, D.C. to avoid being fired. Id. at 227–29. He applied for a job in an Army hospital in Germany which required that he be "credentialed." This involved asking his former employer for information about him. Id. His former supervisor responded to the request for information with a letter which said "that he 'consid-er[ed] Dr. Siegert to be both inept and unethical, perhaps the least trustworthy individual I have supervised in my thirteen years [here].' " Id. The Court held that Siegert had no cause of action for deprivation of liberty under the Due Process Clause because "injury to reputation by itself was not a 'liberty' interest...." Id. at 233; see also Paul v. Davis, 424 U.S. 693, 712 (1976); Cooper v. Dupnik, 924 F.2d 1520, 1532 (9th Cir.1991), cert. denied, 506 U.S. 953 (1992); Ronald D. Rotunda & John E. Nowak, Treatise on Constitutional Law § 17.4(d) (1992).

Like Dr. Siegert's, Peloza's allegations of injury to his reputation are insufficient to support a claim for deprivation of a liberty interest under section 1983. Peloza's citations to dicta in pre-Paul cases that suggest reputation alone is protected in this context are unavailing.

The district court did not err in dismissing the part of Peloza's section 1983 claim which was predicated on an alleged violation of his right to due process under the Fourteenth Amendment.

II.   The Section 1985(3) Claim

In support of his claim under 42 U.S.C. § 1985(3), Peloza alleges in his complaint that the defendants conspired to deprive him of equal protection of the laws under the Fourteenth Amendment; free speech under the First and Fourteenth Amendments; life, liberty "or" property without due process of law under the Fifth and Fourteenth Amendments; and the free exercise of his religious beliefs under the First and Fourteenth Amendments. In addition, he alleges the defendants violated his rights under the Establishment Clause of the First and Fourteenth Amendments. He alleges that the defendants engaged in this conspiracy pursuant to their class-based animus against practicing Christians.

As we stated previously, Peloza's allegations are insufficient to support a claim based on a violation of his constitutional rights of free speech and due process. Accordingly, his allegations of a conspiracy to violate these constitutional rights do not state a claim. See Great American Fed. S & L Ass'n v. Novotny, 442 U.S. 366, 372 (1979) ("Section 1985(3) provides no substantive rights itself; it merely provides a remedy for violation of the rights it designates.").

Because Peloza failed to allege a conspiracy to do something that would violate his free speech or due process rights, or his rights under the Establishment Clause, his section 1985(3) claim predicated on a violation of these rights fails. . . .

IV.   Attorney Fees

Peloza contends the district court erred in awarding the defendants costs and attorney fees of approximately $32,000. This award, made by the district court under Federal Rule of Civil Procedure 11 and 42 U.S.C. 1988, was appropriate if Peloza's complaint is frivolous. Christianburg Garment Co. v. E.E.O.C., 434 U.S. 412 (1978) (under civil rights statutes); Townsend V. Holman Consulting Corp., 929 F.2d 1358, 1362 (9th Cir. 1990) (en banc) (under Fed.R.Civ.P.11). Peloza's complaint is not entirely frivolous. Some of the issues he raises present important questions of first impression in this circuit. His free speech claim involves substantial questions and requires the balancing of rights of free speech against the Establishment Clause, a matter upon which the Supreme Court recently commented in Lamb's Chapel. Accordingly, we reverse the district court's award of attorney fees and costs to the defendants. . . .

POOLE, CIRCUIT JUDGE, concurring in part and dissenting in part: . . . This is an appeal from the granting of a Rule 12(b)(6) motion. As such, we are not permitted to affirm dismissal of the complaint "unless it appears beyond doubt that plaintiff can prove no set of facts in support of his claim which would entitle him to relief." Love v. United States, 915 F.2d 1242, 1245 (9th Cir.1989). At this stage, we know almost nothing about what past or future discussions might involve. I can imagine a wide range of circumstances and questions "regarding religion" which Peloza could permissibly answer without violating the Establishment Clause. For example, a student might come to a teacher during lunch and ask about Malcolm X or Martin Luther King's religious beliefs, and how and why they evolved, or about the origins of Islam, or what the seven great religions of the world were. Such questions would certainly be "regarding religion," student-initiated, and during contract time. As such, they fall within the class of discussions Peloza seeks to be permitted, yet it is hard to see how the descriptive role a teacher would have in responding to these questions would work any violation of the Establishment Clause. . . .

The majority impermissibly attempts to narrow the scope of Peloza's complaint by relying on a written warning from the school district which Peloza has incorporated into the complaint. The letter forbids Peloza from "attempt[ing] to convert students to Christianity or initiating conversations about your religious beliefs." Complaint at ¶ 45. Were this all that the complaint said, I would have little trouble joining the majority. But the complaint alleges more; it contends that "the school district . . . has directed Plaintiff not to discuss any religious matters during any of this 'instructional time,' including student-initiated conversations regarding religion during lunch, class breaks, and before and after school hours." Complaint at ¶ 3. This allegation we must take as true. If all that lies behind it is the far narrower warning the majority cites, then Peloza's case will not be long for this world. But we may not presume that this is so. . . .

NOTES AND QUESTIONS

1. Directly or indirectly, most of the preceding cases involved the rights of students or their parents. Ray Webster and John Peloza were creationist public-school teachers seeking to defend their rights as teachers. They claimed that, as teachers, they had a constitutional right to teach their students about creationism despite school directives, guidelines, or instructions to the contrary. Webster never clearly identified the constitutional basis for his claim, though it sounded generally in free speech and academic freedom. Peloza settled on the Free Speech Clause as the primary basis for his claim. Although both teachers apparently believed that Darwinism was wrong and creation-science was right, their free-speech and academic-freedom claims were rebuffed. In dismissing these claims, the *Webster* and *Peloza* courts stressed that judges should not limit the authority of school boards and administrators over the curriculum and content of public education, which ultimately extends to prescribing what teachers can and cannot say to students at school. This approach left little or no constitutional protection for the academic freedom of teachers in public elementary and secondary schools. Is the situation different for public college and university professors? In explaining their holdings, the *Webster* and *Peloza* courts noted that secondary-school students are at an immature stage of intellectual development and are likely to equate the views of a teacher with those of the school. The intellectual maturity of college students provides one basis for granting greater academic freedom to college professors.

2. Protecting the authority of school boards and administrators over the curriculum and content of public education does not prevent courts from intervening when school officials violate the constitutional rights of students. As a second ground for his action, John Peloza asserted that, by forcing him to teach evolution and barring him from teaching creationism, his school was establishing a religion of "evolutionism, or more generally of 'secular humanism'," in violation of the Establishment Clause rights of students. In a sense, Peloza presented himself as something of a whistleblower whose actions gained constitutional protection by as a means to protect the constitutional rights of students. Why did Peloza's argument fail? The court asserted that evolutionism is not a religion and, as such, even teaching it as a fact would not violate the Establishment Clause. Would Peloza have a constitutional basis to object if his public school had ordered him to provide religious instruction?

3. In *Webster* and *Peloza*, federal district courts granted defendants' pre-trial motions to the plaintiffs' complaints for failing to state claims upon which relief could be granted. Federal appellate courts upheld these rulings. In

considering such motions under Rule 12(b)(6) of the federal rules of civil procedure, plaintiffs' allegations are treated as true and all inferences are made in favor of the plaintiffs. Is it significant that the claims of Webster and Peloza could not satisfy even this least restrictive standard? At least some of the earlier cases brought by creationist students made it to trial, and courts in a few of those lawsuits granted measured relief to the students. Although *Webster* and *Peloza* narrowed the legal options for creationist teachers, they did not discourage all creationist instructors from bring similar actions and, twenty years later, even the Capistrano United School District would be back in court over matters stemming from Peloza's lawsuit.

III. STATE SCHOOL BOARD INITIATIVES

The 1990s brought a new twist the evolution-teaching controversy. It came from the education standards movement. This movement began building in 1983, when the U.S. Department of Education published its seminal *A Nation at Risk* report bewailing the precarious state of public education in America. "The educational foundations of our society are presently being eroded by the rising tide of mediocrity that threatens our very future as a Nation and a people," the report warned.[95] It called for uniform minimum standards for academic content and student performance, particularly in such critical fields as science and mathematics. This Reagan Administration report never mentioned teaching evolution as a way to improve science education, but that seed was planted.

In 1988, Republican presidential nominee George H. W. Bush campaigned on a platform of education reform, the first time this traditionally state and local issue dominated a national election. At a highly publicized "education summit" convened soon after his inauguration in 1989, Bush and the nation's governors, led by then-governor Bill Clinton of Arkansas, committing themselves to the goal of having students demonstrate competency in science, mathematics, English, history, and geography by the end of the century. Bush called the program "America 2000," and it focused the education reform movement squarely on formulating national standards for what should be taught and learned in American public schools. That task, seen as too sensitive for politicians and bureaucrats, passed to professional organizations in each field. Their lists of key concepts and facts for various grades and subjects would become the basis for curriculum development, teacher training, and student testing in the states. In 1991, at the invitation of the National Science Teachers Association and U.S. Department of Education, the National Research Council—the operating arm of the elite National Academy of Sciences (NAS)—assumed responsibility for drafting the standards for science education. Major funding for the project came from the Department of Education and National Science Foundation. Long a champion of rigorous instruction in

---

95. National Commission on Excellence in Education, A Nation At Risk: The Imperative for Educational Reform 5 (1983).

evolution, the NAS now had the mandate to draft modal standards for elementary and secondary science education in American public schools.

Under President Bush's scheme, each state would voluntarily adopt and implement its own education standards, presumably using the national standards as a template. After Clinton became president in 1993, the Democratic-controlled Congress introduced an element of coercion into the program by passing the new administration's "Goals 2000: Educate America Act." As a prerequisite for receiving federal education funds, this Act required states to adopt and implement federally-approved education standards for key subjects, including evolutionary biology. For all practical purposes, Goals 2000 would have made the still-unfinished NAS standards (or something quite like them) mandatory for all public-school science programs in the country. Seventy years after the Scopes trial launched the issue onto the national scene, evolutionists' goals for science education appeared within reach.

The NAS released its draft science-education standards in December, 1994. Running over 250 pages in their final form, these standards identified what science courses should cover from kindergarten through twelfth grade. Under them, all students would receive an education in Darwinism. "Biological evolution accounts for the diversity of species developed through gradual processes over many generations," the life-science standards for grades 5–8 stated. "Natural selection and its evolutionary consequences provide a scientific explanation for the fossil record of ancient life forms, as well as for the striking molecular similarities observed among the diverse species of living organisms," those standards for grades 9–12 explained, leading to the statement that all living species "are related by descent from common ancestors." The earth-science standards for those same grades added, "Evidence for one-celled forms of life—the bacteria—extends back more than 3.5 billion years." A concluding standard for high school students addressed the nature of scientific knowledge. "Science distinguishes itself from other ways of knowing and from other bodies of knowledge though the use of empirical standards, logical arguments, and skepticism.... Explanations on how the natural world changes based on myths, personal beliefs, religious values, mystical inspiration, superstition, or authority ... are not scientific." Linking all the content-specific standards, "evolution and equilibrium" appears as one of five unifying concepts in science. Creationism had no place in science education under these standards; science was strictly limited to systematically investigating for natural causes of physical phenomena.[96]

Two months before the NAS released its science standards in 1994, the overall movement for national education reform nearly derailed when the National Center for History in the Schools released its model standards for American history education. As champions of state's rights and local control, political conservatives (irrespective of their religious beliefs)

---

96. NATIONAL RESEARCH COUNCIL, NATIONAL SCIENCE EDUCATION STANDARDS 15, 115–19, 158, 185, 190, 200 (1996).

had long opposed national curriculum standards for public schools on ideological grounds, but the public clamor for education reform that followed publication of *A Nation at Risk* all but drowned out their objections. These history standards gave conservatives popular new evidence to bolster their arguments for local control. Lynne Cheney, a Republican former leader of the National Endowment for the Humanities and wife of the next Republican vice president, led the assault on the history standards. "They make it sound as if everything in America is wrong and grim," she charged, noting that they contained three dozen references to the Ku Klux Klan and McCarthyism but none to Paul Revere or Thomas Edison. New multi-cultural heroes seemingly replaced the Founding Fathers as the objects of veneration. Senate Republican leader Robert Dole, who became the party's presidential nominee in 1996, joined in the attack, as did countless Republican congressional candidates then in the final weeks of campaigning for the 1994 mid-term elections. The history standards became a campaign issue that helped to elect Republican majorities in both houses of Congress for the first time in over a half century. Once in office, the new Congress gutted the Goals 2000 program by repealing the federal government's power to review or approve state education standards. Each state would still have to adopt standards for its public schools, but could do so without any federal oversight. This process became the flashpoint for the evolution-teaching controversy during the 1990s.

One by one during the decade, the various state boards and departments of education worked through the initial standards-setting process. This typically involved public hearings, open meetings, and committee votes. Many states used the NAS standards as their working draft for science education but others formulated their own frameworks, some of which did little more than list key topics for coverage, and one state— Iowa—turned the process over to local school districts. By 2000, every state (except Iowa) had adopted some form of science standards that at least addressed the topic of biological evolution (though a few avoid using the word itself). Forty-six of them specifically included the concepts of species changing over time and of natural selection; thirty-eight gave evidence for evolution; twenty-one discussed descent with modification; and six raised the issue of human evolution (which the NAS standards did not). In many instances, the exclusion of specific concepts in evolution reflected the abbreviated style of the state's standards rather than hostility toward the topic. Public controversies developed in about one-third of the states over the treatment of evolution in the science standards, with the anti-creationist National Center for Science Education (NCSE) reporting that the greatest public or official opposition to teaching evolution emerged in Alabama, Arizona, Idaho, Illinois, Kansas, Kentucky, Michigan, Nebraska, New Mexico, and Texas. During 2000 and 2001, new or renewed controversies erupted in Alabama, Hawaii, Oklahoma, and Pennsylvania, as efforts were made to revise science standards previously adopted in those states—suggesting that the battle over science standards would not end with their initial adoption. Even in these states, however, evolutionists often prevailed.

On balance, evolution teaching gained ground through the standards-setting process. What is tested tends to be taught and most states tied student-assessment testing to their education standards. Yet the triumph of evolution was not uniform throughout. Based on its study of all the state standards, the pro-standards Fordham Foundation pointed out alleged deficiencies in their treatment of evolution. "Some states treat biological evolution very gingerly or not at all. Some never use the word but do as good as possible given that restriction," the Foundation report observed. "A few states insert items involving such creationist buzzwords as micro- and macro-evolution, as though this minor distinction were worthy of specific mention. Kansas and Alabama are special cases."[97] These two states plus Illinois illustrate places where anti-evolutionism impacted the standards.

Of the three, Illinois made the fewest concessions to popular concern over the teaching of evolution. The Illinois science standards track the NAS model in incorporating evolutionary concepts. Where the NAS standards use the word "evolution" in discussing the origin and development of species, however, the Illinois standards call it "change over time." Expressly teaching "evolution" is left to the discretion of local school districts and the word itself does not appear in state student-assessment tests. Illinois superintendent of public instruction Joseph Spagnolo, a veteran of the evolution-teaching wars from his prior service as Virginia's school chief, opted for this approach to maintain broad support for the standards setting process. Accordingly, the state's initial draft science standards, circulated for public comment in 1996, did not mention "evolution" by name. In response to complaints from some science educators, a revised draft inserted the term. Representatives for the Illinois chapters of two national conservative Christian organizations, Concerned Women for America and Focus on the Family, objected to this late change and threatened to push for offsetting changes of their own that would add creationist doctrine. The state quickly returned to his initial position. "What we were trying to get at here is in fact dealing with theories like evolution," Spagnolo explained, "without creating an offensive word that really in and of itself didn't mean much. We were happy to get the educational aspect built into the standards themselves without offending any group."[98] Over a dozen other states followed a similar approach of using euphemisms for "evolution" in their standards, though not all of them incorporated as much about the underlying concept.

The Alabama Board of Education took a different tack in addressing creationist concerns. Its 1995 science standards included both the term and concept of evolution, but were prefaced by the general disclaimer,

---

97. Lawrence S. Lerner, *The State of State Standards in Science, in* THE STATE OF STATE STANDARDS 2000, 22 (Chester E. Finn, Jr., and Michael J. Petrilli, eds., 2000).

98. Michael Martinez and Jennifer Peltz, *State Skirts Evolution Dispute*, CHICAGO TRIBUNE, Oct. 24, 1999, at 10.

"Explanations of the origin of life and major groups of plants and animals, including humans, shall be treated as theory and not as fact." At the urging of Alabama governor Fob James, the Board then adopted a specific disclaimer for inclusion in biology textbooks. In 1999, the Oklahoma Textbook Committee voted to require an Alabama-style disclaimer for biology texts in its state. A year later, however, the state's attorney general ruled that this exceeded the Committee's statutory authority. The Alabama disclaimer and the Oklahoma Attorney General's opinion follow:

ALABAMA TEXTBOOK DISCLAIMER (1995)
ALABAMA STATE BOARD OF EDUCATION

This textbook discusses evolution, a controversial theory some scientists present as a scientific explanation for the origin of living things, such as plants, animals and humans. No one was present when life first appeared on Earth. Therefore, any statement about life's origins should be considered a theory. The word evolution may refer to many types of change. Evolution describes changes that occur within a species. (White moths, for example, may evolve into gray moths.) This process is micro-evolution, which can be observed and described as fact. Evolution may also refer to the change of one living thing to another, such as reptiles into birds. This process, called macroevolution, has never been observed and should be considered a theory. Evolution also refers to the unproven belief that random, undirected forces produced a world of living things. There are many unanswered questions about the origin of life which are not mentioned in your textbook, including: Why did the major groups of animals suddenly appear in the fossil record, (known as the Cambrian Explosion)? Why have no new major groups of living things appeared in the fossil record in a long time? Why do major groups of plants and animals have no transitional forms in the fossil record? How did you and all living things come to possess such a complete and complex set of instructions for building a living body? Study hard and keep an open mind. Someday you may contribute to the theories of how living things appeared on Earth.

2000 OKLA. ATT'Y GEN. OP. 00–7 (FEB. 2, 2000)

The Honorable Penny Williams
Oklahoma State Senator
2300 North Lincoln Boulevard, Room 309
Oklahoma City, OK 73105
Dear Senator Williams:

This office has received your letter requesting an official Attorney General Opinion addressing, in effect, the following questions:

1. Does the authority delegated to the State Textbook Committee in the Oklahoma Constitution and the Oklahoma Statutes allow the

Committee to require, as a condition for the adoption of the textbooks for Oklahoma public schools, that a statement or pronouncement specified by the Committee be added to or placed in textbooks? ...

The Oklahoma Constitution provides the framework for the textbook system for common schools in Oklahoma:

> The Legislature shall provide for a system of textbooks for the common schools of the State, and the State through appropriate legislation shall furnish such textbooks free of cost for use by all pupils therein. The Legislature shall authorize the Governor to appoint a committee composed of active educators of the State, whose duty it shall be to prepare official multiple textbook lists from which textbooks for use in such schools shall be selected by committees composed of active educators in the local school districts in a manner to be designated by the Legislature.

Okla. Const. art. XIII, § 6.

The Constitution requires certain basics—a committee appointed by the Governor, composed of active educators of the State, which prepares a textbook list from which local textbook committees choose textbooks for their schools, all in a manner to be provided by the Legislature. The provision of a textbook system within those parameters is delegated to the Legislature.

As mandated by Oklahoma's Constitution, the Legislature has provided for a system of textbooks in 70 O.S. 1991 and Supp. 1999, §§ 16–101 through 16–124. The State Textbook Committee's qualifications are set out in pertinent part as follows:

> There is hereby created the State Textbook Committee, which shall be composed of two members from each congressional district, appointed by the Governor with the advice and consent of the Senate and one member, appointed by the Governor with the advice and consent of the Senate, who shall be a lay citizen not having a teaching certificate and having at least one child in the public schools of Oklahoma. A majority of the twelve members appointed from the congressional districts shall be classroom teachers.... Each member appointed from a congressional district shall have had not less than five (5) years' teaching or supervisory experience in the public schools of Oklahoma at the time of appointment, and shall be actively employed in the public schools of Oklahoma during the term of service on said Committee.

70 O.S. Supp. 1999, § 16–101.

The State Textbook Committee (the "Committee") is to select textbooks for subjects taught in the public schools up to and including the twelfth grade, the selections to be for not more than six years for every textbook. See 70 O.S. Supp. 1999, § 16–102(A). Before making the selections, the Committee must advertise for sealed bids from publishers. Each bid, in addition to specifically stating the price at which each book will be furnished, must be accompanied by a sample copy of each book offered in the bid. See 70 O.S. Supp. 1999, § 16–103.

In the first two weeks of October each year the Committee must hold a public hearing on all books being considered for adoption. See 70 O.S. Supp. 1999, § 16–102.1. The Committee shall give consideration to the testimony received at the public hearings and any legislative resolution as to textbook content, and shall select textbooks after careful consideration of all the books presented. See 70 O.S. Supp. 1999, § 16–104. "[T]he books selected for adoption shall be those which, in the opinion of the Committee, are best suited for the public schools in this state." Id. The Committee has the right to reject any and all bids. See 70 O.S. 1991, § 16–109.

The Committee is allowed to adopt a book on a provisional basis under certain circumstances. If the State Textbook Committee determines that significant inaccuracies exist in the contents of a textbook which has been bid or that information contained in the textbook is not current, the Committee may adopt the book on a provisional basis. Final adoption of the textbook and use of textbook money shall be contingent upon the publisher providing a modified or revised textbook which is acceptable by the State Textbook Committee. 70 O.S. Supp. 1999, § 16–104.

The particular statement which gave rise to your questions is set forth below....[99] The statement, while hinting at disagreement with some of the scientific information in the textbooks, does not purport to correct significant inaccuracies or outdated information, and therefore does not fall within this statutory provision.

Once the Committee has selected textbooks for adoption, it must notify those publishers to whom contracts are to be awarded. See 70 O.S. Supp. 1999, § 16–104. All contracts with publishers are then to be signed by the chair and secretary of the Committee. See 70 O.S. Supp. 1999, § 16–106.

---

99. The disclaimer which was ultimately required reads as follows:

A Message from the State Textbook Committee

This textbook discusses evolution, a controversial theory which some scientists present as scientific explanation for the origin of living things, such as plants and humans.

No one was present when life first appeared on earth. Therefore, any statement about life's origins should be considered as theory, not fact.

The word evolution may refer to many types of change. Evolution describes changes that occur within a species. (White moths, for example may evolve into gray moths.) This process is micro evolution, which can be observed and described as fact. Evolution may also refer to the change of one living thing to another, such as reptiles into birds. This process, called macro evolution, has never been observed and should be considered a theory. Evolution also refers to the unproven belief that random, undirected forces produced a world of living things.

There are many unanswered questions about the origin of life which are not mentioned in your textbook, including: Why did the major groups of animals suddenly appear in the fossil record, known as the Cambrian Explosion? Why have no new major groups of living things appeared in the fossil record in a long time? Why do major groups of plants and animals have no transitional forms in the fossil record? How did you and all living things come to possess such a complete and complex set of instructions for building a living body? Study hard and keep an open mind. Someday you may contribute to the theories of how living things appeared on earth.

Your first question asks essentially whether the above constitutional and statutory provisions give the Committee the authority to require the publishers of textbooks to add to or place in those textbooks a statement specified by the Committee. To answer that question, we must look at the nature of the authority of state agencies.

In reaching its decision in the case of Lingo–Leeper Lumber Co. v. Carter, 17 P.2d 365, 368 (Okla. 1932), the Oklahoma Supreme Court cited the following premise: "Public officers have and can exercise only such powers as are conferred on them by law. . . ." A variation of this rule was set forth in a later case when the Court stated, "It is a generally accepted rule, and we think a wholesome one, that Boards created by statute may only exercise the powers granted by statute." Boydston v. State, 277 P.2d 138, 142 (Okla. 1954). Subsequently, the Court has recognized that:

> [G]enerally, an officer or agency has, by implication and in addition to the powers expressly given by statute, such powers as are necessary for the due and efficient exercise of the powers expressly granted, or such as may be fairly implied from the statute granting the express powers. However, an agency created by statute may only exercise the powers granted by statute and cannot expand those powers by its own authority.

Marley v. Cannon, 618 P.2d 401, 405 (Okla. 1980) (citations omitted). Public officers or agencies, then, have only such power as is expressly given by law, is necessary in order to exercise the power given by law, or may be fairly implied from the law giving the express power.

In the case of the Committee and the question you have raised, neither the Oklahoma Constitution nor the applicable statutes provide express authority for the Committee to require an addition of its own making to the textbooks it reviews or adopts. The most the Committee can do outside of rejecting a bid is conditionally adopt a book which contains significant inaccuracies or outdated information, delaying final adoption until the publisher makes the necessary corrections. See 70 O.S. Supp. 1999, § 16–104.

The next inquiry is whether authority to make such additions is 1) necessary in order to execute the Committee's express powers or 2) may be fairly implied from the statutes or constitution which grant the express powers. "In determining what authority may be implied from a statutory scheme, the statute as a whole is considered; and the legislative intent must be determined." City of Hugo v. State ex rel. Public Employees Relations Bd., 886 P.2d 485, 492 (Okla. 1994).

The constitutional mandate to the Legislature is to set up a system of free textbooks for the schools of the State. It requires the objectivity of a Committee of active educators which prepares a list from which local committees are to choose the textbooks for their schools.

The statutory scheme provides for review by professional educators and parents, input by the public, and a system of sealed bids from publishers. It contains strict penalties for bribery. The system provides for a reasoned and controlled process for selecting textbooks. It also provides financial controls for the sizable expenditure of public funds involved in purchasing textbooks for all the schools of the State. Looking at the Constitution and statutes as a whole, the purpose is to provide a system of selection and purchase of textbooks.

The Committee's constitutional duty is to prepare multiple textbook lists. Okla. Const. art. XIII, § 6. The statutory system requires solicitation of bids, review of bids and books, selection or rejection of books, and execution of a contract for books selected. It cannot be said that it is necessary to the execution of any of these duties to add to the books statements or pronouncements formulated by the Committee. Neither can one infer that the review and selection process implies that power.

Since authority for the Committee to require the addition to or placement of a statement in textbooks as a condition of adoption is not granted by Constitution or statute, is not necessary to the exercise of powers expressly granted, and cannot be fairly implied from the provisions granting the express powers, the Committee does not have such authority. . . .

It is, therefore, the official Opinion of the Attorney General that: The Oklahoma State Textbook Committee lacks authority, either express, necessary, or fairly implied, under the Oklahoma Constitution, article XIII, section 6, and the Oklahoma Statutes, 70 O.S. 1991 and Supp. 1999, §§ 16–101 through 16–124, to require that a statement or pronouncement specified by the Committee be added to or placed in textbooks as a condition for their adoption for use in Oklahoma public schools.

W. A. Drew Edmondson
Attorney General of Oklahoma

NOTES AND QUESTIONS

1. In 2001, following the election of a new governor, the Alabama Board of Education revised its textbook disclaimer and added it's language to the science standards. A companion effort to delete any disclaimer from textbooks failed in the face of grass-roots opposition aroused by the Alabama chapter of the conservative Eagle Forum. Rather than depict "evolution" as a controversial theory, the revised disclaimer singled out only "evolution by natural selection" as a controversial theory, stating as follows:

> The theory of evolution by natural selection is a controversial theory that is included in this textbook. It is controversial because it states that natural selection provides the basis for the modern scientific explanation for the diversity of living things. Since natural selection has been observed to play a role in influencing small changes in a population, it is assumed that it produces large changes, even though this has not been directly observed. Because of its importance and implication, students should understand the nature of evolutionary theories. They should learn

to make distinctions between the multiple meanings of evolution, to distinguish between observations and assumptions used to draw conclusions, and to wrestle with the unanswered questions and unresolved problems still faced by evolutionary theory.

The revised disclaimer also replaced the list of allegedly unanswered questions with the following concluding language:

There are many unanswered questions about the origin of life. With the explosion of new scientific knowledge in biochemical and molecular biology and exciting new fossil discoveries, Alabama students may be among those who use their understanding and skills to contribute to knowledge and to answer many unanswered questions. Instructional materials associated with controversy should be approached with an open mind, studied carefully, and critically considered.

Further, the revised disclaimer also deleted any express reference to micro-evolution and macro-evolution. Did these revisions significantly change the disclaimer's likely effect on students and classroom instruction? Do you think that they respond to legal or policy concerns? Micro-evolution and macro-evolution are terms used by "young-earth" creationists to differentiate between changes within the "kinds" of plants and animals created by God as depicted in the Geneses account (micro-evolution) and changes from one basic kind or type of plant or animal to another (macro-evolution). They are not terms recognized in science or by scientists and are inspired by a literal reading of the Bible. The supposedly unanswered questions listed in the original disclaimer included many questions that evolutionary scientists maintain are answered. Many religious critics of Darwinism focus their objections on the supposedly atheistic implications of its theory of evolution by natural selection and some of them accept theistic theories of evolution. As revised, the disclaimer is less patently sectarian and reflects the views of a broader array of theists than the original text. Neither the original nor the revised versions have been challenged in court.

2.   The Alabama State Board of Education was not the first state or local school board to propose or impose a disclaimer for biology textbooks that in some manner identifies Darwinism as a theory rather that a fact. Over a decade before the Alabama Board adopted its disclaimer, Texas Attorney General's Opinion JM–134 (reprinted in Chapter 4) concluded that a similar disclaimer proposed by the Texas Board of Education would violate the Establishment Clause. In ensuing years, cases and opinions arising out of Louisiana, and Georgia would reach similar results. Why has the Alabama disclaimer never been challenged in court? In light of the Texas Attorney General's Opinion and after reviewing *Freiler v. Tangipahoa Parish Board of Education* and *Selman v. Cobb County School District* in the next chapter, consider whether the Alabama disclaimer is constitutional.

3.   What is the purpose of the Oklahoma Textbook Commission? The Commission is charged with approving textbooks for use by local public schools. It is composed of public-school teachers, public-school supervisors, and one parent of a public-school student, all chosen by the governor with the consent of the state senate. Oklahoma Attorney General's Opinion 00–07 concluded that the State Textbook Commission lacked authority under either the state

constitution or state statutes to mandate that, as a condition of its approval, biology textbooks carry a message from the Commission regarding evolution. The Attorney General's Opinion does not comment on whether the message would violate the Establishment Clause of the U.S. Constitution. Proponents of teaching evolution nevertheless hailed the Opinion as a victory. Why? Under the statutes and constitutional provisions quoted in the Opinion, could an Attorney General who supported the Commission's message as matter of public policy have plausible concluded that the Commission had the legal authority to mandate its inclusion in textbooks?

* * * * *

The national media scarcely noted the scattered skirmishes over the treatment of Darwinism in state science standards until the summer of 1999, when the Kansas Board of Education tried to delete the concept from its state standards altogether. Although the episode attracted nationwide attention, its roots were local. In Kansas during the 1990s, the federal mandate of Goals 2000 and a gradual consolidation of state authority over education policies provoked a vocal conservative reaction. By 1996, conservative Republican candidates committed to local and parental control over public schools had won five of the ten seats on the state's elected Board of Education. Not all of these five conservatives came from the religious right, and none campaigned on the evolution issue, but each distrusted the professional education establishment. By displacing moderate Republicans on the Board, they had aroused the ire of the state's mainstream Republican governor, Bill Graves, who supported the Bush Administration's education standards movement. With the Board evenly split along ideological lines, stalemates ensued on such issues as student testing, charter schools, and teacher licensing. Those soon paled before the battle over teaching Darwinism.

In 1998, Graves's commissioner of education assembled a committee of Kansas science educators to draft the state's science standards. The drafting committee hewed close to the NAS model, with its leader expecting to lose only three Board votes over the inclusion of Darwinism. During May 1999, after the committee submitted its 5th Working Draft for Board approval, three Board conservatives offered a creationist alternative authored by Tom Willis, director of the Creation Science Association of Mid–America. His alternative standards reflected the views of young-earth creationism by recommending that students study recent dinosaur life and abrupt geological events. The Board split evenly over the two alternatives, sending both sides back to the drawing boards. For the next three months, public hearings on the science standards became bitter battlegrounds between creationist parents and evolutionist educators. The drafting committee offered an Illinois-style compromise of excising the word "evolution" from its proposal, but the conservatives won the day by taking over the committee's proposal, altering it at various critical points, and offering it as the Compromise Version. The creation-science concept of microevolution within kinds replaced the standard Darwinist theory of common descent. This approach gained the reluctant support of one swing moderate, a devout Mennonite, eager to resolve the impasse. Local schools could still teach Darwinism if they wished, he explained, the state simply would not assess students on it. Despite a statement issued by the presidents of the state's six public universities saying that the proposal would set Kansas back a century in science education, it passed by a margin of six to four on August 11, 1999.

"The reaction from around the world was swift," a network-news broadcast reported, "Congratulations from fundamentalist Christians. Ridicule from everyone else." Governor Graves promptly denounced the new standards as "a terrible, tragic, embarrassing solution to a problem that did not exist." In a *Time* magazine essay, Harvard University paleontologist and popular science writer Stephen Jay Gould commented, "The Board transported its jurisdiction to a never-never land where a Dorothy of the new millennium might explain, 'They still call it Kansas, but I don't think we're in the real world anymore.'" Under the front-page headline, "A Creationist Victory," the *New York Times* tried to put the episode in perspective: "More than a decade after the Supreme Court said states could not compel the teaching of creationism,... many creationists are trying to keep Darwin out of the classroom." A feature article in the magazine *George* observed, "The board's decision made Kansas the butt of late-night talk-show humor and the target of sophisticates' scorn." Refined Republican columnist George Will verbally winced, "Every [political] party at any given time has a certain set of issues on its fringe that can make it look strange, and this is one that can make the Republicans look strange."[100] The complete science standards themselves were over 100 pages long. The relevant changes dealing with evolution were summarized in the following document prepared for the National Center for Science Education comparing the drafting committee's 5th Working Draft with the Compromise Version offered by Board conservatives:

REVISIONS TO KANSAS SCIENCE EDUCATION STANDARDS (1999)
KANSAS STATE BOARD OF EDUCATION

COMPARISON OF 5TH WORKING DRAFT TO THE COMPROMISE VERSION ON EVOLUTION*

The 5th working draft of the standards was based on the National Science Education Standards and listed 5 "unifying concepts and process-

---

100. God and Evolution in Kansas Classrooms, Nightline, July 27, 2000, at ABCNews.com (reporter's quote); Constance Holden, *Kansas Dumps Darwin*, 285 SCIENCE 1186 (1999) (Graves quote); Stephen Jay Gould, *Dorothy, It's Really Oz*, TIME, Aug. 23, 1999; Pam Belluck, *Board for Kansas Deletes Evolution from Curriculum*, NEW YORK TIMES, Aug. 12, 1999, at A1, A13; Peter Keating, *God and Man in Oz*, GEORGE, Oct. 2000, at 85; Geroge Will, *This Week Roundtable*, Aug. 15, 1999, at ABCNews.com; Kate Beem, *Evolution Steals Spotlight*, KANSAS CITY STAR, July 2, 2000, at A1, A6.

* Reprinted with permission from Deborah L. Cunningham, *Creationist Tornado Rips Evolution Out of Kansas Science Standards*, REP. NAT'L CENTER SCI. EDUC., JULY-AUG. 1999, at 10-15.

es": (1) systems, order, and organization; (2) evidence, models, and explanation; (3) constancy, change, and measurement; (4) patterns of cumulative change; and (5) form and function. The explanation of the 4th concept in the working draft reads:

> Accumulated changes through time, some gradual and some sporadic, account for the present form and function of objects, organisms, and natural systems. The general idea is that the present arises from materials and forms of the past. An example of cumulative change is the biological theory of evolution, which explains the process of descent with modification of organisms from common ancestors. Additional examples are continental drift, which is part of plate tectonic theory, fossilization, and erosion. Patterns of cumulative change also help to describe the current structure of the universe (5th Working Draft, p 9).

The compromise version of the standards deletes this 4th concept entirely, as well as other items, including the "Big Bang Theory".

The compromise version . . . also deleted parts of the "Teaching With Tolerance and Respect" section. In the 5th Working Draft of the standards, this section stated:

> If a student should raise a question in a natural science class that the teacher determines to be outside the domain of science, the teacher should treat the question with respect. The teacher should explain why the question is outside the domain of natural science and encourage the student to discuss the question further with his or her family and clergy. Neither the Kansas Constitution nor the United States constitution require time to be given in the science curriculum to accommodate religious views of those who object to certain material or activities presented in science classes. Nothing in the Kansas Statutes Annotated or the Kansas State Board Regulations allows students (or their parents) to excuse class attendance based on disagreement with the curriculum, except as specified for 1) any activity which is contrary to the religious teachings of the child or for 2) human sexuality education (5th Working Draft, p 6).

Instead, the compromise version substituted the following single sentence: "No evidence or analysis of evidence that contradicts a current science theory will be censured" (Compromise Version, p 6).

An additional change was made to an 8th grade benchmark: "The students will observe the diversity of living things and relate their adaptation to their survival or extinction". Instead of "Biological evolution, gradual changes of characteristics of organisms over many generations, has brought variations in populations" (5th Working Draft, p 41), the compromise version substituted "Over time, genetic variation acted upon by natural selection has brought variations in populations. This is termed micro-evolution" (Compromise Version, p 46).

In the next paragraph, the subcommittee deleted: "Students can compare similarities between organisms in different parts of the world, such as tigers in Asia and mountain lions in North America" as was "Students tend to think of all individuals in a population responding to change quickly rather than over a long period of time" (5th Working Draft, p 42). Then this sentence was added to the benchmark: "Natural selection can maintain or deplete genetic variation but does not add new information to the existing genetic code" was added to the description of the benchmark (Compromise Version, p 46). In addition, two indicators were added to that same benchmark in the compromise version, one re-iterating that natural selection acts only on the existing genetic code, and another that natural selection is a valid theoretical framework.

The compromise version also made changes at the 8th-grade level in geologic time indicators.... The result is that they avoid teaching students about the age of the earth. Another indicator was also added, describing the importance of falsification: "No matter how much evidence seems to support a theory, it only takes one proof that it is false to show it to be false. It should be recognized that in the real world it might take years to falsify a theory" (Compromise Version, p 58).

The bulk of the changes occurred at the 12th grade level. The compromise version added an indicator asserting that natural selection and random genetic drift were the primary mechanisms of genotypic change. Other indicators about geologic formation and earth's history were changed in order to include "different methods" of estimating geologic time and evaluating fossils. Finally, another benchmark description was expanded from "As a result of activities in grades 9–12, students should develop an understanding of the universe, its origin, and evolution" (5th Working Draft, p 70) to "Students should develop an understanding of the universe. The origin of the universe remains one of the greatest questions in science. Studies of data regarding fossils, geologic tables, cosmological information are encouraged. But standards regarding origins are not mandated" (Compromise Version, p 78). It is from this section that the "Big Bang" theory was deleted....

The rest of the changes occurred in the Appendices. In Appendix 1, the Glossary, the compromise version of the standards altered several definitions. In the 5th working draft, the definition of "evolution" was subdivided into two sections. In the first, "biological" evolution was defined as:

> A scientific theory that accounts for present day similarity and diversity among living organisms and changes in non-living entities over time. With respect to living organisms, evolution has two major perspectives: The long-term perspective focuses on the branching of lineages; the short-term perspective centers on changes within lineages. In the long term, evolution is the decent [sic] with modification of different lineages from common ancestors. In the short term, evolu-

tion is the on-going adaptation of organisms to environmental challenges and changes (5th Working Draft, p 78).

The second definition of evolution was "cosmological":

> With respect to non-living entities, evolution accounts for sequences of natural stages of development. Such sequences are a natural consequence of the characteristics of matter and energy. Stars, planets, solar systems, and galaxies are examples" (5th Working Draft, p 79).

Instead, the "compromise" version defines "evolution", without subdividing it, as "A scientific theory that accounts for present day similarity and diversity among living organisms and changes in non-living entities over time. With respect to living organisms, evolution has two major perspectives: The long-term perspective (macro-evolution) focuses on the branching of lineages; the short-term perspective (micro-evolution) centers on changes within lineages" (Compromise Version, p 86).

The compromise version changed the definition of "science" from "The human activity of seeking natural explanations for what we observe in the world around us" (5th Working Draft, p 80) to "The human activity of seeking logical explanations for what we observe in the world around us" (Compromise Version, p 88). The definition of "theory" was changed from "In science, a well-substantiated explanation of some aspect of the natural world that can incorporate facts, laws, inferences, and tested hypotheses" (5th Working Draft, p 80) to a version that leaves out "well-substantiated" (Compromise Version, p 88). The compromise version added a definition of "falsification":

> "A method for determining the validity of an hypothesis, theory or law. To be falsifiable a theory must be testable, by others, in such a way that, if it is false, the tests can show that it is false" (Compromise Version, p 87).

The . . . compromise version also replaced the original contents of Appendix 2 with a 2–page treatise on "Falsification—An Essential Verification Strategy". This modified Appendix 2 begins:

> Repeatability is an inadequate criterion and is supplemented with falsification. The reason for falsifiability may not be intuitively obvious. It is fine to make statements like 'this theory is backed by a great body of experiments and observations,' but often overlooked is the fact that such claims are meaningless. **Experiments and observations do not verify theories, they must be evaluated by human reason to determine the degree of verification they provide** (Compromise Version, p 90, bold in original).

The original Appendix 2 contained a diagram explaining the new science standards and a short description illustrating the connections among them. . . .

The final changes were the deletion of Appendix 3, "Scientific Thinking Process", in which specific thinking processes were linked to grade levels, and Appendix 5, "Achievements in the History of Science and Technology", in which *Homo erectus* was listed as existing at 750,000 BCE.

NOTES AND QUESTIONS

1. As suggested by the page references in this summary, state science guidelines are long and detailed documents that cover the entire science curriculum for each grade for Kindergarten through grade 12. At most, evolution is only a small part of those guidelines. Kansas, like most states, started with the NAS's model National Science Education Standards. This model served as the basis for the 5th Working Draft, which a gubernatorially appointed drafting committee submitted to the elected state Board of Education. A sub-committee of creationists on the Board prepared the so-called Compromise Version. Both versions were before the Board when it voted. Except for some minor amendments approved at the meeting, the full Board adopted the Compromise Version. The changes serve as a reference list of issues in Darwinism of concern to creationists. What issues stand out to you?

2. The two versions contained different definitions of science. Reflecting the view of the National Academy of Sciences (NAS), the 5th Working Draft defined science as "The human activity of seeking natural explanations for what we observe in the world around us." Reflecting the view of supporters of creation-science and Intelligent Design (ID), the Compromise Version defined science as "The human activity of seeking logical explanations for what we observe in the world around us." Can you see why this difference is vital to both sides? The NAS approach institutionalizes "methodological naturalism" in science—that is, that science seeks only naturalistic explanations for physical phenomena. The ID approach allows science to also seek supernatural explanations for physical phenomena.

3. The Compromise Version deleted "patterns of cumulative change" as a unifying concept in science. Cumulative change cannot be a unifying concept for creationists who believe that the creation is fundamentally static. Similarly, the Compromise Version inserted a distinction between micro-evolution within lineages or kinds (which many biblical creationists accept from their reading of the Genesis account) and macro-evolution of the branching of lineages into separate kinds (which many biblical creationists dismiss as unscriptural). Accordingly, the Compromise Version affirmed that "genetic variation acted upon by natural selection" produces micro-evolution. Some creationists use this approach to explain how the current array of species could have descended from the few kinds able to fit on Noah's ark. The Compromise Version qualified this role for natural selection, however, by noting that it cannot "add new information to the existing genetic code." Many biblical creationists read the Genesis account to say that the entire extent of that code was created by God in the beginning.

4. The falsification of scientific theories featured prominently in the Compromise Version. Repeatedly, it noted that to be testable, scientific theories needed to be falsifiable and that no amount of evidence can assure that a theory will not later be proven false. Accordingly, the Compromise Version

stated, "No evidence or analysis of evidence that contradicts a current science theory will be censured." Similarly, the Compromise Version added, "The origin of the universe remains one of the greatest questions in science." Why would creationists who reject the prevailing scientific theory of evolution stress the importance of falsification in science and invite uncensored questions about origins? The Compromise Version did not include any mandated standard for teaching about origins or the Big Bang.

5.   The 1999 Kansas Science Education Standards were never tested in court. Instead, they became the defining issue of the state Republican primary election in 2000, when four Board conservatives faced-off against moderate Republicans. The spotlight remained on Kansas through the election. Scores of national science organizations condemned the Board's action. The NAS, as copyright holder of sections drawn from its model, blocked publication of the state's new science standards. The ACLU threatened suit. A *Scientific American* editorial suggested that college-admissions boards question the qualification of Kansas applicants. On the eve of the election, People for the American Way brought home native Kansan Ed Asner to star in a play based on the Scopes trial that ridiculed anti-evolutionism. Asner promised to "yuck-it-up" in his role as William Jennings Bryan. Three thousand people attended, including the state's Republican governor, who endorsed the moderates. Taking the other side, Institute for Creation Research debater Duane Gish, something of a celebrity among creationists worldwide, campaigned on behalf of beleaguered conservative Board Chair Linda Holloway, who raised enough money from a mix of local and out-of-state donors to buy the first-ever television commercial for a Kansas school-board candidate. On both sides, the election focused squarely on the issue of evolution in the science standards. With the nation watching, Kansas voters turned out all but one of the conservatives. Holloway lost by a three-to-two margin. Upon taking office in 2001, the new Board prompted brought the state science standards in line with the NAS model.

CHAPTER 6

DISCLAIMING AND DEFAMING DARWINISM

■ ■ ■

I. LOCAL SCHOOL BOARD ACTION

As shown in the preceding cases, during the twentieth century, state actions and individual responses touched off most of the litigation over the role of creationism in the classroom. Traditionally, however, local school boards and administrators largely supervise what actually happens in American public schools. Perhaps local school districts remained somewhat untouched by the rising tide creation-evolution litigation because, being responsive to the community and operating in relative obscurity, they did not create the sort of controversies that led to lawsuits. When a state legislature passes an anti-evolution statute that applies to all the state's students and teachers, someone in the state is bound to object and everyone is certain to know about it. Especially in small towns or rural areas, when a local school district imposes a similar restriction, virtually the entire community may either agree with it or not want to rock the boat—and outsiders may never notice. Surveys suggest that Darwinism either is not taught or given short shrift in many local school districts throughout America, yet lawsuits rarely ensue. It takes dissenters to challenge governmental actions. Perhaps because it is the seat of Southeastern Louisiana University (SELU)—an institution originally founded by the local school board—Tangipahoa Parish produces dissenters to the otherwise dominant local religious norms and beliefs.

Creationists and conservative Christians were well represented on the Tangipahoa Parish Board of Education during the 1990s. Working closely with a local chapter of the Christian Coalition and the New Orleans-based Origins Research Association (ORA) in 1994, one member of the Tangipahoa board, Enos F. "Jake" Bailey, nearly secured the board's approval of a curriculum guide for science instruction that incorporated such creationist concepts as a young earth, initial complexity, and intelligent design in nature. ORA President Edward Bourdreaux, a chemistry professor at the University of New Orleans, had led the effort to pass the Louisiana Balanced–Treatment Act in 1981 and turned his attention to lobbying local school districts after that statute was declared unconstitutional by the U.S. Supreme Court in 1987. ORA's Models of Origins Curriculum

Guide was a product of Bourdreaux's collaboration with Bailey and others on the Tangipahoa board. An April, 1994, board meeting on the proposal turned angry after several SELU faculty members challenged Bourdreax and defended Darwinism. One of them, philosophy professor and Tangipahoa Parish native Barbara Forrest, would go on to become a national leader in fight against creationist instruction following the publication of her book, *Creationism's Trojan Horse: The Wedge of Intelligent Design*. When it came time to adopt the creationist curriculum guide, a SELU history professor on the board, Howard Nichols, managed to orchestrate its defeat by a single vote. Not to be denied entirely, Bailey promptly joined with a fellow creationist on the board, Arthur Zieske, in demanding at least that the board require teachers, prior to any classroom instruction in evolution, read a disclaimer stating that Darwinism was not being presented to dissuade belief in the biblical account of creation.

Zieske, an articulate retired army officer, served as the point person on the school board in promoting the disclaimer even though Bailey and Bourdreaux were widely perceived as its chief proponents. With the community already divided over the earlier creationism proposal, tensions flared anew over the disclaimer. Bailey rejected a recommendation to delete any explicit reference to religion from the disclaimer's call for critically thinking about Darwinism. Asserting at the April board meeting that up to 90% of local school students were taught by their parents that God created all life, he argued that they would be confused if their science teachers gave a naturalistic account of origins without mentioning the biblical account. By gaining the support of one additional board member, the new proposal won by a margin of five to four. Frustrated opponents immediately threatened to challenge the measure in court.

Herb Freiler, a local realtor with school-aged children, led the charge against the disclaimer just as he often did against perceived intrusions of religion into the Parish's public schools. "What you are doing," he scolded board members at a public meeting prior to their passage of the disclaimer in April, 1994, "is to just foist [your] own fundamentalist Christian viewpoint on the citizens of this parish at great embarrassment to many of us."[101] Securing the assistance of the state ACLU to file suit in federal court, Freiler recruited other plaintiffs, included SELU biologist Robert Okazaki, who joined the lawsuit under the name Sam Smith to protect his children from taunting. The ACLU gave the school board ten days to repeal the disclaimer but the board voted to defend it in court. Both sides dug in their heels. "When the board put this into effect, we had our legal counsels advise us on it. We wanted to make sure the wording was legal," Tangipahoa Parish School Superintendent Ted Cason said at the time. "The board just wanted to make sure that the evolution theory isn't being taken out of context. It's a theory and it is not taught to promote or go against any Christian or religious belief."[102] The constitutionality of this

---

101. Thomas Vinciguerra, *In a Louisiana Parish, Dim Echoes of the 'Monkey Trial'*, NY TIMES, June 25, 2000, at 7.

102. *Tangipahoa Board Faces ACLU Suit Threat*, BATON ROUGE ADVOCATE, Oct. 19, 1994, at 5B.

stance would deeply and bitterly divide the Fifth Circuit Court of Appeals and the U.S. Supreme Court, leading to the following series of increasingly harsh opinions:

FREILER v. TANGIPAHOA PARISH BD. OF EDUC.

United States Court of Appeals for the Fifth Circuit
185 F.3d 337 (5th Cir.1999)

BENAVIDES, CIRCUIT JUDGE: Parents of children in the Tangipahoa Parish Public Schools brought this suit to enjoin their school board from mandating that a disclaimer be read immediately before the teaching of evolution in all elementary and secondary classes. The district court held that the disclaimer constituted an establishment of religion in violation of the First Amendment. We affirm.

The teaching of evolution has created controversy for many years in the Tangipahoa Parish Public Schools ("TPPS"). Following a failed attempt to introduce creation science into the Tangipahoa curriculum as a legitimate scientific alternative to evolution, the Tangipahoa Parish Board of Education ("School Board" or "Board") adopted a resolution disclaiming the endorsement of evolution. The resolution, which passed by a 5–4 vote of the School Board on April 19, 1994, reads:

> Whenever, in classes of elementary or high school, the scientific theory of evolution is to be presented, whether from textbook, workbook, pamphlet, other written material, or oral presentation, the following statement shall be quoted immediately before the unit of study begins as a disclaimer from endorsement of such theory.

> It is hereby recognized by the Tangipahoa Board of Education, that the lesson to be presented, regarding the origin of life and matter, is known as the Scientific Theory of Evolution and should be presented to inform students of the scientific concept and not intended to influence or dissuade the Biblical version of Creation or any other concept.

> It is further recognized by the Board of Education that it is the basic right and privilege of each student to form his/her own opinion and maintain beliefs taught by parents on this very important matter of the origin of life and matter. Students are urged to exercise critical thinking and gather all information possible and closely examine each alternative toward forming an opinion.

Preceding the adoption of the resolution, School Board members and parents who were present at the April 19, 1994, meeting discussed the language of the disclaimer. In particular, debate centered on the inclusion of the phrase "Biblical version of Creation." A School Board member, Logan Guess, voiced concerns that the reference to the Bible excluded non-Christian viewpoints from the disclaimer. He argued that, even though the disclaimer also included the phrase "or any other concept," School Board members were concerned only with declining to endorse evolution because of its inconsistency with the Biblical version of creation. Bailey, the board member who proposed the disclaimer, justified including the phrase, arguing that because "there are two basic concepts out there" (presumably creation science and evolution), and because he believed that "perhaps 95 percent" of the community "fall into the category of believing [in] divine creation," the Board should not "shy away, or hide away from saying that this is not to dissuade from the Biblical version." In his closing remarks immediately before the Board voted to adopt the disclaimer, Bailey further suggested that evolution theory as taught in science class should not be confused with fact and that the School Board should explicitly decline to endorse evolution theory because of its inconsistency with the faith of the larger community.

On November 7, 1994, approximately seven months after the resolution passed, several parents of children in the TPPS brought suit in the U.S. District Court for the Eastern District of Louisiana, challenging the validity of the disclaimer under provisions in the United States and Louisiana constitutions barring laws "respecting an establishment of religion." U.S. Const. amends., I, XIV; La. Const. art. I, § 8. The district court concluded that the resolution was devoid of secular purpose and therefore ran afoul of the first prong of the three-part test of Lemon v. Kurtzman, 403 U.S. 602 (1971). In reaching this conclusion, the district court discredited the School Board's assertion that its secular purpose in adopting the disclaimer was to promote critical thinking and information gathering by students on the subject of the origin of life. The court noted that School Board members did not mention this purported purpose during the adoption debate and that the Tangipahoa Parish Public Schools already encouraged students to think critically about all issues before the adoption of the disclaimer. The district court found that the statements made by School Board members both during the adoption debate and while testifying at trial revealed that the disclaimer, in fact, had a religious purpose—i.e., to satisfy the religious concerns of the majority that the teaching of evolution in public school contradicted lessons taught in Sunday school. Accordingly, the court held the resolution invalid under the federal and state constitutions and enjoined the reading of the disclaimer. The School Board and the named individual defendants then brought this appeal.

The sole issue for our resolution is whether the specific disclaimer adopted by the Tangipahoa Parish Board of Education contravenes the First Amendment. We limit our analysis to the precise language of the disclaimer and the context in which it was adopted. We do not confront the broader issue of whether the reading of any disclaimer before the teaching of evolution would amount to an unconstitutional establishment of religion. . . .

Although widely criticized and occasionally ignored, the Lemon test continues to govern Establishment Clause cases. In Agostini v. Felton, 521 U.S. 203 (1997), the Supreme Court laid to rest rumors of the Lemon test's demise when it exclusively applied Lemon analysis to a school aid program. The Court acknowledged the continued viability of the general Lemon principles used to evaluate whether government action violates the Establishment Clause and noted in particular that the nature of the inquiry under Lemon's purpose prong has "remained largely unchanged." Id. at 223.

A.

The first prong of the Lemon test requires that challenged state action have a secular purpose. See Lemon, 403 U.S. at 612. Lemon's first prong does not require that challenged state action have been enacted in furtherance of exclusively, or even predominately, secular objectives. See Wallace v. Jaffree, 472 U.S. 38, 56 (1985) (explaining that a statute motivated in part by a religious purpose may satisfy Lemon's purpose prong). In order for state activity to pass muster under Lemon's first criterion a sincere secular purpose for the contested state action must exist; even if that secular purpose is but one in a sea of religious purposes. See id. at 56.

The School Board has articulated three distinct, albeit intertwined, purposes for the contested disclaimer. According to the Board, the disclaimer serves (1) to encourage informed freedom of belief, (2) to disclaim any orthodoxy of belief that could be inferred from the exclusive placement of evolution in the curriculum, and (3) to reduce offense to the sensibilities and sensitivities of any student or parent caused by the teaching of evolution. . . .

We find that the contested disclaimer does not further the first articulated objective of encouraging informed freedom of belief or critical thinking by students. Even though the final sentence of the disclaimer urges students "to exercise critical thinking and gather all information possible and closely examine each alternative toward forming an opinion," we find that the disclaimer as a whole furthers a contrary purpose, namely the protection and maintenance of a particular religious viewpoint. In the first paragraph to be read to school children, the Tangipahoa Board of Education declares that the "Scientific Theory of Evolution . . . should be presented to inform students of the scientific concept" but that such teaching is "not intended to influence or dissuade the Biblical version of Creation or any other concept." From this, school children hear that evolution as taught in the classroom need not affect what they already know. Such a message is contrary to an intent to encourage critical thinking, which requires that students approach new concepts with an open mind and a willingness to alter and shift existing viewpoints. This conclusion is even more inescapable when the message of the first paragraph is coupled with the statement in the last that it is "the basic right and privilege of each student to . . . maintain beliefs taught by parents on [the] . . . matter of the origin of life. . . ." We, therefore, find that the disclaimer as a whole does not serve to encourage critical thinking and that the School Board's first articulated purpose is a sham.

We find that the disclaimer does further the second and third purposes articulated by the School Board. The disclaimer explicitly acknowledges the existence of at least one alternative theory for the origin of life, i.e., the Biblical version of creation. Additionally, the disclaimer reminds school children that they can rightly maintain beliefs taught by their parents on the subject of the origin of life. We have no doubt that the disclaimer will further its second and third avowed objectives of disclaiming any orthodoxy of belief that could be implied from the exclusive place of evolution in the public school curriculum and reducing student/parent offense caused by the teaching of evolution. Accordingly, we conclude that these two purposes are sincere. . . .

In order to avoid the "callous indifference" first cautioned against by the Supreme Court in Zorach v. Clauson, 343 U.S. 306, 314 (1952), we conclude that, under the instant facts, the dual objectives of disclaiming orthodoxy of belief and reducing student/parent offense are permissible secular objectives that the School Board could rightly address. Cf. Bethel School District No. 403 v. Fraser, 478 U.S. 675, 681 (1986) (noting that, in the context of a civil rights action, fundamental values essential to a democratic society include "tolerance of divergent political and religious views" and "consideration of the sensibilities of others, and, in the case of a school, the sensibilities of fellow students"). In so doing, we acknowledge that local school boards need not turn a blind eye to the concerns of students and parents troubled by the teaching of evolution in public classrooms.

B.

Lemon's second prong asks whether, irrespective of the School Board's actual purpose, "the practice under review in fact conveys a message of endorsement or disapproval." Doe v. Santa Fe Independent School District, 168 F.3d 806, 817 (5th Cir.1999). This is similar to analysis pursuant to the endorsement test. Under either the second Lemon prong or the endorsement test, the Supreme Court has cautioned that a government practice may not aid one religion, aid all religions, or favor one religion over another. See, e.g., County of Allegheny v. ACLU, 492 U.S. 573, 605 (1989) ("Whatever else the Establishment Clause may mean (and we have held it to mean no official preference even for religion over nonreligion), it certainly means at the very least that government may not demonstrate a preference for one particular sect or creed (including a preference for Christianity over other religions)." (citation omitted)). Nonetheless, where the benefit to religion or to a church is no more than indirect, remote, or incidental, the Supreme Court has advised that "no realistic danger [exists] that the community would think that the [contested government practice] was endorsing religion or any particular creed." Lamb's Chapel v. Center Moriches Union Free School District, 508 U.S. 384, 395 (1993). . . .

In assessing the primary effect of the contested disclaimer, we focus on the message conveyed by the disclaimer to the students who are its intended audience. See County of Allegheny, 492 U.S. at 620. After careful consideration of the oral arguments, the briefs, the record on appeal, and the language of the disclaimer, we conclude that the primary effect of the disclaimer is to protect and maintain a particular religious viewpoint, namely belief in the Biblical version of creation. In reaching this conclusion, we rely on the interplay of three factors: (1) the juxtaposition of the disavowal of endorsement of evolution with an urging that students contemplate alternative theories of the origin of life; (2) the reminder that students have the right to maintain beliefs taught by their parents regarding the origin of life; and (3) the "Biblical version of Creation" as the only alternative theory explicitly referenced in the disclaimer.

We note that the term "disclaimer," as used by the School Board to describe the passage to be read to students before lessons on evolution, is not wholly accurate. Beyond merely "disclaiming" endorsement of evolution, the two paragraph passage urges students to take action—to "exercise critical thinking and gather all information possible and closely examine each alternative" to evolution. The disclaimer, taken as a whole, encourages students to read and meditate upon religion in general and the "Biblical version of Creation" in particular.

Although it is not per se unconstitutional to introduce religion or religious concepts during school hours, there is a fundamental difference between introducing religion and religious concepts in "an appropriate study of history, civilization, ethics, comparative religion, or the like" and the reading of the School Board-mandated disclaimer now before us. Stone v. Graham, 449 U.S. 39, 42 (1980). The TPPS disclaimer does not encourage students to think about religion in order to provide context for a political controversy studied in a history class, see, e.g., Aguillard, 482 U.S. at 607 n. 8 (Powell, J., concurring) ("For example, the political controversies in Northern Ireland, the Middle East, and India cannot be understood properly without reference to the underlying religious beliefs and the conflicts they tend to generate."), or to promote understanding of different religions, see, e.g., School District of Abington v. Schempp, 374 U.S. 203, 225 (1963) ("[I]t might well be said that one's education is not complete without a study of comparative religion or the history of religion and its relationship to the advancement of civilization."). Instead, the disclaimer-including the directive to "exercise critical thinking" in the second paragraph, together with the explicit reference to the "Biblical version of Creation" in the first paragraph-urges students to think about religious theories of "the origin of life and matter" as an alternative to evolution, the State-mandated curriculum. . . .

The School Board's reliance on Lamb's Chapel is misplaced. . . . In that case, the Court held that using a public school after school hours for the showing of religiously oriented films did not violate the Establishment Clause. See Lamb's Chapel, 508 U.S. at 395. The Court found that "this film series would not have been during school hours, would not have been sponsored by the school, and would have been open to the public, not just to church members." Id. at 395. The Court concluded that, under these circumstances, there was no realistic danger that the community would think that the school district was endorsing religion.

There are few, if any, parallels between the instant case and Lamb's Chapel. Here, the disclaimer approved by the School Board is to be read during school hours by school teachers and explicitly encourages students to consider religious alternatives to evolution, a part of the state-mandated curriculum. Unlike in Lamb's Chapel, there is a much greater danger of students and parents perceiving that the School Board endorses religion, specifically those creeds that teach the Biblical version of creation.

The benefit to religion conferred by the reading of the Tangipahoa disclaimer is more than indirect, remote, or incidental. As such, we conclude that the disclaimer impermissibly advances religion, thereby violating the second prong of the Lemon test as well as the endorsement test.

FREILER v. TANGIPAHOA PARISH BD. OF EDUC.

United States Court of Appeals for the Fifth Circuit
201 F.3d 602 (5th Cir.2000)

PER CURIUM En Banc: The School Board contends that the panel opinion misquoted the disclaimer's language, substituting and for or in a disclaimer passage. The School Board is correct. The particular passage as stated in the disclaimer reads as follows:

> It is further recognized by the Board of Education that it is the basic right and privilege of each student to form his/her own opinion or maintain beliefs taught by parents on this very important matter of the origin of life and matter.

The improper substitution of "and" for "or" does not affect the outcome of this case.

In denying rehearing, we emphasize that we do not decide that a state-mandated statement violates the Constitution simply because it disclaims any intent to communicate to students that the theory of evolution is the only accepted explanation of the origin of life, informs students of their right to follow their religious principles, and encourages students to evaluate all explanations of life's origins, including those taught outside the classroom. We decide only that under the facts and circumstances of this case, the statement of the Tangipahoa Parish School Board is not sufficiently neutral to prevent it from violating the Establishment Clause.

Treating the Petition for Rehearing En Banc as a Petition for Panel Rehearing, the Petition for Panel Rehearing is DENIED. The court having been polled at the request of one of the members of the court and a majority of the judges who are in regular active service not having voted in favor (Fed.R.App.P. and 5th Cir. R. 35), the Petition for Rehearing En Banc is DENIED.

RHESA HAWKINS BARKSDALE, CIRCUIT JUDGE, joined by E. GRADY JOLLY, PATRICK E. HIGGINBOTHAM, EDITH H. JONES, JERRY E. SMITH, EMILIO M. GARZA and HAROLD R. DEMOSS, JR., CIRCUIT JUDGES, dissenting from the denial of rehearing en banc:.... The theory of evolution may be viewed by some as anti-religious. The disclaimer recognizes this historic tension between evolution (scientific concept) and other theories or concepts about the origin of life and matter, using the "Biblical version of Creation" as but an example of such other concepts. And, it affirmatively notes that evolution is the only theory taught. In furtherance of the purposes to disclaim any orthodoxy of belief that could be inferred from the exclusive placement of evolution in the curriculum, and to reduce any resulting offense to students who adhere to concepts other than evolution, the disclaimer points out that the fact that evolution is the only such concept taught—"presented to inform students of [that] scientific concept"—is not intended to influence or dissuade any other concept, including the Biblical version. The disclaimer balances; it neutralizes; it is consistent with the requisite neutrality.

The panel reasoned that, because the only alternative theory identified in the disclaimer is a religious one, the disclaimer "serves only to promote a religious alternative to evolution." Freiler, 185 F.3d at 348. The reliance on this factor is misplaced, because the panel fails to take into account the disclaimer's audience....

The record reflects that an estimated 95% of the parish students are adherents to the Biblical concept of creation. Accordingly, use of the "Biblical version of Creation" as an illustration of an alternative concept to evolution is hardly surprising. Because the overwhelming majority of the students expected to hear the disclaimer were familiar with that alternative concept, the reference serves to give context to the message, but without promoting that concept or expressing intolerance for any other. Surely, giving context to a message is an admirable method of instruction.

Contrary to the panel's interpretation, the disclaimer expressly encourages examination of "each alternative" concept for life's origin, including evolution, the Biblical version, and others that are not identified. Moreover, the panel erroneously assumes that all alternatives to evolution are religious in nature, ignoring the existence of non-religious theories, such as the "Big Bang" and panspermia (reproductive bodies of living organisms exist throughout the universe and develop wherever the environment is favorable).

Based on my review of the record, the language of the disclaimer, and the context in which it was intended to be used, the primary effect of the disclaimer is not to advance religion; instead, it is to advance tolerance and respect for diverse viewpoints. The record reflects that, to the overwhelming majority of the parish students, the scientific concept of evolution conflicts with their (or their parents') beliefs about the origin of life and matter; and its exclusive place in the curriculum had caused concern among students and parents. The disclaimer's message is one of respect for diverse viewpoints, informing students that teaching evolution as the sole concept for the origin of life and matter is not intended to influence or dissuade them from forming their own opinions about the subject or from maintaining beliefs taught by their parents. . . .

TANGIPAHOA PARISH BD. OF EDUC. v. FREILER

Supreme Court of the United States
530 U.S. 1251 (2000)

Petition for writ of certiorari to the United States Court of Appeals for the Fifth Circuit denied.

JUSTICE SCALIA, with whom THE CHIEF JUSTICE and JUSTICE THOMAS join, dissenting:

I

On April 19, 1994, the Tangipahoa Parish, Louisiana, Board of Education (Board) passed the following resolution:

"Whenever, in classes of elementary or high school, the scientific theory of evolution is to be presented, whether from textbook, workbook, pamphlet, other written material, or oral presentation the following statement shall be quoted immediately before the unit of study begins as a disclaimer from endorsement of such theory.

"It is hereby recognized by the Tangipahoa Parish Board of Education, that the lesson to be presented, regarding the origin of life and matter, is known as the Scientific Theory of Evolution and should be presented to inform students of the scientific concept and not intended to influence or dissuade the Biblical version of Creation or any other concept.

"It is further recognized by the Board of Education that it is the basic right and privilege of each student to form his/her own opinion or maintain beliefs taught by parents on this very important matter of the origin of life and matter. Students are urged to exercise critical thinking and gather all information possible and closely examine each alternative toward forming an opinion." Pet. for Cert. 2.

Approximately seven months after this resolution was adopted, respondents, three parents of children attending the Tangipahoa Parish Public Schools, brought suit in the United States District Court for the Eastern District of Louisiana against petitioners, the Board, its members, and the superintendent of the school district. They brought a facial challenge to the disclaimer contained in the last two paragraphs of the resolution, claiming that it violated the coextensive Establishment Clauses of the United States and Louisiana Constitutions. The District Court ruled in favor of respondents. 975 F.Supp. 819 (1997). It concluded that the disclaimer lacked a secular purpose, and thus failed the first prong of the three-prong test outlined in Lemon v. Kurtzman, 403 U.S. 602 (1971), because the Board's articulated purpose—that it adopted the disclaimer to promote critical thinking by students on the subject of the origin of life-was a sham. See 975 F.Supp., at 829. It therefore held the disclaimer unconstitutional under both the Federal and the Louisiana Constitutions. See id., at 830.

The Fifth Circuit affirmed. 185 F. 3d 337 (1999). It began by noting that, in the context of public education, this Court has used three different tests to evaluate state actions challenged on Establishment Clause grounds: the three-prong test of Lemon; the "endorsement" test of County of Allegheny v. American Civil Liberties Union, Greater Pittsburgh Chapter, 492 U.S. 573 (1989); and the "coercion" test of Lee v. Weisman, 505 U.S. 577 (1992). See 185 F.3d, at 343. Although noting that the Lemon test has been "widely criticized and occasionally ignored," the court opted to apply it. 185 F.3d, at 344. The court first concluded that the disclaimer had a secular purpose and therefore survived the first prong of the Lemon test. See 185 F.3d, at 344–346. While agreeing with the District Court that the purpose of promoting critical thinking by students on the subject of the origin of life was a sham, the court concluded that the disclaimer served two other, legitimate secular purposes: disclaiming any orthodoxy of belief that could be inferred from the exclusive place of evolution in the curriculum, and reducing offense to any student or parent caused by the teaching of evolution. See ibid.

The Fifth Circuit then turned to the second prong of the Lemon test-the so-called "effects" prong. See 185 F.3d, at 346–348. The court concluded that the disclaimer failed this prong because "the primary effect of the disclaimer is to protect and maintain a particular religious viewpoint, namely belief in the Biblical version of creation." Id., at 346. It based this conclusion on three factors: "(1) the juxtaposition of the disavowal of endorsement of evolution with an urging that students contemplate alternative theories of the origin of life; (2) the reminder that students have the right to maintain beliefs taught by their parents regarding the origin of life; and (3) the 'Biblical version of Creation' as the only alternative theory explicitly referenced in the disclaimer." Ibid. (Finally, the court noted, albeit in passing and without elaboration, that, because the disclaimer failed the second prong of the Lemon test, it would also fail the endorsement test. See 185 F.3d, at 348.)

Petitioners unsuccessfully moved for rehearing by the panel and by the en banc Fifth Circuit. 201 F.3d 602 (2000). Judge Barksdale, joined by six other judges, dissented from the denial of rehearing en banc. See id., at 603–608.

II

Like a majority of the Members of this Court, I have previously expressed my disapproval of the Lemon test. See Lamb's Chapel v. Center Moriches Union Free School Dist., 508 U.S. 384, 398–400 (1993) (SCALIA, J., joined by THOMAS, J., concurring in judgment); County of Allegheny, supra, at 655–657 (KENNEDY, J., concurring in judgment in part and dissenting in part); Corporation of Presiding Bishop of Church of Jesus Christ of Latter–Day Saints v. Amos, 483 U.S. 327, 346–349 (1987) (O'CONNOR, J., concurring in judgment); Wallace v. Jaffree, 472 U.S. 38, 107–113 (1985) (REHNQUIST, J., dissenting). I would grant certiorari in this case if only to take the opportunity to inter the Lemon test once for all.

Even assuming, however, that the Fifth Circuit correctly chose to apply the Lemon test, I believe the manner of its application so erroneous as independently to merit the granting of certiorari, if not summary reversal. Under the second prong of Lemon, the "principal or primary effect [of a state action] must be one that neither advances nor inhibits religion." Lemon, supra, at 612. Far from advancing religion, the "principal or primary effect" of the disclaimer at issue here is merely to advance freedom of thought. At the outset, it is worth noting that the theory of evolution is the only theory actually taught in the Tangipahoa Parish schools. As the introductory paragraph of the resolution suggests, the disclaimer operates merely as a (perhaps not too believable) "disclaimer from endorsement" of that single theory, and not as an affirmative endorsement of any particular religious theory as to the origin of life, or even of religious theories as to the origin of life generally. The only allusion to religion in the entire disclaimer is a reference to the "Biblical version of Creation," mentioned as an illustrative example—surely the most obvious example—of a "concept" that the teaching of evolution was "not intended to influence or dissuade." The disclaimer does not refer again to the "Biblical version of Creation," much less provide any elaboration as to what that theory entails; instead, it merely reaffirms that "it is the basic right and privilege of each student to form his/her own opinion or maintain beliefs taught by parents on this very important matter of the origin of life and matter," and neutrally encourages students "closely [to] examine each alternative" before forming an opinion.

As even this cursory discussion of the disclaimer amply demonstrates, the Fifth Circuit's conclusion that "[t]he disclaimer ... encourages students to read and meditate upon religion in general and the 'Biblical version of Creation' in particular," 185 F.3d, at 346, lacks any support in the text of the invalidated document. In view of the fact that the disclaimer merely reminds students of their right to form their own beliefs on the subject, or to maintain beliefs taught by their parents—not to mention the fact that the theory of evolution is the only theory actually taught in the lesson that follows the disclaimer—there is "no realistic danger that the community would think that the [School Board] was endorsing religion or any particular creed, and any benefit to religion or to the Church would have been no more than incidental." Lamb's Chapel, supra, at 395. At bottom, the disclaimer constitutes nothing more than "simply a tolerable acknowledgment of beliefs widely held among the people of this country," Marsh v. Chambers, 463 U.S. 783, 792 (1983). See also Lynch v. Donnelly, 465 U.S. 668, 673, (1984) ("Nor does the Constitution require complete separation of church and state; it affirmatively mandates accommodation, not merely tolerance, of all religions, and forbids hostility toward any'').

In denying the petition for rehearing, the Fifth Circuit panel took another tack: "In denying rehearing, we emphasize that we do not decide that a state-mandated statement violates the Constitution simply because it disclaims any intent to communicate to students that the theory of evolution is the only accepted explanation of the origin of life, informs students of their right to follow their religious principles, and encourages students to evaluate all explanations of life's origins, including those taught outside the classroom. We decide only that under the facts and circumstances of this case, the statement of the Tangipahoa Parish School Board is not sufficiently neutral to prevent it from violating the Establishment Clause." 201 F.3d, at 603. Inasmuch as what the disclaimer contains is nothing more than what this statement purports to allow, the explanation is incoherent. Reference to unnamed "facts and circumstances of this case" is not a substitute for judicial reasoning. The only aspect of the disclaimer that could conceivably be regarded as going beyond what the rehearing statement purports to approve is the explicit mention—as an example—of "the Biblical version of Creation." To think that this reference to (and plainly not endorsement of) a reality of religious literature—and this use of an example that is not a contrived one, but to the contrary the example most likely to come into play—somehow converts the otherwise innocuous disclaimer into an establishment of religion is quite simply absurd.

In Epperson v. Arkansas, 393 U.S. 97 (1968), we invalidated a statute that forbade the teaching of evolution in public schools; in Edwards v. Aguillard, 482 U.S. 578 (1987), we invalidated a statute that required the teaching of creationism whenever evolution was also taught; today we permit a Court of Appeals to push the much beloved secular legend of the Monkey Trial one step further. We stand by in silence while a deeply divided Fifth Circuit bars a school district from even suggesting to students that other theories besides evolution—including, but not limited to, the Biblical theory of creation—are worthy of their consideration. I dissent.

NOTES AND QUESTIONS

1. In *Freiler*, a pro-creationist state or local school-board action finally passed the *Lemon* test's purpose prong. According to the Fifth Circuit Court of Appeals, what was the Tangipahoa Parish School Board's acceptable "sincere secular purpose" for adopting the anti-evolution disclaimer? Asserting that schools "need not turn a blind eye to the concerns of students and parents troubled by the teaching of evolution," the court ruled that public schools may seek to address those concerns by telling students that the Bible offers a religious accounts of origins that they may believe instead of the scientific theory of evolution. In doing so, the School Board was motivated by religious reasons in the sense that it was responding to religious concerns and

was motivated by religious beliefs. Nevertheless, as described by the court, the Board did not have an *unconstitutional* religious purpose under the *Lemon* test because it did not seek to *advance* religious belief. Can you see the difference? Although it may seem like a fine line, it has proved decisive in some Establishment Clause cases. It assumes that legislators or school-board members may adopt laws or policies for religious reasons without necessarily seeking to advance religion. For example, school officials may simply want to accommodate the religious beliefs of students, such as by closing the school on religious holidays, or neutralize a possible impression that school activities favor or disfavor particular religious beliefs, such as by including a variety of religious and non-religious symbols in December holiday pageants and displays. In support of its holding, the *Freiler* court cited a 1952 Supreme Court decision, *Zorach v. Clauson*, upholding "release-time programs" in which public schools allowed some students to leave school during school hours to receive religious instruction while requiring others to stay in school. "Our institutions presume a Supreme Being," Justice William O. Douglass famously wrote in *Zorach*, and presumably those institutions will incorporate religious values. In evaluating the secular purpose in *Freilier*, consider Justice Black's concurring opinion in *Epperson*, suggesting that Arkansas's 1927 anti-evolution law had the secular purpose of removing a controversial subject from the curriculum, and Justice Scalia's dissenting opinion in *Edwards*, arguing that Louisiana's 1981 Balanced Treatment Act had the secular purpose of promoting students' freedom from indoctrination. Yet the Supreme Court struck down both of those laws for not having a sincere secular purpose. How did the purposes for the Tangipahoa disclaimer differ from those attributed to the Arkansas initiative by Justice Black or to the Louisiana act by Justice Scalia? Perhaps a majority of the justices simply did not believe the alleged secular purposes in *Epperson* and *Edwards* while the Fifth Circuit judges believed the alleged secular purposes in *Freiler*.

2.   Despite surviving the treacherous shoals of the *Lemon* test's purpose prong, the Tangipahoa disclaimer ran aground on the *Lemon* test's effect prong. This prong, the *Freiler* court noted, asks whether a challenged government action has the primary effect of conveying "a message of endorsement or disapproval" of religion. To answer this question, a court first identifies the intended audience and then assesses what primary message that audience would likely receive. What is the disclaimer's intended audience? If students, what message would they likely receive from the disclaimer? The panel decision stated that, by singling out the "Biblical version of Creation" as the only named alternative to the "Scientific Theory of Evolution," the disclaimer had the primary effect of communicating the School Board's endorsement of biblical creationism to students. As such, the court ruled, it violated both the *Lemon* test's purpose prong and a stand-alone "endorsement test." In denying the School Board's motion for rehearing en banc or by the panel, the court stressed that its ruling would not necessarily apply to a disclaimer that simply urged students to keep an open mind about origins without singling out a particular religious alternative to for special consideration. Consider again the Alabama textbook disclaimer reprinted in the previous chapter, especially as it was revised by the Alabama Board of Education in 2001. Would it run afoul of

the *Lemon* test's effect prong as depicted in *Frieler*? Particularly as revised, the Alabama disclaimer did not single out an alternative to Darwinism.

3.   Although it was not reviewed en banc or by the Supreme Court, the panel opinion in *Frieler* excited strong opposition. Seven of the fifteen judges on Fifth Circuit Court of Appeals—one shy of a number needed for rehearing—dissented from the court's denial of the School Board's motion for a rehearing en banc. Three of the nine justices on the U.S. Supreme Court—one shy of number needed for review—dissented from the High Court's denial of the School Board's petition for Supreme Court review. The dissenters argued that the disclaimer urged students to consider all alternatives to Darwinism and simply named the biblical version of creation as one example. Given the widespread local belief in biblical creationism, the Fifth Circuit dissenters noted, the use of this example "is hardly surprising." Do you agree or was the School Board signaling its endorsement of biblical creationism? *Frieler* turned out to be the first of six lawsuits brought by the ACLU against the Tangipahoa Parish Board of Education over religious activities in public education, including repeated complaints about teacher-led prayer and official prayers at athletic events.

II.   DISCIPLINING CREATIONIST TEACHERS

Faribault, Minnesota, is a small town some 60 miles south of Minneapolis—"Minnesota nice" was how local science teacher Rodney LeVake depicted it—but the steel-side of Minnesota stubborn showed itself in 1998 when LeVake refused to teach Darwinism in the manner prescribed by his superiors.[103] LeVake had taught science at Faribault Junior High School for thirteen years when an opening arose to teach 10th grade biology at Faribault High School in 1997. Certified to teach the subject and with sufficient seniority for promotion to the position, LeVake requested the job despite harboring doubts about Darwinism. "I believe that the Bible is God's word," LeVake stated in a later television interview, "and there isn't [sic] any mistakes in it. I believe that God created the world around us and the plants and animals and so forth."[104] In his view, revealed biblical truth denied Darwinism and, rightly understood, evidence from nature did too. The theory of evolution, however, was a prescribed element in the course syllabus, the course registration guide, and the state graduation standards. Although LeVake would later say that his predecessor in the position had devoted only a day to teaching evolution, that predecessor had co-authored the course syllabus and was said by others to give the subject extended coverage. Darwinism was also featured in the assigned textbook. Nevertheless, in his first year teaching biology, LeVake rarely mentioned evolution. "Other biology teachers were devoting two-three weeks to evolution, but Rodney wasn't covering it," recalled his

---

103. Randy Moore, *When a Biology Teacher Refuses to Teach Evolution: A Talk with Rod LeVake*, 66 AM. BIOLOGY TCHR. 246, 249 (2004).

104. *In the Beginning* (CNN television broadcast, Mar. 12, 2000) (interview of Rodney LeVake).

department co-chair, Ken Hubert.[105] LeVake also kept creationist material in his classroom and gave extra credit to one student for summarizing a creationist article.

After talking with LeVake about the issue and hearing LeVake's objections to teaching evolution, Hubert reported the matter to the high-school principal and the district curriculum director. Over the spring following LaVake's first year teaching biology, meetings were held with LaVake, school officials, and the school's other science teachers to try to resolve the issue. LeVake made it clear that he could not in good conscience teach Darwinism without also telling students about the difficulties and inconsistencies with the theory. He maintained that large-scale evolution was impossible and gave his fellow teachers books supporting that position. None of the other science teachers agreed with him. At the same time, LeVake assured his superiors that he had not talked about God in the classroom and would not teach creation-science—only about problems with Darwinism. Concluding that LeVake would not follow the district-approved curriculum, the principal reassigned him to teach 9th grade physical science for the next year. Teaching reassignments were authorized under school-district contracts.

Feeling that he had been reassigned unjustly for his religious beliefs or for what school administrators thought that he might teach rather than for what he did or would teach, LeVake asked for legal aid from three conservative Christian defense organizations, The Rutherford Institute (which had assisted creationist teacher John Peloza), Focus on the Family, and the American Center for Law and Justice (ACLJ), which was founded in 1990 by televangelist Pat Robertson as a Christian counterweight to the ACLU. The ACLJ agreed to help and soon Robertson's Christian Broadcasting Network was spreading LeVake's story nationwide. After the school superintendent once again refused to reinstate LeVake in his former position, he filed suit in state court against the school district and various school officials charging that they had violated his state and constitutional rights by reassigning him to teach physical science. Although a surface cordiality persisted, local students, parents, and even teachers split over the lawsuit, with some supporting and others opposing LeVake. Even though he was not named as a defendant in the case, Hubert reported receiving hate mail because of his role in it.

National interest in the lawsuit built over time. CNN featured the story in March, 2000, followed by an article in the popular news magazine, *Time*. "LeVake is so profoundly nonconfrontational that he inspires trust," the *Time* article reported, "which is why he is the perfect weapon in the new war over how evolution is—or isn't—being taught in public schools across the U.S. LeVake believes evolution is flat-out bad science. He can be very convincing." Predicting a landmark ruling, LeVake's attorney sought to distance the suit from prior creation-science litigation:

---

105. Randy Moore, *Standing up for Our Profession: A Talk with Ken Hubert*, 66 AM. BIOLOGY TCHR. 325, 326 (2004).

"For the first time, we have a teacher who is not asking to teach creationism. He simply wants to teach science the way he thinks—and the way a lot of people think—it should be taught, in a more balanced way."[106] For its part, the school district countered that the issue was not about evolution but solely about the authority of school districts to establish and enforce the curriculum. LeVake wanted his case decided by a jury composed of local Minnesotans but the court granted the school district's motion for summary judgment in June, 2000, and flatly rejected all of LeVake's claims. On appeal, the Minnesota Court of Appeals issued the following opinion:

LeVAKE v. INDEPENDENT SCHOOL DIST. #656

Court of Appeals for Minnesota
625 N.W.2d 502 (Minn. Ct. App. 2001)

FOLEY, J.: . . . In 1984, appellant Rodney LeVake was hired by respondent Independent School District #656 as a high school science and math teacher. According to LeVake's contract, he could be assigned to teach any topic for which he has licensure. During the summer of 1997, LeVake was offered a position to teach tenth-grade biology for the 1997–98 academic year. Before accepting the position, LeVake met with Ken Hubert, cochairman of the high school science department, and Dave Johnson, the high school principal, to discuss the course and its curriculum requirements. As part of the tenth-grade biology course, LeVake was required to teach evolution. The curriculum for the course is governed by the "Biology Program Curriculum Proposal" (the proposal) and the "Course Syllabus" (the syllabus). The proposal states that upon completion of the class, students will be able to understand that evolution involves natural selection and mutations, which constantly cause changes in living things. In the required course book for the biology class, three chapters dealt with evolution but only one was required as part of the curriculum. None of the chapters addressed alternative theories to or criticisms of evolution. The syllabus provided examples of topics that should be covered in class, which included evolution. Minnesota's high school graduation standards do not specifically refer to evolution; rather, the standards provide that a student must demonstrate an understanding of biological change over time. Minn. R. 3501.0446, subp. 2 (1999).

LeVake accepted the position and began teaching the class with full knowledge of the curriculum requirements. In spring 1998, when LeVake arrived at the evolution component of the course, he spent only one day covering the topic, which included a correlating lab. The school year was cut short that year, so none of the other biology teachers spent a significant amount of time teaching the evolution chapters either. Hubert expressed concern to Johnson that LeVake did not adequately cover evolution and also discussed the situation with LeVake. LeVake essentially

---

106. Josh Tyrangiel, *A Teacher Is Stirring Up Trouble About Darwin—In a Very Minnesota Way*, TIME, July 10, 2000, at 60.

told Hubert that he could not teach evolution according to the prescribed curriculum.[107] On April 1, 1998, LeVake met with Hubert, Johnson, and Cheryl Freund, the curriculum director, to discuss the issue. LeVake indicated that he did not regard evolution as a viable scientific concept. At that time, Freund asked if LeVake mentioned God or the Bible in class because she wanted to be sure that LeVake was not discussing religion in a manner that would give the impression that the school was not religiously neutral.

On April 7, 1998, LeVake, Hubert, Johnson, Freund, and the rest of the high school's science department met to discuss LeVake's teaching methods. At that meeting Johnson asked LeVake to write a position paper on how he proposed to teach evolution in his biology class. LeVake completed this paper on April 15. In his paper, LeVake articulated that he believes evolution is impossible from a "biological, anatomical, and physiological standpoint" and that there is "no evidence to show that it actually occurred." LeVake's paper also contends that the "complexity of life that we see around us is a testimony that evolution, as it is currently being handled in our text, is impossible." LeVake concludes by writing:

> I don't believe an unquestioning faith in the theory of evolution is foundational to the goals I have stated in teaching my students about themselves, their responsibilities, and gaining a sense of awe for what they see around them. I will teach, should the department decide that it is appropriate, the theory of evolution. *I will also accompany that treatment of evolution with an honest look at the difficulties and inconsistencies of the theory without turning my class into a religious one.*

(Emphasis added.)

On April 28, 1998, after meeting with the school district's lawyers and consulting with Freund and others, Johnson decided that LeVake should be reassigned to teach ninth-grade natural science for the following academic year. LeVake was informed of this decision the following day. As the basis for the school's decision, Johnson expressed concern that a basic concept of biology, meaning the theory of evolution, would be diluted and that students would "lose the gist" of the theory.

LeVake appealed his reassignment to Superintendent Keith Dixon. On May 14, 1998, Dixon wrote LeVake a letter, affirming his reassignment. Dixon believed that LeVake differed fundamentally with the "com-

---

107. [The trial court opinion expanded on these facts in part as follows:

At some point in the second semester of the academic year, Ken Hubert noticed that, while he and Mr. Koehler had covered chapter nine, Plaintiff appeared to have skipped that chapter, Mr. Hubert was concerned by this because he believed evolution was part of the state graduation standards, and, in his opinion, a failure to teach it amounted to a problem with the curriculum. Sometime in February or Much of 1998, Mr. Hubert approached Plaintiff and asked him how he was going to handle the topic of evolution. In his own deposition, Plaintiff stated that "in essence ... said to him I can't teach evolution. That's what I said to him." Mr. Hubert expressed his concerns to Principal Johnson that Plaintiff was not teaching evolution. Principal Johnson informed Ms. Freund of Mr. Hubert's concerns.

LeVake v. Ind. School Dist. #656, No. CX–99–793, slip op. at 4–5 (Minn. Dist. Ct. June 20, 2000).]

monly held principles of the curriculum as outlined." Dixon further articulated that LeVake's insistence on teaching the inconsistencies of evolution was not an appropriate method for teaching the approved curriculum.

On May 24, 1999, LeVake filed a lawsuit against respondents Independent School District #656, Keith Dixon, Dave Johnson, and Cheryl Freund (respondents). Based on 42 U.S.C. § 1983, LeVake alleged that respondents violated his right to free exercise of religion, free speech, due process, freedom of conscience, and academic freedom. Respondents moved for summary judgment, which the district court granted. The district court dismissed all of LeVake's claims with prejudice on the merits. LeVake now appeals from the district court's grant of summary judgment. . . .

I. Free Exercise of Religion

The First Amendment to the United States Constitution provides that "Congress shall make no law respecting an establishment of religion, or prohibiting the free exercise thereof." U.S. Const. amend. I. The First Amendment applies to the states by virtue of the Fourteenth Amendment. *Cantwell v. Connecticut*, 310 U.S. 296, 303 (1940).

> The right to believe as one wishes and to practice that belief according to the dictates of conscience, without violating the personal rights of others, is fundamental to our system.

Murphy v. Murphy, 574 N.W.2d 77, 80 (Minn. App. 1998). If a law of general application "incidentally infringes on religious practices," it does not contravene the free exercise clause. *Id.* The party asserting a free exercise violation has the initial burden of proving that the state's requirement imposes a burden on the party's religious belief or practice. *Abington Sch. Dist. v. Schempp*, 374 U.S. 203, 223 (1963).

It is unclear on what basis LeVake argues that his right to free exercise of religion was violated. LeVake does not contend that respondents prohibited him from practicing the religion of his choice. He does not assert that respondents demanded that he refrain from practicing his religion outside of the scope of his duties as a public school teacher in order to retain his teaching position, and he does not assert that the curriculum requirements incidentally infringed on his religious practice. *Cf. Hazelwood Sch. Dist. v. Kuhlmeier*, 484 U.S. 260, 273 (1988) (stating educators do not offend First Amendment so long as their actions are reasonably related to pedagogical concerns).

By analogy, LeVake focuses on employment discrimination cases to argue that circumstantial evidence of discrimination based on his religious belief exists, and he concludes that this alleged discrimination equates to respondents' violation of his right to free exercise of religion. *See Sigurdson v. Isanti Co.*, 386 N.W.2d 715, 720 (Minn. 1986) (setting out standard for showing circumstantial evidence of employment discrimination). But LeVake did not bring an employment discrimination action, and he has not provided authority demonstrating how use of this standard raises a genuine issue of material fact regarding his free exercise claim. Consequently, he has not articulated how an argument based on religious discrimination equates to a violation of his right to free exercise of religion. . . . [108]

Given respondents' important pedagogical interest in establishing the curriculum and its legitimate concern with ensuring that the school remained religiously neutral, we conclude that LeVake has not presented a genuine issue of material fact as to whether respondents' decision to assign him to teach a different class violated his right to free exercise of religion.

II. Free Speech

. . . The classroom is a "marketplace of ideas," and academic freedom should be safeguarded. *Keyishian v. Board of Regents*, 385 U.S. 589, 603 (1967). But LeVake, in his role as a public school teacher rather than as a private citizen, wanted to discuss the criticisms of evolution. LeVake's position paper established that he does not believe the theory of evolution is credible. Further, LeVake's proposed method of teaching evolution is in direct conflict with respondents' curriculum requirements. *See Clark v. Holmes*, 474 F.2d 928, 931 (7th Cir. 1972) (recognizing teacher had no First Amendment right to override judgment of superiors regarding proper course content). Accordingly, the established curriculum and LeVake's responsibility as a public school teacher to teach evolution in the manner prescribed by the curriculum overrides his First Amendment rights as a private citizen.[109] *See Webster v. New Lenox Sch. Dist. No. 122*, 917 F.2d

---

108. [The trial court opinion expanded on the Free Exercise analysis in this case in part as follows:

. . . Plaintiff's analogy to a Black at-will employee who is fired for racial considerations is apt. However, the black employee would still have the burden of bringing forth specific facts that establish his racial discrimination claim. Plaintiff here has the burden of bringing forth specific facts that create a genuine issue of fact that Defendants may have considered Plaintiff's religious belief when making their decision to reassign him.

Plaintiff has not come forth with any facts demonstrating a genuine issue. . . . The pieces of evidence (i.e. deposition testimony, documents) to which Plaintiff points as support for his position actually support Defendants' position that they based Plaintiff's reassignment upon doubts concerning Plaintiffs' efficacy as a biology teacher. Superintendent Dixon referred in his letter to Plaintiff to statements by Plaintiff in his position paper characterizing evolution as "impossible" and stating that he would teach evolution, but with an "honest look" at the difficulties and inconsistencies. Superintendent Dixon asserted that Plaintiff had made it clear that he could not teach the curriculum. Principal Johnson, discussing the April 7th meeting, stated in his deposition that Defendants were concerned that Plaintiff would overemphasize the difficulties with the theory of evolution at the expense of allowing the theory itself to slip into obscurity. Ms. Freud's memo to the school board members made no reference to religious views but justified the decision "to reassign Defendant based on fears that he would not properly teach the biology curriculum. Plaintiff has failed to adduce any specific disputed facts to justify a finding that Defendants reassigned him based, even in part, upon their attitudes toward his religious beliefs and their preconception of how those beliefs affected him as a biology teacher. Without any facts demonstrating religious factors in Defendants" decision-making, Plaintiff cannot make out violation of the Free Exercise Clause in this case, and Defendants are entitled to judgment as a matter of law on that claim.

LeVake v. School Dist., No. CX–99–793, slip op. at 14–16.]

109. [The trial court opinion expanded on the Free Speech analysis in this case in part as follows:

1004, 1007 (7th Cir. 1990) (recognizing compelling state interest in choice and adherence to suitable curriculum for benefit of young students overrides individual teachers' desire to teach what they please).

Based on LeVake's belief that evolution is not a viable theory, respondents' concern about his inability to teach the prescribed curriculum was well-founded. Thus, the district court did not err in granting respondents' motion for summary judgment because LeVake did not demonstrate a genuine issue of material fact regarding his claim that respondents violated his right to free speech.

III. Due Process

. . . LeVake's due process claim is premised on his belief that respondents deprived him of his liberty interest to teach his class free "from state action which impinges upon and violated his constitutional rights to free speech and free exercise" by failing to provide him with adequate notice of what types of expression were prohibited before reassigning him.

The cases LeVake relies on in making this argument involve the termination of teachers, but LeVake was not terminated. In fact, he was not even demoted. Further, before accepting the position to teach tenthgrade biology, LeVake understood that respondents' prescribed curriculum included teaching students about evolution.

LeVake was given sufficient notice about what he could and could not teach through the established curriculum and the syllabus. In addition, LeVake's contract specifically required him to "faithfully perform the teaching . . . *prescribed by the School Board*," but LeVake articulated that he could not teach the class according to the existing curriculum requirements. (Emphasis added.) In fact, LeVake admitted in his deposition testimony that "in essence [he] said to [Hubert] that [*he could not*] *teach evolution*." (Emphasis added.) Also, LeVake's position paper demonstrates that he does not believe that evolution is a credible theory. More importantly, LeVake's proposal of how he wanted to teach evolution conflicted with respondents' curriculum goals, which dictated that evolution should be taught as the *accepted* theory for how life has changed over time.

Thus, the district court did not err in granting respondents' summary judgment motion because LeVake did not demonstrate a genuine issue of

---

. . . Plaintiff's classroom at the high school is a nonpublic forum, and the District has the right to limit the speech in that classroom to the teaching of the designated curriculum. The District has the responsibility of assuring "that participants learn whatever lessons the activity is designed to teach." Miles v. Denver Public Schools, 944 F.2d 773, 777 (10th Cir. 1991) (quoting Hazelwood School District v. Kuhlmeier, 484 U.S. 260 (1988)). In the District's 10th grade biology curriculum, one of those lessons is evolution. When Plaintiff is standing before his students in the classroom, he is not in the position of a citizen on the public square with a right freely to express his opinion as he sees fit. Rather, he is acting as an employee of the school charged with teaching the prescribed curriculum and is in a location which the District has reserved for the purpose of teaching students the prescribed curriculum. To rule that Plaintiff has a free speech right to teach the curriculum as he sees fit would be literally to make a federal case out of every dispute between a teacher and his superiors. This the Court will not do. Defendants are entitled to judgment as a matter of law on this claim.

LeVake v. School Dist., No. CX–99–793, slip op. at 20–21.]

material fact regarding his claim that his due process rights had been
violated. . . .

NOTES AND QUESTIONS

1.   How does Rodney LeVake differ from Ray Webster and John Peloza,
whose cases appear in the preceding chapter? All three were public school
teachers. Webster and Peloza were directed by their school supervisors either
to teach Darwinism or not to teach creationism and responded with lawsuits
claiming that these directives violated their constitutional rights. They lost.
LeVake was also directed by his supervisor to teach Darwinism but, rather
than file a lawsuit at this point, LeVake simply disobeyed the directive. After
it became clear that LeVake would not teach the required curriculum, his
supervisors reassigned him to teach other science courses that did not cover
Darwinism. Then LeVake sued, claiming that the reassignment violated his
constitutional rights. Which set of facts is more compelling? Should a public
school teacher challenge school policies before violating them or violate those
policies and then fight any disciplinary action? LeVake's civil disobedience
underscored his sincerity yet his approach deprived his students of a fundamental part of the required curriculum.

2.   LeVake claimed that he was reassigned because of his religious beliefs in
violation of the Free Exercise Clause. According to the court, why did this
claim fail? Was he reassigned because of his religious beliefs or because those
beliefs prevented him from doing his job? Consider the hypothetical of a city
or state food inspector who is required to taste various different foods. Many
religions prohibit consuming certain types of food. If, because of his religion, a
particular food inspector could not taste certain foods, would it violate the
Free Exercise Clause for the government to assign that inspector to taste
other foods? In the a landmark opinion authored by Justice Antonin Scalia,
Employment Division, Oregon Department of Human Resources v. Smith, 494
U.S. 872 (1990), the U.S. Supreme Court held that the Free Exercise Clause
does not authorize a person to use religious motivation as a reason not to obey
neutral law of general applicability. "To permit this would be to make the
professed doctrines of religious belief superior to the law of the land, and in
effect to permit every citizen to become a law unto himself," Justice Scalia
wrote. In fact, school supervisors accommodated LeVake's religious beliefs by
reassigning him to teach other classes at the same pay but *Smith* suggests
that they could have dismissed him. Minnesota's high-school graduation
standards require students to demonstrate an understanding of biological
change over time. LeVake's school addressed this standard by teaching
Darwinism in tenth-grade biology. If LeVake could not teach Darwinism, the
court reasoned, he could not do his job. LeVake's suit ended in 2002, after
first the Minnesota Supreme Court and then the U.S. Supreme Court rejected
his appeals for discretionary review.

3.   If anything, the Minnesota courts gave even less credence to LeVake's
Free Speech claim than to his Free Exercise claim. "The high school is
nonpublic forum," the trial court wrote. As a teacher, the court noted, LeVake
"is acting as an employee of the school charged with teaching the prescribed
curriculum and is in a location which the District has reserved for the purpose

of teaching students the prescribed curriculum.'' It refused to grant public-school teachers any free speech rights over the content of the classroom curriculum. The appellate court was somewhat less absolutist in its language but no less conclusive in its holding. It wrote, ''LeVake's responsibility as a public school teacher to teach evolution in the manner prescribed by the curriculum overrides his First Amendment rights as a private citizen.'' In addressing LeVake's due process claim, the court observed that his supervisors must provide adequate notice to LeVake of what could and could not be taught under the school's prescribed curriculum. Many states provide so-called conscience exceptions to otherwise neutral laws of general applicability. For example, by law in some states, hospital nurses who object to performing abortions may not be compelled to assist in such procedures by their public or private employers. If applied to classroom speech by public-school teachers, could such a conscience exception protect LeVake? Would it be advisable? In this case, school administers effectively accommodated LeVake's religious beliefs by reassigning him to teach courses that did not cover Darwinism. Fourteen years after being reassigned and twelve years after losing his lawsuit over that reassignment, LeVake continued to teach ninth-grade physical science at Faribault High School. Living in the same affable Minnesota town, his kids and the children of the teacher who reported him, Ken Hubert, are friends and the two teachers remain cordial.

III. STICKER SHOCK IN GEORGIA

By 2002, the situation could readily confuse school officials and citizens alike. On the one hand, the federal courts had struck down Tangipahoa Parish's 1994 ''exercise-critical-thinking'' disclaimer ostensibly for identifying biblical creationism as an alternative to Darwinism. On the other hand, no one had filed suit challenging the constitutionality of Alabama's 1995 ''keep-an-open-mind'' disclaimer that did not mention any specific alternative to evolution.

Further complicating the situation, in 2001, Congress added the so-called Santorum Amendment to the conference report for the ''No Child Left Behind'' education bill, but the Amendment's legal significance was disputed. Without fanfare during a late-night session, conservative Catholic U.S. Senator Rick Santorum quietly secured Senate passage for a floor amendment to the education bill stating, in part, ''Where biological evolution is taught, the curriculum should help students to understand why the subject generates so much controversy.'' To many creationists, this language invited public schools to encourage critical thinking about Darwinism. Once they heard about the Amendment, which had been drafted by critics of evolutionary instruction, virtually every national scientific organization lobbied to have it stripped from the final legislation. In conference, lawmakers seeking to work out differences between versions of bill passed by the Senate and House of Representatives removed the Amendment from the bill but included a watered-down version of it in their non-binding explanatory report. In pertinent part, the Conference Report stated,

The Conferees recognize that a quality science education should prepare students to distinguish the data and testable theories from religious or philosophical claims that are made in the name of science.

Where topics are taught that may generate controversy (such as biological evolution), the curriculum should help students to understand the full range of scientific views that exist, why such topics may generate controversy, and how scientific discoveries can profoundly affect society.[110]

Although not carrying the force of law, some creationists argued that the report language authorized state and local school districts to teach the controversy over evolution. Defenders of Darwinism uniformly dismissed the language as meaningless. This confusing legal landscape confronted the elected school board of suburban Cobb County, Georgia, when it entered the disclaimer thicket in 2002.

A traditionally conservative, largely rural area recently transformed into an affluent bedroom community for Atlanta with its own growing commercial infrastructure, Cobb County had a long history of restricting Darwinian instruction in its schools. Prior to 2002, the local school board had maintained a policy of strictly excluding the theory of human evolution from required science courses. After Georgia's Department of Education adopted state science guidelines that mandated teaching evolutionary concepts, Cobb County School District began a process of adopting new science textbooks that led to its selection of the popular Prentice Hall high-school text *Biology* by Kenneth Miller and Joseph Levine for use beginning in the 2002–03 school year. Adopting the Miller and Levine text necessitated a loosening of the district's restrictions on Darwinian instruction, which triggered a reaction by some conservative Christian parents and taxpayers. Several of them expressly complained about the absence of alternative theories of origins or criticism of Darwinism in the approved book. Before placing them in use and acting on the advice of counsel, the Cobb County Board of Education drew on the experience of Alabama to direct that school personal paste a sticker inside each of the new biology books advising readers that material about evolution "should be approached with an open mind, studied carefully, and critically considered." The stickers made no mention of creationism. When adopting them, the Board acted so quickly and quietly that few people took notice until they began appearing in the books.

Having more than doubled in population to over 600,000 persons during the preceding two decades, with many of the new residents coming from the North for good jobs in metropolitan Atlanta, Cobb County was a far less homogeneous community by 2000 than when its school district first imposed restrictions on teaching evolution. Founded as Cobb County Junior College in 1963, Kennesaw State University had grown into the third largest four-year university in Georgia and was assembling a faculty

---

110. H.R. Doc. No. 334, 107th Cong., 1st Sess. 703 (2001) (Conf. Rep.), *reprinted* in 2001 U.S.C.C.A.N. 1230, 1249.

appropriate to its size. By 2002, someone in Cobb County was virtually certain to complain about the stickers. As word of them spread, many residents were outraged or embarrassed. The first to file suit was Jeffrey Selman, a computer programmer who had moved to Cobb County from New York, largely drifted away from his Orthodox Jewish upbringing, and complained regularly about the pervasiveness of evangelical Christian influences in local and state government. Other plaintiffs later joined him. The ACLU handled the litigation.

Even as Selman's suit was simmering early in the 2002–03 academic year, the Cobb County Board of Education stirred the pot by publicly debating a proposal to authorized classroom discussion of disputed views on origins as part of providing a balanced education to students. "We've been told by our attorney we're not allowed to teach creationism," Board Chair Curt Johnson commented, "but the point is that we want free and open discussion in the classroom."[111] The proposal touched off what Johnson depicted as "the most difficult and polarized debate" that he had experienced as a board member.[112] Marjorie Rogers, one the parents who had complained about the adoption of the Miller and Levine text, now submitted a petition signed by some 2000 local parents in support of added restrictions on Darwinian instruction. Selman countered by threatening to expand his lawsuit. Gradually the media took notice and made the Cobb County sticker wars into a national story. Following a bench trial that featured expert testimony on Darwinism by *Biology* co-author Kenneth Miller, the district and appellate courts issued the following opinions:

SELMAN v. COBB COUNTY SCHOOL DIST.

United States District Court for the Northern District of Georgia
390 F. Supp. 2d 1286 (N.D. Ga. 2005)

COOPER, DISTRICT JUDGE: Plaintiffs Jeffrey Michael Selman, Kathleen Chapman, Jeff Silver, Paul Mason, and Terry Jackson (collectively referred to herein as "Plaintiffs") bring this action under 42 U.S.C. § 1983 against Defendants Cobb County School District and Cobb County Board of Education (collectively referred to herein as "Defendants") to challenge the constitutionality of a sticker commenting on evolution, which the Cobb County Board of Education (referred to herein as the "School Board") adopted in March of 2002 and placed in certain science textbooks later that year. Plaintiffs contend that the sticker violates the Establishment Clause of the First Amendment, as incorporated by the Fourteenth Amendment, and the Constitution of the State of Georgia. Plaintiffs are all parents of students attending Cobb County schools, and Plaintiffs are residents and taxpayers of Cobb County, Georgia. Plaintiffs seek declaratory and injunctive relief, nominal damages, costs, and attorneys' fees.

---

111. *Discussing Creationism is issue in Georgia*, ST. LOUIS POST-DISPATCH, Aug. 24, 2002, at 24.

112. Mary MacDonald, *Cobb Dads Head Call to War on Evolution*, ATLANTA JOURNAL-CONSTITUTION, Sept. 8, 2002, at IA.

This matter involves one of those instances where science and religion both offer an explanation to resolve a controversial issue-namely, the origin of the human species. This issue historically has generated intense controversy and debate precisely because of its religious implications and the belief of some that science and religion cannot coexist. Since at least the 1920s, courts throughout the Nation have been struggling to determine the constitutional limitations that should be placed on public school curriculum concerning the origin of the human species and to delineate clearly the line that separates church and state.

Due to the various challenges that arise in this area, the Court believes it prudent to state from the outset what the instant case is not about. First, the Court is not resolving in this case whether science and religion are mutually exclusive, and the Court takes no position on the origin of the human species. Second, the issue before the Court is not whether it is constitutionally permissible for public school teachers to teach intelligent design, the theory that only an intelligent or supernatural cause could be responsible for life, living things, and the complexity of the universe. Third, this case does not resolve the ongoing debate regarding whether evolution is a fact or theory or whether evolution should be taught as fact or theory.

To be clear, this opinion resolves only a legal dispute. Specifically, the narrow issue raised by this facial challenge is whether the sticker placed in certain Cobb County School District science textbooks violates the Establishment Clause of the First Amendment of the United States Constitution and/or Article I, Section II, Paragraph VII of the Constitution of the State of Georgia.

The findings of fact and conclusions of law adduced below are based on the Court's review of the evidence presented at trial, the testimony of the witnesses at trial, the parties' trial briefs, the parties' proposed findings of fact and conclusions of law, the other documents and evidence in the record, and the applicable law.

FINDINGS OF FACT

Evolution is the dominant scientific theory regarding the origin of the diversity of life and is accepted by the majority of the scientific community (Miller Trial Test; Moreno Trial Test, McCoy Trial Test, Sticker Trial Test).[113] The inclusion of this theory in the curriculum of Cobb County Schools has been a source of controversy for quite some time. In 1995, the Cobb County School District maintained a policy, which was adopted in 1979 and revised on several occasions thereafter, stating the following:

---

113. "Miller" refers to Dr. Kenneth Miller, the co-author of one of the biology textbooks used in the Cobb County School District "Moreno" refers to Dr. Carlos S. Moreno, an assistant professor at Emory University, who has a Ph. D in genetics and molecular biology from Emory. "McCoy" refers to Dr. Roger W. McCoy, the science department chair at North Cobb High School, who teaches genetics, biology, and astronomy "Stickel" refers to George Stickel, the high school science supervisor for Cobb County schools....

The Cobb County School District acknowledges that some scientific accounts of the origin of human species as taught in public schools are inconsistent with the family teachings of a significant number of Cobb County citizens. Therefore, the instructional program and curriculum of the school system shall be planned and organized with respect for these family teachings. The Constitutional principle of separation of church and state shall be preserved and maintained as established by the United States Supreme Court and defined by judicial decisions.

Defs' Ex. 1.

A more specific statement regarding the practicality of teaching theories of origin in Cobb County public school classrooms, the Cobb County School District's regulation concerning theories of origin read as follows in 1995:

In respect for the family teachings of a significant number of Cobb County citizens, the following regulations are established for the teaching of theories of the origin of human species in the Cobb County School District:

(1) The curriculum of the Cobb County School District shall be organized so as to avoid the compelling of any student to study the subject of the origin of human species.

(2) The origin of human species shall be excluded as a topic of curriculum for the elementary and middle schools of the Cobb County School District.

(3) No course of study dealing with theories of the origin of human species shall be required of students for high school graduation.

(4) Elective opportunities for students to investigate theories of the origin of human species shall be available both through classroom studies and library collections which shall include, but not be limited to, the creation theory.

(5) All high school courses offered on an elective basis which include studies of the origin of human species theories shall be noted in curriculum catalogs and listings which are provided for students and parents for the purpose of course selection.

Defs' Ex. 2.

Neither the former policy nor regulation explicitly references evolution, but both imply that a significant number of Cobb County citizens maintain beliefs that are deemed to conflict with evolution. Not all Cobb County teachers interpreted the former policy and regulation to require teaching on evolution, although the state curriculum apparently mandated such teaching. (McCoy Trial Test, Searcy Trial Test)[114] In fact, it was

---

114. "Searcy" refers to Laura Searcy, one of the members of the School Board at the time the textbook adoption process was taking place. The other members of the School Board at that time included Gordon O'Neill, Betty Gray, Johnny Johnson, Lindsey Tippins, Curt Johnston, and Teresa Plenge (Redden Aff ¶ 7). Joseph Redden is the Superintendent of the Cobb County School District and was in that position at the time of the textbook adoption (Redden Aff ¶ 2).

common practice in some science classes for textbook pages containing material on evolution to be removed from the students' textbooks (Tippins Dep., p. 86, ll. 11–15; Searcy Trial Test). With respect to human evolution specifically, teachers were asked not to discuss that topic in required courses for graduation but to restrict the topic to those courses that were considered electives (McCoy Trial Test).

In the Fall of 2001, the Cobb County School District began the process of adopting new science textbooks (Redden Aff. ¶ 3). The textbook adoption process started with the formation of a textbook adoption committee, which read and studied various books and then recommended certain books for adoption (Redden Dep., p. 5, ll. 18–20, p. 6, ll. 5–8, McCoy Trial Test). In October of 2001, the textbook adoption committee raised concerns regarding curriculum and instruction on theories of the origin of life (Redden Aff. ¶ 3). One concern of the committee was that a textbook adoption might conflict with the existing policy and regulation on theories of origin (Redden Trial Test). After a legal review of the issues raised by the textbook adoption committee, the school administration determined that revisions to the policy and regulation would be recommended (Redden Aff. ¶¶ 5–6, Redden Trial Test). These revisions would strengthen evolution instruction and bring Cobb County into compliance with statewide curriculum requirements (Redden Aff. ¶ 6, Redden Trial Test).

Prior to the presentation of the new policy and regulation and based on recommendations received from the textbook adoption committee, the administration recommended science textbooks for adoption by the School Board (Redden Aff. ¶ 7, Redden Trial Test). The committee believed that the textbook written by Kenneth Miller and Joseph Levine, which was one of the books ultimately adopted by the School Board and the textbook that has taken the forefront in this litigation, was the best they had seen for high school students (McCoy Trial Test) George Stickel, Supervisor of High School Science Curriculum, agreed and saw the textbook as offering a comprehensive perspective of current scientific thinking regarding theory of origins (Stickel Aff. ¶¶ 7–8, Ex. A, B; Stickel Trial Test).

Once parents of Cobb County students learned that instruction on evolution was being strengthened and that the School Board was in the process of adopting new science textbooks containing material on evolution, certain parents began to express their concerns to School Board members about this issue. (Johnston Dep., p. 7, ll. 14–18, Johnston Trial Test). In accordance with School Board regulation, parents were permitted to review and comment upon the recommended textbooks (Redden Dep., p. 5, ll. 21–25, Gray Trial Test). Only three parents reviewed the books containing material on evolution at the formal review session conducted on February 26, 2002 (Doc. No. 77, Ex. 42). Of these three parents, one parent submitted a comment form stating that he was "very happy w/ the inclusion of evolution, even if not by that term we must teach this." (Id.). The second parent, Marjorie Rogers, submitted several comment forms that criticized the presentation of evolution in various textbooks and condemned the books for not mentioning any alternate theories, such as one involving a creator. (Id.) The third parent made no comment regarding the presentation of evolution. (Id.)

Although the evidence shows only three parents submitted official comment forms regarding the textbooks, the School Board heard complaints from several parents that the textbooks did not present the theories of origin in a fair manner. (Johnston Dep., p. 9, ll. 3–8; Johnston Trial Test, Searcy Trial Test; Redden Trial Test) Similar to Ms Rogers' complaint, most of the complaints were that the textbooks presented only the theory of evolution and did not offer any information regarding alternate theories or criticisms of evolution. (Johnston Dep., p. 7, ll. 21–24, Johnston Trial Test; Redden Dep., p. 12, ll. 24–25, p. 13, ll. 1–4, p. 24, ll. 19–25.) For some of the parents, such as Ms Rogers, the alternate theories would have included the theories of creationism and intelligent design. (Redden Dep., p. 18, ll. 24–25, p. 19, ll. 1–4; Rogers Trial Test)

Ms. Rogers, who identifies herself as a six-day biblical creationist, was the most vocal of the parents who complained to the School Board. Opposed to the presentation of evolution as a fact rather than as a theory, Ms. Rogers organized and presented a petition to the School Board that contained the signatures of about 2,300 Cobb County residents (Redden Dep., p. 27, ll. 17–23, p. 28, ll. 3–5, Rogers Trial Test, Redden Trial Test). The petition requested that the School Board "clearly identify presumptions and theories and distinguish them from fact" (Rogers Trial Test). The petition also requested, among other things, that the Board ensure the presentation of all theories regarding the origin of life and place a statement prominently at the beginning of the text that warned students that the material on evolution was not factual but rather was a theory. (Id.)

Mr. Tippins, who is the current chairman of the School Board, initially brought to the School Board's attention the concerns of those parents who had problems with the proposed textbooks. (Redden Dep., p. 24, ll. 19–25, Tippins Trial Test). In response to the outcry from these parents, certain unidentified members of the School Board consulted legal counsel to determine if there was any language that would help to address parent concerns within the confines of the law (Johnston Dep., p. 7, l. 25, p. 8, ll. 1–12; Johnston Trial Test, Searcy Trial Test). The Cobb County School District's legal counsel recommended language that they thought would be constitutional. (Johnston Dep., p. 7, l. 21, p. 8, ll. 15–18, Tippins Dep., p. 77, ll. 8–11). The language, which now appears on the sticker (referred to herein as the "Sticker"), reads as follows:

> This textbook contains material on evolution. Evolution is a theory, not a fact, regarding the origin of living things. This material should be approached with an open mind, studied carefully, and critically considered.

Pls' Ex. 1. Evolution is the only theory mentioned in the Sticker, and there is no sticker placed in textbooks related to any other theory, topic, or subject covered in the Cobb County School District's curriculum (Plenge Dep., p. 12, ll. 14–21; Tippins Dep., p. 81, ll. 14–17, Johnston Dep., p. 18, ll. 8–14; Plenge Trial Test). However, there are other scientific topics taught that have religious implications, such as the theories of gravity, relativity, and Galilean heliocentrism (Miller Trial Test; McCoy Trial Test, Stickel Trial Test).

On March 28, 2002, the School Board unanimously adopted the textbooks recommended by the administration with the condition that the Sticker would be placed in certain of the science textbooks (Compl. ¶ 13; Pls' Ex. 1; Plenge Dep., p. 16, ll. 6–12, Tippins Trial Test, Plenge Trial Test). With respect to this issue, the School Board minutes from a meeting held on March 27, 2002, reflect only that citizen concerns prompted the School Board to consider the idea of putting a statement at the beginning of the textbooks. (Doc. No. 77, Ex. 43). There are no School Board minutes detailing any of the discussions had by the School Board members about the Sticker. The School Board's collective purpose in adopting the Sticker is not stated on the Sticker, and the School Board did not issue any statement regarding the purpose of the Sticker contemporaneous with its adoption. . . .

The School Board did not solicit expert opinion on scientific theories of origin or do research outside of the School Board sessions before voting on the Sticker, but they did hear from scientists via materials sent to them via e-mail and through the mail (Redden Dep., p. 30, ll. 23–25, p. 31, ll. 1–6; Johnston Trial Test, Searcy Trial Test). Among other things, the School Board received material from the Discovery Institute, which included a pro-intelligent design book called Icons of Evolution (Searcy Trial Test; Johnston Test). Mr. Johnston also received correspondence from Dr. West of the Discovery Institute in which Dr. West offered to assist the Board in, among other things, drafting a sticker presumably to go into textbooks (Johnston Test). Mr. Johnston did not take Dr. West up on his offer, but Mr. Johnston did refer Dr. West to the Cobb County School District's legal counsel. (Id.) There is no evidence that Dr. West ever conferred with the Cobb County School District's legal counsel. . . .

Between the Summer and Fall of 2002, the School Board had the Stickers produced with monies from the general fund (Plenge Dep, p. 30, ll. 20–23, Searcy Trial Test). The Stickers were then sent to the schools, and personnel at the schools physically affixed the Stickers into all of the science textbooks that contained material regarding the origin of life (Redden Dep., p. 29, ll. 13–19, p. 30, ll. 1–5, Stickel Trial Test).

Following the adoption of the new science textbooks and the Sticker, the Board adopted its revised policy on theories of origin in September of 2002. (Johnston Dep., p. 24, ll. 14–17, Ex. 1) The pertinent part of the policy states the following:

> [I]t is the educational philosophy of the Cobb County School District to provide a broad based curriculum; therefore, the Cobb County School District believes that discussion of disputed views of academic

subjects is a necessary element of providing a balanced education, including the study of the origin of the species. This subject remains an area of intense interest, research, and discussion among scholars. As a result, the study of this subject shall be handled in accordance with this policy and with objectivity and good judgment on the part of teachers, taking into account the age and maturity level of their students.

The purpose of this policy is to foster critical thinking among students, to allow academic freedom consistent with legal requirements, to promote tolerance and acceptance of diversity of opinion, and to ensure a posture of neutrality toward religion. It is the intent of the Cobb County Board of Education that this policy not be interpreted to restrict the teaching of evolution, to promote or require the teaching of creationism, or to discriminate for or against a particular set of religious beliefs, religion in general, or non-religion.

Defs.' Ex. 5....

In over two years since the adoption of the science textbooks and the placement of the Sticker in the textbooks, neither the Superintendent of the Cobb County School District, the Supervisor of High School Science Curriculum, nor the Board members who testified at trial have received complaints about the teaching of religion or religious theories of origin in science classes (Redden Trial Test; Stickel Trial Test, Johnston Trial Test, Tippins Trial Test.; Searcy Trial Test, Plenge Test). Moreover, students have brought up the topic of religion as it relates to the theory of evolution no more frequently than they did before the Sticker was placed in textbooks (McCoy Trial Test).

Notwithstanding the foregoing, it appears that the Sticker is impacting science instruction on evolution Some students have pointed to the language on the Sticker to support arguments that evolution does not exist. (McCoy Trial Test) In addition, Dr. McCoy testified that the Board's misuse of the word "theory" in the Sticker causes "confusion" in his science class and consequently requires him to spend significantly more time trying to distinguish "fact" and "theory" for his students. (Id.) Dr. McCoy stated that some of his students translate the Sticker to state that evolution is "just" a theory, which he believes has the effect of diminishing the status of evolution among all other theories. (Id.)

Some parents who saw the Sticker were alarmed by its contents. Plaintiff Kathy Chapman's "alarm bells went off" when she saw the Sticker in her child's textbook, and she immediately felt that the Sticker "came from a religious source" because, in her opinion, religious people are the only people who ever challenge evolution. (Chapman Trial Test) She viewed the Sticker as promoting the religious view of origin and questioning the science in the textbooks. (Id.) Plaintiff Jeff Silver perceived the effect of the Sticker to "open [ ] the door to introducing schools of thought based in faith and religion into science classes." (Silver Trial Test) He also believed that the Sticker disparaged evolution and implicitly asked students to think about alternative theories. (Id.) Not surprisingly, the Sticker also raised a red flag for Plaintiff Jeffrey Selman because the Sticker singled out evolution and was, in his opinion, obviously religious (Selman Trial Test). Thus, the Sticker is now before this Court for consideration of its constitutionality.

CONCLUSIONS OF LAW

. . . To determine whether the Sticker at issue violates the Establishment Clause, Supreme Court and Eleventh Circuit precedent direct the Court to apply the three-prong test articulated in Lemon v. Kurtzman, 403 U.S. 602 (1971). See Santa Fe Ind. Sch. Dist. v. Doe, 530 U.S. 290, 314 (2000) (applying the Lemon test in analyzing an Establishment Clause challenge); Glassroth v. Moore, 335 F.3d 1282, 1295–96 (11th Cir. 2003) (same). Under the Lemon test, a government-sponsored message violates the Establishment Clause of the First Amendment if: (1) it does not have a secular purpose, (2) its principal or primary effect advances or inhibits religion, or (3) it creates an excessive entanglement of the government with religion. Lemon, 403 U.S. at 612–13. If the government-sponsored action or message fails to meet either of these three prongs, then the challenge under the Establishment Clause succeeds Glassroth, 335 F.3d at 1295. As the Eleventh Circuit unequivocally recognizes, however, "there is no bright-line rule for evaluating Establishment Clause challenges" and "each challenge calls for line-drawing based on a fact-specific, case-by-case analysis". King, 331 F.3d at 1275–76 (citing Lynch v. Donnelly, 465 U.S. 668, 679 (1984)).

Both the Supreme Court and the Eleventh Circuit have acknowledged that the second and third prongs of the Lemon test are interrelated insofar as courts often consider similar factors in analyzing them. See Agostini v. Felton, 521 U.S. 203, 232–33 (1997); Holloman v. Harland, 370 F.3d 1252, 1284–85 (11th Cir. 2004). In fact, the Eleventh Circuit, like several other circuit courts, has combined the second and third prongs of the Lemon analysis into a single "effect" inquiry. See Harland, 370 F.3d at 1285, accord Child Evangelism Fellowship of New Jersey, Inc. v. Stafford Township Sch. Dist., 386 F.3d 514, 534 (3d Cir. 2004); Commack Self–Service Kosher Meats, Inc. v. Weiss, 294 F.3d 415, 424 (2d Cir. 2002); Columbia Union College v. Clarke, 159 F.3d 151, 157 (4th Cir. 1998). The Court will do the same in the instant Order. . . .

A. Purpose

"The purpose prong of the Lemon test asks whether government's actual purpose is to endorse or disapprove of religion." Lynch, 465 U.S. at 690 (O'Connor, J., concurring). To survive this Establishment Clause challenge, the Sticker in dispute must have a "clearly secular purpose." Wallace, 472 U.S. at 56; Bown v. Gwinnett County Sch. Dist., 112 F.3d 1464, 1469 (11th Cir.1997). However, the purpose of the Sticker "need not be exclusively secular." Bown, 112 F.3d at 1469 (citing Lynch, 465 U.S. at 681 n. 6). The Sticker runs afoul of the Establishment Clause only if it is "entirely motivated by a purpose to advance religion." Wallace, 472 U.S. at 56; King, 331 F.3d at 1278; Bown, 112 F.3d at 1469. Thus, it logically follows that a state-sponsored message may satisfy this first prong "even if it is 'motivated in part by a religious purpose.'" Adler, 206 F.3d at 1084 (quoting Wallace, 472 U.S. at 56). However, the religious purpose must not be preeminent. Stone, 449 U.S. at 41.

The court should defer to a state's articulation of a secular purpose, so long as the statement is sincere and not a sham. Edwards, 482 U.S. at 586–87. A determination of the statement's purpose should involve a look at the language of the statement itself, enlightened by its context and contemporaneous legislative history. Edwards, 482 U.S. at 594. As Justice O'Connor advised in Wallace, the inquiry into the purpose "should be deferential and limited. Even if the text and official history of a [statement] express no secular purpose, the [statement] should be held to have an improper purpose only if it is beyond purview that endorsement of religion or a religious belief 'was and is the . . . reason for [the statement's] existence.'" 472 U.S. at 75–6 (O'Connor, J., concurring).

Based on the evidence before this Court at the summary judgment stage, the Court ruled that the School Board did not act with the purpose of promoting or advancing religion in placing the Sticker in the science textbooks. To the contrary, the Court found that the School Board sought to advance two secular purposes. First, the School Board sought to encourage students to engage in critical thinking as it relates to theories of origin. Second, given the movement in Cobb County to strengthen teaching on evolution and to make it a mandatory part of the curriculum, the School Board adopted the Sticker to reduce offense to those students and parents whose personal beliefs might conflict with teaching on evolution. The Court was satisfied on summary judgment that these two purposes were secular and not a sham. However, both parties made arguments in their trial briefs and presented evidence at trial relevant to the purpose inquiry. Therefore, having considered all of the arguments and evidence presented by the parties and upon closer review of the applicable law, the Court will revisit the purpose prong of the Lemon test to provide a more thorough analysis.

In most Establishment Clause cases involving challenges to statutes or school board policies, there is a stated purpose for the statute or policy. See, e.g., Edwards, 482 U.S. at 586 (stated purpose of statute requiring equal treatment of evolution and creation science in science classroom was to protect academic freedom); Adler, 206 F.3d at 1085 (stated purpose of policy allowing student-initiated messages at commencement exercises was to give "graduating students an opportunity to direct their own graduation ceremony by selecting a student speaker to express a message"); Bown, 112 F.3d at 1469 (stated purpose of statute requiring moment for quiet reflection in public schools was to give students the opportunity to reflect quietly on the events to come during the day). The Sticker in this case does not include a statement regarding its purpose. Likewise, there is no contemporaneous legislative history, such as detailed meeting minutes, which would aid the Court in determining the School Board's purpose for voting for the Sticker. The dearth of such evidence makes the Court's factual inquiry regarding the purpose somewhat difficult, but it does not mean that Defendants fail the purpose prong. King, 331 F.3d at 1277 (government does not fail purpose prong simply because "there is no available evidence of the original intent").

In this case, Defendants state that the Cobb County School District's revised policy concerning theories of origin is consistent with the School Board's purposes for adopting the Sticker. Notably, the School Board did not adopt the revised policy until almost six (6) months after adopting the Sticker, and the revised policy does not reference the Sticker. However, the majority of the School Board members either knew the policy was being revised to reflect the strengthening of the evolution curriculum in Cobb County or they testified during the litigation that the policy was consistent with their purpose in voting for the Sticker.

Courts generally frown upon evidence of purpose that is not contemporaneous with the challenged action. See Edwards, 482 U.S. at 595 (concluding that post-enactment testimony from outside experts would be of little benefit in determining legislature's purpose for enacting balanced treatment statute); Adler, 206 F.3d at 1088 (post-enactment comments by individual board members did not outweigh other evidence of a secular purpose); Adland v. Russ, 307 F.3d 471, 483 n. 3 (6th Cir. 2002) (refusing to rely on post-enactment comments of legislator in evaluating asserted secular purpose of statute challenged under Establishment Clause); Friedman v. Board of County Comm'rs of Bernalillo County, 781 F.2d 777, 781 n. 3 (10th Cir.1985) ("all courts must be wary of accepting after-the-fact justifications by government officials in lieu of genuinely considered and recorded reasons for actions challenged on Establishment Clause grounds"). However, in these cases, the evidence offered consisted of either testimony from individuals who were not a part of the decision-making process or comments made by individual legislators or decision-makers regarding their particular motivations. In contrast, the post-adoption evidence in this case is an official policy of the Cobb County School District, which was revised and adopted by the School Board as a collective unit. Thus, while the Court examines the secular purposes asserted following the adoption of the Sticker with caution, the Court will not refuse to consider them altogether.

The revised policy states, in pertinent part, that its purpose "is to foster critical thinking among students, to allow academic freedom consistent with legal requirements, to promote tolerance and acceptance of diversity of opinion, and to ensure a posture of neutrality toward religion." Defs' Ex. 5. To evaluate the sincerity of these articulated purposes in relation to the Sticker, the Court relies on the text of the Sticker and the circumstances giving rise to the Sticker's adoption. The Court also considers the testimony of the School Board members whom the Court found to be highly credible.

Fostering critical thinking is a clearly secular purpose for the Sticker, which the Court finds is not a sham. First, it is important to note that prior to the adoption of the new textbooks and Sticker and the revision of the related policy and regulation, many students in Cobb County were not being taught evolution or the origin of the human species in school. Further, the School Board was aware that a large population of Cobb County citizens maintained beliefs that would potentially conflict with the teaching of evolution. Against this backdrop, the Sticker appears to have the purpose of furthering critical thinking because it tells students to approach the material on evolution with an open mind, to study it carefully, and to give it critical consideration. The other language on the Sticker, which states that evolution is a theory and not a fact, somewhat undermines the goal of critical thinking by predetermining that students should think of evolution as a theory when many in the scientific community would argue that evolution is factual in some respects. However, the testimony of the School Board members persuades the Court that the School Board did not seek to disclaim evolution by encouraging students to consider it critically. Rather, the School Board sought to encourage students to analyze the material on evolution themselves and make their own decision regarding its merit.

In Freiler v. Tangipahoa Parish Bd. of Educ., a case involving a similar challenge to an oral disclaimer regarding evolution, the Fifth Circuit rejected a school board's avowed purpose of critical thinking. 185 F.3d 337 (5th Cir.1999). The disclaimer in that case instructed students "to exercise critical thinking and gather all information possible and closely examine each alternative toward forming an opinion," but the disclaimer also stated that the teaching of evolution was "not intended to influence or dissuade the Biblical version of Creation or any other concept." Id. at 341. The court concluded that the disclaimer did not further the purpose of critical thinking but encouraged "the protection and maintenance of a particular religious viewpoint" by communicating to students that the teaching of evolution "need not affect what they already know." Id. at 344–45. The Fifth Circuit went on to state that "critical thinking requires that students approach new concepts with an open mind and a willingness to alter and shift existing viewpoints." Id. at 345.

Unlike the disclaimer in the Freiler case, the Sticker in this case does not contain a reference to religion in general, any particular religion, or any religious theory. This weighs heavily in favor of upholding the Sticker as constitutional. See Adler, 206 F.3d at 1083 ("For the most part, statutes which the Supreme Court has invalidated for lack of secular purpose have openly favored religion or demonstrated a religious purpose on their face."). Moreover, the Sticker here does not explicitly mention any alternative theories of origin. The Sticker specifically tells students to keep an open mind and to study evolution carefully. Plaintiffs urge that encouraging students to critically consider only evolution suggests that the School Board's asserted purpose of promoting critical thinking is a sham. However, evolution is the only theory of origin being taught in

Cobb County classrooms. Thus, it makes sense that the School Board is not suggesting that students critically consider other theories of origin. Moreover, as School Board member Laura Searcy pointed out at trial, evolution was the only topic in the curriculum, scientific or otherwise, that was creating controversy at the time of the adoption of the textbooks and Sticker. The School Board's singling out of evolution is understandable in this context, and the undisputed fact that there are other scientific theories with religious implications that are not mentioned in this Sticker or in others supports the Court's conclusion that the Board was not seeking to endorse or advance religion. Therefore, the Court continues to believe that the School Board sincerely sought to promote critical thinking in adopting the Sticker to go in the textbooks.

Having found a secular purpose for the Sticker that is not a sham, the Court is not required to proceed further in analyzing this prong. See Lynch, 465 U.S at 681 n. 6 (stating that Lemon requires only one secular purpose to exist). However, the Court does not believe that the promotion of critical thinking is the Sticker's main purpose. Rather, the chief purpose of the Sticker is to accommodate or reduce offense to those persons who hold beliefs that might be deemed inconsistent with the scientific theory of evolution. The School Board did not articulate this purpose as such in the revised policy it adopted, but the arguments of the Defendants and the evidence in this case overwhelmingly show that this is the primary purpose of the Sticker. Because this purpose is intertwined with religion, the Court discusses this purpose in detail below.

Evidence in the record suggests that the idea of placing a sticker in the textbooks originated with parents who opposed the presentation of only evolution in science classrooms and sought to have other theories, including creation theories, included in the curriculum. Namely, Marjorie Rogers wrote a letter to the School Board over two weeks before the adoption of the Sticker recommending, among other things, that the School Board place a disclaimer in each book. Moreover, Ms. Rogers and over 2,300 other Cobb County citizens submitted a petition to the School Board also asking the School Board to place a statement at the beginning of the texts that warned that the material on evolution was not factual. There is no dispute that a large number of Cobb County citizens opposed the teaching of evolution in a rigid fashion, and it is clear to the Court that many of these citizens were motivated by their religious beliefs.

However, the Court does not rely on communications from these individuals, who apparently sought to advance religion, to determine whether the School Board itself sought to endorse or advance religion when it voted to place the Sticker in science textbooks. See Adler 206 F.3d at 1086 (stating that courts should not discern legislative purpose from letters written by community members to school officials). Rather, the highly credible testimony of the School Board members, although not contemporaneous with the sticker adoption, made it clear that the School Board adopted the Sticker to placate their constituents and to communicate to them that students' personal beliefs would be respected and tolerated in the classroom

The Court notes that well-established law holds that the government may not "undertake religious instruction nor blend secular and sectarian education nor use secular institutions to force one or some religion on any person". Id. Additionally, "the First Amendment does not permit the State to require that teaching and learning must be tailored to the principles or prohibitions of any religious sect or dogma." Epperson, 393 U.S. at 106. Still, the Constitution does not require the government to "show a callous indifference to religious groups." Zorach v. Clauson, 343 U.S. 306, 314 (1952). As the Fifth Circuit stated in Freiler, "local school boards need not turn a blind eye to the concerns of students and parents troubled by the teaching of evolution in public classrooms." 185 F.3d at 346.

Here, the School Board did not implement other recommendations, such as making theories of origin that posit the existence of a creator or supreme being a part of the curriculum or obtaining specially-printed textbooks from publishers that omit materials that some would consider "objectionable." Instead, the School Board adopted a sticker that is not openly religious but served to put students, parents, and teachers on notice that evolution would be taught in a manner that is inclusive rather than exclusive. The School Board sought to show consideration for their constituents' personal beliefs regarding the origin of life while still maintaining a posture of neutrality towards religion. The School Board's decision to adopt the Sticker was undisputably influenced by sectarian interests, but the Constitution forbids only a purpose to endorse or advance religion. Wallace, 472 U.S. at 56; King, 331 F.3d at 1278; Bown, 112 F.3d at 1469. Here, even Plaintiffs concede that "[t]he intention of the Board was to accommodate parents who held a belief contrary to evolution," Plaintiffs' Amended Findings of Fact and Conclusions of Law ¶ 36, and the law clearly holds that mere accommodation of religion is insufficient to render the Sticker unconstitutional. See Hobbie v. Unemployment Appeals Comm'n, 480 U.S. 136, 144 (1987) (stating that the Supreme Court "has long recognized that the government may accommodate religious practices and that it may do so without violating the Establishment Clause"); Lynch, 465 U.S. at 673 (stating that the Constitution "affirmatively mandates accommodation, not merely tolerance, of all religions, and forbids hostility toward any"); cf. Smith v. Board of Sch. Comm'rs, 827 F.2d 684, 691 (11th Cir.1987) (stating that mere accommodation of religion is not sufficient to violate the primary effect prong of the Lemon analysis).

Notwithstanding Plaintiffs' concession that the School Board's purpose was to accommodate the religious views held by parents, Plaintiffs argue that inquiries by School Board members concerning whether creationism and intelligent design could be taught in public classrooms are evidence of the School Board's desire to advance religion. It is undisputed that School Board member Lindsey Tippins posed questions regarding the teaching of creationism and intelligent design. However, it is also the case that this became a moot issue once the School Board received the legal opinion of the Cobb County School District's counsel that such theories could not be taught. While one still might assume from these inquiries that at least one School Board member may have seen the Sticker as the first step in getting religion into the classrooms, the Eleventh Circuit has advised that "[t]here is nothing inappropriate about a school system attempting to understand its constitutional obligations." Adler, 206 F.3d at 1086. Moreover, the religious motivations of individual School Board members cannot invalidate the Sticker. See Bown, 112 F.3d at 1471–72 (holding that motivations of individual legislators could not alone invalidate statute requiring period for silent reflection).

Relying heavily upon McLean v. Arkansas Bd. of Educ., 529 F.Supp. 1255 (E.D.Ark. 1982), a case in which a balanced treatment statute was held unconstitutional, Plaintiffs also assert that the Court should infer a purpose to advance religion by the School Board's failure to seek out expert opinion from scientists before adopting the Sticker. McLean, however, is distinguishable from the instant case because McLean involved a statute requiring the teaching of creation-science, which was a substantial change to the curriculum. In this case on the other hand, the Sticker only speaks generally about evolution and does not change the curriculum. While the School Board may have acted more prudently by consulting educators and scientists to determine whether evolution should properly be referenced as a theory, fact, or combination thereof, and to get expert opinion regarding what impact, if any, the Sticker might have on the teaching of evolution, the School Board's failure to do so does not prove that the School Board sought to advance religion. . . .

Therefore, after considering the additional arguments and evidence presented by the parties and evaluating the evidence in light of the applicable law, the Court remains convinced that the Sticker at issue serves at least two secular purposes. First, the Sticker fosters critical thinking by encouraging students to learn about evolution and to make their own assessment regarding its merit. Second, by presenting evolution in a manner that is not unnecessarily hostile, the Sticker reduces offense to students and parents whose beliefs may conflict with the teaching of evolution. For the foregoing reasons, the Court concludes that the Sticker satisfies the first prong of the Lemon analysis.

B. Effect

Regardless of the School Board's actual subjective purpose in voting for the Sticker, the effects prong asks whether the statement at issue in fact conveys a message of endorsement or disapproval of religion to an informed, reasonable observer. Wallace, 472 U.S. at 56 n. 42; Glassroth, 335 F.3d at 1297; Bown, 112 F.3d at 1472. "Endorsement sends a message to nonadherents that they are outsiders, not full members of the political community, and an accompanying message to adherents that they are insiders, favored members of the political community." Lynch, 465 U.S. at

688. Borrowing from the analysis typically applied in religious display cases, to which this case bears great similarities, the Court is mindful that the informed, reasonable observer is someone who personifies the "community ideal of reasonable behavior" and is familiar with the origins and context of the government-sponsored message at issue and the history of the community where the message is displayed. See Capitol Square Review & Advisory Bd. v. Pinette, 515 U.S. 753, 779–81 (1995) (O'Connor, J., concurring). Whether the Sticker communicates a message of endorsement of religion is not really based on the Court's factual findings but is "in large part a legal question to be answered on the basis of judicial interpretation of social facts." Lynch, 465 U.S. at 693–94 (O'Connor, J., concurring). Thus, the Court's focus here is not on the particular views or reactions held by the Plaintiffs or the numerous citizens and organizations who wrote to the School Board. The Court's focus is on ascertaining the view of a disinterested, reasonable observer.

In this case, the Court believes that an informed, reasonable observer would interpret the Sticker to convey a message of endorsement of religion. That is, the Sticker sends a message to those who oppose evolution for religious reasons that they are favored members of the political community, while the Sticker sends a message to those who believe in evolution that they are political outsiders. This is particularly so in a case such as this one involving impressionable public school students who are likely to view the message on the Sticker as a union of church and state. Given that courts should be "particularly vigilant in monitoring compliance with the Establishment Clause in elementary and secondary schools," Edwards, 482 U.S. at 583–84, the Court is of the opinion that the Sticker must be declared unconstitutional. See also Smith, 827 F.2d at 690 (stating that courts must use "particular care" when "many of the citizens perceiving the governmental message are children in their formative years").

Members of certain religious denominations historically have opposed the teaching of evolution in public schools. See McLean, 529 F.Supp. at 1259–60 (setting forth the history of the movement by Christian fundamentalists and creationists in opposition to evolution). As early as the 1920s and continuing into the late 1960s, the judicial system was resolving challenges to anti-evolution statutes, which made it criminal to teach evolution in school. See Epperson, 393 U.S. at 97; Scopes v. State, 154 Tenn. 105, 126 (1927); see also McLean, 529 F.Supp. at 1259. In Epperson, the Supreme Court declared such statutes unconstitutional. In the 1970s and 1980s, there was a movement by anti-evolutionists to have creationism taught alongside evolution. See Edwards, 482 U.S. at 578; McLean, 529 F.Supp. at 1255, 1259. However, the Supreme Court held in Edwards that the teaching of creation-science in public schools would constitute an establishment of religion in violation of the First Amendment. Most recently, the judicial system has witnessed efforts by anti-evolutionists motivated by religion to discredit or disclaim the theory of evolution. See Freiler, 185 F.3d at 337.

Just as citizens around the country have been aware of the historical debate between evolution and religion, an informed, reasonable observer in this case would be keenly aware of the sequence of events that preceded the adoption of the Sticker. See Capitol Square, 515 U.S. at 780 (O'Connor, J., concurring) (noting that the reasonable observer is "presumed to possess a certain level of information that all citizens might not share"). Based on Justice O'Connor's description of what the reasonable observer would be deemed to know, the Court believes these events are key to ascertaining the primary effect of the Sticker. Specifically, the informed, reasonable observer would know that a significant number of Cobb County citizens had voiced opposition to the teaching of evolution for religious reasons. The informed, reasonable observer would also know that despite this opposition, the Cobb County School District was in the process of revising its policy and regulation regarding theories of origin to reflect that evolution would be taught in Cobb County schools. Further, the informed, reasonable observer would be aware that citizens and parents largely motivated by religion put pressure on the School Board to implement certain measures that would nevertheless dilute the teaching of evolution, including placing a disclaimer in the front of certain textbooks that distinguished evolution as a theory, not a fact. Finally, the informed, reasonable observer would be aware that the language of the Sticker essentially mirrors the viewpoint of these religiously-motivated citizens.

While the School Board may have considered the request of its constituents and adopted the Sticker for sincere, secular purposes, an informed, reasonable observer would understand the School Board to be endorsing the viewpoint of Christian fundamentalists and creationists that evolution is a problematic theory lacking an adequate foundation. Of course, the amicus brief filed by certain biologists and Georgia scientists indicates that there are some scientists who have questions regarding certain aspects of evolutionary theory, and the informed, reasonable observer would be aware of this also. On the whole, however, the Sticker would appear to advance the religious viewpoint of the Christian fundamentalists and creationists who were vocal during the textbook adoption process regarding their belief that evolution is a theory, not a fact, which students should critically consider.

The critical language in the Sticker that supports the conclusion that the Sticker runs afoul of the Establishment Clause is the statement that "[e]volution is a theory, not a fact, concerning the origin of living things." This statement is not problematic because of its truth or falsity, although testimony from various witnesses at trial and the amicus brief submitted by the Colorado Citizens for Science, et al., suggest that the statement is not entirely accurate. Rather, the first problem with this language is that there has been a lengthy debate between advocates of evolution and proponents of religious theories of origin specifically concerning whether evolution should be taught as a fact or as a theory, and the School Board appears to have sided with the proponents of religious theories of origin in violation of the Establishment Clause. As the Supreme Court stated in

County of Allegheny v. American Civil Liberties Union, 492 U.S. 573, 593–94 (1989), "[t]he Establishment Clause, at the very least, prohibits government from appearing to take a position on questions of religious belief," and this is exactly what the School Board appears to have done.

This Court's review of anti-evolution cases indicates that whether evolution is referenced as a theory or a fact is certainly a loaded issue with religious undertones. See, e.g., Edwards, 482 U.S. at 624 (Scalia, J., dissenting) (noting that senator who sponsored balanced treatment legislation opposed evolution being taught as a fact because it would communicate to students that "science has proved their religious beliefs false"); Peloza v. Capistrano Unified Sch. Dist., 37 F.3d 517, 520 (9th Cir.1994) (high school biology teacher who was a practicing Christian brought § 1983 action to oppose the teaching of "evolutionism" because, among other things, the school district allegedly required him to teach "evolutionism" as a fact rather than a theory); Mozert v. Hawkins County Bd. of Educ., 827 F.2d 1058, 1062 (6th Cir.1987) (witness in Free Exercise case brought by born again Christians complained that teachers presented evolution in a factual manner, although there were disclaimers in textbooks stating that "evolution is a theory, not a proven scientific fact"); Freiler v. Tangipahoa Parish Bd. of Educ., 975 F.Supp. 819, 824 (E.D.La. 1997) (noting concern of school board members with teaching of evolution as fact because many students in school district believed in Biblical version of creation).

Because the Court is examining social facts to aid in its analysis of the effect of the Sticker, the Court may also consider secondary sources that shed light on relevant facts. See County of Allegheny, 492 U.S. at 614 n. 60; Lynch, 465 U.S. at 709–12, 721–24 (Brennan, J., dissenting). The Court's review of pertinent law review articles affirms that encouraging the teaching of evolution as a theory rather than as a fact is one of the latest strategies to dilute evolution instruction employed by anti-evolutionists with religious motivations. See Kent Greenawalt, Establishing Religious Ideas: Evolution, Creationism, and Intelligent Design, 17 Notre Dame J.L. Ethics & Pub Pol'y 321, 329 (2003); Wendy F. Hanakahi, Comment, Evolution–Creationism Debate: Evaluating the Constitutionality of Teaching Intelligent Design in Public Classrooms, 25 U. Haw. L. Rev. 9, 28, 50–51 (2002); Deborah A. Reule, The New Face of Creationism: The Establishment Clause and the Latest Efforts to Suppress Evolution in Public Schools, 54 Vand. L. Rev. 2555, 2558 (2001); cf. Jay D. Wexler, Darwin, Design, and Disestablishment Teaching the Evolution Controversy in Public Schools, 56 Vand. L. Rev. 751, 752 (2003) (referring to "critics of evolution" generally without specifying whether they have a religious intent)....

The Sticker also has the effect of implicitly bolstering alternative religious theories of origin by suggesting that evolution is a problematic theory even in the field of science. In this regard, the Sticker states, in part, that "[e]volution is a theory, not a fact, concerning the origin of living things" that should be "approached with an open mind, studied carefully, and critically considered." Pls' Ex. 1. This characterization of evolution might be appropriate in other contexts, such as in an elective course on theories of origin or a religious text. However, the evidence in the record and the testimony from witnesses with science backgrounds, including the co-author of one of the textbooks into which the Sticker was placed and Defendants' own witness, Dr. Stickel, reflect that evolution is more than a theory of origin in the context of science. To the contrary, evolution is the dominant scientific theory of origin accepted by the majority of scientists. While evolution is subject to criticism, particularly with respect to the mechanism by which it occurred, this Sticker misleads students regarding the significance and value of evolution in the scientific community for the benefit of the religious alternatives. By denigrating evolution, the School Board appears to be endorsing the well-known prevailing alternative theory, creationism or variations thereof, even though the Sticker does not specifically reference any alternative theories.

In addition to the foregoing, the Sticker targets only evolution to be approached with an open mind, carefully studied, and critically considered without explaining why it is the only theory being isolated as such.... In light of the historical opposition to evolution by Christian fundamentalists and creationists in Cobb County and throughout the Nation, the informed, reasonable observer would infer the School Board's problem with evolution to be that evolution does not acknowledge a creator.

In Epperson, the Supreme Court declared an anti-evolution statute unconstitutional because it "select[ed] from the body of knowledge a particular segment which it proscribe[d] for the sole reason that it is deemed to conflict with a particular religious doctrine." 393 U.S. at 103. Similarly, in Edwards, the Supreme Court declared that a balanced treatment statute was unconstitutional because "[o]ut of many possible science subjects taught in the public schools, the legislature chose to affect the teaching of the one scientific theory that historically has been opposed by certain religious sects." 482 U.S. at 592 n. 7. This case is distinguishable from Epperson and Edwards inasmuch as those statutes clearly impacted the teaching of evolution and the theories of origin curriculum, whereas the Sticker in this case does not preclude evolution from being taught and has not resulted in any complaints that religion is being taught in science classrooms. This case is further distinguishable because the Supreme Court found that the government actors in those cases did act with a purpose to advance religion. However, just as evolution was isolated in the statutes in Epperson and Edwards, evolution is isolated in the Sticker in this case. In the absence of an explicit explanation on the Sticker for evolution's isolation, the Court believes the Sticker sends an impermissible message of endorsement.

Due to the manner in which the Sticker refers to evolution as a theory, the Sticker also has the effect of undermining evolution education to the benefit of those Cobb County citizens who would prefer that students maintain their religious beliefs regarding the origin of life. As Plaintiffs argue and Dr. Miller, the co-author of the science textbook, testified, the use of "theory" in the Sticker plays on the colloquial or popular understanding of the term and suggests to the informed, reasonable observer that evolution is only a highly questionable "opinion" or a "hunch." The Sticker thus has a great potential to prompt confusion among the students. While there may be an educational benefit to students spending time learning the general difference between a theory and a fact as a scientific matter, teachers have less time to teach the substance of evolution. Thus, although evolution is required to be taught in Cobb County classrooms as a technical matter, distracting tangential issues effectively dilute evolution instruction to the benefit of the anti-evolutionists who are motivated to advance their religious beliefs.

Parents for Truth in Education, participating as amici curiae, argue that the Sticker properly references evolution as a theory because prior case law, the dictionary, and other sources do the same. See Brief of Parents for Truth in Education 7–9. In this regard, amici note that the Supreme Court referred to evolution as a "theory" in both the Edwards and Epperson decisions and that Justice Brennan, concurring in the Edwards decision, cited a dictionary that defined "evolution" as a "theory." Id. at 7. Amici also argue that the Edwards Court implicitly acknowledged that evolution is not a fact by making the statement that "[w]e do not imply that a legislature could never require that scientific critiques of prevailing scientific theories be taught." Id. at 8 (citing Edwards, 482 U.S. at 593. While the foregoing may be true, the basis for this Court's conclusion that the Sticker violates the effects prong is not that the School Board should not have called evolution a theory or that the School Board should have called evolution a fact. Rather, the distinction of evolution as a theory rather than a fact is the distinction that religiously-motivated individuals have specifically asked school boards to make in the most recent anti-evolution movement, and that was exactly what parents in Cobb County did in this case. By adopting this specific language, even if at the direction of counsel, the Cobb County School Board appears to have sided with these religiously-motivated individuals. . . .

In sum, the Sticker in dispute violates the effects prong of the Lemon test and Justice O'Connor's endorsement test, which the Court has incorporated into its Lemon analysis. Adopted by the school board, funded by the money of taxpayers, and inserted by school personnel, the Sticker conveys an impermissible message of endorsement and tells some citizens that they are political outsiders while telling others that they are political insiders. Regardless of whether teachers comply with the Cobb County School District's regulation on theories of origin and regardless of the discussions that actually take place in the Cobb County science classrooms, the Sticker has already sent a message that the School Board agrees with the beliefs of Christian fundamentalists and creationists. The School Board has effectively improperly entangled itself with religion by appearing to take a position. Therefore, the Sticker must be removed from all of the textbooks into which it has been placed. . . .

CONCLUSION

For the above-stated reasons, the Court hereby FINDS and CON-CLUDES that the Sticker adopted by the Cobb County Board of Education violates the Establishment Clause of the First Amendment. . . . In light of this conclusion, the Court hereby ORDERS as follows:

1. Defendants shall immediately remove the Sticker from all science textbooks into which the Sticker has been placed.

2. Defendants are permanently enjoined from disseminating the Sticker in any form.

3. Because Plaintiffs seek nominal damages, Plaintiffs shall file with the Court and serve upon Defendants their claim for damages and a verified statement of any fees and/or costs to which they claim entitlement. Defendants shall have the right to object to any such fees and costs as provided in the applicable statutes and court rules.

SELMAN v. COBB COUNTY SCHOOL DIST.

United States Court of Appeals for the Eleventh Circuit
449 F.3d 1320 (11th Cir. 2006)

CARNES, CIRCUIT JUDGE: . . . There are serious problems with two major sequence of events findings that underlie the district court's decision that the school board's adoption of the sticker violated the Establishment Clause. The court decided that while the purpose behind the board action passed muster so that there was no Lemon first prong problem, Selman, 390 F.Supp.2d at 1305, the effects of the action did not, rendering it unconstitutional under the second prong. Id. at 1312. The court collapsed the third prong into the second, apparently believing that any action with a forbidden religious effect also constituted excessive entanglement. Id. at 1299, 1312. In other words, the court's decision that the sticker violated the Establishment Clause turned on its conclusion that the adoption and use of the sticker had the effect of advancing and endorsing religion. That conclusion was heavily influenced by the court's findings about the se-quence of events that led to the adoption of the sticker. The court stated: "in light of the sequence of events that led to the Sticker's adoption, the Sticker communicates to those who endorse evolution that they are political outsiders, while the Sticker communicates to the Christian funda-mentalists and creationists who pushed for a disclaimer that they are political insiders." Id. at 1308 (emphasis added).

The two key facts that the district court stressed as defining the sequence of events leading to the board's adoption of the sticker were a letter from Marjorie Rogers and a 2,300 name petition the court thought she submitted to the board, both asking that the board place a "disclaim-er" about evolution in the textbooks discussing the subject. Id. at 1303. In discussing the events that led to the board's adoption of the sticker, the district court stated:

Opposed to the presentation of evolution as a fact rather than as a theory, Ms. Rogers organized and presented a petition to the School Board that contained the signatures of about 2,300 Cobb County residents. The petition requested that the School Board "clearly identify presumptions and theories and distinguish them from fact." The petition also requested, among other things, that the Board ensure the presentation of all theories regarding the origin of life and place a statement prominently at the beginning of the text that warned students that the material on evolution was not factual but rather was a theory. . . .

In response to the outcry from these parents, certain unidentified members of the School Board consulted legal counsel to determine if there was any language that would help to address parent concerns within the confines of the law. . . .

Id. at 1291–92 (emphasis added). The actual wording of the sticker derived from the board's request to its counsel and counsel's response to that. Id. at 1292. . . .

Later in its opinion the district court again stressed what it understood to be the sequence of events that led to the adoption of the sticker:

Evidence in the record suggests that the idea of placing a sticker in the textbooks originated with parents who opposed the presentation of only evolution in science classrooms and sought to have other theories, including creation theories, included in the curriculum. Namely, Marjorie Rogers wrote a letter to the School Board over two weeks before the adoption of the Sticker recommending, among other things, that the School Board place a disclaimer in each book. Moreover, Ms. Rogers and over 2,300 other Cobb County citizens submitted a petition to the School Board also asking the School Board to place a statement at the beginning of the texts that warned that the material on evolution was not factual. There is no dispute that a large number of Cobb County citizens opposed the teaching of evolution in a rigid fashion, and it is clear to the Court that many of these citizens were motivated by their religious beliefs.

Id. at 1303 (emphasis added). The court thought that the board's decision to have a sticker placed in the textbooks came about because of the letter Marjorie Rogers wrote to the board and the 2,300 name petition it thought that she had submitted to the board. Having outlined the sequence of events in its factfinding and purpose inquiry, the district court specifically relied on the timing of events in concluding that the sticker had the effect of advancing or endorsing religion. Id. at 1308 (stressing the sequence of events).

There is a serious problem with that reasoning. The findings on which it is based are not adequately supported by the evidence in the record before us. The evidence in the record before us does not establish that the Rogers letter was submitted to the board before it adopted the sticker.

And the only petition in the record that resembles the one the court described came well after the board's action. . . .

We are convinced from our painstaking review of the record and the parties' various submissions to us that: no copy of any 2,300 name petition was ever put into the record; when plaintiffs' trial counsel questioned Marjorie Rogers about the petition he used some other document; and in describing to the court the petition that it had heard so much about he read from one that was not submitted to the board until at least six months after the sticker was adopted. The record, even as supplemented, does not support a finding that the board was presented with a 2,300 name, anti-evolution, pro-sticker petition-or any other petition-before it adopted the sticker. Our conclusion in this regard is consistent with the findings of fact and conclusions of law that the plaintiffs submitted to the district court, which do not suggest otherwise. As plaintiffs' counsel on appeal has acknowledged: "Perhaps because the 2300-signature Rogers Petition is missing from the record, both parties have confused it with the September Petition." He also made this remark: "The trial transcript is replete with testimony about documents where the absence of identification by exhibit number and other foundational information make it difficult to ascertain with certainty from the appellate record what is being discussed." That is, if anything, an understatement. . . .

In vacating the district court's judgment and remanding the case for additional proceedings, we want to make it clear that we do not intend to make any implicit rulings on any of the legal issues that arise from the facts once they are found on remand. We intend no holding on any of the legal premises that may have shaped the district court's conclusions on the three Lemon prongs. Mindful that in this area factual context is everything, we simply choose not to attempt to decide this case based on a less than a complete record on appeal or fewer than all the facts.

NOTES AND QUESTIONS

1.   On appeal, the U.S. Court of Appeals for the Eleventh Circuit overturned the trial court ruling in *Selman* for deficiencies in the findings of fact and sent the case back to the trial judge, Clarence Cooper, for additional evidentiary inquiry and new findings. As noted in the foregoing opinion, the deficiency involved the role of Margorie Rogers's letter and petition in influencing the Cobb County School Board's decision to adopt the anti-evolution sticker. On appeal, questions were raised as to whether the letter and petition were submitted before or after the Board acted. After this discrepancy was resolved and Judge Cooper made clear that his ruling would stand whether or not Rogers's petition was submitted before or after the board's action, the case was settled out of court in favor of the plaintiffs. Under the settlement, Cobb County school officials agreed not to order the placement of "any stickers, labels, stamps, inscriptions, or other warnings or disclaimers bearing language substantially similar to that used on the sticker that is the subject of this action." The school district also agreed to pay $166,659 towards plaintiffs'

attorney fees in the case. Given the appellate court's action on the initial appeal—which expressly did not rule on any constitutional issues—why did the School District settle the case rather than let Judge Cooper rule again and appeal his decision on legal (rather than factual) grounds? Could the threat of added attorney fees be a factor?

2.   Cobb County is an affluent suburban county near Atlanta, Georgia. Prior to adopting the stickers at issue in this case, the Cobb County School District maintained a written policy against compelling any student to study the subject of human origins. This policy, which was reprinted in Judge Cooper's decision, was never challenged in court. Many districts around the country formally or informally maintain similar policies. Why was it never challenged in court? The policy did not mention religion but suggested that teaching human origins might conflict with the "family teachings of a significant number of Cobb County citizens." Is this a valid secular reason for omitting it from the curriculum? In light of preceding judicial opinions beginning with *Epperson*, was Cobb County's policy an unconstitutional establishment of religion or a constitutional accommodation of religion?

3.   In effect repealing its longstanding policy of not compelling any student to study the subject of human origins, in 2001, the Cobb County School District adopted a widely used evolutionary high-school biology textbook by Kenneth Miller and Joseph Levine, *Biology: the Living Science*. When some parents and taxpayers objected to the expanded teaching of Darwinism, the School District ordered that a sticker be placed in the textbooks stating in pertinent part, "Evolution is a theory, not a fact, regarding the origin of living things." Thus, unlike in the previous cases presented in this book, the anti-evolution disclaimer was adopted in the context of expending (rather than restricting) the teaching of Darwinism. Yet it was precisely in this context that Judge Cooper held the sticker to be unconstitutional. "Just as citizens around the country have been aware of the historical debate between evolution and religion," he wrote, "an informed, reasonable observer in this case would be keenly aware of the sequence of events that preceded the adoption of the Sticker." What was the sequence of events that tainted the sticker with the unconstitutional effect of endorsing religion? Given the religious motives of those objecting to the new Darwinist textbooks, Judge Cooper concluded that by adopting the sticker, "the School Board appears to have sided with the proponents of religious theories of origin in violation of the Establishment Clause." Do you agree that high-school students, who were the intended audience for the sticker, would perceive that the School District was endorsing religious creationism over Darwinism?

4.   Much like the *Freiler* court, the *Selman* court held that the Cobb County School District did not violate the *Lemon* test's purpose prong. Both courts found that the school boards, in adopting their respective disclaimers, sought to reduce offense to creationist students and parents. This, the courts ruled, was a valid secular purpose. In doing so, Judge Cooper wrote, "The School Board's decision to adopt the Sticker was indisputably influenced by sectarian interests, but the Constitution forbids only a purpose to endorse or advance religion." This reasoning mirrored the reasoning in *Freiler* and followed the instructions of the Supreme Court in *Wallace v. Jaffree*, 472 U.S. 38, 46 (1985), that a government action violated the purpose prong only if it was

"entirely motivated by a purpose to advance religion." Acting with religious interests is not necessarily acting to promote religion. In *Freiler*, however, the court rejected the additional claim that the Tangipahoa Parish disclaimer was adopted with a sincere secular purpose of promoting critical thinking. In contrast, in *Selman*, Judge Cooper concluded that the Cobb County School Board did seek to promote critical thinking through its sticker. What considerations led to the different conclusions regarding critical thinking? Two factors appeared important. First, unlike the Tangipahoa Parish disclaimer, the Cobb County sticker was adopted in the context of strengthening teaching about evolution. Second, also unlike the Tangipahoa Parish disclaimer, the Cobb County sticker did not mention any alternative religious theory of origins. Given these findings regarding purpose, why did the *Selman* court nevertheless find that the Cobb County sticker would have the primary effect of advancing or endorsing a particular religious viewpoint? In *Freiler*, the disclaimer's identification of the "Biblical version of Creation" as an acceptable alternative to Darwinism appeared to be the most important factor in finding that the disclaimer would have the primary effect of communicated the school board's endorsement of a religious belief—but this factor was lacking in *Selman*.

CHAPTER 7

ANTI-EVOLUTIONISM IN THE TWENTY-FIRST CENTURY

■ ■ ■

I. THE RISE OF INTELLIGENT DESIGN

Lawyers are trained to look for similarities and differences in the application of legal precedent, and they can strain gnats for willing clients. For example, the Arkansas Balanced Treatment Act defined "creation-science" to mean scientific evidence supporting a biblical view of biological and geological history, including "changes only within fixed limits of originally created kinds of plants and animals, ... the occurrence of a worldwide flood, and a relatively recent inception of the earth and living kinds." After *McLean* struck the Arkansas statute for unconstitutionally authorizing religious instruction in public schools, Wendell Bird, as special counsel for Louisiana, argued that Louisiana's Balanced Treatment Act was not doomed by this ruling because the Louisiana statute defined "creation-science" as scientific evidence for the abrupt appearance of the universe, life, and living kinds, without any direct biblical references. The U. S. Supreme Court saw it differently. Writing for the majority in *Edwards*, Justice William Brennan concluded "that the term 'creation science,' as contemplated by the legislature that adopted the Act, embodied the religious belief that a supernatural creation was responsible for the creation of humankind."[115] In his concurring opinion, Justice Louis Powell linked creation-science to the fundamentalist religious teachings of the Institute for Creation Research (ICR). The Court freely associated creation-science with Protestant fundamentalism.

Clearly the creation-science of the Louisiana statute was too similar to the creationism of the Arkansas law to pass constitutional muster. In commentary written in 1990, before his book *Darwin on Trial* launched him to the forefront of the Intelligent Design (ID) movement, University of California law professor Phillip E. Johnson observed that "Bird labored unsuccessfully to rescue scientific creationism from its fatal association with Biblical fundamentalism." Whatever valid arguments Bird may have raised against Darwinism as a self-sufficient theory of biological origins,

---

115. Edwards v. Aguillard, 482 U.S. 578, 592 (1987).

Johnson observed, were "thoroughly obscured by all the attention paid to Noah's flood." To succeed at law after *Edwards*, he suggested, Darwin's critics must distance themselves from creation-science. Johnson's target became the basic methodology that limits science to the study of natural explanations for physical phenomena. "It is not only 'fundamentalists'," he contended, "but theists of any description who believe that an intelligent artificer made humanity with a purpose, whether through evolution or otherwise."[116] As an evangelical Presbyterian, he placed himself among these theists. Science should be open to supernatural answers of this sort. Much as Bird's 1978 *Yale Law Journal* article provided a road map to creationist legal strategies for the 1980s, Johnson's 1990 commentary anticipated the basic pattern of anti-evolution legal activities into the next century. There would be challenges to the sufficiency of purely naturalistic theories of evolution to explain origins, programs to open science education to teaching evidence of intelligent design, claims that Darwinism is only a theory, and calls to teach the controversy over evolutionary naturalism.

Many scientists and science organizations addressed this new challenge to Darwinian instruction by affirming the comparability of methodological naturalism with belief in God. The National Academy of Sciences (NAS), a self-selecting body of the nation's premiere scientists, had asserted as much in a glossy brochure distributed to school teachers during the 1980s in reaction to the creation-science movement. In 1998, the NAS mass-produced a new booklet reasserting that, while science is committed to methodological naturalism, it does not conflict with religion. They simply represent separate ways of knowing. "Science," the booklet stated, "is limited to explaining the natural world through natural causes. Science can say nothing about the supernatural. Whether God exists or not is a question about which science is neutral." In response to the rhetorical query, "Can a person believe in God and still accept evolution?" the NAS booklet carefully replied, "Many do."[117] The 8,000–member National Association of Biology Teachers (NABT) took a similar tact. In a position statement initially adopted in opposition to the creation-science movement and always controversial among theists, the NABT had defined evolution as "an unsupervised, impersonal, unpredictable and natural process of temporal descent with gradual modification." In 1997, responding to heightened sensitivity to the atheistic implications of Darwinism, the NABT's executive committee voted to delete the words "unsupervised" and "impersonal" from the statement. "To say that evolution is unsupervised is to make a theological statement," the NABT's executive director explained, and that exceeds the bounds of science.[118]

---

116. Phillip E. Johnson, *The Origin of Species Revisited*, 7 CONST. COMMENTARY 427, 431, 433 (1990). See also, Phillip E. Johnson, *Evolution as Dogma: The Establishment of Naturalism*, FIRST THINGS, Oct. 1990, at 22.

117. NATIONAL ACADEMY OF SCIENCES, TEACHING ABOUT EVOLUTION AND THE NATURE OF SCIENCE 58 (1998).

118. Laurie Goodstein, *New Light for Creationism*, NEW YORK TIMES, Dec. 21, 1997, at 4–1, 4–4.

Johnson was known mostly as a conservative criminal-law scholar in 1991, when his first popular book, *Darwin on Trial*, propelled the nascent ID movement into national prominence. An adult convert to evangelical Christianity, Johnson only began thinking critically about Darwinism four years earlier, after reading *The Blind Watchmaker* by British evolutionary biologist and popular science writer Richard Dawkins. The book's message—that modern biology justifies atheism—enraged Johnson. In *Darwin on Trial*, he set about to discredit it. "I could see that Dawkins achieved his word magic with the very tools that are familiar to us lawyers," Johnson reasoned: using definitions to determine results. "We define *science* as the pursuit of materialist alternatives. Now what kind of answers do we come up with? By gosh, we come up with materialist answers!"[119] Natural selection may be the best naturalistic answer to the origin of species, he argued, but not the correct one. If we admit that supernatural forces could shape the natural world, he claimed, then the apparent abrupt appearance of species in the fossil record and the intricate complexity of natural systems should favor intelligent design over natural selection, and public schools should be able to teach this alternative so long as they do not promote any particular religious view.

Johnson's work attracted the attention of Stephen Meyer, an assistant professor of philosophy at a small Christian college in Washington State. With Johnson's support, Meyer launched an ID think tank, the Center for the Renewal of Science and Culture (later renamed the Center for Science and Culture), as part of the Seattle-based Discovery Institute. Among the Center's Senior Fellows, Michael J. Behe, William A. Dembski, and Jonathan Wells have attracted the most attention. Behe's writings do not question the evolutionary concept of common descent but assert that some biochemical processes (such as the cascade of multiple proteins required for blood clotting) and biological features (such as the bacterial flagellum) are too irreducibly complex to have originated in the step-by-step fashion envisioned by Darwinism. This is a logical argument, not a scientific proof of design, and Behe has not conducted any original scientific research on the matter. His contribution comes in assembling various examples of biological complexity and popularizing them in his 1996 book, *Darwin's Black Box*. Seeking to break the stalemate in God's favor, Dembski's writings deploy probability filters (of the type used to sift radio signals from outer space for messages sent by intelligent beings) to detect whether the complexity within various biological systems is more likely the product of random chance or intelligent design. They claim that the probabilities underlying some biochemical systems are statistically small enough to serve as evidence for intelligent design—though the probabilistic nature of such evidence inevitably makes its weight dependant on one's conception of the age, size, and dimensions of the universe. Given enough time, enough planets in our universe, and enough universes, no probability is too small too be discarded as unlikely to happen. Wells

---

119. Phillip Johnson interviewed in Tim Stafford, *The Making a Revolution*, CHRISTIANITY TODAY, Dec. 8, 1997, at 18.

is best known for a 2002 book, *Icons of Evolution,* which attempted to undermine popular acceptance of Darwinism by discrediting some of the classic evidence once used to support it, such the comparative embryo drawings of nineteenth century German evolutionist Ernst Haeckel and the 1952 Miller–Urey experiment on the origin of organic molecules. By pointing out that some of this long-discredited evidence for Darwinism still appeared in textbooks, Wells suggested that scientists were complicit in propping up a failed theory for ideological reasons. Collectively, the work of Johnson, Behe, Dembski, Wells, and their colleagues became the modern doctrine of Intelligent Design.

Along with sponsoring writing and research about intelligent design in nature, the Discovery Institute provides advice and materials to school boards and teachers on both alternatives to Darwinism and teaching what it depicts as the "controversy" over evolutionary materialism. In 2004, it began advising members of the Dover, Pennsylvania, School Board. Dover is in the conservative Appalachian heartland of Pennsylvania. Without expressly campaigning on the issue of Darwinism in the school, religious conservatives had won a majority of seats on Dover's school board. In 2003, some of them began seeking ways to incorporated creationism into the science curriculum before discovering the legal obstacles to doing so and turning instead to Intelligent Design. One school board member persuaded donors at his church to contribute funds to purchase sixty copies of the ID-text *Of Pandas and People* for the local public high school. In October, 2004, the Board voted to make ninth-grade biology students "aware of gaps/problems with Darwin's theory and of other theories of evolution, including, but not limited to intelligent design." Before beginning the section on Darwinism, biology teachers were directed to read their students a prescribed statement about those problems and alerting them to the donated ID texts. When the teachers refused to read the statement, school administrators did so and a lawsuit followed.

Represented by the ACLU, the Americans United for the Separation of Church and State, and an elite Philadelphia law firm, eleven parents filed suit in federal district court against the school district in December, 2004. Clearly outgunned, the school district accepted the services of the Thomas More Law Center, a conservative Catholic legal rights organization based in Michigan that bills itself as the "sword and shield for people of faith." A trial ensued in October, 2005, before federal district Judge John E. Jones III, sitting without a jury. With ample resources for plaintiffs and defendant alike and the promise of a definitive legal test for teaching ID objections to Darwinism, the trial attracted prominent expert witnesses on both sides, including Michael Behe for the school board and, for the plaintiffs, Brown University biologist Kenneth Miller, co-author of the biology textbook at issue in *Selman* and a practicing Catholic who had long championed the compatibility of Darwinism and Christianity. Reporters from as far away as Europe and Asia descended on Harrisburg to cover the trial, which attracted non-stop media attention across the United States and spawned several books and a television documentary. After hearing six weeks of testimony and reviewing dozens of legal briefs, Judge Jones issued the following opinion in January, 2005:

KITZMILLER v. DOVER AREA SCHOOL DIST.

United States District Court for the Middle District of Pennsylvania
400 F.Supp.2d 707 (M.D. Pa. 2005)

JONES, DISTRICT JUDGE: On October 18, 2004, the Defendant Dover Area School Board of Directors passed by a 6–3 vote the following resolution:

> Students will be made aware of gaps/problems in Darwin's theory and of other theories of evolution including, but not limited to, intelligent design. Note: Origins of Life is not taught.

On November 19, 2004, the Defendant Dover Area School District announced by press release that, commencing in January 2005, teachers would be required to read the following statement to students in the ninth grade biology class at Dover High School:

> The Pennsylvania Academic Standards require students to learn about Darwin's Theory of Evolution and eventually to take a standardized test of which evolution is a part.

> Because Darwin's Theory is a theory, it continues to be tested as new evidence is discovered. The Theory is not a fact. Gaps in the Theory exist for which there is no evidence. A theory is defined as a well-tested explanation that unifies a broad range of observations.

> Intelligent Design is an explanation of the origin of life that differs from Darwin's view. The reference book, Of Pandas and People, is available for students who might be interested in gaining an understanding of what Intelligent Design actually involves.

> With respect to any theory, students are encouraged to keep an open mind. The school leaves the discussion of the Origins of Life to individual students and their families. As a Standards-driven district, class instruction focuses upon preparing students to achieve proficiency on Standards-based assessments.

A.   Background and Procedural History

On December 14, 2004, Plaintiffs filed the instant suit challenging the constitutional validity of the October 18, 2004 resolution and November 19, 2004 press release (collectively, "the ID Policy"). It is contended that the ID Policy constitutes an establishment of religion prohibited by the First Amendment to the United States Constitution, which is made applicable to the states by the Fourteenth Amendment....

C.   Federal Jurisprudential Legal Landscape

As we will review the federal jurisprudential legal landscape in detail below, we will accordingly render only an abbreviated summary of that terrain by way of an introduction at this juncture. The religious movement known as Fundamentalism began in nineteenth century America as a response to social changes, new religious thought and Darwinism. McLean v. Ark. Bd. of Educ., 529 F.Supp. 1255, 1258 (E.D.Ark. 1982). Religiously motivated groups pushed state legislatures to adopt laws prohibiting public schools from teaching evolution, culminating in the Scopes "monkey trial" of 1925. McLean, 529 F.Supp. at 1259; see Scopes v. State, 154 Tenn. 105 (1927) (criminal prosecution of public-school teacher for teaching about evolution).

In 1968, a radical change occurred in the legal landscape when in Epperson v. Arkansas, 393 U.S. 97 (1968), the Supreme Court struck down Arkansas's statutory prohibition against teaching evolution. Religious proponents of evolution thereafter championed "balanced treatment" statutes requiring public-school teachers who taught evolution to devote equal time to teaching the biblical view of creation; however, courts realized this tactic to be another attempt to establish the Biblical version of the creation of man. Daniel v. Waters, 515 F.2d 485 (6th Cir.1975).

Fundamentalist opponents of evolution responded with a new tactic suggested by Daniel's reasoning which was ultimately found to be unconstitutional under the First Amendment, namely, to utilize scientific-sounding language to describe religious beliefs and then to require that schools teach the resulting "creation science" or "scientific creationism" as an alternative to evolution.

In Edwards v. Aguillard, 482 U.S. 578 (1987), five years after McLean, the Supreme Court held that a requirement that public schools teach "creation science" along with evolution violated the Establishment Clause. The import of Edwards is that the Supreme Court turned the proscription against teaching creation science in the public school system into a national prohibition.

D. The Endorsement and Lemon Tests

Having briefly touched upon the salient legal framework, it is evident that as the cases and controversies have evolved over time, so too has the methodology that courts employ in evaluating Establishment Clause claims.... After a searching review of Supreme Court and Third Circuit Court of Appeals precedent, it is apparent to this Court that both the endorsement test and the Lemon test should be employed in this case to analyze the constitutionality of the ID Policy under the Establishment Clause.... We will therefore initially analyze the constitutionality of the ID Policy under the endorsement test and will then proceed to the Lemon test as it applies to this case.

E. Application of the Endorsement Test to the ID Policy

The endorsement test recognizes that when government transgresses the limits of neutrality and acts in ways that show religious favoritism or sponsorship, it violates the Establishment Clause. As Justice O'Connor first elaborated on this issue, the endorsement test was a gloss on Lemon that encompassed both the purpose and effect prongs:

The central issue in this case is whether [the government] has endorsed [religion] by its [actions].

To answer that question, we must examine both what [the government] intended to communicate ... and what message [its conduct] actually conveyed. The purpose and effect prongs of the Lemon test represent these two aspects of the meaning of the [government's] action.

Lynch v. Donnelly, 465 U.S. 668, 690 (1984) (O'Connor, J., concurring).

As the endorsement test developed through application, it is now primarily a lens through which to view "effect," with purpose evidence being relevant to the inquiry derivatively. In Allegheny, the Supreme Court instructed that the word "endorsement is not self-defining" and further elaborated that it derives its meaning from other words that the Court has found useful over the years in interpreting the Establishment Clause. County of Allegheny v. ACLU, 492 U.S. 573, 593 (1989). The endorsement test emanates from the "prohibition against government endorsement of religion" and it "preclude[s] government from conveying or attempting to convey a message that religion or a particular religious belief is *favored* or *preferred*." Id. (citations omitted) (emphasis in original). The test consists of the reviewing court determining what message a challenged governmental policy or enactment conveys to a reasonable, objective observer who knows the policy's language, origins, and legislative history, as well as the history of the community and the broader social and historical context in which the policy arose. McCreary County, Ky. v. ACLU, 545 U.S. 844 (2005) (objective observer "presumed to be familiar with the history of the government's actions and competent to learn what history has to show"); Santa Fe Ind. Sch. Dist. v. Doe, 530 U.S. 290, 308 (2000) (objective observer familiar with "implementation of" governmental action); Selman, 390 F.Supp.2d at 1306 (objective observer "familiar with the origins and context of the government-sponsored message at issue and the history of the community where the message is displayed")....

1. An Objective Observer

The history of the intelligent design movement (hereinafter "IDM") and the development of the strategy to weaken education of evolution by focusing students on alleged gaps in the theory of evolution is the historical and cultural background against which the Dover School Board acted in adopting the challenged ID Policy. As a reasonable observer, whether adult or child, would be aware of this social context in which the ID Policy arose, and such context will help to reveal the meaning of Defendants' actions, it is necessary to trace the history of the IDM.

It is essential to our analysis that we now provide a more expansive account of the extensive and complicated federal jurisprudential legal landscape concerning opposition to teaching evolution, and its historical origins. As noted, such opposition grew out of a religious tradition,

Christian Fundamentalism that began as part of evangelical Protestant-ism's response to, among other things, Charles Darwin's exposition of the theory of evolution as a scientific explanation for the diversity of species. McLean, 529 F.Supp. at 1258; see also, e.g., Edwards, 482 U.S. at 590–92. Subsequently, as the United States Supreme Court explained in Epperson, in an "upsurge of fundamentalist religious fervor of the twenties," 393 U.S. at 98, state legislatures were pushed by religiously motivated groups to adopt laws prohibiting public schools from teaching evolution. McLean, 529 F.Supp. at 1259; see Scopes, 154 Tenn. 105 (1927). Between the 1920s and early 1960s, anti-evolutionary sentiment based upon a religious social movement resulted in formal legal sanctions to remove evolution from the classroom. McLean, 529 F.Supp. at 1259 (discussing a subtle but pervasive influence that resulted from anti-evolutionary sentiment concerning teaching biology in public schools).

As we previously noted, the legal landscape radically changed in 1968 when the Supreme Court struck down Arkansas's statutory prohibition against teaching evolution in Epperson, 393 U.S. 97. Although the Arkan-sas statute at issue did not include direct references to the Book of Genesis or to the fundamentalist view that religion should be protected from science, the Supreme Court concluded that "the motivation of the [Arkansas] law was the same . . .: to suppress the teaching of a theory which, it was thought, 'denied' the divine creation of man." Edwards, 482 U.S. at 590 (quoting Epperson, 393 U.S. at 109) (Arkansas sought to prevent its teachers from discussing the theory of evolution as it is contrary to the belief of some regarding the Book of Genesis.).

Post–Epperson, evolution's religious opponents implemented "bal-anced treatment" statutes requiring public school teachers who taught evolution to devote equal time to teaching the biblical view of creation; however, such statutes did not pass constitutional muster under the Establishment Clause. See, e.g., Daniel, 515 F.2d at 487, 489, 491. In Daniel, the Sixth Circuit Court of Appeals held that by assigning a "preferential position for the Biblical version of creation" over "any account of the development of man based on scientific research and reasoning," the challenged statute officially promoted religion, in violation of the Establishment Clause. Id. at 489.

Next, and as stated, religious opponents of evolution began cloaking religious beliefs in scientific sounding language and then mandating that schools teach the resulting "creation science" or "scientific creationism" as an alternative to evolution. However, this tactic was likewise unsuccess-ful under the First Amendment. "Fundamentalist organizations were formed to promote the idea that the Book of Genesis was supported by scientific data. The terms 'creation science' and 'scientific creationism' have been adopted by these Fundamentalists as descriptive of their study of creation and the origins of man." McLean, 529 F.Supp. at 1259. In 1982, the district court in McLean reviewed Arkansas's balanced-treat-ment law and evaluated creation science in light of Scopes, Epperson, and the long history of Fundamentalism's attack on the scientific theory of evolution, as well as the statute's legislative history and historical context. The court found that creation science organizations were fundamentalist religious entities that "consider[ed] the introduction of creation science into the public schools part of their ministry." Id. at 1260. The court in McLean stated that creation science rested on a "contrived dualism" that recognized only two possible explanations for life, the scientific theory of evolution and biblical creationism, treated the two as mutually exclusive such that "one must either accept the literal interpretation of Genesis or else believe in the godless system of evolution," and accordingly viewed any critiques of evolution as evidence that necessarily supported biblical creationism. Id. at 1266. The court concluded that creation science "is simply not science" because it depends upon "supernatural intervention," which cannot be explained by natural causes, or be proven through empirical investigation, and is therefore neither testable nor falsifiable. Id. at 1267. Accordingly, the United States District Court for the Eastern District of Arkansas deemed creation science as merely biblical creationism in a new guise and held that Arkansas' balanced-treatment statute could have no valid secular purpose or effect, served only to advance religion, and violated the First Amendment. Id. at 1264, 1272–74.

Five years after McLean was decided, in 1987, the Supreme Court struck down Louisiana's balanced-treatment law in Edwards for similar reasons. After a thorough analysis of the history of fundamentalist attacks against evolution, as well as the applicable legislative history including statements made by the statute's sponsor, and taking the character of organizations advocating for creation science into consideration, the Supreme Court held that the state violated the Establishment Clause by "restructur[ing] the science curriculum to conform with a particular religious viewpoint." Edwards, 482 U.S. at 593. . . .

The concept of intelligent design (hereinafter "ID"), in its current form, came into existence after the Edwards case was decided in 1987. For the reasons that follow, we conclude that the religious nature of ID would be readily apparent to an objective observer, adult or child.

We initially note that John Haught, a theologian who testified as an expert witness for Plaintiffs and who has written extensively on the subject of evolution and religion, succinctly explained to the Court that the argument for ID is not a new scientific argument, but is rather an old religious argument for the existence of God. He traced this argument back to at least Thomas Aquinas in the 13th century, who framed the argument as a syllogism: Wherever complex design exists, there must have been a designer; nature is complex; therefore nature must have had an intelligent designer. (Trial Tr. vol. 9, Haught Test., 7–8, Sept. 30, 2005). Dr. Haught testified that Aquinas was explicit that this intelligent designer "everyone understands to be God." Id. The syllogism described by Dr. Haught is essentially the same argument for ID as presented by defense expert witnesses Professors Behe and Minnich who employ the phrase "purposeful arrangement of parts."

Dr. Haught testified that this argument for the existence of God was advanced early in the 19th century by Reverend Paley and defense expert witnesses Behe and Minnich admitted that their argument for ID based on the "purposeful arrangement of parts" is the same one that Paley made for design. (9:7–8 (Haught); Trial Tr. vol. 23, Behe Test., 55–57, Oct. 19, 2005; Trial Tr. vol. 38, Minnich Test., 44, Nov. 4, 2005). The only apparent difference between the argument made by Paley and the argument for ID, as expressed by defense expert witnesses Behe and Minnich, is that ID's "official position" does not acknowledge that the designer is God. However, as Dr. Haught testified, anyone familiar with Western religious thought would immediately make the association that the tactically unnamed designer is God, as the description of the designer in *Of Pandas and People* (hereinafter "*Pandas*") is a "master intellect," strongly suggesting a supernatural deity as opposed to any intelligent actor known to exist in the natural world. (P–11 at 85). Moreover, it is notable that both Professors Behe and Minnich admitted their personal view is that the designer is God and Professor Minnich testified that he understands many leading advocates of ID to believe the designer to be God. (21:90 (Behe); 38:36–38 (Minnich)).

Although proponents of the IDM occasionally suggest that the designer could be a space alien or a time-traveling cell biologist, no serious alternative to God as the designer has been proposed by members of the IDM, including Defendants' expert witnesses. (20:102–03 (Behe)). In fact, an explicit concession that the intelligent designer works outside the laws of nature and science and a direct reference to religion is *Pandas'* rhetorical statement, "what kind of intelligent agent was it [the designer]" and answer: "On its own science cannot answer this question. It must leave it to religion and philosophy." (P–11 at 7; 9:13–14 (Haught)).

A significant aspect of the IDM is that despite Defendants' protestations to the contrary, it describes ID as a religious argument. In that vein, the writings of leading ID proponents reveal that the designer postulated by their argument is the God of Christianity. Dr. Barbara Forrest, one of Plaintiffs' expert witnesses, is the author of the book *Creationism's Trojan Horse*. She has thoroughly and exhaustively chronicled the history of ID in her book and other writings for her testimony in this case. Her testimony, and the exhibits which were admitted with it, provide a wealth of statements by ID leaders that reveal ID's religious, philosophical, and cultural content. The following is a representative grouping of such statements made by prominent ID proponents.

Phillip Johnson, considered to be the father of the IDM, developer of ID's "Wedge Strategy," which will be discussed below, and author of the 1991 book entitled *Darwin on Trial*, has written that "theistic realism" or "mere creation" are defining concepts of the IDM. This means "that God is objectively real as Creator and recorded in the biological evidence ..." (Trial Tr. vol. 10, Forrest Test., 80–81, Oct. 5, 2005; P–328). In addition, Phillip Johnson states that the "Darwinian theory of evolution contradicts not just the Book of Genesis, but every word in the Bible from beginning to end. It contradicts the idea that we are here because a creator brought about our existence for a purpose." (11:16–17 (Forrest); P–524 at 1). ID proponents Johnson, William Dembski, and Charles Thaxton, one of the editors of *Pandas*, situate ID in the Book of John in the New Testament of the Bible, which begins, "In the Beginning was the Word, and the Word was God." (11:18–20, 54–55 (Forrest); P–524; P–355; P–357). Dembski has written that ID is a "ground clearing operation" to allow Christianity to receive serious consideration, and "Christ is never an addendum to a scientific theory but always a completion." (11:50–53 (Forrest); P–386; P–390). Moreover, in turning to Defendants' lead expert, Professor Behe, his testimony at trial indicated that ID is only a scientific, as opposed to a religious, project for him; however, considerable evidence was introduced to refute this claim. Consider, to illustrate, that Professor Behe remarkably and unmistakably claims that the plausibility of the argument for ID depends upon the extent to which one believes in the existence of God. (P–718 at 705). As no evidence in the record indicates that any other scientific proposition's validity rests on belief in God, nor is the Court aware of any such scientific propositions, Professor Behe's assertion constitutes substantial evidence that in his view, as is commensurate with other prominent ID leaders, ID is a religious and not a scientific proposition.

Dramatic evidence of ID's religious nature and aspirations is found in what is referred to as the "Wedge Document." The Wedge Document, developed by the Discovery Institute's Center for Renewal of Science and Culture (hereinafter "CRSC"), represents from an institutional standpoint, the IDM's goals and objectives, much as writings from the Institute for Creation Research did for the earlier creation-science movement, as discussed in McLean. (11:26–28 (Forrest)); McLean, 529 F.Supp. at 1255. The Wedge Document states in its "Five Year Strategic Plan Summary" that the IDM's goal is to replace science as currently practiced with "theistic and Christian science." (P–140 at 6). As posited in the Wedge Document, the IDM's "Governing Goals" are to "defeat scientific materialism and its destructive moral, cultural, and political legacies" and "to replace materialistic explanations with the theistic understanding that nature and human beings are created by God." Id. at 4. The CSRC expressly announces, in the Wedge Document, a program of Christian apologetics to promote ID. A careful review of the Wedge Document's goals and language throughout the document reveals cultural and religious goals, as opposed to scientific ones. (11:26–48 (Forrest); P–140). ID aspires to change the ground rules of science to make room for religion, specifically, beliefs consonant with a particular version of Christianity.

In addition to the IDM itself describing ID as a religious argument, ID's religious nature is evident because it involves a supernatural designer. The courts in Edwards and McLean expressly found that this characteristic removed creationism from the realm of science and made it a religious proposition. Edwards, 482 U.S. at 591–92; McLean, 529 F.Supp.

at 1265–66. Prominent ID proponents have made abundantly clear that the designer is supernatural.

Defendants' expert witness ID proponents confirmed that the existence of a supernatural designer is a hallmark of ID. First, Professor Behe has written that by ID he means "not designed by the laws of nature," and that it is "implausible that the designer is a natural entity." (P–647 at 193; P–718 at 696, 700). Second, Professor Minnich testified that for ID to be considered science, the ground rules of science have to be broadened so that supernatural forces can be considered. (38:97 (Minnich)). Third, Professor Steven William Fuller testified that it is ID's project to change the ground rules of science to include the supernatural. (Trial Tr. vol. 28, Fuller Test., 20–24, Oct. 24, 2005). Turning from defense expert witnesses to leading ID proponents, Johnson has concluded that science must be redefined to include the supernatural if religious challenges to evolution are to get a hearing. (11:8–15 (Forrest); P–429). Additionally, Dembski agrees that science is ruled by methodological naturalism and argues that this rule must be overturned if ID is to prosper. (Trial Tr. vol. 5, Pennock Test., 32–34, Sept. 28, 2005).

Further support for the proposition that ID requires supernatural creation is found in the book *Pandas*, to which students in Dover's ninth grade biology class are directed. *Pandas* indicates that there are two kinds of causes, natural and intelligent, which demonstrate that intelligent causes are beyond nature. (P–11 at 6). Professor Haught, who as noted was the only theologian to testify in this case, explained that in Western intellectual tradition, non-natural causes occupy a space reserved for ultimate religious explanations. (9:13–14 (Haught)). Robert Pennock, Plaintiffs' expert in the philosophy of science, concurred with Professor Haught and concluded that because its basic proposition is that the features of the natural world are produced by a transcendent, immaterial, non-natural being, ID is a religious proposition regardless of whether that religious proposition is given a recognized religious label. (5:55–56 (Pennock)). It is notable that not one defense expert was able to explain how the supernatural action suggested by ID could be anything other than an inherently religious proposition. Accordingly, we find that ID's religious nature would be further evident to our objective observer because it directly involves a supernatural designer.

A "hypothetical reasonable observer," adult or child, who is "aware of the history and context of the community and forum" is also presumed to know that ID is a form of creationism. Child Evangelism, 386 F.3d at 531; Allegheny, 492 U.S. at 624–25. The evidence at trial demonstrates that ID is nothing less than the progeny of creationism. What is likely the strongest evidence supporting the finding of ID's creationist nature is the history and historical pedigree of the book to which students in Dover's ninth grade biology class are referred, *Pandas*. *Pandas* is published by an organization called FTE, as noted, whose articles of incorporation and filings with the Internal Revenue Service describe it as a religious, Christian organization. (P–461; P–28; P–566; P–633; Buell Dep. 1:13, July

8, 2005). *Pandas* was written by Dean Kenyon and Percival Davis, both acknowledged creationists, and Nancy Pearcey, a Young Earth Creationist, contributed to the work. (10:102–08 (Forrest)).

As Plaintiffs meticulously and effectively presented to the Court, *Pandas* went through many drafts, several of which were completed prior to and some after the Supreme Court's decision in Edwards, which held that the Constitution forbids teaching creationism as science. By comparing the pre and post Edwards drafts of *Pandas*, three astonishing points emerge: (1) the definition for creation science in early drafts is identical to the definition of ID; (2) cognates of the word creation (creationism and creationist), which appeared approximately 150 times were deliberately and systematically replaced with the phrase ID; and (3) the changes occurred shortly after the Supreme Court held that creation science is religious and cannot be taught in public school science classes in Edwards. This word substitution is telling, significant, and reveals that a purposeful change of words was effected without any corresponding change in content, which directly refutes FTE's argument that by merely disregarding the words "creation" and "creationism," FTE expressly rejected creationism in *Pandas*. In early pre-Edwards drafts of *Pandas*, the term "creation" was defined as "various forms of life that began abruptly through an intelligent agency with their distinctive features intact-fish with fins and scales, birds with feathers, beaks, and wings, etc.," the very same way in which ID is defined in the subsequent published versions. (P–560 at 210; P–1 at 2–13; P–562 at 2–14, P–652 at 2–15; P–6 at 99–100; P–11 at 99–100; P–856.2.). This definition was described by many witnesses for both parties, notably including defense experts Minnich and Fuller, as "special creation" of kinds of animals, an inherently religious and creationist concept. (28:85–86 (Fuller); Minnich Dep. at 34, May 26, 2005; Trial Tr. vol. 1, Miller Test., 141–42, Sept. 26, 2005; 9:10 (Haught); Trial Tr. vol. 33, Bonsell Test., 54–56, Oct. 31, 2005). Professor Behe's assertion that this passage was merely a description of appearances in the fossil record is illogical and defies the weight of the evidence that the passage is a conclusion about how life began based upon an interpretation of the fossil record, which is reinforced by the content of drafts of *Pandas*.

The weight of the evidence clearly demonstrates, as noted, that the systemic change from "creation" to "intelligent design" occurred sometime in 1987, after the Supreme Court's important Edwards decision. This compelling evidence strongly supports Plaintiffs' assertion that ID is creationism re-labeled. Importantly, the objective observer, whether adult or child, would conclude from the fact that *Pandas* posits a master intellect that the intelligent designer is God.

Further evidence in support of the conclusion that a reasonable observer, adult or child, who is "aware of the history and context of the community and forum" is presumed to know that ID is a form of creationism concerns the fact that ID uses the same, or exceedingly similar arguments as were posited in support of creationism. One significant difference is that the words "God," "creationism," and "Genesis" have been systematically purged from ID explanations, and replaced by an unnamed "designer." Dr. Forrest testified and sponsored exhibits showing six arguments common to creationists. (10:140–48 (Forrest); P–856.5–856.10). Demonstrative charts introduced through Dr. Forrest show parallel arguments relating to the rejection of naturalism, evolution's threat to culture and society, "abrupt appearance" implying divine creation, the exploitation of the same alleged gaps in the fossil record, the alleged inability of science to explain complex biological information like DNA, as well as the theme that proponents of each version of creationism merely aim to teach a scientific alternative to evolution to show its "strengths and weaknesses," and to alert students to a supposed "controversy" in the scientific community. (10:140–48 (Forrest)). In addition, creationists made the same argument that the complexity of the bacterial flagellum supported creationism as Professors Behe and Minnich now make for ID. (P–853; P–845; 37:155–56 (Minnich)). The IDM openly welcomes adherents to creationism into its "Big Tent," urging them to postpone biblical disputes like the age of the earth. (11:3–15 (Forrest); P–429). Moreover and as previously stated, there is hardly better evidence of ID's relationship with creationism than an explicit statement by defense expert Fuller that ID is a form of creationism. (Fuller Dep. at 67, June 21, 2005) (indicated that ID is a modern view of creationism).

Although contrary to Fuller, defense experts Professors Behe and Minnich testified that ID is not creationism, their testimony was primarily by way of bare assertion and it failed to directly rebut the creationist history of *Pandas* or other evidence presented by Plaintiffs showing the commonality between creationism and ID. The sole argument Defendants made to distinguish creationism from ID was their assertion that the term "creationism" applies only to arguments based on the Book of Genesis, a young earth, and a catastrophic Noaich flood; however, substantial evidence established that this is only one form of creationism, including the chart that was distributed to the Board Curriculum Committee, as will be described below. (P–149 at 2; 10:129–32 (Forrest); P–555 at 22–24).

Having thus provided the social and historical context in which the ID Policy arose of which a reasonable observer, either adult or child would be aware, we will now focus on what the objective student alone would know. We will accordingly determine whether an objective student would view the disclaimer read to the ninth grade biology class as an official endorsement of religion.

2. An Objective Student

... After a careful review of the record and for the reasons that follow, we find that an objective student would view the disclaimer as a strong official endorsement of religion. Application of the objective student standard pursuant to the endorsement test reveals that an objective Dover High School ninth grade student will unquestionably perceive the text of the disclaimer, "enlightened by its context and contemporary legislative history," as conferring a religious concept on "her school's seal of approval." Selman, 390 F.Supp.2d at 1300; Santa Fe, 530 U.S. at 308; Edwards, 482 U.S. at 594 (in addition to "[t]he plain meaning of the [enactment's] words, enlightened by their context and the contemporaneous legislative history," the Supreme Court also looks for legislative purpose in "the historical context of the [enactment], and the specific sequence of events leading to [its] passage") (internal citations omitted); see also Santa Fe, 530 U.S. at 308 ("Regardless of the listener's support for, or objection to, the message, an objective Santa Fe High School student will unquestionably perceive the inevitable pregame prayer as stamped with her school's seal of approval.").

We arrive at this conclusion by initially considering the plain language of the disclaimer, paragraph by paragraph. The first paragraph reads as follows:

> The Pennsylvania Academic Standards require students to learn about Darwin's Theory of Evolution and eventually to take a standardized test of which evolution is a part.

P–124. The evidence in this case reveals that Defendants do not mandate a similar pronouncement about any other aspect of the biology curriculum or the curriculum for any other course, despite the fact that state standards directly address numerous other topics covered in the biology curriculum and the students' other classes, and despite the fact that standardized tests cover such other topics as well. Notably, the unrefuted testimony of Plaintiffs' science education expert Dr. Alters, the only such expert to testify in the case sub judice explains, and the testimony of Drs. Miller and Padian confirms, the message this paragraph communicates to ninth grade biology students is that:

> [W]e have to teach this stuff[.] The other stuff we're just going to teach you, but now this one we have to say the Pennsylvania academic standards require[ ] students to ... eventually take a test. We'd rather not do it, but Pennsylvania academic standards ... require students to do this.

Trial Tr. vol. 14, Alters Test., 110–11, Oct. 12, 2005.

Stated another way, the first paragraph of the disclaimer directly addresses and disavows evolutionary theory by telling students that they have to learn about evolutionary theory because it is required by "Pennsylvania Academic Standards" and it will be tested; however, no similar disclaimer prefacing instruction is conducted regarding any other portion of the biology curriculum nor any other course's curriculum.

The second paragraph of the disclaimer reads as follows:

> Because Darwin's Theory is a theory, it continues to be tested as new evidence is discovered. The Theory is not a fact. Gaps in the Theory exist for which there is no evidence. A theory is defined as a well-tested explanation that unifies a broad range of observations.

P–124. This paragraph singles out evolution from the rest of the science curriculum and informs students that evolution, unlike anything else that they are learning, is "just a theory," which plays on the "colloquial or popular understanding of the term ['theory'] and suggest[ing] to the informed, reasonable observer that evolution is only a highly questionable 'opinion' or a 'hunch.'" Selman, 390 F.Supp.2d at 1310; 14:110–12 (Alters); 1:92 (Miller). Immediately after students are told that "Darwin's Theory" is a theory and that it continues to be tested, they are told that "gaps" exist within evolutionary theory without any indication that other scientific theories might suffer the same supposed weakness. As Dr. Alters explained this paragraph is both misleading and creates misconceptions in students about evolutionary theory by misrepresenting the scientific status of evolution and by telling students that they should regard it as singularly unreliable, or on shaky ground. (14:117 (Alters)). Additionally and as pointed out by Plaintiffs, it is indeed telling that even defense expert Professor Fuller agreed with this conclusion by stating that in his own expert opinion the disclaimer is misleading. (Fuller Dep. 110–11, June 21, 2005). Dr. Padian bluntly and effectively stated that in confusing students about science generally and evolution in particular, the disclaimer makes students "stupid." (Trial Tr. vol. 17, Padian Test., 48–52, Oct. 14, 2005).

In summary, the second paragraph of the disclaimer undermines students' education in evolutionary theory and sets the groundwork for presenting students with the District's favored religious alternative.

Paragraph three of the disclaimer proceeds to present this alternative and reads as follows:

> Intelligent Design is an explanation of the origin of life that differs from Darwin's view. The reference book, *Of Pandas and People*, is available for students who might be interested in gaining an understanding of what Intelligent Design actually involves.

P–124. Students are therefore provided information that contrasts ID with "Darwin's view" and are directed to consult *Pandas* as though it were a scientific text that provided a scientific account of, and empirical scientific evidence for, ID. The theory or "view" of evolution, which has been discredited by the District in the student's eyes, is contrasted with an alternative "explanation," as opposed to a "theory," that can be offered without qualification or cautionary note. The alternative "explanation" thus receives markedly different treatment from evolutionary "theory." In other words, the disclaimer relies upon the very same "contrived dualism" that the court in McLean recognized to be a creationist tactic that has "no scientific factual basis or legitimate educational purpose." McLean, 529 F.Supp. at 1266.[120]

> The two model approach of creationists is simply a contrived dualism which has no scientific factual basis or legitimate educational purpose.

---

120. The McLean court explained that: The approach to teaching "creation science" and "evolution science" ... is identical to the two-model approach espoused by the Institute for Creation Research and is taken almost verbatim from ICR writings. It is an extension of Fundamentalists' view that one must either accept the literal interpretation of Genesis or else believe in the godless system of evolution.

It assumes only two explanations for the origins of life and existence of man, plants and animals: it was either the work of a creator or it was not. Application of these two models, according to creationists, and the defendants, dictates that all scientific evidence which fails to support the theory of evolution is necessarily scientific evidence in support of creationism and is, therefore, creation science "evidence[.]"

529 F.Supp. at 1266.

The overwhelming evidence at trial established that ID is a religious view, a mere re-labeling of creationism, and not a scientific theory. As the Fifth Circuit Court of Appeals held in Freiler, an educator's "reading of a disclaimer that not only disavows endorsement of educational materials but also juxtaposes that disavowal with an urging to contemplate alternative religious concepts implies School Board approval of religious principles." Freiler, 185 F.3d at 348.

In the fourth and final paragraph of the disclaimer, students are informed of the following:

With respect to any theory, students are encouraged to keep an open mind. The school leaves the discussion of the Origins of Life to individual students and their families. As a Standards-driven district, class instruction focuses upon preparing students to achieve proficiency on Standards-based assessments.

P–124....

In summary, the disclaimer singles out the theory of evolution for special treatment, misrepresents its status in the scientific community, causes students to doubt its validity without scientific justification, presents students with a religious alternative masquerading as a scientific theory, directs them to consult a creationist text as though it were a science resource, and instructs students to forego scientific inquiry in the public school classroom and instead to seek out religious instruction elsewhere. Furthermore, as Drs. Alters and Miller testified, introducing ID necessarily invites religion into the science classroom as it sets up what will be perceived by students as a "God-friendly" science, the one that explicitly mentions an intelligent designer, and that the "other science," evolution, takes no position on religion. (14:144–45 (Alters)). Dr. Miller testified that a false duality is produced: It "tells students ... quite explicitly, choose God on the side of intelligent design or choose atheism on the side of science." (2:54–55 (Miller)). Introducing such a religious conflict into the classroom is "very dangerous" because it forces students to "choose between God and science," not a choice that schools should be forcing on them. Id. at 55.

Our detailed chronology of what a reasonable, objective student is presumed to know has made abundantly clear to the Court that an objective student would view the disclaimer as a strong official endorsement of religion or a religious viewpoint. We now turn to whether an objective adult observer in the Dover community would perceive Defendants' conduct similarly.

3.   An Objective Dover Citizen

The Court must consider whether an objective adult observer in the Dover community would perceive the challenged ID Policy as an endorsement of religion because the unrefuted evidence offered at trial establishes that although the disclaimer is read to students in their ninth grade biology classes, the Board made and subsequently defended its decision to implement the curriculum change publicly, thus casting the entire community as the "listening audience" for its religious message. Santa Fe, 530 U.S. at 308. We are in agreement with Plaintiffs that when a governmental practice bearing on religion occurs within view of the entire community, the reasonable observer is an objective, informed adult within the community at large, even if the specific practice is directed at only a subset of that community, as courts routinely look beyond the government's intended audience to the broader listening audience. Otherwise, government would be free and able to sponsor religious messages simply by declaring that those who share in the beliefs that it is espousing are the message's only intended recipients. See Allegheny, 492 U.S. at 597 ("when evaluating the effect of government conduct under the Establishment Clause, we must ascertain whether 'the challenged governmental action is sufficiently likely to be perceived by adherents of the controlling denominations as an endorsement, and by the nonadherents as a disapproval, of their individual religious choice' ") (quoting Grand Rapids Sch. Dist. v. Ball, 473 U.S. at 373 (1985)). Accordingly, not only are parents and other Dover citizens part of the listening audience for the Board's curriculum change, but they are part of its "intended audience" as well.

First, the Board brought the public into the debate over whether to include ID in the curriculum as it proposed, advocated, and ultimately approved the ID Policy in public school board meetings. These meetings were such that members of the public not only attended them, but also had the opportunity to offer public comment on the proposal. In those Board meetings, open to the public at large, several Dover School Board members advocated for the ID Policy in expressly religious terms, with their comments reported extensively in the local newspapers, as will be discussed in detail below. Second, at least two Board members, William Buckingham and Heather Geesey, defended the proposed curriculum change in the media in expressly religious terms.

Moreover, it is notable that the Board sent a newsletter to every household in Dover in February 2005 "produced to help explain the changes in the biology curriculum" and prepared in conjunction with defense counsel, the Thomas More Law Center. (P–127). Typically, the Board sent out a newsletter in the Dover area approximately four times a year and in February 2005, the Board unanimously voted to mail a specialized newsletter to the community. (Trial Tr. vol. 15, C. Sneath Test., 98–99, 136, Oct. 12, 2005; P–82). Although formatted like a typical district newsletter, an objective adult member of the Dover community is presumed to understand this mailing as an aggressive advocacy piece denigrating the scientific theory of evolution while advocating ID. Within this newsletter, the initial entry under the heading "Frequently Asked Questions" demeans Plaintiffs for protecting their Constitutional rights as it states, "A small minority of parents have objected to the recent curriculum change by arguing that the Board has acted to impose its own religious beliefs on students." (P–127 at 1). Religion is again mentioned in the second "Frequently Asked Question" as it poses the question "Isn't ID simply religion in disguise?" Id. The newsletter suggests that scientists engage in trickery and doublespeak about the theory of evolution by stating, "The word evolution has several meanings, and those supporting Darwin's theory of evolution use that confusion in definition to their advantage." Id. The newsletter additionally makes the claim that ID is a scientific theory on par with evolution and other scientific theories by explaining, "The theory of intelligent design (ID) is a scientific theory that differs from Darwin's view, and is endorsed by a growing number of credible scientists." Id. at 2. Evolution is subsequently denigrated and claims that have not been advanced, must less proven in the scientific community, are elaborated upon in the newsletter. "In simple terms, on a molecular level, scientists have discovered a purposeful arrangement of parts, which cannot be explained by Darwin's theory. In fact, since the 1950s, advances in molecular biology and chemistry have shown us that living cells, the fundamental units of life processes, cannot be explained by chance." Id. The newsletter suggests that evolution has atheistic implications by indicating that "Some have said that before Darwin, 'we thought a benevolent God had created us. Biology took away our status as made in the image of God' . . . or 'Darwinism made it possible to be an intellectually fulfilled atheist.' " Id. Finally and notably, the newsletter all but admits that ID is religious by quoting Anthony Flew, described as a "world famous atheist who now believes in intelligent design," as follows: "My whole life has been guided by the principle of Plato's Socrates: Follow the evidence where it leads." Id.

The February 2005 newsletter was mailed to every household in Dover. Even those individuals who had no children, never attended a Dover Board meeting, and never concerned themselves with learning about school policies, were directly confronted and made the "listening audience" for the District's announcement of its sponsorship of a religious viewpoint. Thus, the February 2005 newsletter was an astonishing propaganda discourse which succeeded in advising the few individuals who were by that time not aware that a firestorm had erupted over ID in Dover. . . .

Third, it is readily apparent to the Court that the entire community became intertwined in the controversy over the ID Policy. The Board's actions from June 2004 through October 18, 2004, the date the Board approved the curriculum change, were consistently reported in news articles in the two local newspapers, the *York Daily Record* and the *York Dispatch*. . . . The news reports in the York newspapers were followed by numerous letters to the editor and editorials published in the same papers. . . .

The 225 letters to the editor and sixty-two editorials from the *York Daily Record* and *York Dispatch* that Plaintiffs offered at trial and which we have admitted for consideration in our analysis of the endorsement test and Lemon's effect prong, show that hundreds of individuals in this small community felt it necessary to publish their views on the issues presented in this case for the community to see. Moreover, a review of the letters and editorials at issue reveals that in letter after letter and editorial after editorial, community members postulated that ID is an inherently religious concept, that the writers viewed the decision of whether to incorporate it into the high school biology curriculum as one which implicated a religious concept, and therefore that the curriculum change has the effect of placing the government's imprimatur on the Board's preferred religious viewpoint. (P–671–72, 674–75). These exhibits are thus probative of the fact that members of the Dover community perceived the Board as having acted to promote religion, with many citizens lined up as either for the curriculum change, on religious grounds, or against the curriculum change, on the ground that religion should not play a role in public school science class. Accordingly, the letters and editorials are relevant to, and provide evidence of, the Dover community's collective social judgment about the curriculum change because they demonstrate that "[r]egardless of the listener's support for, or objection to," the curriculum change, the community and hence the objective observer who personifies it, cannot help but see that the ID Policy implicates and thus endorses religion. . . .

Accordingly, taken in the aggregate, the plethora of letters to the editor and editorials from the local York newspapers constitute substantial additional evidence that the entire community became intertwined in the controversy of the ID Policy at issue and that the community collectively perceives the ID Policy as favoring a particular religious view. As a result of the foregoing analysis, we conclude that an informed, objective adult member of the Dover community aware of the social context in which the ID Policy arose would view Defendants' conduct and the challenged Policy to be a strong endorsement of a religious view.

We have now found that both an objective student and an objective adult member of the Dover community would perceive Defendants' conduct to be a strong endorsement of religion pursuant to the endorsement test. Having so concluded, we find it incumbent upon the Court to further address an additional issue raised by Plaintiffs, which is whether ID is science.To be sure, our answer to this question can likely be predicted based upon the foregoing analysis. While answering this question compels us to revisit evidence that is entirely complex, if not obtuse, after a six week trial that spanned twenty-one days and included countless hours of detailed expert witness presentations, the Court is confident that no other tribunal in the United States is in a better position than are we to traipse into this controversial area. Finally, we will offer our conclusion on whether ID is science not just because it is essential to our holding that an Establishment Clause violation has occurred in this case, but also in the hope that it may prevent the obvious waste of judicial and other resources which would be occasioned by a subsequent trial involving the precise question which is before us.

4.   Whether ID is Science

After a searching review of the record and applicable caselaw, we find that while ID arguments may be true, a proposition on which the Court takes no position, ID is not science. We find that ID fails on three different levels, any one of which is sufficient to preclude a determination that ID is science. They are: (1) ID violates the centuries-old ground rules of science by invoking and permitting supernatural causation; (2) the argument of irreducible complexity, central to ID, employs the same flawed and illogical contrived dualism that doomed creation science in the 1980's; and (3) ID's negative attacks on evolution have been refuted by the scientific community. As we will discuss in more detail below, it is additionally important to note that ID has failed to gain acceptance in the scientific community, it has not generated peer-reviewed publications, nor has it been the subject of testing and research.

Expert testimony reveals that since the scientific revolution of the 16th and 17th centuries, science has been limited to the search for natural causes to explain natural phenomena. (9:19–22 (Haught); 5:25–29 (Pennock); 1:62 (Miller)). This revolution entailed the rejection of the appeal to authority, and by extension, revelation, in favor of empirical evidence. (5:28 (Pennock)). Since that time period, science has been a discipline in which testability, rather than any ecclesiastical authority or philosophical coherence, has been the measure of a scientific idea's worth. (9:21–22 (Haught); 1:63 (Miller)). In deliberately omitting theological or "ultimate" explanations for the existence or characteristics of the natural world, science does not consider issues of "meaning" and "purpose" in the world. (9:21 (Haught); 1:64, 87 (Miller)). While supernatural explanations may be important and have merit, they are not part of science. (3:103 (Miller); 9:19–20 (Haught)). This self-imposed convention of science, which limits inquiry to testable, natural explanations about the natural world, is referred to by philosophers as "methodological naturalism" and is sometimes known as the scientific method. (5:23, 29–30 (Pennock)). Methodological naturalism is a "ground rule" of science today which requires scientists to seek explanations in the world around us based upon what we can observe, test, replicate, and verify. (1:59–64, 2:41–43 (Miller); 5:8, 23–30 (Pennock)).

As the National Academy of Sciences (hereinafter "NAS") was recognized by experts for both parties as the "most prestigious" scientific association in this country, we will accordingly cite to its opinion where appropriate. (1:94, 160–61 (Miller); 14:72 (Alters); 37:31 (Minnich)). NAS is in agreement that science is limited to empirical, observable and ultimately testable data: "Science is a particular way of knowing about the world. In science, explanations are restricted to those that can be inferred from the confirmable data—the results obtained through observations and experiments that can be substantiated by other scientists. Anything that can be observed or measured is amenable to scientific investigation. Explanations that cannot be based upon empirical evidence are not part of science." (P–649 at 27).

This rigorous attachment to "natural" explanations is an essential attribute to science by definition and by convention. (1:63 (Miller); 5:29–31 (Pennock)). We are in agreement with Plaintiffs' lead expert Dr. Miller, that from a practical perspective, attributing unsolved problems about nature to causes and forces that lie outside the natural world is a "science stopper." (3:14–15 (Miller)). As Dr. Miller explained, once you attribute a cause to an untestable supernatural force, a proposition that cannot be disproven, there is no reason to continue seeking natural explanations as we have our answer. Id.

ID is predicated on supernatural causation, as we previously explained and as various expert testimony revealed. (17:96 (Padian); 2:35–36 (Miller); 14:62 (Alters)). ID takes a natural phenomenon and, instead of accepting or seeking a natural explanation, argues that the explanation is supernatural. (5:107 (Pennock)). Further support for the conclusion that ID is predicated on supernatural causation is found in the ID reference book to which ninth grade biology students are directed, Pandas. Pandas states, in pertinent part, as follows:

> Darwinists object to the view of intelligent design because it does not give a natural cause explanation of how the various forms of life started in the first place. Intelligent design means that various forms of life began abruptly, through an intelligent agency, with their distinctive features already intact-fish with fins and scales, birds with feathers, beaks, and wings, etc.

P–11 at 99–100. Stated another way, ID posits that animals did not evolve naturally through evolutionary means but were created abruptly by a non-natural, or supernatural, designer. Defendants' own expert witnesses acknowledged this point. (21:96–100 (Behe); P–718 at 696, 700) ("implausible that the designer is a natural entity"); 28:21–22 (Fuller) (". . . ID's rejection of naturalism and commitment to supernaturalism . . ."); 38:95–96 (Minnich) (ID does not exclude the possibility of a supernatural designer, including deities).

It is notable that defense experts' own mission, which mirrors that of the IDM itself, is to change the ground rules of science to allow supernatural causation of the natural world, which the Supreme Court in Edwards and the court in McLean correctly recognized as an inherently religious concept. Edwards, 482 U.S. at 591–92; McLean, 529 F.Supp. at 1267. First, defense expert Professor Fuller agreed that ID aspires to "change the ground rules" of science and lead defense expert Professor Behe admitted that his broadened definition of science, which encompasses ID, would also embrace astrology. (28:26 (Fuller); 21:37–42 (Behe)). Moreover, defense expert Professor Minnich acknowledged that for ID to be considered science, the ground rules of science have to be broadened to allow consideration of supernatural forces. (38:97 (Minnich)).

Prominent IDM leaders are in agreement with the opinions expressed by defense expert witnesses that the ground rules of science must be changed for ID to take hold and prosper. William Dembski, for instance, an IDM leader, proclaims that science is ruled by methodological naturalism and argues that this rule must be overturned if ID is to prosper. (5:32–37 (Pennock)); P–341 at 224 ("Indeed, entire fields of inquiry, including especially in the human sciences, will need to be rethought from the ground up in terms of intelligent design.").

The Discovery Institute, the think tank promoting ID whose CRSC developed the Wedge Document, acknowledges as "Governing Goals" to "defeat scientific materialism and its destructive moral, cultural and political legacies" and "replace materialistic explanations with the theistic understanding that nature and human beings are created by God." (P–140 at 4). In addition, and as previously noted, the Wedge Document states in its "Five Year Strategic Plan Summary" that the IDM's goal is to replace science as currently practiced with "theistic and Christian science." Id. at 6. The IDM accordingly seeks nothing less than a complete scientific revolution in which ID will supplant evolutionary theory.[121]

Notably, every major scientific association that has taken a position on the issue of whether ID is science has concluded that ID is not, and cannot be considered as such. (1:98–99 (Miller); 14:75–78 (Alters); 37:25 (Minnich)). Initially, we note that NAS, the "most prestigious" scientific association in this country, views ID as follows:

> Creationism, intelligent design, and other claims of supernatural intervention in the origin of life or of species are not science because they are not testable by the methods of science. These claims subordinate observed data to statements based on authority, revelation, or religious belief. Documentation offered in support of these claims is typically limited to the special publications of their advocates. These publications do not offer hypotheses subject to change in light of new data, new interpretations, or demonstration of error. This contrasts

---

121. Further support for this proposition is found in the Wedge Strategy, which is composed of three phases: Phase I is scientific research, writing and publicity; Phase II is publicity and opinion-making; and Phase III is cultural confrontation and renewal. (P–140 at 3). In the "Five Year Strategic Plan Summary," the Wedge Document explains that the social consequences of materialism have been "devastating" and that it is necessary to broaden the wedge with a positive scientific alternative to materialistic scientific theories, which has come to be called the theory of ID. "Design theory promises to reverse the stifling dominance of the materialist worldview, and to replace it with a science consonant with Christian and theistic convictions." Id. at 6. Phase I of the Wedge Strategy is an essential component and directly references "scientific revolutions." Phase II explains that alongside a focus on influential opinion-makers, "we also seek to build up a popular base of support among our natural constituency, namely, Christians. We will do this primarily through apologetics seminars. We intend these to encourage and equip believers with new scientific evidence that support the faith, as well as to 'popularize' our ideas in the broader culture." Id. Finally, Phase III includes pursuing possible legal assistance "in response to resistance to the integration of design theory into public school science curricula." Id. at 7.

with science, where any hypothesis or theory always remains subject to the possibility of rejection or modification in the light of new knowledge.

P–192 at 25. Additionally, the American Association for the Advancement of Science (hereinafter "AAAS"), the largest organization of scientists in this country, has taken a similar position on ID, namely, that it "has not proposed a scientific means of testing its claims" and that "the lack of scientific warrant for so-called 'intelligent design theory' makes it improper to include as part of science education . . ." (P–198). Not a single expert witness over the course of the six week trial identified one major scientific association, society or organization that endorsed ID as science. What is more, defense experts concede that ID is not a theory as that term is defined by the NAS and admit that ID is at best "fringe science" which has achieved no acceptance in the scientific community. (21:37–38 (Behe); Fuller Dep. at 98–101, June 21, 2005; 28:47 (Fuller); Minnich Dep. at 89, May 26, 2005).

It is therefore readily apparent to the Court that ID fails to meet the essential ground rules that limit science to testable, natural explanations. (3:101–03 (Miller); 14:62 (Alters)). Science cannot be defined differently for Dover students than it is defined in the scientific community as an affirmative action program, as advocated by Professor Fuller, for a view that has been unable to gain a foothold within the scientific establishment. Although ID's failure to meet the ground rules of science is sufficient for the Court to conclude that it is not science, out of an abundance of caution and in the exercise of completeness, we will analyze additional arguments advanced regarding the concepts of ID and science.

ID is at bottom premised upon a false dichotomy, namely, that to the extent evolutionary theory is discredited, ID is confirmed. (5:41 (Pennock)). This argument is not brought to this Court anew, and in fact, the same argument, termed "contrived dualism" in McLean, was employed by creationists in the 1980's to support "creation science." The court in McLean noted the "fallacious pedagogy of the two model approach" and that "[i]n efforts to establish 'evidence' in support of creation science, the defendants relied upon the same false premise as the two model approach . . . all evidence which criticized evolutionary theory was proof in support of creation science." McLean, 529 F.Supp. at 1267, 1269. We do not find this false dichotomy any more availing to justify ID today than it was to justify creation science two decades ago.

ID proponents primarily argue for design through negative arguments against evolution, as illustrated by Professor Behe's argument that "irreducibly complex" systems cannot be produced through Darwinian, or any natural, mechanisms. (5:38–41 (Pennock); 1:39, 2:15, 2:35–37, 3:96 (Miller); 16:72–73 (Padian); 10:148 (Forrest)). However, we believe that arguments against evolution are not arguments for design. Expert testimony revealed that just because scientists cannot explain today how biological systems evolved does not mean that they cannot, and will not, be able to explain them tomorrow. (2:36–37 (Miller)). As Dr. Padian aptly noted, "absence of evidence is not evidence of absence." (17:45 (Padian)). To that end, expert testimony from Drs. Miller and Padian provided multiple examples where Pandas asserted that no natural explanations exist, and in some cases that none could exist, and yet natural explanations have been identified in the intervening years. It also bears mentioning that as Dr. Miller stated, just because scientists cannot explain every evolutionary detail does not undermine its validity as a scientific theory as no theory in science is fully understood. (3:102 (Miller)).

As referenced, the concept of irreducible complexity is ID's alleged scientific centerpiece. Irreducible complexity is a negative argument against evolution, not proof of design, a point conceded by defense expert Professor Minnich. (2:15 (Miller); 38:82 (Minnich)) (irreducible complexity "is not a test of intelligent design; it's a test of evolution"). Irreducible complexity additionally fails to make a positive scientific case for ID, as will be elaborated upon below.

We initially note that irreducible complexity as defined by Professor Behe in his book *Darwin's Black Box* and subsequently modified in his 2001 article entitled "Reply to My Critics," appears as follows:

> By irreducibly complex I mean a single system which is composed of several well-matched, interacting parts that contribute to the basic function, wherein the removal of any one of the parts causes the system to effectively cease functioning. An irreducibly complex system cannot be produced directly by slight, successive modifications of a precursor system, because any precursor to an irreducibly complex system that is missing a part is by definition nonfunctional ... Since natural selection can only choose systems that are already working, then if a biological system cannot be produced gradually it would have to arise as an integrated unit, in one fell swoop, for natural selection to have anything to act on.

P–647 at 39; P–718 at 694. Professor Behe admitted in "Reply to My Critics" that there was a defect in his view of irreducible complexity because, while it purports to be a challenge to natural selection, it does not actually address "the task facing natural selection." (P–718 at 695). Professor Behe specifically explained that "[t]he current definition puts the focus on removing a part from an already-functioning system," but "[t]he difficult task facing Darwinian evolution, however, would not be to remove parts from sophisticated pre-existing systems; it would be to bring together components to make a new system in the first place." Id. In that article, Professor Behe wrote that he hoped to "repair this defect in future work;" however, he has failed to do so even four years after elucidating his defect. Id.; 22:61–65 (Behe).

In addition to Professor Behe's admitted failure to properly address the very phenomenon that irreducible complexity purports to place at issue, natural selection, Drs. Miller and Padian testified that Professor Behe's concept of irreducible complexity depends on ignoring ways in which evolution is known to occur. Although Professor Behe is adamant in his definition of irreducible complexity when he says a precursor "missing a part is by definition nonfunctional," what he obviously means is that it will not function in the same way the system functions when all the parts are present. For example in the case of the bacterial flagellum, removal of a part may prevent it from acting as a rotary motor. However, Professor Behe excludes, by definition, the possibility that a precursor to the bacterial flagellum functioned not as a rotary motor, but in some other way, for example as a secretory system. (19:88–95 (Behe)).

As expert testimony revealed, the qualification on what is meant by "irreducible complexity" renders it meaningless as a criticism of evolution. (3:40 (Miller)). In fact, the theory of evolution proffers exaptation as a well-recognized, well-documented explanation for how systems with multiple parts could have evolved through natural means. Exaptation means that some precursor of the subject system had a different, selectable function before experiencing the change or addition that resulted in the subject system with its present function (16:146–48 (Padian)). For instance, Dr. Padian identified the evolution of the mammalian middle ear bones from what had been jawbones as an example of this process. (17:6–17 (Padian)). By defining irreducible complexity in the way that he has, Professor Behe attempts to exclude the phenomenon of exaptation by definitional fiat, ignoring as he does so abundant evidence which refutes his argument.

Notably, the NAS has rejected Professor Behe's claim for irreducible complexity by using the following cogent reasoning:

> [S]tructures and processes that are claimed to be "irreducibly" complex typically are not on closer inspection. For example, it is incorrect to assume that a complex structure or biochemical process can function only if all its components are present and functioning as we see them today. Complex biochemical systems can be built up from simpler systems through natural selection. Thus, the "history" of a protein can be traced through simpler organisms ... The evolution of complex molecular systems can occur in several ways. Natural selection can bring together parts of a system for one function at one time and then, at a later time, recombine those parts with other systems of components to produce a system that has a different function. Genes can be duplicated, altered, and then amplified through natural selection. The complex biochemical cascade resulting in blood clotting has been explained in this fashion.

P–192 at 22.

As irreducible complexity is only a negative argument against evolution, it is refutable and accordingly testable, unlike ID, by showing that there are intermediate structures with selectable functions that could have evolved into the allegedly irreducibly complex systems. (2:15–16 (Miller)). Importantly, however, the fact that the negative argument of irreducible complexity is testable does not make testable the argument for

ID. (2:15 (Miller); 5:39 (Pennock)). Professor Behe has applied the concept of irreducible complexity to only a few select systems: (1) the bacterial flagellum; (2) the blood-clotting cascade; and (3) the immune system. Contrary to Professor Behe's assertions with respect to these few bio-chemical systems among the myriad existing in nature, however, Dr. Miller presented evidence, based upon peer-reviewed studies, that they are not in fact irreducibly complex.

First, with regard to the bacterial flagellum, Dr. Miller pointed to peer-reviewed studies that identified a possible precursor to the bacterial flagellum, a subsystem that was fully functional, namely the Type–III Secretory System. (2:8–20 (Miller); P–854.23–854.32). Moreover, defense expert Professor Minnich admitted that there is serious scientific research on the question of whether the bacterial flagellum evolved into the Type–III Secretory System, the Type–III Secretory System into the bacterial flagellum, or whether they both evolved from a common ancestor. (38:12–16 (Minnich)). None of this research or thinking involves ID. (38:12–16 (Minnich)). In fact, Professor Minnich testified about his research as follows: "we're looking at the function of these systems and how they could have been derived one from the other. And it's a legitimate scientific inquiry." (38:16 (Minnich)).

Second, with regard to the blood-clotting cascade, Dr. Miller demon-strated that the alleged irreducible complexity of the blood-clotting cas-cade has been disproven by peer-reviewed studies dating back to 1969, which show that dolphins' and whales' blood clots despite missing a part of the cascade, a study that was confirmed by molecular testing in 1998. (1:122–29 (Miller); P–854.17–854.22). Additionally and more recently, sci-entists published studies showing that in puffer fish, blood clots despite the cascade missing not only one, but three parts. (1:128–29 (Miller)). Accordingly, scientists in peer-reviewed publications have refuted Profes-sor Behe's predication about the alleged irreducible complexity of the blood-clotting cascade. Moreover, cross-examination revealed that Profes-sor Behe's redefinition of the blood-clotting system was likely designed to avoid peer-reviewed scientific evidence that falsifies his argument, as it was not a scientifically warranted redefinition. (20:26–28, 22:112–25 (Behe)).

The immune system is the third system to which Professor Behe has applied the definition of irreducible complexity. Although in *Darwin's Black Box*, Professor Behe wrote that not only were there no natural explanations for the immune system at the time, but that natural expla-nations were impossible regarding its origin. (P–647 at 139; 2:26–27 (Miller)). However, Dr. Miller presented peer-reviewed studies refuting Professor Behe's claim that the immune system was irreducibly complex. Between 1996 and 2002, various studies confirmed each element of the evolutionary hypothesis explaining the origin of the immune system. (2:31 (Miller)). In fact, on cross-examination, Professor Behe was ques-tioned concerning his 1996 claim that science would never find an evolu-tionary explanation for the immune system. He was presented with fifty-eight peer-reviewed publications, nine books, and several immunology textbook chapters about the evolution of the immune system; however, he simply insisted that this was still not sufficient evidence of evolution, and that it was not "good enough." (23:19 (Behe)).

We find that such evidence demonstrates that the ID argument is dependent upon setting a scientifically unreasonable burden of proof for the theory of evolution. As a further example, the test for ID proposed by both Professors Behe and Minnich is to grow the bacterial flagellum in the laboratory; however, no-one inside or outside of the IDM, including those who propose the test, has conducted it. (P–718; 18:125–27 (Behe); 22:102–06 (Behe)). Professor Behe conceded that the proposed test could not approximate real world conditions and even if it could, Professor Minnich admitted that it would merely be a test of evolution, not design. (22:107–10 (Behe); 2:15 (Miller); 38:82 (Minnich)).

We therefore find that Professor Behe's claim for irreducible complexity has been refuted in peer-reviewed research papers and has been rejected by the scientific community at large. (17:45–46 (Padian); 3:99 (Miller)). Additionally, even if irreducible complexity had not been rejected, it still does not support ID as it is merely a test for evolution, not design. (2:15, 2:35–40 (Miller); 28:63–66 (Fuller)).

We will now consider the purportedly "positive argument" for design encompassed in the phrase used numerous times by Professors Behe and Minnich throughout their expert testimony, which is the "purposeful arrangement of parts." Professor Behe summarized the argument as follows: We infer design when we see parts that appear to be arranged for a purpose. The strength of the inference is quantitative; the more parts that are arranged, the more intricately they interact, the stronger is our confidence in design. The appearance of design in aspects of biology is overwhelming. Since nothing other than an intelligent cause has been demonstrated to be able to yield such a strong appearance of design, Darwinian claims notwithstanding, the conclusion that the design seen in life is real design is rationally justified. (18:90–91, 18:109–10 (Behe); 37:50 (Minnich)). As previously indicated, this argument is merely a restatement of the Reverend William Paley's argument applied at the cell level. Minnich, Behe, and Paley reach the same conclusion, that complex organisms must have been designed using the same reasoning, except that Professors Behe and Minnich refuse to identify the designer, whereas Paley inferred from the presence of design that it was God. (1:6–7 (Miller); 38:44, 57 (Minnich)). Expert testimony revealed that this inductive argument is not scientific and as admitted by Professor Behe, can never be ruled out. (2:40 (Miller); 22:101 (Behe); 3:99 (Miller)).

Indeed, the assertion that design of biological systems can be inferred from the "purposeful arrangement of parts" is based upon an analogy to human design. Because we are able to recognize design of artifacts and objects, according to Professor Behe, that same reasoning can be employed to determine biological design. (18:116–17, 23:50 (Behe)). Professor Behe testified that the strength of the analogy depends upon the degree of similarity entailed in the two propositions; however, if this is the test, ID completely fails.

Unlike biological systems, human artifacts do not live and reproduce over time. They are non-replicable, they do not undergo genetic recombination, and they are not driven by natural selection. (1:131–33 (Miller); 23:57–59 (Behe)). For human artifacts, we know the designer's identity, human, and the mechanism of design, as we have experience based upon empirical evidence that humans can make such things, as well as many other attributes including the designer's abilities, needs, and desires. (D–251 at 176; 1:131–33 (Miller); 23:63 (Behe); 5:55–58 (Pennock)). With ID, proponents assert that they refuse to propose hypotheses on the designer's identity, do not propose a mechanism, and the designer, he/she/it/they, has never been seen. In that vein, defense expert Professor Minnich agreed that in the case of human artifacts and objects, we know the identity and capacities of the human designer, but we do not know any of those attributes for the designer of biological life. (38:44–47 (Minnich)). In addition, Professor Behe agreed that for the design of human artifacts, we know the designer and its attributes and we have a baseline for human design that does not exist for design of biological systems. (23:61–73 (Behe)). Professor Behe's only response to these seemingly insurmountable points of disanalogy was that the inference still works in science fiction movies. (23:73 (Behe)).

It is readily apparent to the Court that the only attribute of design that biological systems appear to share with human artifacts is their complex appearance, i.e. if it looks complex or designed, it must have been designed. (23:73 (Behe)). This inference to design based upon the appearance of a "purposeful arrangement of parts" is a completely subjective proposition, determined in the eye of each beholder and his/her viewpoint concerning the complexity of a system. Although both Professors Behe and Minnich assert that there is a quantitative aspect to the inference, on cross-examination they admitted that there is no quantitative criteria for determining the degree of complexity or number of parts that bespeak design, rather than a natural process. (23:50 (Behe); 38:59 (Minnich)). As Plaintiffs aptly submit to the Court, throughout the entire trial only one piece of evidence generated by Defendants addressed the strength of the ID inference: the argument is less plausible to those for whom God's existence is in question, and is much less plausible for those who deny God's existence. (P–718 at 705).

Accordingly, the purported positive argument for ID does not satisfy the ground rules of science which require testable hypotheses based upon natural explanations. (3:101–03 (Miller)). ID is reliant upon forces acting outside of the natural world, forces that we cannot see, replicate, control or test, which have produced changes in this world. While we take no position on whether such forces exist, they are simply not testable by scientific means and therefore cannot qualify as part of the scientific process or as a scientific theory. (3:101–02 (Miller)).

It is appropriate at this juncture to address ID's claims against evolution. ID proponents support their assertion that evolutionary theory cannot account for life's complexity by pointing to real gaps in scientific knowledge, which indisputably exist in all scientific theories, but also by misrepresenting well-established scientific propositions. (1:112, 1:122, 1:136–37 (Miller); 16:74–79, 17:45–46 (Padian)).

Before discussing Defendants' claims about evolution, we initially note that an overwhelming number of scientists, as reflected by every scientific association that has spoken on the matter, have rejected the ID proponents' challenge to evolution. Moreover, Plaintiffs' expert in biology, Dr. Miller, a widely-recognized biology professor at Brown University who has written university-level and high-school biology textbooks used prominently throughout the nation, provided unrebutted testimony that evolution, including common descent and natural selection, is "overwhelmingly accepted" by the scientific community and that every major scientific association agrees. (1:94–100 (Miller)). As the court in Selman explained, "evolution is more than a theory of origin in the context of science. To the contrary, evolution is the dominant scientific theory of origin accepted by the majority of scientists." Selman, 390 F.Supp.2d at 1309 (emphasis in original). Despite the scientific community's overwhelming support for evolution, Defendants and ID proponents insist that evolution is unsupported by empirical evidence. Plaintiffs' science experts, Drs. Miller and Padian, clearly explained how ID proponents generally and *Pandas* specifically, distort and misrepresent scientific knowledge in making their anti-evolution argument.

In analyzing such distortion, we turn again to *Pandas*, the book to which students are expressly referred in the disclaimer. Defendants hold out *Pandas* as representative of ID and Plaintiffs' experts agree in that regard. (16:83 (Padian); 1:107–08 (Miller)). A series of arguments against evolutionary theory found in *Pandas* involve paleontology, which studies the life of the past and the fossil record. Plaintiffs' expert Professor Padian was the only testifying expert witness with any expertise in paleontology. His testimony therefore remains unrebutted. Dr. Padian's demonstrative slides, prepared on the basis of peer-reviewing scientific literature, illustrate how *Pandas* systematically distorts and misrepresents established, important evolutionary principles.

We will provide several representative examples of this distortion. First, *Pandas* misrepresents the "dominant form of understanding relationships" between organisms, namely, the tree of life, represented by classification determined via the method of cladistics. (16:87–97 (Padian); P–855.6–855.19). Second, *Pandas* misrepresents "homology," the "central concept of comparative biology," that allowed scientists to evaluate comparable parts among organisms for classification purposes for hundreds of years. (17:27–40 (Padian); P–855.83–855.102). Third, *Pandas* fails to address the well-established biological concept of exaptation, which involves a structure changing function, such as fish fins evolving fingers and bones to become legs for weight-bearing land animals. (16:146–48 (Padian)). Dr.

Padian testified that ID proponents fail to address exaptation because they deny that organisms change function, which is a view necessary to support abrupt-appearance. Id. Finally, Dr. Padian's unrebutted testimony demonstrates that *Pandas* distorts and misrepresents evidence in the fossil record about pre-Cambrian-era fossils, the evolution of fish to amphibians, the evolution of small carnivorous dinosaurs into birds, the evolution of the mammalian middle ear, and the evolution of whales from land animals. (16:107–17, 16:117–31, 16:131–45, 17:6–9, 17:17–27 (Padian); P–855.25–855.33, P–855.34–855.45, P–855.46–855.55, P–855.56–866.63, P–855.64–855.82).

In addition to Dr. Padian, Dr. Miller also testified that *Pandas* presents discredited science. Dr. Miller testified that *Pandas'* treatment of biochemical similarities between organisms is "inaccurate and downright false" and explained how *Pandas* misrepresents basic molecular biology concepts to advance design theory through a series of demonstrative slides. (1:112 (Miller)). Consider, for example, that he testified as to how *Pandas* misinforms readers on the standard evolutionary relationships between different types of animals, a distortion which Professor Behe, a "critical reviewer" of *Pandas* who wrote a section within the book, affirmed. (1:113–17 (Miller); P–854.9–854.16; 23:35–36 (Behe)). In addition, Dr. Miller refuted *Pandas'* claim that evolution cannot account for new genetic information and pointed to more than three dozen peer-reviewed scientific publications showing the origin of new genetic information by evolutionary processes. (1:133–36 (Miller); P–245). In summary, Dr. Miller testified that *Pandas* misrepresents molecular biology and genetic principles, as well as the current state of scientific knowledge in those areas in order to teach readers that common descent and natural selection are not scientifically sound. (1:139–42 (Miller)).

Accordingly, the one textbook to which the Dover ID Policy directs students contains outdated concepts and badly flawed science, as recognized by even the defense experts in this case.

A final indicator of how ID has failed to demonstrate scientific warrant is the complete absence of peer-reviewed publications supporting the theory. Expert testimony revealed that the peer review process is "exquisitely important" in the scientific process. It is a way for scientists to write up their empirical research and to share the work with fellow experts in the field, opening up the hypotheses to study, testing, and criticism. (1:66–69 (Miller)). In fact, defense expert Professor Behe recognizes the importance of the peer review process and has written that science must "publish or perish." (22:19–25 (Behe)). Peer review helps to ensure that research papers are scientifically accurately, meet the standards of the scientific method, and are relevant to other scientists in the field. (1:39–40 (Miller)). Moreover, peer review involves scientists submitting a manuscript to a scientific journal in the field, journal editors soliciting critical reviews from other experts in the field and deciding whether the scientist has followed proper research procedures, employed up-to-date methods, considered and cited relevant literature and generally, whether the researcher has employed sound science.

The evidence presented in this case demonstrates that ID is not supported by any peer-reviewed research, data or publications. Both Drs. Padian and Forrest testified that recent literature reviews of scientific and medical-electronic databases disclosed no studies supporting a biological concept of ID. (17:42–43 (Padian); 11:32–33 (Forrest)). On cross-examination, Professor Behe admitted that: "There are no peer reviewed articles by anyone advocating for intelligent design supported by pertinent experiments or calculations which provide detailed rigorous accounts of how intelligent design of any biological system occurred." (22:22–23 (Behe)). Additionally, Professor Behe conceded that there are no peer-reviewed papers supporting his claims that complex molecular systems, like the bacterial flagellum, the blood-clotting cascade, and the immune system, were intelligently designed. (21:61–62 (complex molecular systems), 23:4–5 (immune system), and 22:124–25 (blood-clotting cascade) (Behe)). In that regard, there are no peer-reviewed articles supporting Professor Behe's argument that certain complex molecular structures are "irreducibly complex."[122] (21:62, 22:124–25 (Behe)). In addition to failing to produce papers in peer-reviewed journals, ID also features no scientific research or testing. (28:114–15 (Fuller); 18:22–23, 105–06 (Behe)).

After this searching and careful review of ID as espoused by its proponents, as elaborated upon in submissions to the Court, and as scrutinized over a six week trial, we find that ID is not science and cannot be adjudged a valid, accepted scientific theory as it has failed to publish in peer-reviewed journals, engage in research and testing, and gain acceptance in the scientific community. ID, as noted, is grounded in theology, not science. Accepting for the sake of argument its proponents', as well as Defendants' argument that to introduce ID to students will encourage critical thinking, it still has utterly no place in a science curriculum. Moreover, ID's backers have sought to avoid the scientific scrutiny which we have now determined that it cannot withstand by advocating that the controversy, but not ID itself, should be taught in science class. This tactic is at best disingenuous, and at worst a canard. The goal of the IDM is not to encourage critical thought, but to foment a revolution which would supplant evolutionary theory with ID.

To conclude and reiterate, we express no opinion on the ultimate veracity of ID as a supernatural explanation. However, we commend to the attention of those who are inclined to superficially consider ID to be a true "scientific" alternative to evolution without a true understanding of the concept the foregoing detailed analysis. It is our view that a reason-

---

122. The one article referenced by both Professors Behe and Minnich as supporting ID is an article written by Behe and Snoke entitled "Simulating evolution by gene duplication of protein features that require multiple amino acid residues." (P–721). A review of the article indicates that it does not mention either irreducible complexity or ID. In fact, Professor Behe admitted that the study which forms the basis for the article did not rule out many known evolutionary mechanisms and that the research actually might support evolutionary pathways if a biologically realistic population size were used. (22:41–45 (Behe); P–756).

able, objective observer would, after reviewing both the voluminous record in this case, and our narrative, reach the inescapable conclusion that ID is an interesting theological argument, but that it is not science.

F.   Application of the Lemon Test to the ID Policy

Although we have found that Defendants' conduct conveys a strong message of endorsement of the Board members' particular religious view, pursuant to the endorsement test, the better practice in this Circuit is for this Court to also evaluate the challenged conduct separately under the Lemon test. See Child Evangelism, 386 F.3d at 530–35; Modrovich, 385 F.3d at 406; Freethought, 334 F.3d at 261.

As articulated by the Supreme Court, under the Lemon test, a government-sponsored message violates the Establishment Clause of the First Amendment if: (1) it does not have a secular purpose; (2) its principal or primary effect advances or inhibits religion; or (3) it creates an excessive entanglement of the government with religion. Lemon, 403 U.S. at 612–13. As the Lemon test is disjunctive, either an improper purpose or an improper effect renders the ID Policy invalid under the Establishment Clause.[123]

We will therefore consider whether (1) Defendants' primary purpose was to advance religion or (2) the ID Policy has the primary effect of promoting religion.

1.   Purpose Inquiry

. . . The disclaimer's plain language, the legislative history, and the historical context in which the ID Policy arose, all inevitably lead to the conclusion that Defendants consciously chose to change Dover's biology curriculum to advance religion. We have been presented with a wealth of evidence which reveals that the District's purpose was to advance creationism, an inherently religious view, both by introducing it directly under the label ID and by disparaging the scientific theory of evolution, so that creationism would gain credence by default as the only apparent alternative to evolution, for the reasons that follow.

We will begin the Lemon purpose inquiry by providing a detailed chronology of the events that transpired in Dover leading up to the enactment of the ID Policy at issue.

We will initially supply background information on the composition of the Board, which consists of nine seats. The nine members of the Board in 2004 were Alan Bonsell, William Buckingham, Sheila Harkins, Jane Cleaver, Heather Geesey, Angie Yingling, Noel Wenrich, Jeff Brown, and Casey Brown. Wenrich and Cleaver resigned on October 4, 2004, Casey and Jeff Brown resigned on October 18, 2004, and Yingling resigned verbally in November 2004 and in writing February 2005. (Trial Tr. vol. 34, Harkins Test., 113, Nov. 2, 2005; Cleaver Dep. at 15, June 9, 2005).

---

123.   Plaintiffs are not claiming excessive entanglement. Accordingly, Plaintiffs argue that the ID Policy is violative of the first two prongs of the Lemon test, the purpose and effect prongs.

During 2004, Bonsell was President of the Board and as President, he appointed Buckingham to be Chair of the Board's Curriculum Committee. (32:86–87 (Bonsell); 34:39 (Harkins)). As Board President, Bonsell also served as an ex officio member of the Curriculum Committee. (32:116 (Bonsell)).

a.   Expressions of Interest to Inject Religion

The Board held a retreat on January 9, 2002, several weeks after Bonsell joined the Board. Superintendent Nilsen's contemporaneous notes reveal that Bonsell identified "creationism" as his number one issue and "school prayer" as his number two issue. (P–21). Although Bonsell claims he cannot recall raising such subjects but does not dispute that he did, in fact, raise them, the overwhelming evidence indicates that he raised the issues of creationism and school prayer during the January 2002 Board retreat.

The Board held another retreat the following year, on March 26, 2003, in which Bonsell again raised the issue of "creationism" as an issue of interest as reflected in Dr. Nilsen's contemporaneous notes. (35:50–53 (Baksa); P–25). For the second, consecutive time, Bonsell does not dispute that he raised the issue but his testimony indicates that he cannot recall doing so, despite the fact that Jeff Brown, Barrie Callahan, Bertha Spahr, and Assistant Superintendent Baksa testified otherwise. (32:75 (Bonsell); Trial Tr. vol. 8, J. Brown Test., 50–51, Sept. 29, 2005) (Recalled Bonsell say at the March 26, 2003 retreat that he felt creationism "belonged in biology class alongside evolution."); 3:126–27 (B. Callahan) (Her testimony and notes took during the March 26, 2003 retreat reveal that Bonsell said he wanted creationism taught 50/50 with evolution in biology class.). . . .

Apart from two consecutive Board retreats, Bonsell raised the issue of creationism on numerous other occasions as well. When he ran for the Board in 2001, Bonsell told Jeff Brown he did not believe in evolution, that he wanted creationism taught side-by-side with evolution in biology class, and that taking prayer and Bible reading out of school was a mistake which he wanted reinstated in the Dover public schools. (8:48–49 (J. Brown)). Subsequently, Bonsell told Jeff Brown he wanted to be on the Board Curriculum Committee because he had concerns about teaching evolution and he wanted to see some changes in that area. (8:55 (J. Brown)). Additionally, Nilsen complained to Jeff Brown that each Board President had a new set of priorities and Bonsell's priority was that of creationism. (8:53 (J. Brown)). It is notable, and in fact incredible that Bonsell disclaimed any interest in creationism during his testimony, despite the admission by his counsel in Defendants' opening statement that Bonsell had such an interest. (1:19). Simply put, Bonsell repeatedly failed to testify in a truthful manner about this and other subjects. Finally, Bonsell not only wanted prayer in schools and creationism taught in science class, he also wanted to inject religion into the social studies curriculum, as evidenced by his statement to Baksa that he wanted students to learn more about the Founding Fathers and providing Baksa with a book entitled Myth of Separation by David Barton. (36:14–15, 17 (Baksa), P–179). . . .

c. Early 2004–Buckingham's Contacts with the Discovery Institute

At some point before June 2004, Seth Cooper, an attorney with the Discovery Institute contacted Buckingham and two subsequent calls occurred between the Discovery Institute and Buckingham. Although Buckingham testified that he only sought legal advice which was provided in the phone calls, for which Defendants asserted the attorney-client privilege, Buckingham and Cooper discussed the legality of teaching ID and gaps in Darwin's theory. (29:133–143 (Buckingham); 30:9 (Buckingham)). The Discovery Institute forwarded Buckingham a DVD, videotape, and book which he provided to Nilsen to give the science teachers. (29:130–131 (Buckingham); 25:100–01 (Nilsen); 26:114–15 (Baksa)). Late in the 2003–04 school year, Baksa arranged for the science teachers to watch a video from the Discovery Institute entitled "Icons of Evolution" and at a subsequent point, two lawyers from the Discovery Institute made a legal presentation to the Board in executive session. (Trial Tr. vol. 4, B. Rehm Test., 48–49, Sept. 27, 2005; 33:111–12 (Bonsell)). . . .

e. June 2004 Board Meetings

Plaintiffs introduced evidence that at public school board meetings held on June 7, 2004 and June 14, 2004, members of the Board spoke openly in favor of teaching creationism and disparaged the theory of evolution on religious grounds. On these important points, Plaintiffs introduced the testimony of Plaintiffs Fred and Barrie Callahan, Bryan and Christy Rehm, Beth Eveland, former school Board members Casey and Jeff Brown and William Buckingham, teachers Bertha Spahr and Jennifer Miller, and newspaper reporters Heidi Bernhard–Bubb and Joseph Maldonado. We are in agreement with Plaintiffs that with the exception of Buckingham, the testimony of these witnesses was both credible and convincing, as will be discussed below.

We will now provide our findings regarding the June 7, 2004 Board meeting. First, the approval of several science textbooks appeared on the agenda for the meeting, but not approval for the biology textbook. (P–42 at 8–9). After Barrie Callahan asked whether the Board would approve the purchase of the 2002 edition of the textbook entitled Biology, Buckingham told Callahan that the book was "laced with Darwinism" and spoke in favor of purchasing a textbook that included a balance of creationism and evolution. (P–46/P–790; 35:76–78 (Baksa); 24:45–46 (Nilsen); 3:135–36 (B. Callahan); 4:51–52 (B. Rehm); 6:62–63 (Rehm); 7:25–26 (Brown)). With surprising candor considering his otherwise largely inconsistent and non-credible testimony, Buckingham did admit that he made this statement. Second, Buckingham said that the Board Curriculum Committee would look for a book that presented a balance between creationism and evolution. (P–45/P–805; Trial Tr. vol. 30, Bernhard–Bubb Test., 96, Oct. 27, 2005; P–46/P–790; Trial Tr. vol. 31, Maldonado Test., 59–60, Oct. 28,

2005). Third, Bonsell said that there were only two theories that could possibly be taught, creationism and evolution, and as long as both were taught as theories there would be no problems for the District. (P–46/P–790; 6:65 (Rehm)). Fourth, Buckingham spoke in favor of having a biology book that included creationism. (P–47/P–791; 8:60–61 (J. Brown); 7:33 (Brown); 3:137–38 (B. Callahan); 30:89–90, 105–06, 110–11 (Bernhard–Bubb); 31:60, 66 (Maldonado)). Fifth, both Wenrich and Bonsell spoke in favor of having a biology book that included creationism. (P–47/P–791; 8:60 (J. Brown); 7:33 (Brown); 30:89–90, 105–06, 110–11 (Bernhard–Bubb); 31:66 (Maldonado); 3:137–38 (B. Callahan)). Sixth, Superintendent Nilsen said that the District was looking for a textbook that presented "all options and theories" and never challenged the accuracy of that quotation. (25:119–20 (Nilsen)). Seventh, Buckingham testified that he had previously said the separation of church and state is a myth and not something that he supports. (P–44/P–804; P–47/P–791; 3:141–42 (B. Callahan); 7:32–33 (Brown); 31:66–67 (Maldonado)). Buckingham also said: "It is inexcusable to have a book that says man descended from apes with nothing to counterbalance it." (P–44/P–804; 30:77–78 (Bernhard–Bubb)). Finally, after the meeting, Buckingham stated: "This country wasn't founded on Muslim beliefs or evolution. This country was founded on Christianity and our students should be taught as such." (P–46/P–790; 31:63 (Maldonado)).

We will now provide our findings regarding the June 14, 2004 Board meeting. Initially, we note that the subject of the biology textbook did not appear on the agenda of the meeting but members of the public made comments, and the Board continued to debate the subject of the biology textbook. Second, Buckingham's wife, Charlotte, gave a speech that exceeded the normal time protocols during the public comment section in which she explained that "evolution teaches nothing but lies," quoted from Genesis, asked "how can we allow anything else to be taught in our schools," recited gospel verses telling people to become born again Christians, and stated that evolution violated the teachings of the Bible. (P–53/P–793; 4:55–56 (B.Rehm); 6:71 (Rehm); 7:34–35 (Brown); 8:104–05 (F.Callahan); 8:63 (J. Brown); 30:107–08 (Bernhard–Bubb); 31:76–77 (Maldonado); 33:37–43 (Bonsell); 29:82–83 (Buckingham); 12:125 (J. Miller); 13:84 (Spahr)). In her deposition, Charlotte Buckingham admitted that she made a speech at the June 14, 2004 Board meeting in which she argued that creationism as set forth in Genesis should be taught at Dover High School and that she read quotations from scripture as part of her speech. Buckingham Dep. at 19–22, April 15, 2005. During this religious speech at a public Board meeting, Board members Buckingham and Geesey said "amen." (7:35 (Brown)). Third, Buckingham stood by his opposition to the 2002 edition of the textbook entitled Biology. Fourth, Bonsell and Wenrich said they agreed with Buckingham that creationism should be taught to balance evolution. (P–806/P–54). Fifth, Buckingham made several outwardly religious statements, which include the following remarks. "Nowhere in the Constitution does it call for a separation of church and state." He explained that this country was founded on

Christianity. Buckingham concedes that he said "I challenge you (the audience) to trace your roots to the monkey you came from." He said that while growing up, his generation read from the Bible and prayed during school. He further said "liberals in black robes" were "taking away the rights of Christians" and he said words to the effect of "2,000 years ago someone died on a cross. Can't someone take a stand for him?" (P–806/P–54; 12:126 (J. Miller); 13:85 (Spahr); 30:105–07 (Bernhard–Bubb); P–793/P–53; 31:75–76, 78–79 (Maldonado); 29:71 (Buckingham); 35:81–82 (Baksa); 6:73 (Rehm); 4:54–55 (B. Rehm); 6:96 (Eveland); 7:26–27 (Brown); 8:63 (J. Brown); 8:105–06 (F. Callahan)).

Finally, although Buckingham, Bonsell, and other defense witnesses denied the reports in the news media and contradicted the great weight of the evidence about what transpired at the June 2004 Board meetings, the record reflects that these witnesses either testified inconsistently, or lied outright under oath on several occasions, and are accordingly not credible on these points. . . .

g. July 2004–Buckingham Contacted Richard Thompson

At some point before late July 2004, Buckingham contacted the Thomas More Law Center (hereinafter "TMLC") for the purpose of seeking legal advice and spoke with Richard Thompson, President and Chief Counsel for the TMLC. (30:10–12 (Buckingham)). The TMLC proposed to represent the Board, and Buckingham accepted the offer on the Board's behalf. Buckingham and the Board first learned of the creationist textbook *Pandas* from Richard Thompson at some point before late July 2004. (29:107–08 (Buckingham); 30:10–12, 15–16 (Buckingham)). . . .

i. August 2004–Buckingham Tried to Prevent Purchase

On August 2, 2004 the Board met and one of the agenda items was the approval of the 2004 edition of *Biology*. A few days prior to this meeting, Casey Brown received a telephone call from Baksa who told her that Buckingham recommended that the District purchase *Pandas* as a supplemental textbook. (7:52–53 (Brown); 8:64 (J. Brown)). Jeff Brown then went to Harkins' home to pick up a copy of *Pandas* at which point she told him that she wanted the School District to purchase the book. (8:65 (J. Brown)).

Subsequently, at the August 2, 2004 meeting, Buckingham opposed the purchase of *Biology*, which was recommended by the faculty and administration, unless the Board also approved the purchase of *Pandas* as a companion text. Only eight members of the Board were present on August 2, 2004 and the initial vote to approve the purchase of *Pandas* failed on a four to four vote with Buckingham, Harkins, Geesey, and Yingling voting for it. (8:68 (J. Brown); 29:105–06 (Buckingham); P–67). After Buckingham stated that he had five votes in favor of purchasing *Pandas* and if the Board approved the purchase of *Pandas*, he would release his votes to also approve the purchase of *Biology*, Yingling changed her vote and the motion to approve the purchase of *Biology* passed. (P–67;

8:68–69 (J. Brown)). At trial, Buckingham testified that at the meeting he specifically said "if he didn't get his book, the district would not get the biology book." (29:106 (Buckingham))....

k. August 30, 2004–Board Curriculum Committee

On August 30, 2004, the Board Curriculum Committee met with Spahr, Miller, Nilsen, Baksa, Bonsell, Buckingham, Harkins, and Casey Brown with the principal subject of discussion being *Pandas* and how it would be used in the classroom. (12:134 (J. Miller)). Although Spahr expressed concern that the textbook taught ID, which she equated with creationism, Buckingham wanted *Pandas* to be used in the classroom as a comparison text side-by-side the standard biology textbook. (12:135 (J. Miller); 29:104–05 (Buckingham)). Despite the fact that the teachers strongly opposed using *Pandas* as a companion text, they agreed that *Pandas* could be placed in the classroom as a reference text as a compromise with the Board. (29:111 (Buckingham); 12:136 (J. Miller); 13:88 (Spahr)). Baksa testified that no one could construe the teachers as having supported *Pandas* in any way, reference text or otherwise, which is evidenced by Jen Miller's statement that if the teachers compromised with the Board, "maybe this will go away again." (35:120 (Baksa); 12:136 (J. Miller)). It is patently evident that by this point, the teachers were both weary from the extended contention concerning the teaching of evolution, and wary of retribution in the event they persisted in opposing Buckingham and his cohorts on the Board....

l. October 2004–Arrangement for Donation of *Pandas*

The October 4, 2004 Board meeting agenda indicated that Nilsen had accepted a donation of 60 copies of the text *Pandas*. (P–78 at 9). There is no evidence that Bonsell, Buckingham or any other individual disclosed the source of the donation until it was finally admitted at trial, despite the fact that Larry Snook, a former Board member, inquired as to the source of the donation at a November 2004 Board meeting. (30:47 (Buckingham); 33:30 (Bonsell)).

The testimony at trial stunningly revealed that Buckingham and Bonsell tried to hide the source of the donations because it showed, at the very least, the extraordinary measures taken to ensure that students received a creationist alternative to Darwin's theory of evolution. To illustrate, we note that at January 3, 2005 depositions taken pursuant to an order of this Court so Plaintiffs could decide whether to seek a temporary restraining order, upon repeated questioning by Plaintiffs' counsel on this point, neither Buckingham nor Bonsell provided any information about Buckingham's involvement in the donation or about a collection he took at his church. (30:50–56 (Buckingham); 33:31–35 (Bonsell) (emphasis added)). Buckingham actually made a plea for donations to purchase *Pandas* at his church, the Harmony Grove Community Church, on a Sunday before services and a total of $850 was collected as a result. (30:38–40 (Buckingham))....

m.　October 7, 2004–Board Curriculum Committee

. . . The Board Curriculum Committee met on October 7, 2004 to discuss changing the biology curriculum, without inviting the science teachers. (35:124 (Baksa)). As Casey Brown was absent, the Board members present with Baksa were Buckingham, Bonsell, and Harkins, and the meeting involved a discussion of various positions regarding the proposed curriculum change. (P–81; 35:125 (Baksa); 29:113 (Buckingham)). The Board Curriculum Committee ultimately adopted, within a matter of minutes, Bonsell's alternative, which states: "Students will be made aware of gaps/problems in Darwin's theory and of other theories of evolution, including but not limited to intelligent design." (P–82; 35:125 (Baksa)). The Board Curriculum Committee's proposed change also called for Pandas to be cited as a reference text. (35:125 (Baksa)). The curriculum change proposed by the Board Curriculum Committee and the change proposed by the administration and accepted by the science faculty, were circulated to the full Board by memoranda dated October 13, 2004. (P–84A; P–84B).

n.　October 18, 2004–Curriculum Change Resolution Passed

On October 18, 2004, the Board passed by a 6–3 vote, a resolution that amended the biology curriculum as follows:

> Students will be made aware of gaps/problems in Darwin's theory and of other theories of evolution including, but not limited to, intelligent design. Note: Origins of Life is not taught.

In addition, the Board resolution stated that this subject is to be covered in lecture form with *Pandas* to be a reference book. (7:89–90 (Brown); P–88; P–209 at 1646; P–84C). Board members Bonsell, Buckingham, Harkins, Geesey, Cleaver, and Yingling voted for the resolution with Noel Wenrich and Casey and Jeff Brown voting against it. (7:89–90 (Brown); P–88). . . .

Although the resolution passed, it was not without opposition. Both the Superintendent and Assistant Superintendent, Nilsen and Baksa, opposed the curriculum change. (35:126 (Baksa)). Baksa testified that he still feels the curriculum change was wrong. (35:127 (Baksa)). Both Casey and Jeff Brown, who voted against the resolution, resigned at the conclusion of the October 18, 2004 Board meeting. The following excerpt from Casey Brown's poignant resignation speech speaks volumes about what had occurred within the Board by that time:

> There has been a slow but steady marginalization of some board members. Our opinions are no longer valued or listened to. Our contributions have been minimized or not acknowledged at all. A measure of that is the fact that I myself have been twice asked within the past year if I was "born again." No one has, nor should have the right, to ask that of a fellow board member. An individual's religious beliefs should have no impact on his or her ability to serve as a school board director, nor should a person's beliefs be used as a yardstick to

measure the value of that service. However, it has become increasingly evident that it is the direction the board has now chosen to go, holding a certain religious belief is of paramount importance. 7:92–93 (Brown). . . .

o.   Development of Statement to be Read to Students

After the curriculum was changed, Baksa was given the task of preparing a statement to be read to students before the evolution unit in biology commenced. The persuasive evidence presented at trial demonstrates that the final version of the statement communicated a very different message about the theory of evolution than the language that Baksa and senior science teacher Jen Miller proposed. (36:27 (Baksa)). . . .

Subsequently, on January 6, 2005, the teachers sent a memo to the Board requesting that they be released from any obligation to read the statement. (36:97 (Linker)). The memo provides, in relevant part, as follows:

> You have indicated that students may "opt-out" of this portion [the statement read to students at the beginning of the biology evolution unit] of the class and that they will be excused and monitored by an administrator. We respectfully exercise our right to "opt-out" of the statement portion of the class. We will relinquish the classroom to an administrator and we will monitor our own students. This request is based upon our considered opinion that reading the statement violates our responsibilities as professional educators as set forth in the Code of Professional Practice and Conduct for Educators[.]
>
> INTELLIGENT DESIGN IS NOT SCIENCE. INTELLIGENT DESIGN IS NOT BIOLOGY. INTELLIGENT DESIGN IS NOT AN ACCEPTED SCIENTIFIC THEORY.
>
> I believe that if I as the classroom teacher read the required statement, my students will inevitably (and understandably) believe that Intelligent Design is a valid scientific theory, perhaps on par with the theory of evolution. That is not true. To refer the students to *Of Pandas and People* as if it is a scientific resource breaches my ethical obligation to provide them with scientific knowledge that is supported by recognized scientific proof or theory.

P–121.

Administrators were thus compelled to read the statement to ninth graders at Dover High School in January 2005 because of the refusal by the teachers to do so. (25:56–57 (Nilsen); 35:38 (Baksa)). The administrators read the statement again in June 2005. . . .

r.   No Convincing Evidence [of] Valid Secular Purpose

Although Defendants attempt to persuade this Court that each Board member who voted for the biology curriculum change did so for the secular purpose of improving science education and to exercise critical thinking skills, their contentions are simply irreconcilable with the record evidence. Their asserted purposes are a sham, and they are accordingly unavailing, for the reasons that follow.

We initially note that the Supreme Court has instructed that while courts are "normally deferential to a State's articulation of a secular purpose, it is required that the statement of such purpose be sincere and not a sham." Edwards, 482 U.S. at 586–87 (citing Wallace, 472 U.S. at 64 (Powell, J., concurring); id. at 75 (O'Connor, J., concurring in judgment). Although as noted Defendants have consistently asserted that the ID Policy was enacted for the secular purposes of improving science education and encouraging students to exercise critical thinking skills, the Board took none of the steps that school officials would take if these stated goals had truly been their objective. The Board consulted no scientific materials. The Board contacted no scientists or scientific organizations. The Board failed to consider the views of the District's science teachers. The Board relied solely on legal advice from two organizations with demonstrably religious, cultural, and legal missions, the Discovery Institute and the TMLC. Moreover, Defendants' asserted secular purpose of improving science education is belied by the fact that most if not all of the Board members who voted in favor of the biology curriculum change conceded that they still do not know, nor have they ever known, precisely what ID is. To assert a secular purpose against this backdrop is ludicrous.

Finally, although Defendants have unceasingly attempted in vain to distance themselves from their own actions and statements, which culminated in repetitious, untruthful testimony, such a strategy constitutes additional strong evidence of improper purpose under the first prong of the Lemon test. . . .

Accordingly, we find that the secular purposes claimed by the Board amount to a pretext for the Board's real purpose, which was to promote religion in the public school classroom, in violation of the Establishment Clause.

2.   Effect Inquiry

. . . While the Third Circuit formally treats the endorsement test and the Lemon test as distinct inquiries to be treated in succession, it has continued to recognize the relationship between the two. Moreover, because the Lemon effect test largely covers the same ground as the endorsement test, we will incorporate our extensive factual findings and legal conclusions made under the endorsement analysis by reference here, in accordance with Third Circuit practice. Freethought, 334 F.3d at 269 (The court noted that "effect under the Lemon test is cognate to endorsement," and hence the court did not hesitate simply to "incorporate [its] discussion of endorsement" into the effect analysis.).

To briefly reiterate, we first note that since ID is not science, the conclusion is inescapable that the only real effect of the ID Policy is the advancement of religion. See McLean, 529 F.Supp. at 1272. Second, the disclaimer read to students "has the effect of implicitly bolstering alternative religious theories of origin by suggesting that evolution is a problematic theory even in the field of science." Selman, 390 F.Supp.2d at 1308–09. Third, reading the disclaimer not only disavows endorsement of educational materials but also "juxtaposes that disavowal with an urging to contemplate alternative religious concepts implies School Board approval of religious principles." Freiler, 185 F.3d at 348.

The effect of Defendants' actions in adopting the curriculum change was to impose a religious view of biological origins into the biology course, in violation of the Establishment Clause.

H.   Conclusion

The proper application of both the endorsement and Lemon tests to the facts of this case makes it abundantly clear that the Board's ID Policy violates the Establishment Clause. In making this determination, we have addressed the seminal question of whether ID is science. We have concluded that it is not, and moreover that ID cannot uncouple itself from its creationist, and thus religious, antecedents.

Both Defendants and many of the leading proponents of ID make a bedrock assumption which is utterly false. Their presupposition is that evolutionary theory is antithetical to a belief in the existence of a supreme being and to religion in general. Repeatedly in this trial, Plaintiffs' scientific experts testified that the theory of evolution represents good science, is overwhelmingly accepted by the scientific community, and that it in no way conflicts with, nor does it deny, the existence of a divine creator.

To be sure, Darwin's theory of evolution is imperfect. However, the fact that a scientific theory cannot yet render an explanation on every point should not be used as a pretext to thrust an untestable alternative hypothesis grounded in religion into the science classroom or to misrepresent well-established scientific propositions.

The citizens of the Dover area were poorly served by the members of the Board who voted for the ID Policy. It is ironic that several of these individuals, who so staunchly and proudly touted their religious convictions in public, would time and again lie to cover their tracks and disguise the real purpose behind the ID Policy.

With that said, we do not question that many of the leading advocates of ID have bona fide and deeply held beliefs which drive their scholarly endeavors. Nor do we controvert that ID should continue to be studied, debated, and discussed. As stated, our conclusion today is that it is unconstitutional to teach ID as an alternative to evolution in a public school science classroom.

Those who disagree with our holding will likely mark it as the product of an activist judge. If so, they will have erred as this is manifestly not an activist Court. Rather, this case came to us as the result of the activism of an ill-informed faction on a school board, aided by a national public interest law firm eager to find a constitutional test case on ID, who in combination drove the Board to adopt an imprudent and ultimately unconstitutional policy. The breathtaking inanity of the Board's decision is evident when considered against the factual backdrop which has now been fully revealed through this trial. The students, parents, and teachers of the Dover Area School District deserved better than to be dragged into this legal maelstrom, with its resulting utter waste of monetary and personal resources.

To preserve the separation of church and state mandated by the Establishment Clause of the First Amendment to the United States Constitution, . . . we will enter an order permanently enjoining Defendants from maintaining the ID Policy in any school within the Dover Area School District, from requiring teachers to denigrate or disparage the scientific theory of evolution, and from requiring teachers to refer to a religious, alternative theory known as ID. We will also issue a declaratory judgment that Plaintiffs' rights under the Constitutions of the United States and the Commonwealth of Pennsylvania have been violated by Defendants' actions. Defendants' actions in violation of Plaintiffs' civil rights as guaranteed to them by the Constitution of the United States and 42 U.S.C. § 1983 subject Defendants to liability with respect to injunctive and declaratory relief, but also for nominal damages and the reasonable value of Plaintiffs' attorneys' services and costs incurred in vindicating Plaintiffs' constitutional rights. . . .

NOTES AND QUESTIONS

1. Even though earlier creation-teaching cases dealt with the general concept of supernatural causation in nature, why was *Kitzmiller* the first case to address directly the constitutionality of teaching Intelligent Design? As discussed above, by 2005, Intelligent Design, or ID, had become a term of art. It referred to the work of Phillip Johnson, Michael Behe, William Dembski, and others associated with the Discovery Institute's Center for Science and Culture. At a minimum, ID included the essential element that some biological organisms, organs, features, or functions were intelligently designed rather than evolved naturally from prior elements. It also sought to expand the definition of science from strictly the study of natural causes for physical phenomena to also the study of supernatural ones. Creation-science, in contrast, narrowly focused on uncovering evidence from nature supportive of the biblical account of creation, literally read. Thus, for example, creation-scientists look for evidence of a recent creation while ID theorists can accept an ancient earth. Much as the *McLean* court was the first court to rule on the constitutionality of a law providing balanced treatment to creation-science in public schools, the *Kitzmiller* court became the first to confront a school-board policy that expressly mandated the introduction of ID into public-school biology classes. The *Kitzmiller* court thus faced the question, was ID a religious concept?

2. Addressing the issue of creation-science as a matter of first impression in reviewing the constitutionality of Arkansas's 1980 Balanced Treatment Act, the *McLean* court conducted a factual inquiry into the status of creation-science as both a scientific theory and a religious doctrine. The *Kitzmiller* court did much the same analysis for Intelligent Design. How did Judge Jones reach the conclusion that ID was a religious doctrine? On this point, his opinion began by discussing the history of natural theology from Thomas Aquinas through William Paley to the Intelligent Design Movement. Natural theology consists of using evidence of complexity in creation to show the existence of a creator and examining the characteristics of creation for clues to creator's qualities. Judge Jones's opinion then turned to the writings of prominent ID leaders and organizations, particularly the Discovery Institute's Wedge Document, suggesting or stating that the IDM's purpose was to promote religious belief. Finally, the decision concluded that ID is not science. Judge Jones wrote, "After this searching and careful review of ID as espoused by its proponents, as elaborated upon in submissions to the Court, and as scrutinized over a six week trial, we find that ID is not science and cannot be adjudged a valid, accepted scientific theory as it has failed to publish in peer-reviewed journals, engage in research and testing, and gain acceptance in the scientific community. ID, as noted, is grounded in theology, not science." In making this point, Judge Jones stressed that he was not equating science with truth. Indeed, he wrote, "After a searching review of the record and applicable case law, we find that while ID arguments may be true, a proposition on which the Court takes not position, ID is not science."

3. Was it necessary for the *Kitzmiller* court to find that ID was not science in order to conclude that Dover's policy violated the Establishment Clauses or should it have been enough simply to find that ID was a religious doctrine? Finding that ID was not a scientific theory logically supported the conclusion that it was a religious doctrine—but it should not have been determinative. Many unscientific ideas have nothing whatsoever to do with religion and some scientific theories, such as the Big Bang Theory, can arise in part from religious sources, have religious implications, and support particular religious beliefs. Certainly the Establishment Clause does not bar public schools from teaching bad science or even non-science in science classes so long as doing so does not have the purpose or effect of promoting or inhibiting religious belief. Further, it should be constitutional for public schools to teach scientific theories that have religious implications unless they do so with the sole propose or primary effect of promoting or inhibiting religion.

4. In many prior opinions reprinted in this casebook, the courts assessed the constitutionality of challenged policies and practices under the Lemon test, with at most a nod to the endorsement test. *Kitzmiller* reversed this approach by analyzing the Dover policy first under the endorsement test and then under the Lemon test. How do these tests differ? The endorsement test originated with the 1984 concurring opinion of Justice Sandra Day O'Conner in *Lynch v. Donnelly*. It asks wither the government, by its challenged actions, has communicated the message of endorsing a particular religious or irreligious viewpoint. "As the endorsement test developed though application, it is now primarily a lens through which to view 'effect,' with purpose evidence being relevant to the inquiry derivatively," the *Kitzmiller* court noted. Re-

flecting its function as a lens for viewing effects under the Lemon test, the endorsement test leads to the same result as the Lemon test's effect prong by focusing that prong on whither the challenged policy or practice has a primary effect of endorsing religion or irreligion.

5. After losing in the trial court, why didn't the Dover Area School District appeal? Like most public school districts, Dover had an elected school board. In Dover, the regular school-board elections fell four days after the trial concluded and a month before Judge Jones issued his decision in December, 2005. Because of resignations and scheduled turn-over, eight seats on the nine-seat board were up for grabs in the elections of November, 2005. Typically such elections are low-key. Not so in 2005. A unified slate of eight candidates opposed to the ID policy swept the election. Among the losers, the principal proponents of the ID policy had the fewest votes. After the election and before the court announced its decision, the new board members declared that the district would not appeal Judge Jones's ruling.

6. Anticipating objections from creationists and ID supporters, the *Kitzmiller* opinion concluded with the observation that "this is manifestly not an activist court." Prior to becoming a federal district court judge, John E. Jones III served as the campaign manager of Pennsylvania Republican gubernatorial candidate Tom Ridge and, following Ridge's election, asked for and received appointment to one of the highest paid state positions—Chair of the Pennsylvania Liquor Control Board. Because Pennsylvania is the most populated state to limit sales of distilled liquors to state stores, the Pennsylvania Liquor Control Board is the largest retailer of spirits in the United States. Governor Ridge actively supported the presidential campaign of George W. Bush and eventually joined Bush's cabinet as Secretary of Homeland Security. At Ridge's urging and with the endorsement of Pennsylvania's U.S. Senator Rick Santorum, a vocal proponent of the Intelligent Design Movement and critic of Darwinism, President Bush nominated Jones as a federal judge for the middle district of Pennsylvania in 2002. Only five months after his nomination, Jones was unanimously confirmed by the Senate. Following his decision in *Kitzmiller*, ID activists associated with the Discovery Institute publicly criticized Jones as an activist judge. For his ruling, *Time* magazine named Jones one of the 100 most influential persons of 2005.

II. TEACHING THE "CONTROVERSY"

Critics of Darwinian instruction in public schools have proved extraordinarily resilient in the face of legal setbacks. Fellows and staff members from the Seattle-based ID think tank, the Discovery Institute, advised school officials in Tangipahoa Parish, Louisiana, and Dover, Pennsylvania, in drafting their anti-Darwinism disclaimers. Those disclaimers expressly referred to either creationism or Intelligent Design as an alternative to the scientific theory of evolution in a manner that courts concluded unconstitutionally commandeered public schools to promoted specific religious beliefs. Deprived of this alternative, the Discovery Institute persevered in its efforts to advise and encourage public schools to teach the controversy over Darwinism. Advocates of teaching evolution inevitably counter that there is no scientific controversy over the theory of evolution in that virtually all scientists accept it. The controversy over Darwinism is religious, political, or ideological, they argue, not scientific. ID advocates do cite these non-scientific controversies as meriting classroom discussion but maintain that there are scientific holes in evolution theory as well, most of which allegedly involve the sufficiency of random genetic mutations and natural selection to account for evolutionary development. ID theorists want to plug these holes with intelligently designed modifications or creations. To the extent that scientists recognize holes in the classical neo-Darwinian synthesis, they instead generally look for naturalistic alternatives to random genetic mutations as sources for genetic variation, such as hybridization and other gene flows among organisms.

The Discovery Institute embodied its teach-the-controversy approach to science education in its Model Academic Freedom Statute, which served as the basis for dozens of bills introduced in various state legislatures during the first decade of the 21st century. In 2008 alone, academic-freedom bills surfaced in six Southern or Midwestern state legislatures. While some of these bills explicitly referred to Intelligent Design or creation, typically they asserted the rights of public-school teachers and students to hold and express different views on biological origins and other controversial scientific topics without the bills themselves identifying any specific alternative theories.

Most of these bills stalled but, in the wake of the 2005 *Freiler* decision involving Tangipahoa Parish schools and the 2006 adoption of a local academic freedom policy by the state's Ouachita Parish Board of Education, a proposed Academic Freedom Act found traction in the Louisiana legislature during it 2008 session. The text of both the Ouachita Parish policy and state Act came from the Louisiana Family Forum, a local evangelical Christian advocacy group known for supporting pro-life and pro-traditional-family causes, which in turn drew on recourses from the Discovery Institute. In 2007, Louisiana's U.S. Senator David Vitter unsuccessfully sought to earmark federal funds for the Family Forum's science education efforts. Early in 2008, the Forum's "Academic Freedom Act" was introduced into the Louisiana State Senate by the chair of its education committee, Ben Nevers, who had previously sponsored balanced-treatment legislation. In committee, the bill was renamed the Louisiana Science Education Act and stripped of its most contentious features, including an itemized list of controversial theories and the language about teaching the strengths and weakness of them. Little remained beyond a provision authorizing state education officials to assist local school districts in promoting critical thinking skills in science. In the Senate, Nevers managed to reinsert a non-exclusive list of theories subject to critical analysis that included "evolution, the origins of life, global warming, and human cloning." Representatives from the Louisiana Family Forum and the Discovery Institute testified in favor of the measure. With two-thirds of the members joining as co-sponsors, Nevers's bill sailed through both houses of the state legislature with only three dissenting votes and was signed into law by Governor Bobby Jindal on June 25, 2008.

Although similar bills were introduced in others state legislatures during the years following the enactment of Louisiana's Science Education Act, none of them passed until 2012. Returning full circle to the state that in 1925 enacted the first anti-evolution law and in 1973 enacted the first equal-time or balanced-treatment statute for creationism, in 2011 the Tennessee House of Representatives easily passed an Academic Freedom bill designed to protect and encourage critical study of such "controversial" scientific theories as "biological evolution, the chemical origins of life, global warming, and human cloning." Responding to the widespread characterization of measure as a second Scopes Monkey law, one supporter spoke for many when he declared on the House floor, "since the late '50s, early '60s when we let the intellectual bullies hijack our education system, we've been on a slippery slope."[124] After the House action drew sharp protests from scientists at Vanderbilt University, the University of Tennessee system, and Oak Ridge National Laboratory, the bill was bottled up in the Senate Education Committee for nearly a year before emerging in somewhat revised form early in 2012. Passing the Senate by a three-to-one margin, the bill became law when Governor Bill Haslam declined either to sign or veto it—making it the first bill enacted in that manner during his tenure. "I do not believe that this legislation changes the scientific standards that are taught in our school or the curriculum that is used by our teachers," he wrote in an attempt to explain his unusual decision to let the bill become law without his signature, "but good legislation should bring clarity and not confusion. My concern is that this bill has not met this objective."[125] The Louisiana and Tennessee statutes follow:

LOUISIANA SCIENCE EDUCATION ACT (2008)

§ 285.1.   Science education; development of critical thinking skills:

A.   This Section shall be known and may be cited as the "Louisiana Science Education Act."

B.   (1) The State Board of Elementary and Secondary Education, upon request of a city, parish, or other local public school board, shall allow and assist teachers, principals, and other school administrators to create and foster an environment within public elementary and secondary schools that promotes critical thinking skills, logical analysis, and open and objective discussion of scientific theories being studied including, but not limited to, evolution, the origins of life, global warming, and human cloning.

---

124.   Andy Sher, *Tennessee House OKs Bill Shielding Teachers Who Doubt Evolution, Global Warming*, CHATTANOOGA TIMES FREE PRESS, Apr. 7, 2011, at 1.

125.   Chas Sisk, *Gov. Haslam Allows Evolution Bill to Become TN Law*, NASHVILLE TENNESSEAN, Apr. 11, 2012, at 1.

(2) Such assistance shall include support and guidance for teachers regarding effective ways to help students understand, analyze, critique, and objectively review scientific theories being studied, including those enumerated in Paragraph (1) of this Subsection.

C. A teacher shall teach the material presented in the standard textbook supplied by the school system and thereafter may use supplemental textbooks and other instructional materials to help students understand, analyze, critique, and review scientific theories in an objective manner, as permitted by the city, parish, or other local public school board unless otherwise prohibited by the State Board of Elementary and Secondary Education.

D. This Section shall not be construed to promote any religious doctrine, promote discrimination for or against a particular set of religious beliefs, or promote discrimination for or against religion or nonreligion.

E. The State Board of Elementary and Secondary Education and each city, parish, or other local public school board shall adopt and promulgate the rules and regulations necessary to implement the provisions of this Section prior to the beginning of the 2008–2009 school year.

TENNESSEE ACADEMIC FREEDOM STATUTE (2012)

WHEREAS, the general assembly finds that:

(1) An important purpose of science education is to inform students about scientific evidence and to help students develop critical thinking skills necessary to become intelligent, productive, and scientifically informed citizens;

(2) The teaching of some scientific subjects required to be taught under the curriculum framework developed by the state board of education may cause debate and disputation including, but not limited to, biological evolution, the chemical origins of life, global warming, and human cloning; and

(3) Some teachers may be unsure of the expectation concerning how they should present information when debate and disputation occur on such subjects; now, therefore,

SECTION 1. Tennessee Code Annotated, Title 49, Chapter 6, Part 10, is amended by adding the following as a new, appropriately designated section:

(a) The state board of education, public elementary and secondary school governing authorities, directors of schools, school system administrators, and public elementary and secondary school principals and administrators shall endeavor to create an environment within public elementary and secondary schools that encourages students to explore scientific questions, learn about scientific evidence, develop critical thinking skills, and respond appropriately and respectfully to differences of opinion about scientific subjects required to be taught under the curriculum framework developed by the state board of education.

(b) The state board of education, public elementary and secondary school governing authorities, directors of schools, school system administrators, and public elementary and secondary school principals and administrators shall endeavor to assist teachers to find effective ways to present the science curriculum taught under the curriculum framework developed by the state board of education as it addresses scientific subjects that may cause debate and disputation.

(c) Neither the state board of education, nor any public elementary or secondary school governing authority, director of schools, school system administrators, or any public elementary or secondary school principal or administrators shall prohibit any teacher in a public school system of this state from helping students understand, analyze, critique, and review in an objective manner the scientific strengths and scientific weaknesses of existing scientific theories covered in the course being taught within the curriculum framework developed by the state board of education.

(d) This section only protects the teaching of scientific information, and shall not be construed to promote any religious or non-religious doctrine, promote discrimination for or against a particular set of religious beliefs or non-beliefs, or promote discrimination for or against religion or non-religion.

SECTION 2. By no later than the start of the 2012–2013 school term, the department of education shall notify all directors of schools of the provisions of this act. Each director shall notify all employees within the director's school system of the provisions of this act.

SECTION 3. This act shall take effect upon becoming a law, the public welfare requiring it.

NOTES AND QUESTIONS

1. Are the provisions of the Louisiana Science Education Act triggered by the State Board of Education, public-school districts, or public-school teachers? Whose rights does this Act protect? Under the Act, a local school board initiates a request to the State Board of Elementary and Secondary Education on behalf of its school district. The State Board then allows and assists public-school teachers and administrators in that district to promoted critical thinking about evolution, origin of life, global warming, human cloning, and other scientific theories. Within limits prescribed by their school board and the State Board of Education, public-school teachers are permitted to use supplemental materials to help students critique scientific theories. Presumably the State Board will recommend supplementary material for this purpose as part of its role in assisting teachers to promote critical thinking about science. Under the Act, school boards retained control over public education. How could the Tangipahoa Parish Board of Education use the Louisiana Science Education Act to foster critical thinking about Darwinism?

2.   Does the 2012 Tennessee law impose greater duties on public-school teachers and administrators than the Louisiana Act? Unlike the Louisiana Act, which is triggered by local school officials, the Tennessee law imposes an affirmative duty on school administrators to create an environment in public elementary and secondary schools that encourages critical thinking skills about controversial subjects in science. They must assist and may not hinder teachers from helping students to understand and critique existing scientific theories. Arguably, teachers play a more central role in triggering the Tennessee law than the Louisiana Act.

3.   Why do the Louisiana and Tennessee statutes single out the scientific subjects of evolution, origins of life, global warming, and human cloning for analysis and critique? Assuming that all four subjects are controversial in Louisiana and Tennessee, state legislators may simply want to encourage students to think critically about them. Significantly, however, controversy surrounding the theory of global warming is more political, economic, or ideological than religious and disputation over human cloning raises ethical issues of concern to secular and religious people alike. In *Freiler*, the Fifth Circuit Court of Appeals struck down Tangipahoa Parish's evolution-teaching disclaimer at least in part because, by singling out Darwinism for critical analysis, it had the effect of promoting religious alternatives. Naming other subjects, especially ones that are controversial for non-religious reasons, may lessen the likelihood that these laws violate the Establishment Clause. Although some scientists and scientific organizations have lobbied the Louisiana and Tennessee legislatures to repeal their science-education statutes, including by boycotting those states for scientific conventions, no individuals or organizations have challenged them in court. Considering the decisions in *Freiler*, *Selman*, and *Kitzmiller* as well as the lack of legal challenges to the 1976 Kentucky Creationism Statute and the Alabama Textbook disclaimer, are the Louisiana and Tennessee laws constitutional?

III.   CREATIONIST SCHOOLS AND STUDENTS

Opposition to Darwinian instruction is widely perceived as one reason why the number of students attending conservative Christian elementary and secondary schools increased during the twenty-year period from 1990 to 2010 even as the total number of students attending private schools declined. Other factors undoubtedly contributed to this development, and may have predominated, but in their endorsement of Christian schooling and critique of public education such influential American evangelicals as James Dobson, Charles Colson, and Pat Robertson have stressed the fundamental significance of how science courses handle the issue of biological origins. Many conservative Christian high schools use biology textbooks published by either A Beka Book, which bills itself as a ministry of Pensacola Christian College, or Bob Jones University Press, the publishing house of an unabashedly fundamentalist Protestant institution.

At the same time, proponents of Darwinian instruction and critics of narrowly sectarian schools have long argued that students without a proper education in evolutionary science are ill-prepared for college.

Taking this argument to the extreme during the 1925 Scopes trial, Columbia University President Nicholas Murray Butler threatened to bar Tennessee public-school graduates from admission to his university so long as the state's anti-evolution law remained in effect. Some evolutionists made similar comments about Kansas public-school graduates in 1999, after that state's board of education deleted Darwinism for its science-education standards. The concern is greatest with respect to graduates of those conservative Christian schools in which Darwinism is either not taught in biology courses or taught in a way that disparages it. Some universities have denied credit for such courses and looked askance at applicants from such schools. Christian school students and parents have little recourse against such practices by private colleges and universities, which generally are free to set their own admissions policies, but may object when they are done by state universities supported by their tax dollars.

In California, the issue came to a head in 2004, after the University of California (UC) system began scrutinizing private school courses and their textbooks based on their religious viewpoint. Although interested parties disagreed on exactly how the process operated, the UC system clearly denied admissions credit for courses that taught any subject from only a single religious perspective, including ones that relied on the Bible as an unerring source for facts and analysis. Such courses, university officials maintained, would not teach the substantive content and methods of inquiry needed by students entering the UC system. For admission to a school in the UC system, unless they test-out of a particular subject or graduate in the top 4% their class at a participating high school, applicants must pass a certain number of college preparatory courses in various subjects, including one year of laboratory science in at least two of three disciplines—biology, physics, or chemistry. If a school's courses in these required subjects are not approved for admissions credit, then their students are effectively precluded from attending a UC school. For admissions credit in biology, the UC system would not approve any high-school course taught from either A Beka's textbook, *Biology: God's Living Creation*, or Bob Jones University Press' *Biology for Christian Schools*. Both texts took a strictly creationist approach that denied Darwinism and embraced a literal reading of the Bible as authoritative in matters of science. "Since the day that Darwinism invaded the classroom," the A Beka biology textbook boosted in its Preface, "God's Glory has been hidden from students. Now there is an opportunity in the Christian classroom to declare that glory with *Biology: God's Living Creation*."[126]

Following the rejection of four of its courses for admissions credit in 2004, Calvary Chapel Christian School filed suit in federal court claiming that the UC course-approval policy violated its rights of free speech, religious freedom, and equal protection under U.S. Constitution. Five Calvary Chapel students and the Association of Christian Schools International, a member organization including over 800 California parochial

---

126. GREGORY PARKER ET AL., BIOLOGY: GOD'S LIVING CREATION iii (2d ed. 1997).

schools, joined as co-plaintiffs. The UC system had approved 43 courses at Calvary Chapel for admission credit but rejected the school's courses in English, History, Government, and Religion. In their complaint, plaintiffs objected to the UC policy on its face and as applied to Calvary Chapel. They also objected to UC's decision to deny approval for a biology course at Calvary Baptist School that exclusively used the A Beka textbook. In all, out of over 150 courses rejected by UC for admissions credit, they identified 38 as proposed by religious schools. In their suit, plaintiffs were represented by former ICR counsel Wendell Bird, who had written and defended the Louisiana Balanced Treatment Act, and a local religious-rights legal group, Advocates for Faith and Freedom. As their expert witness reviewing the two disapproved biology textbooks, they hired Intelligent Design biologist and former witness for the school district in the Dover ID case, Michael Behe. In 2008, District Judge S. James Otero decided the case in two stages on separate motions for summary judgment, first on the facial challenge to the UC policy and then on the policy as applied. A Stanford Law School graduate who had served for 13 years on the Los Angeles Superior Court, Judge Otero was nominated to the federal bench by President George W. Bush in 2003. The following are substantial portions of Judge Otero's two opinions, particularly as they relate to the disapproved biology course and textbooks:

ASSOCIATION OF CHRISTIAN SCHOOLS v. STEARNS

United States District Court for the Central District of California
679 F. Supp. 2d 1083 (C.D. Ca. 2008)

OTERO, DISTRICT JUDGE: This matter is before the Court on Plaintiffs' Motion for Summary Judgment and Defendants' Motion for Partial Summary Judgment, both filed on August 27, 2007. Oppositions and Replies have been filed as to both Motions. After hearing argument on February 14, 2008 and carefully considering all admissible documents and the arguments made in support of and in opposition to each Motion, the Court DENIES Plaintiffs' Motion for Summary Judgment and GRANTS Defendants' Motion for Partial Summary Judgment.

I. BACKGROUND

Defendants are the University of California ("UC") employees responsible for developing and implementing the admissions policy by which applicants are selected to attend UC. Plaintiffs are the Calvary Chapel Christian School ("Calvary"), five Calvary students, and the Association of Christian Schools International ("ACSI").

Plaintiffs have brought suit against Defendants, alleging that the UC admissions policy is unconstitutional under the Free Speech Clause, the Free Exercise Clause, the Establishment Clause, and the Equal Protection Clause.

A. The UC Admissions Process

Each year, UC must decide which of California's more than 360,000 high school graduates will be admitted to attend one of UC's ten campuses. (Defs.' MSJ 2.) California applicants are admitted to UC only if they qualify through one or more of the following four "Paths":

Path 1: By meeting specified requirements for coursework, grade point average, and test scores.

Path 2: By ranking in the top four percent at participating California high schools.

Path 3: By scoring exceptionally high on standardized tests.

Path 4: By demonstrating the potential to succeed at UC despite not falling in any other category.

(Lynch Decl. No. 1 Exs. 1 (describing Paths 1, 2, and 3), 19 (describing Path 4).)

About eighty-two percent of California applicants who are admitted to UC qualify only through Path 1 or Path 2. (Pls.' Exs. 62, 64.) To qualify through Path 1 or 2, the applicant must demonstrate proficiency in seven specific subjects: (a) history and social science; (b) English; (c) mathematics; (d) laboratory science; (e) foreign languages; (f) the visual or performing arts; and (g) electives. (Lynch Decl. No. 1 Exs. 4, 17.) UC refers to these seven subjects as the "A–G Subjects." ... Nearly all of the applicants qualifying through Paths 1 and 2 demonstrate proficiency in the A–G Subjects by taking UC-approved high school courses. (Defs.' MSJ 4.) Plaintiffs' constitutional claims center on UC's method for approving high school courses.

B.   The A–G Guidelines

For an applicant to demonstrate proficiency in the A–G Subjects through high school courses, she must take a minimum number of UC-approved courses. The number of courses a student must take to demonstrate proficiency varies by subject, ranging from a year-long course in the arts to four year-long courses in English. (Lynch Decl. No. 1 Ex. 4.)

UC requires applicants to take approved courses "to make [the UC] eligibility standards substantively meaningful and to ensure that the students whom it guarantees a spot have earned their relevant grades in courses that are sufficiently rigorous to prepare the students for study at UC." (Defs.' MSJ 2 (citing Rashid Decl. ¶ 7).)

High schools seeking course approval must provide UC with a satisfactory course description. (Defs.' Opp'n 6; *see also* Lynch Decl. No. 2 Ex. 93.) The typical course description is three to five pages in length. (Pls.' MSJ 2.) UC evaluates this course description in light of the A–G Guidelines, which provide about one page of general principles per subject area (Pls.' Ex. 61) and hundreds of pages of examples of approved course outlines for each subject (Lynch Decl. No. 1 Ex. 2).

In deciding whether to approve a course, UC reviews the submitted course descriptions to determine whether the course challenges students academically, involves substantial reading and writing, teaches critical thinking skills, emphasizes both analytical thinking and factual content, and develops students' oral and listening skills. (Lynch Decl. No. 1 Ex. 6, at 4; Wilbur Decl. ¶ 10.) UC also seeks to ensure that the course will sufficiently prepare students for UC study. (Lynch Decl. No. 1 Ex. 6, at 4.) Courses that meet these standards are approved. However, UC will not approve courses that "fail[ ] to teach topics with sufficient accuracy and depth" or "fail[ ] to teach relevant analytical thinking skills." (Defs.' Opp'n 7.)

Occasionally, UC reviews individual textbooks where the subject area is one where "selected texts tend strongly to guide course content" (such as history, mathematics, and science) and the "course outline[ ] raise[s] concerns about whether the course meets faculty guidelines...." (Pls.' Ex. 241.) UC does not interview the teachers, observe classroom instruction, or test the students. (Pls.' MSJ 2.) UC does not review courses taken by applicants from out-of-state high schools (Pls.' MSJ 2), which comprise approximately fourteen percent of the applicant pool and about nine percent of admitted students (Pls.' Ex. 80; Wilbur Decl. No. 2 ¶ 53).

C. The "A–G Policies"

Plaintiffs allege that Defendants, in applying the A–G Guidelines, have established a set of binding "A–G Policies" that are used to routinely deny courses submitted by religious high schools. The official-sounding term "A–G Policies" is a label Plaintiffs created to describe what they believe are secret rules by which Defendants deny Plaintiffs' courses. (Pls.' Opp'n 3.) The extent to which these "A–G Policies" exist is discussed in Part II.A of this Order.

Plaintiffs contend that "[t]hese policies require rejection of courses, regardless of their standard content, that add a single religious viewpoint, any instance of God's guidance of history, or any alternative ... to evolution." (Pls.' Reply 1.) ... Defendants admit to creating UC Position Statements and form rejection language, but deny Plaintiffs' assertion that UC has a policy of "den[ying] students a-g credit for otherwise acceptable courses that teach standard content and that add religious viewpoints...." (Defs.' Opp'n 1.)

D. The Parties' Motions for Summary Judgment

Now, both parties move for summary judgment. Plaintiffs seek summary judgment that the UC course review process is unconstitutional on its face and as applied to Plaintiffs. Defendants seek summary judgment on Plaintiffs' facial claims, reserving for trial their proof that they constitutionally applied their regulations to Plaintiffs' courses.

II. DISCUSSION

. . .

A. The Scope of Plaintiffs' Facial Challenge

The parties disagree as to the scope of Plaintiffs' facial challenge. Defendants argue that a facial challenge is limited to the text of the A–G

Guidelines, while Plaintiffs contend that a facial challenge must include analysis of the A–G Policies. Neither party supports its argument with legal authority.... In addition, Plaintiffs ask the Court to find that Defendants have three specific A–G Policies.

1. The "Single Religious Viewpoint Policy"

First, Plaintiffs contend that Defendants have a policy of rejecting courses that contain standard content, but add a single religious viewpoint. (Pls.' MSJ 6; Pls.' Opp'n 2; Pls.' Reply 1.) Yet, the evidence establishes otherwise.

Defendants have approved many high school courses that include religious material and viewpoints, including courses such as "The Prophetic Voice" (Hargrove Decl. Ex. 3, at 430), "Western Civilization: The Jewish Experience" (Hargrove Decl. Ex. 6, at 574), and "The Bible as Literature" (Hargrove Decl. Ex. 3, at 535). Western Christian Academy submitted its "Language Arts 12" course for approval as an English course. (Hargrove Decl. Ex. 3, at 459.) This course relies on a Christian textbook published by Alpha Omega Publications. (Hargrove Decl. Ex. 3, at 461.) The course description includes assignments such as "Write an essay on the Christian view of nature as demonstrated in Jesus' use of elements of nature in His parables" and "Write an essay contrasting the Byronic manner of facing guilt with the way the Bible says Christians should deal with guilt." (Hargrove Decl. Ex. 3, at 462.) Despite its religious content, this course was approved. (Hargrove Decl. ¶ 10.)

Although Defendants disapprove of some Christian "science" textbooks that "prioritize religion over science" when used as the primary or sole text in an A–G Subject course (Hargrove Decl. ¶ 10), they do approve many courses that utilize these texts as secondary texts (Hargrove Decl. ¶ 14; Wilber Decl. No. 2 ¶ 7). Further, Defendants reviewed and approved some Christian textbooks for use as the primary or sole text, including *Chemistry for Christian Schools* and *Physics for Christian Schools*. (Pls.' Ex. 100.) This indicates that Defendants are not withholding approval solely because the course includes a religious viewpoint.

For example, Defendants have approved biology, physics, and chemistry courses using Christian texts, including a chemistry course taught at Calvary that utilized two texts—*Modern Chemistry and Chemistry for Christians* (Hargrove Decl. Ex. 5, at 565) and a biology course taught by Kings Christian High School that utilized three texts—*Biology: God's Living Creation, Biology,* and *Health Biology* (Hargrove Decl. Ex. 3, at 540–44)....

2. The "History and Social Science Policy"

Second, Plaintiffs contend that Defendants have a policy of rejecting history and social science courses that "add a Christian god" or that are "limited to one denomination or viewpoint." (Pls.' MSJ 9–13.) To the contrary, Defendants provide evidence of approved history courses taught from the perspective of a single religious denomination. (Wilbur Decl. No. 2 ¶¶ 33, 42; Hargrove Decl. ¶ 16, Ex. 6.) In addition to the "Western Civilization: The Jewish Experience" course described above, UC approved courses such as Sierra Christian Academy's "World History" course, which seeks to "understand[ ] and appreciate[ ] the beginnings of Western Civilization from a Judeo–Christian point of view" (Hargrove Decl. Ex. 6, at 592), and Valley Christian High School's "Ancient World History" course, which "cover[ ]s the time frame of *Creation* through the Reformation" (Hargrove Decl. Ex. 6, at 597 (emphasis added)).

Further, Defendants explain that the mention of God in the explanation of a historical event does not "automatically disqualify a course for approval." (Given Decl. ¶ 5 (noting that supernatural-based explanations of history do not "automatically disqualify a course for approval," but "excessive reliance" on these explanations may prevent approval).) Rather, the focus is on whether the course as a whole meets the UC standards. (Wilbur Decl. No. 2 ¶ 32 ("[T]he mention of God as the explanation of [a] historical event may or may not cause rejection of a course for [history] credit, depending on whether the course, as a whole, meets the UC faculty's expectations for college preparatory history. . . .").)

Again, there is no genuine issue of material fact as to this issue. Defendants do not have a "well-established practice" of rejecting history courses because they "add a Christian god" or "one religious perspective."

3.   The "Science Policy"

Finally, Plaintiffs contend that Defendants have a policy of rejecting biology courses that, in addition to evolution, contain topics such as theistic evolution, intelligent design, creation, or weaknesses of evolution. (Pls.' MSJ 13–17.) Again, Defendants deny this allegation, explaining that biology courses may include scientific discussion of the weaknesses of evolution, creationism, or intelligent design. (Wilbur Decl. No. 2 ¶ 43 ("A biology course could be approved for [science] credit if it included both an adequate treatment of the theory of evolution and discussion of creationism.").) For example, biology courses that use Christian texts that discuss perceived weaknesses of evolution, creationism, and intelligent design as *supplemental* texts can and have been approved. (Wilbur Decl. No. 2 ¶ 7; Hargrove Decl. Ex. 3, at 540–44 (approving Kings Christian High School's biology course, which used A Beka's *Biology: God's Living Creation* as a supplemental text).)

Once more, there is no genuine issue of material fact as to this issue. Defendants do not have a "well-established practice" of rejecting biology courses that add theistic evolution, intelligent design, creation, or weaknesses of evolution.

In evaluating Plaintiffs' facial challenge, the Court will consider the A–G Guidelines, the UC Position Statements, and form rejection language (collectively referred to as the "A–G Guidelines and Policies").

B. Plaintiffs' Facial Constitutional Claims

Plaintiffs have brought a variety of constitutional claims against Defendants. They claim that the A–G Guidelines and Policies are unconstitutional on their face because these regulations violate rights guaranteed to religious schools under: (1) the Free Speech Clause; (2) the Free Exercise Clause; (3) the Establishment Clause; and (4) the Equal Protection Clause. Each clause is addressed in turn.

1. The Free Speech Clause

... Plaintiffs vigorously attack the A–G Guidelines and Policies as viewpoint discrimination and content regulation. According to Plaintiffs, "UC policies, confirmed by hundreds of course rejections, discriminate by viewpoint and are content-based in regulation." (Pls.' Reply 3.) Plaintiffs' briefs rely on Rosenberger v. Rector & Visitors of University of Virginia, 515 U.S. 819 (1995), and other public forum cases as the cornerstone of their argument, insisting that " '[v]iewpoint discrimination is ... an egregious form of content discrimination' " (Pls.' MSJ 4 (quoting Rosenberger, 515 U.S. at 829)) and that " '[d]iscrimination against speech because of its message is presumed to be unconstitutional' " (Pls.' MSJ 21 (quoting Rosenberger, 515 U.S. at 828)).

Yet, not all content-based regulations are subject to strict scrutiny. The Supreme Court has repeatedly rejected a heightened standard where the government is providing a public service that by its nature requires evaluations of, and distinctions based upon, the content of speech. See, e.g., United States v. Am. Library Ass'n, 539 U.S. 194, 204–05 (2003); Nat'l Endowment for the Arts v. Finley, 524 U.S. 569, 580 (1998); cf. Ark. Educ. Television Comm'n v. Forbes, 523 U.S. 666, 672–73 (1998) (generalizing that governmental functions that require content-based judgments, such as selecting programming for a public television station, are not subject to heightened scrutiny). Instead, these regulations are constitutional if they are reasonably related to the government's goal of providing the public service and are not the product of government animus....

In National Endowment for the Arts v. Finley, the Supreme Court held that a government agency could make aesthetic judgments in allocating competitive funding for art projects that demonstrated "excellence." 524 U.S. at 586. After all, determinations of "excellence" are "inherently content-based." Id. Because limited funding was allocated according to a competitive process, the Supreme Court specifically noted that reliance on Rosenberger was "misplaced." Id.

The distribution of grants in Finley is the closest parallel to the UC admissions process. In both scenarios, the government is providing a public benefit that is allocated to a limited number of persons through a competitive process. Like the government agency that must judge the excellence of prospective art projects, UC must judge the excellence of prospective students who apply for a guaranteed spot at UC.

It is undisputed that the content of an applicant's high school courses is an important factor in evaluating the merit of that applicant. According to defense expert Dr. Michael Kirst, the content of high school courses is a "crucial variable in predicting whether students will succeed at very selective post-secondary institutions such as the University of California." (Kirst Decl. Ex. A, at 2.) Plaintiffs' experts concur that it is "educationally reasonable" for Defendants to condition admittance on content and skill requirements. For example, Dr. Donald Erickson, one of Plaintiffs' education experts, finds it reasonable for UC to expect admitted students to know, among other things, about "plants," "evolution," "accurate carbon dating," and "the roles of Latinos in United States history." (Lynch Decl. No. 1 Ex. 57.)

Dr. Derek Keenan, another of Plaintiffs' education experts, testified that "critical thinking and analysis skills are legitimate concerns of [UC] in evaluating student preparation." (Lynch Decl. No. 1 Ex. 63.) According to Dr. Keenan, "it's educationally appropriate for [UC] to set standards for the content and skills that need to be mastered for students to attend" (Keenan Dep. 46–47), and "high school course content is an important factor in student preparation for college work" (Keenan Dep. 47)....

It is undisputed that UC can reasonably reject courses that either (1) fail to teach important topics with sufficient accuracy and depth of coverage or (2) fail to teach relevant analytical skills. Now, the Court must consider whether the contested A–G Guidelines and Policies reasonably apply this standard, both substantively and procedurally. Because the test of reasonableness "is not capable of precise definition or mechanical application," its proper application "requires careful attention to the facts and circumstances of each particular case." Graham v. Connor, 490 U.S. 386, 396 (1989)....

Plaintiffs base their claims against the UC Position Statements on Science and History Courses on the false assertion that these Position Statements require a secular curriculum without religious viewpoints. (Pls.' MSJ 11 ("In other words, there *must* be a 'secular history curriculum' without religious viewpoints."), 16 ("The [Science] Position Statement also means that *only* a 'secular science curriculum' (no religious viewpoint added) is approved.").) Yet, the Position Statements do not use the word "must"; rather, they use the word "can" (Pls.' Exs. 241–42), indicating that a "secular" curriculum is not mandatory for approval. Indeed, as discussed in Part II.A, Defendants have approved numerous science and history courses that incorporate religious viewpoints.

The rest of the Position Statements reinforce the purpose of the A–G Guidelines: Admitted students must attain "essential critical thinking and study skills," "the necessary preparation for courses, majors, and programs offered at [UC]," and "a body of knowledge that will provide breadth and perspective to new, more advanced studies." (Pls.' Exs. 241–42.)

There is no genuine issue of material fact as to this issue. The UC Position Statements on Science and History Courses are reasonable....

Even if the A–G Guidelines and Policies are rationally related to UC's educational purpose, Plaintiffs can still prevail if they demonstrate that the regulations are the result of government animus towards religious viewpoints. In Finley, the Supreme Court repeatedly emphasized that the government may not punish disfavored viewpoints under the guise of legitimate regulations. 524 U.S. at 587. Although there is no guidance from the Ninth Circuit or the Supreme Court regarding government animus in the specific arena of free speech, two Supreme Court decisions have addressed the issue in the context of the Free Exercise Clause: Church of the Lukumi Babalu Aye, Inc. v. City of Hialeah, 508 U.S. 520 (1993), and Locke v. Davey, 540 U.S. 712 (2004).

In Lukumi, the plaintiffs challenged a city ordinance that targeted the Santeria religion under the guise of a legitimate regulation on animal slaughter. 508 U.S. 520. Leaning on "the principle that the First Amendment forbids an official purpose to disapprove of a particular religion or of religion in general," the Supreme Court invalidated the ordinance because it was not neutral and it was not a law of general applicability. Id. at 532.

In Locke, the plaintiff challenged a state scholarship program that was available to all qualifying college students except for those "pursuing a degree in theology." 540 U.S. at 716. Over Justice Scalia's vigorous dissent, the Supreme Court extended the Lukumi test to require an element of animus, even if the government regulation was not neutral. Id. at 724 ("Far from evincing the hostility toward religion which was manifest in Lukumi, [the scholarship program] goes a long way toward including religion in its benefits."); see also id. at 731 (Scalia, J., dissenting) ("The Court makes no serious attempt to defend the program's neutrality...."). Requiring strict scrutiny solely because a government regulation was not neutral "would extend the Lukumi line of cases well beyond not only their facts but their reasoning." Id. at 720.

Although decided under the Free Exercise Clause, Lukumi and Locke guide this Court's analysis of Plaintiffs' claim under the Free Speech Clause. The animus requirement is equally applicable whether the government is punishing disfavored viewpoints or disfavored religious practices. In this case, importing the test used in free exercise cases is particularly appropriate because Plaintiffs complain of discrimination against religious speech. Cf. Capitol Square Review & Advisory Bd. v. Pinette, 515 U.S. 753, 767 (1995) (observing that "private religious expression receives preferential treatment under the Free Exercise Clause"); Widmar v. Vincent, 454 U.S. 263 (1981) (invalidating restrictions on religious speech under both the Free Speech and Free Exercise Clauses).

Here, the A–G Guidelines and Policies are more like the scholarship program in Locke than the criminal prohibition in Lukumi. In Locke, the Supreme Court noted that the challenged scholarship program was distinguishable from the invalidated criminal statute in Lukumi in three fundamental ways. First, the scholarship program imposed a "far milder" burden on religion. 540 U.S. at 720. Second, the scholarship program went "a long way" to include religion. Id. at 724. Finally, the history of the ordinance did not reveal animus toward religion. Id. at 725. The Supreme Court upheld the scholarship program even though it expressly discriminated against theology majors.

The A–G Guidelines and Policies share the same critical distinctions found in Locke. First, any burden on religious schools or their students is mild, particularly when compared to the heavy criminal penalties at stake in Lukumi. UC does not penalize students for taking non-approved courses or attending schools that teach non-approved courses. Should a student attend a religious school that does not offer approved courses in the A–G Subjects, that student may demonstrate proficiency in a number of alternative ways.

Second, UC "goes a long way" to accommodate religious school students. Defendants offer students alternative ways of demonstrating proficiency in the A–G Subjects (see Part I.A) and offer religious schools personalized assistance in creating curriculums that would earn approval. (Pls.' Ex. 240 (UC Position Statement) ("[UC] is happy to provide additional assistance to high schools, including Christian schools, through a collaborative consultation process, in order to help the schools create course outlines that meet the faculty's 'a-g' course requirements.").)

Finally, there is little in the history of the A–G Guidelines and Policies to demonstrate that Defendants were motivated by an improper purpose. Plaintiffs' best evidence of animus is their characterization of the deposition testimony from the former chair of the UC board responsible for the A–G Guidelines and Policies, Michael Brown, that the "subtext" of Defendants' discussion in adopting the UC Position Statement on science was "antagonism toward the Christian schools," and that religious schools' "right wing perspectives were highly objectionable." Brown's actual deposition testimony was as follows:

> Q: Did the emotional tenor of any others on the BOARS committee in your view reflect antagonism toward the Christian schools or what they taught?

> A: It was my assessment that that was the subtext. It wasn't that anybody ever said they're Christian schools, we ain't approving them, but I had the sense that their feelings about radical or fundamentalist ... right wing perspectives were highly objectionable. (Brown Dep. 143–44.)

Even construing this evidence in the light most favorable to Plaintiffs, Brown's testimony is insufficient to create a genuine issue of material fact. Brown's "assessment" and "sense" that the committee was antagonistic is of little value without concrete factual support. In addition, the power of Plaintiffs' quotation is tempered by their omission of the words "radical" and "fundamentalist." These adjectives suggest the Board's "feelings" concerned extreme views inconsistent with knowledge generally accepted in the relevant academic community rather than antagonism toward religion. Further, Brown admitted in his deposition that his "assessment" did not apply to the entire board. (Brown Dep. 144 ("Most [board members] were quiet.... Trying to, in my view, reason it out.... I was actually honored by that. I really appreciated being in that context to see [board members] trying to grapple with it.").) An email Brown sent to the board after the allegedly antagonistic discussion confirms his appreciation: "I remain deeply appreciative of the tenor of [the] discussion ... regarding the issue of approving science courses ... submitted from 'Christian' schools.... I thought the [board members] participated in a frank, thoughtful, and sensitive manner." (Pls.' Ex. 157.) ...

2. Free Exercise and Establishment Clauses

... Although Establishment Clause claims typically challenge government action that allegedly benefits religion, the clause also governs "a claim brought under a hostility to religion theory." Am. Family Ass'n v. City & County of San Francisco, 277 F.3d 1114, 1121 (9th Cir. 2002); see also Vernon v. City of Los Angeles, 27 F.3d 1385, 1396 (9th Cir.1994) ("The government neutrality required under the Establishment Clause is ... violated as much by government disapproval of religion as it is by government approval of religion.").

"Notwithstanding its 'checkered career,' Lemon v. Kurtzman, 403 U.S. 602 (1971), continues to set forth the applicable constitutional standard for assessing governmental actions challenged under the Establishment Clause." Vasquez v. Los Angeles County, 487 F.3d 1246, 1254 (9th Cir.2007) (quoting Santa Fe Indep. Sch. Dist. v. Doe, 530 U.S. 290, 319 (2000) (Rehnquist, C.J., dissenting)). Under Lemon, government action does not violate the Establishment Clause if it: (1) has a secular purpose, (2) has a primarily secular effect; and (3) does not excessively entangle the government with religion. 403 U.S. at 612–13.

Government action "will stumble on the purpose prong 'only if it is motivated wholly by [the] impermissible purpose' " of endorsing or disapproving religion. Kreisner v. City of San Diego, 1 F.3d 775, 782 (1993) (quoting Bowen v. Kendrick, 487 U.S. 589, 602 (1988)). The Court must focus "solely on purpose" and cannot "question the propriety of the means to achieve that purpose or whether the defendants were correct or even reasonable in the assumptions underlying their actions...." Am. Family, 277 F.3d at 1121. In addition, the court "must be 'reluctant to attribute unconstitutional motives' to government actors in the face of a plausible secular purpose." Kreisner, 1 F.3d at 782 (quoting Mueller v. Allen, 463 U.S. 388, 394–95 (1983)). Here, a secular purpose is plainly evident. UC aims to admit the most qualified students and ensure that those students have the knowledge and skills necessary to succeed at UC.

Under the effect prong of the Lemon test, the Court must determine whether, from the perspective of an informed and reasonable observer, the government's action has "the principal or primary effect of advancing or inhibiting religion." Am. Family, 277 F.3d at 1122. Here, a reasonable person would not find the primary effect of the UC course review process to be inhibition of religion. UC approves many courses that include religious perspectives or are submitted by religious schools. Additionally, an informed observer would be aware of the controversial nature of intelligent design and creation as scientific beliefs. See Kitzmiller v. Dover Area School District, 400 F.Supp.2d 707, 764 (E.D.Pa.2005); McLean v. Ark. Bd. of Educ., 529 F.Supp. 1255, 1259 (E.D.Ark.1982) (dismissing "creation science" as "simply not a science"). No reasonable and informed observer could conclude that refusing to recognize intelligent design as science or other religious beliefs as academics has the primary effect of inhibiting religion. Therefore, Defendants meet the secular effect prong of the Lemon test.

Plaintiffs contend that government evaluations of religious content excessively entangle the government with religion. (Pls.' MSJ 26.) This argument is undermined by two Supreme Court cases in which public schools argued that they must exclude religious speech because allowing the speech would result in excessive entanglement. See Bd. of Educ. v. Mergens, 496 U.S. 226, 253 (1990) (invalidating a public high school policy excluding religious after school clubs); Widmar, 454 U.S. 263 (invalidating a state university policy prohibiting the use of buildings or grounds for religious worship). In both cases, the Supreme Court recognized that excluding religious speech posed a *greater* risk of "entanglement" because the public schools would have to determine what words and activities fell within the prohibited categories of religious worship and religious teaching. Widmar, 454 U.S. at 272 n. 11; see also Mergens, 496 U.S. at 253 ("[D]enial of equal access to religious speech might well create greater entanglement problems in the form of invasive monitoring to prevent religious speech. . . .").

While "invasive monitoring" designed to root out religious speech may constitute impermissible entanglement, application of the A–G Guidelines and Policies to private schools does not implicate this potentially unconstitutional consequence. First, these regulations do not require Defendants to identify religious speech. Rather, Defendants are charged with determining what content and skills are necessary for college preparation, and whether high school courses adequately teach the necessary content and skills. Second, there is no invasive monitoring. See Widmar, 454 U.S. at 272 n. 11 ("There would also be a continuing need to monitor group meetings to ensure compliance with the rule."). Religious schools seeking course approval need only submit a course description to UC. Defendants do not monitor classroom instruction to ensure that students are taught the approved content. The A–G Guidelines and Policies do not excessively entangle the government with religion.

There is no genuine issue of material fact here. Defendants are entitled to judgment as a matter of law on Plaintiffs' facial Establishment Clause claim.

Plaintiffs also argue that the UC course review process violates the Free Exercise Clause because UC imposes a substantial burden on religious school students' right to practice their religion. The analysis under the Free Exercise Clause has changed drastically over the past twenty years. Formerly, Sherbert v. Verner, 374 U.S. 398 (1963), governed Free Exercise claims. Under Sherbert, any government conduct or regulation that substantially burdened a religious practice was unconstitutional unless it was narrowly tailored to achieve a compelling state interest. 374 U.S. at 402–03. The government's burden was high. Id. at 407. ("[I]n this highly sensitive constitutional area, 'only the gravest abuses, endangering paramount interests, give occasion for permissible limitation.'") (quoting Thomas v. Collins, 323 U.S. 516, 530 (1945)).

In 1990, the Supreme Court radically changed course, effectively overruling Sherbert in Department of Human Resources of Oregon v. Smith, 494 U.S. 872 (1990). Under Smith, if prohibiting the exercise of religion is not the object of the law, but merely the incidental effect of a generally applicable law, then there is no Free Exercise violation. Id. at 884 ("To make an individual's obligation to obey [otherwise valid laws of general application] contingent upon the law's coincidence with his religious beliefs, except where the State's interest is 'compelling' . . . contradicts both constitutional tradition and common sense."). The Smith Court held that the Free Exercise Clause does not require a case-by-case assessment of the religious burdens imposed by facially constitutional laws. Id. at 883–90.

In Lukumi, the Supreme Court clarified its holding in Smith, observing that a free exercise violation would exist if the plaintiff showed that the challenged law is either not neutral or not generally applicable. 508 U.S. at 531–34. Finally, in Locke, the Supreme Court went a step further. Under Locke, the law must be the product of animosity toward religion. 540 U.S. at 724.

Because Plaintiffs' free exercise claim is subject to the same test as their free speech claim—the regulations must be rationally related to a legitimate state interest and not motivated by animus—the results are identical as well. As discussed in Part II.B.1, the A–G Guidelines and Policies are closer to the civil regulation in Locke than the criminal prohibition in Lukumi because of the relatively mild burden placed on religious schools and their students, Defendants' attempts to accommodate religion, and the lack of evidence concerning animus.

Accordingly, there is no genuine issue of material fact as to animus or the reasonableness of the A–G Guidelines and Policies under the Free Exercise Clause. . . .

3. Equal Protection Clause

As an alternative basis for relief, Plaintiffs argue that the A–G Guidelines and Policies violate the Equal Protection Clause by discriminating against religious schools. (Pls.' Reply 10.) As to claims of religious discrimination, if the defendant's actions do not violate the Free Exercise Clause, then courts will apply only rational basis scrutiny to equal protection claims based on religion. Locke, 540 U.S. at 720 n. 3 ("Because we hold that the program is not a violation of the Free Exercise Clause, . . . we apply rational basis scrutiny to [the plaintiffs] equal protection claims."); see also Johnson v. Robison, 415 U.S. 361, 375 n. 14 (1974) (applying "the traditional rational-basis test" to an equal protection claim premised on religious discrimination that did not violate the Free Exercise Clause). As discussed in Part II.B.1, there is no genuine issue of material fact as to whether the UC course review process satisfies rational basis scrutiny.

C.   Plaintiffs' "As Applied" Constitutional Claims

Plaintiffs also challenge Defendants' application of the A–G Guidelines and Policies to specific courses for which Plaintiffs sought approval and were rejected under the Free Speech, Free Exercise, Establishment, and Equal Protection Clauses. . . . Plaintiffs do not provide an analysis as to why any of the more than 150 courses rejected by UC should have been approved. Rather, Plaintiffs only claim that the courses were unconstitutionally rejected pursuant to UC's unconstitutional policies, such as the "Single Religious Viewpoint Policy." However, the Court earlier found that these policies did not exist. Therefore, Plaintiffs have not supplied any basis for their summary judgment request on the as-applied challenges to the rejection of specific courses. The Court is not obligated to consider matters not specifically brought to its attention. See Carmen v. S.F. Unified Sch. Dist., 237 F.3d 1026, 1029 (9th Cir.2001) ("A district court is 'not required to comb the record [when ruling on] a motion for summary judgment.' "). Still, the Court will determine whether Defendants supply a rational basis for their rejection of Plaintiffs' courses. . . .

Plaintiffs challenge Defendants' decision to reject biology courses that used *Biology: God's Living Creation* (published by A Beka) or *Biology for Christian Schools* (published by Bob Jones University ("BJU")) as the primary text. (Defs.' Opp'n 8.) Around early 2003, UC Professor Barbara Sawrey reviewed these two Christian biology textbooks and concluded that they were inappropriate for use as primary texts in college-preparatory science classes. (Sawrey Decl. ¶ 3.) Professor Sawrey found these texts problematic because they characterized religious doctrine as scientific evidence, included scientific inaccuracies, failed to encourage critical thinking, and took an "overall un-scientific approach to the subject matter." (Defs.' Opp'n 9; Sawrey Decl. ¶ 3.)

Sawrey's "judgment was based not on the fact that the textbooks contained religious references and viewpoints, but on [her] conclusion that [the texts] would not adequately teach students the scientific principles, methods, and knowledge necessary for them to successfully study those subjects at UC." (Sawrey Decl. ¶ .) After forming her conclusions, Professor Sawrey shared her findings with other members of the course review committee, who supported her conclusions. (Sawrey Decl. ¶ 4.)

Defendants' biology experts, Professors Donald Kennedy and Francisco Ayala, concur in her judgment. Professor Kennedy determined that "[b]y teaching students to reject scientific evidence and methodology whenever they might be inconsistent with the Bible ... both texts fail to encourage critical thinking and the skills required for careful scientific analysis." (Kennedy Decl. Ex. A, at 8.) Professor Ayala found that the texts "reject the methodology generally accepted in science, which relies on observation and experimentation and on the formulation of laws and theories that need to be tested rather than accepted on the basis of the Bible or any other authority." (Ayala Decl. Ex. A, at 4.)

Both professors concluded that neither of the two Christian textbooks are appropriate for use as the principal text in a college preparatory biology course. (Ayala Decl. Ex. A, at 28; Kennedy Decl. Ex. A, at 20.) In making this finding, Professor Kennedy reiterated Professor Sawrey's initial conclusion that "the problem is not ... that the creationist view is taught as an alternative to scientific explanations, but that the nature of science, the theory of evolution, and critical thinking are not taught adequately." (Kennedy Decl. Ex. A, at 7.)

Plaintiffs' evidence also supports Defendants' conclusion that these biology texts are inappropriate for use as the primary or sole text. Plaintiffs' own biology expert, Professor Michael Behe, testified that "it is personally abusive and pedagogically damaging to de facto require students to subscribe to an idea.... Requiring a student to, effectively, consent to an idea violates [her] personal integrity. Such a wrenching violation [may cause] a terrible educational outcome." (Behe Decl. ¶ 59.)

Yet, the two Christian biology texts at issue commit this "wrenching violation." For example, *Biology for Christian Schools* declares on the very first page that:

(1) " 'Whatever the Bible says is so; whatever man says may or may not be so,' is the only [position] a Christian can take...."

(2) "If [scientific] conclusions contradict the Word of God, the conclusions are wrong, no matter how many scientific facts may appear to back them."

(3) "Christians must disregard [scientific hypotheses or theories] that contradict the Bible." (Phillips Decl. Ex. B, at xi.)

Defendants have raised a genuine issue of material fact as to whether their rejection of Plaintiffs' biology courses was reasonable....

III. RULING

For the foregoing reasons, Plaintiffs' Motion for Summary Judgment is DENIED and Defendants' Motion for Partial Summary Judgment is GRANTED as to Plaintiffs' facial claims. Remaining as issues for trial are the reasonableness of Defendants' challenged decisions to deny approval for specific religious school courses under the A–G Guidelines and Policies and Plaintiffs' other "as applied" challenges.

ASSOCIATION OF CHRISTIAN SCHOOLS v. STEARNS

United States District Court for the Central District of California
678 F. Supp. 2d 980 (C.D. Ca. 2008)

OTERO, DISTRICT JUDGE: This matter is before the Court on Defendants' "Motion for Summary Judgment on Plaintiffs' As–Applied Claims," filed May 28, 2008. Plaintiffs filed an Opposition, to which Defendants replied. The Court heard oral argument from the parties on July 18, 2008. (Docket No. 221.) Because Plaintiffs fail to raise a genuine issue of material fact in support of their "as-applied" claims, Defendants' Motion is GRANTED.

I. BACKGROUND

. . . Earlier this year, the Court ruled on one round of summary judgment motions brought by the parties. In those motions, Defendants requested summary judgment only on Plaintiffs' facial claims, while Plaintiffs requested summary judgment on all of their claims—both facial and as-applied. After determining that Defendants' policies and actions are subject to rational basis review, the Court granted summary judgment in favor of Defendants on Plaintiffs' facial claims. Plaintiffs' request for summary judgment was denied in its entirety, leaving Plaintiffs' as-applied claims remaining for adjudication. Upon the parties' request, the Court granted Defendants leave to file a second summary judgment motion concerning Plaintiffs' as-applied claims. Now, Defendants move for summary judgment on Plaintiffs' as-applied claims.

II. DISCUSSION

. . . Plaintiffs primarily argue that Defendants engaged in viewpoint discrimination and content regulation prohibited by the Free Speech Clause. As discussed in the Prior Order, Defendants necessarily facilitate some viewpoints over others in judging the excellence of those students applying to UC. Therefore, the decision to reject a course is constitutional as long as: (1) UC did not reject the course because of animus; and (2) UC had a rational basis for rejecting the course.

a. Animus

Defendants argue that Plaintiffs waived any animus argument when Plaintiffs' counsel stated "We do not intend to argue the case based on proving animus" at the hearing on the parties' first round of summary judgment motions. (Tr. of Feb. 14, 2008 MSJ Hearing 39.) Plaintiffs dispute this argument, explaining that they did not intend to argue animus until this Court used that term to describe the punishment of disfavored viewpoints prohibited by National Endowment for the Arts v. Finley, 524 U.S. 569, 587 (1998).

Regardless of whether Plaintiffs waived this issue, they fail to present evidence of animus sufficient to raise a genuine issue of material fact. The prototypical example of government animus is found in Church of the

Lukumi Babalu Aye, Inc. v. City of Hialeah, 508 U.S. 520 (1993). There, the city council passed an ordinance prohibiting some, but not all, forms of animal killing so that members of the Santeria religion could not sacrifice animals during their worship ceremonies at a local church. "[T]he record . . . compel[led] the conclusion that suppression of the central element of the Santeria worship service was the object of the [city] ordinance," id. at 534, in part because of comments made at a city meeting at which the issue was addressed.

One councilman said that Santeria devotees "are in violation of everything this country stands for" and another asked "[w]hat can we do to prevent the Church from opening?" Id. at 541. A city official told the city council that Santeria was a sin, "foolishness," "an abomination to the Lord," and the worship of "demons" and urged the city council "not to permit this Church to exist." Id. at 541–42. Also, the city attorney commented that the ordinance indicated that "[t]his community will not tolerate religious practices which are abhorrent to its citizens." Id. at 542.

This evidence of animus demonstrated that the city used an ordinance that otherwise has a rational basis to punish a disfavored viewpoint. Similarly, Plaintiffs would have to show that Defendants rejected the challenged courses to punish religious viewpoints rather than out of rational concern about the academic merit of those religious viewpoints.

Here, Plaintiffs provide no evidence of animus. Instead, Plaintiffs essentially argue that Defendants had no rational basis for their actions and therefore they must have been motivated by animus. This argument adds nothing to the constitutional analysis; if Defendants had no rational basis, the Court need not reach the issue of animus.

Accordingly, there is no genuine issue of material fact as to this issue. Defendants' decisions to reject the courses challenged by Plaintiffs were not motivated by animus.

b. Rational Basis Review

Defendants' course approval decisions are subject to rational basis review. (Prior Order 37.) Under rational basis review, government regulation is "accorded a strong presumption of validity." Heller v. Doe by Doe, 509 U.S. 312, 319 (1993). . . . "When judges are asked to review the substance of a genuinely academic decision . . . , they should show great respect for the faculty's professional judgment." Regents of Univ. of Mich. v. Ewing, 474 U.S. 214, 225 (1985). "Plainly, [courts] may not override [this judgment] unless it is such a substantial departure from accepted academic norms as to demonstrate that the person or committee responsible did not actually exercise professional judgment." Id. Indeed, "restrained judicial review of the substance of academic decisions" enables academic freedom to thrive. Id.; see also id. at 226 n. 12 ("Academic freedom thrives not only on the independent and uninhibited exchange of ideas among teachers and students, but also, and somewhat inconsistently, on autonomous decisionmaking by the academy itself. . . .") . . .

Plaintiffs challenge Defendants' decision to deny approval for the Biology course submitted by Calvary Baptist School. Although Calvary Baptist has a similar name, it is not the same school as Calvary.

This course proposed a primary text published by A Beka titled *Biology: God's Living Creation.* (Pls.' Ex. 624, at 40.) UC Professor Barbara Sawrey reviewed this text and concluded that it was inappropriate for use as the primary text in college-preparatory science classes. (Sawrey Decl. ¶ 3.) Professor Sawrey found the text problematic because it characterized religious doctrine as scientific evidence, included scientific inaccuracies, failed to encourage critical thinking, and took an "overall un-scientific approach to the subject matter." (Sawrey Decl. ¶ 3.)[127]

Sawrey's "judgment was based not on the fact that the textbooks contained religious references and viewpoints, but on [her] conclusion that [the texts] would not adequately teach students the scientific principles, methods, and knowledge necessary for them to successfully study those subjects at UC." (Sawrey Decl. ¶ 3.)[128] After forming her conclusions, Professor Sawrey shared her findings with other members of the course review committee, who supported her conclusions. (Sawrey Decl. ¶ 4.)

Defendants' biology experts, Professors Donald Kennedy and Francisco Ayala, reviewed the A Beka text and a second Biology text published by BJU and concurred in her judgment. Professor Kennedy determined that "[b]y teaching students to reject scientific evidence and methodology whenever they might be inconsistent with the Bible ... both texts fail to encourage critical thinking and the skills required for careful scientific analysis." (Kennedy Decl. Ex. A, at 8.) Professor Ayala found that the texts "reject the methodology generally accepted in science, which relies on observation and experimentation and on the formulation of laws and theories that need to be tested rather than accepted on the basis of the Bible or any other authority." (Ayala Decl. Ex. A, at 4.)

Both professors concluded that neither the A Beka nor the BJU Biology texts are appropriate for use as the principal text in a college preparatory biology course. (Ayala Decl. Ex. A, at 28; Kennedy Decl. Ex. A, at 20.) In making this finding, Professor Kennedy reiterated Professor Sawrey's initial conclusion that "the problem is not ... that the creation-

---

127. The UC Position Statement on Science Courses reflects these concerns:

The texts in question are primarily religious texts; science is secondary.... Courses that utilize these texts teach students that their conclusions must conform to the Bible, and that scientific material and methods are secondary. Students who [are] taught to discount the scientific process and the scientific conclusions validated by a wealth of scientific research are not being provided with an understanding of scientific principles expected by the UC faculty.

128. Similarly, some Christian schools have declined to use BJU and A Beka textbooks because of concerns about the texts' academic merit. (Lynch Decl. No. 1 Exs. 47B ("[Valley Christian School] felt that the A Beka books ... did not represent the same level of academic rigor as we could find in some other texts."), 47C ("[Patten Academy declined to use A Beka and BJU textbooks] because they didn't provide the content that the principal and faculty believed would prepare the youngsters to meet their post-high school goals."); cf. Lynch Decl. No. 1 Ex. 47A ("[Oaks Christian School] acknowledge[s] that there was a much fuller treatment of evolution in the secular book that [it] used [than the BJU biology textbook, which it did not use].").)

ist view is taught as an alternative to scientific explanations, but that the nature of science, the theory of evolution, and critical thinking are not taught adequately." (Kennedy Decl. Ex. A, at 7.)

Plaintiffs offer little admissible evidence to the contrary. Plaintiffs' Biology expert, Dr. Michael Behe, submitted a declaration concluding that the BJU text mentions standard scientific content. (Watters Decl. Ex. U.) However, Professor Behe "did not consider how much detail or depth" the texts gave to this standard content. (Watters Decl. Ex. U ¶ 4.) Therefore, Professor Behe fails to refute one of Professor Kennedy's primary concerns that the nature of science, the theory of evolution, and critical thinking are not taught adequately.

Accordingly, there is no genuine issue of material fact as to this issue. Defendants had a rational basis for rejecting Calvary Baptist's proposed Biology course. . . .

III. RULING

Because Plaintiffs fail to raise any genuine issue of material fact to support their as-applied claims, Defendants' Motion is GRANTED.

NOTES AND QUESTIONS

1. The Ninth Circuit Court of Appeal affirmed the district court's rulings in *Stearns* on both facial and as-applied claims in an unpublished opinion that did not address the biology course specifically. *Association of Christian Schools v. Stearns*, 2010 WL 107035 (9th Cir. 2010). With respect to the facial claims, the appellate court wrote:

> The plaintiffs have not alleged facts showing any risk that UC's policy will lead to the suppression of speech. Nor can they. It is undisputed that UC's policy does not prohibit or otherwise prevent high schools, including Calvary, from teaching whatever and however they choose or students from taking any course they wish. High schools can, and do, continue to teach courses even when they are denied UC approval. UC does not punish a school for teaching, or a student for taking, an unapproved course.

> The plaintiffs devote much of their appeal to arguing that UC's policy on religion and ethics courses constitutes viewpoint discrimination. This policy provides that in order to receive UC approval, religion and ethics courses should "treat the study of religion or ethics from the standpoint of scholarly inquiry, rather than in a manner limited to one denomination or viewpoint." Aside from pointing out that UC's policy includes the word "viewpoint," the plaintiffs fail to allege facts showing that this policy is discriminatory in any way. It is not. As UC's expert explained, UC's policy is necessary because the "academic study of religion is multidisciplinary in nature" and "[p]rivileging one tradition or point of view is considered unacceptable and counter-productive in the scholarly study of religion at UC and similar colleges and universities."

Going beyond UC's written policies, the plaintiffs contend that UC has a well established practice of rejecting courses with standard content solely because they add a religious viewpoint. The evidence, however, is to the contrary. It is undisputed that UC has approved courses with religious content and viewpoints as well as courses that used religious textbooks as the primary and secondary course texts.

Id., slip at 4–6 (citations omitted). Following the appellate court ruling, the U.S. Supreme Court declined to hear plaintiffs' appeal. As a public university, should the University of California be able to determine what high-school courses it approves for admissions or credit? Even though the university apparently approved courses with religious content and viewpoints, could it have declined to do so on the grounds that such courses were insufficiently academic?

2.   What difference does it make whether the University of California (UC) approves a high-school course? UC uses high-school transcripts as part of its admission process. Both grade-point average and course selection matter. Unapproved courses are excluded from consideration. Taking an unapproved religion course may make little difference for an applicant. It means one less grade from an elective subject. Taking an unapproved biology course may make a great difference for an applicant. It means no grade or course credit for an essential subject. Students hoping to gain admission to UC may have second thoughts about attending private high schools with unapproved courses.

3.   *Stearns*, like *McLean* and *Kitzmiller*, involved a battle of expert witnesses. In reviewing the two disapproved biology textbooks, UC offered two of California's most renowned biologists, UC–Irvine professor and former American Association for the Advancement of Science President Francisco Ayala, a recipient of the famed Templeton Prize, and *Science* editor and retired Stanford University President Donald Kennedy, a former Commissioner of the U.S. Food and Drug Administration. Both defense experts concluded that both texts relied on scriptural authority rather than methodological naturalism to explain physical phenomena like the origin of organic types and the age of the earth. "The problem is not . . . that the creationist view is taught as an alternative to scientific explanations," Kennedy wrote, "but that the nature of science, the theory of evolution, and critical thinking are not taught adequately." In other words, the plaintiffs' biology textbooks did not even provide balanced treatment for Darwinism. The Christian schools countered with one biology expert, Lehigh University biology professor and ID theorist Michael Behe whose earlier testimony at the *Kitzmiller* trial had been largely rebutted and widely ridiculed. Further, Behe did not address the extent of coverage in the textbooks of standard subjects like evolution. Did the authority and testimony of these battling experts foreordain the outcome of the case? Why didn't the plaintiffs secure more authoritative experts or at least have them give more compelling testimony? Under the criteria for course approval apparently applied by UC and discussed by its experts, would it have been sufficient for the biology courses to use textbooks that provided balanced treatment for Darwinism and creation-science or ID?

* * * * *

Orange County California's pacific San Capistrano Unified School District, rocked during the 1990s by a highly-publicized case brought by creationist teacher John Peloza, was hit by an even more politicized suit filed in 2008 by creationist student Chad Farnan. The student's complaint alleged that James Corbett, one of the teachers accused in the earlier case of harassing Peloza, unconstitutionally disparaging creationism and other Christian beliefs in class. Corbett was an experienced teacher with a Ph.D. from Ohio State University known for using provocative comments and contemporary analogies to make history come alive for students in his popular Advanced Placement European History course, which boosted a 90%–plus pass rate for its students taking the AP Euro exam. His comments frequently disparaged traditional religious, social, and political practices. Farnan was a politically conservative Christian and all-star swimmer who secretly recorded Corbett's sophomore AP Euro class after Corbett had denied permission for doing so. Without discussing his concerns with his teacher or school administrators, Farnan dropped out of the class during the fall semester and, represented by the conservative Christian legal-rights group Advocates for Freedom and Faith, filed suit in federal court against Corbett and the school district for classroom remarks hostile toward religion in violation of the Establishment Clause.

Farnan's lawsuit quickly became a cause célèbre, especially in conservative circles. Excerpts from Farnan's recordings of Corbett's lectures soon began appearing on Fox News and conservative talk radio, including Corbett's depiction of talk-show host Rush Limbaugh as a "fat, pain-in-the-ass liar." Even before the lawsuit ended, Farnan was speaking at Republican campaign rallies and a fundraiser at the nearby Nixon Presidential Library. Corbett, in contrast, lost 45–pounds during the lawsuit and his son was jeered as an atheist even though hundreds of students rallied to the teacher's side and the school district paid the legal fees. Ultimately, renowned constitutional-law scholar Erwin Chemerinsky, dean of a nearby law school, volunteered to assist Corbett's defense.

Twenty-two classroom comments touching on religion stood at the heart of Farnan's Establishment Clause case, which was decided in response to cross motions for summary judgment by Judge James Selna, a former Orange County Superior Court judge nominated to the federal bench by President George W. Bush in 2003. Media attention focused on Corbett's statement, "When you put on your Jesus glasses, you can't see the truth." In context, however, Judge Selna ruled that this comment did not express hostility to Christianity because Corbett said it in the course of explained why Catholic peasants opposed the land reform efforts of eighteenth-century Austrian Emperor Joseph II that were designed for their benefit but opposed by the Church. Similarly contextualized, all of the other comments fell away in the eyes of Judge Selna except one about the earlier case in which Corbett said of his creationist colleague, "I will not leave John Peloza alone to propagandize kids with this religious, superstitious nonsense." While ruling that this unequivocal classroom statement about creationism by a public-school teacher violated the Establishment Clause, Judge Selna absolved the school district from liability, denied Farnan's request for an injunction prohibiting Corbett from making future classroom comments that could be perceived as hostile to religion, and found Corbett not financially liable for the comment under a qualified immunity defense. Both sides appealed to the Ninth Circuit Court of Appeals, which issued the following opinion:

C.F. ET AL. v. CAPISTRANO UNIFIED SCHOOL DIST.

United States Court of Appeals for the Ninth Circuit
654 F.3d 975 (9th Cir. 2011)

FISHER, CIRCUIT JUDGE: The First Amendment provides that "Congress shall make no law respecting the establishment of religion, or prohibiting the free exercise thereof." U.S. Const. amend. I. The government runs afoul of the Establishment Clause through disparagement as well as endorsement of religion. See Catholic League for Religious & Civil Rights v. City & Cnty. of S.F., 624 F.3d 1043, 1060 (9th Cir.2010) (en banc) (Silverman, J., concurring); id. at 1053–54 (Kleinfeld, J., dissenting); see also Church of the Lukumi Babalu Aye, Inc. v. City of Hialeah, 508 U.S. 520, 532 (1993). In this case, a former public high school student alleges that his history teacher violated his rights under the Establishment Clause by making comments during class that were hostile to religion in general, and to Christianity in particular. Mindful that there has never been any prior reported case holding that a teacher violated the Constitution under comparable circumstances, we affirm the district court's conclusion that the teacher is entitled to qualified immunity. Because it is readily apparent that the law was not clearly established at the time of the events in question, and because we may resolve the appeal on that basis alone, we decline to pass upon the constitutionality of the teacher's challenged statements. See Pearson v. Callahan, 555 U.S. 223 (2009).

BACKGROUND

In fall 2007, Chad Farnan was a 15–year–old sophomore enrolled in Dr. James Corbett's Advanced Placement European History (AP Euro) class at Capistrano Valley High School. Corbett has taught in the Capistrano Unified School District (District) for more than 20 years, and has taught AP Euro for more than 16 years. He is presently the only teacher who teaches AP Euro at Capistrano Valley High School. Corbett is a Christian who regularly prays and attends church services. Farnan is also a Christian, and believes in creationism. He was offended by comments Corbett made during class that Farnan characterizes as "derogatory, disparaging, and belittling regarding religion and Christianity in particular." Neither Farnan nor his parents ever discussed this concern with Corbett or any other school official. Rather, before completing the first semester of AP Euro, Farnan withdrew from the class and filed this lawsuit under 42 U.S.C. § 1983 alleging a violation of his First Amendment rights under the Establishment Clause....

District Judge Selna's thoughtful decision, C.F. v. Capistrano Unified Sch. Dist., 615 F.Supp.2d 1137 (C.D.Cal.2009) ("Farnan I"), describes in detail the statements made by Corbett that Farnan takes issue with, and we quote from a selection of them here.[129] Farnan challenges, for example, Corbett's commentary on how religion influenced serfs' reactions to Joseph II's attempts to spearhead reform in the Holy Roman Empire:

> [H]ere is Joseph II. He's trying, for example, to end serfdom. Serfdom in which the peasants, the Ser[f] class, on these estates [were], literally, property. They had no rights to speak of at all. He doesn't just go that far. I mean, he tries to get them land. He ... really has the interest of this class of people at heart, and the—the reforms that he makes really are going to make the lives of these peasants massively better. So why do the peasants oppose him? ... Because he also tried to reform religion, and the peasants love their church.
>
> It's the same thing here. You know, you go down to Georgia, Alabama, Mississippi, all these states that are as red as they could possibly be, as right-wing Republican as you could possibly be. [But] [w]hen you first present these people with the economic policies of the Democratic party, they are all Democrats. Virtually all the social programs they like....
>
> How do you get the peasants to oppose something that is in their best interest? Religion. You have to have something that is irrational to counter that rational approach. No problem.... [W]hen you put on your Jesus glasses, you can't see the truth. Um, Joseph made these reforms with no consultation, with no consent. (Inaudible) in the state.
>
> Now, the father of modern conservatism is [Edmund] Burke. He's in this chapter. And [Edmund] Burke made a very good point here that Joseph II should have paid attention to. You cannot overturn long-held traditions overnight without causing chaos, you know. You need to approach it by getting people some education, and you need to move it in a way that gets their support before you do anything....

Farnan also takes issue with statements Corbett made about the relationship between religion and the Scientific Revolution:

> [B]y 1543 we got religious wars going on. These are the religious wars that Charles V was involved with with the German princes, right? And those wars are going to end with the peace of Augsburg in 1555. Okay. (Inaudible). [O]kay. So we're talking about the beginnings here, starting at a time of real religious upheaval.... But what was the consequence? You know the consequence is that mankind becomes—

---

129. These quotations come from transcripts of audio recordings Farnan made during class without Corbett's knowledge. We recognize that Corbett alleges some of the recordings and transcripts have been edited and the statements have been taken out of the context of the classes in which they occurred. See Farnan I, 615 F.Supp.2d at 1141 n. 3. Corbett also suggests that Farnan violated California Education Code section 51512 by recording his lectures without written permission. Because Corbett does not argue that this affects our analysis of this case, we do not address that allegation.

because of the seismic revolution—a kind of cog in a cosmic clock instead of God's most important creation.

Um, see, people believed before the scientific revolution that the Bible was literal and that anything that happened, God did it. They didn't understand. They didn't have the scientific method. They didn't approach truth. The explanation to everything literally was that God did it. And the ultimate authority ... was the Bible....

[T]hink how humbling it's going to be, you know, when all these people who have been talking about Adam and Eve and creation and all of this stuff for all that time when eventually something happens, and they find out that there are people on another planet, six billion light years away, who don't look like us, worshipping huge geckos. (Students laughing.)

It's—I mean, it's profoundly disturbing (inaudible). You have (inaudible) people who are deep believers and find out that maybe we're not so important. Aristotle was a physicist. He said, "No movement without movers." And he argued that, you know, there sort of has to be a God. Of course that's nonsense. I mean, that's what you call deductive reasoning, you know. And you hear it all the time with people who say, "Well, if all this stuff that makes up the universe is here, something must have created it." Faulty logic. Very faulty logic. What's another explanation? ...

Yeah. The answer is—the other possibility is, it's always been here.... Your call as to which one of those notions is scientific and which one is magic. (Inaudible) the spaghetti monster behind the moon. I mean, all I'm saying is that, you know, the people who want to make the argument that God did it, there is as much evidence that God did it as there is that there is a giant spaghetti monster living behind the moon who did it....[130]

Because I can say to you, you know at least one of the laws of physics: Matter, can matter be—[Student: Created or destroyed.] Therefore, no creation, unless you invoke magic. Science doesn't invoke magic. If we can't explain something, we do not uphold that position. It's not, ooh, then magic. That's not the way we work. If we can't find a rational explanation, we go looking for other rational explanations. We do not invoke a supernatural every time we get stymied.

It's okay for religious people to, you know, or a magician (inaudible). There may be a distinction, but there is no difference. What was it that Mark Twain said? "Religion was invented when the first con man met the first [fool]."

---

130. Intervenors note that "spaghetti monster" is a term coined by evolution proponents who criticized the logic of teaching "creation science" in public schools. See, e.g., Cornelia Dean, Helping Out Darwin's Cause With a Little Pointed Humor, N.Y. Times, Dec. 27, 2005.

Anyway, um, he argued that all movement—no movement without a mover in a natural state, all objects at rest.... [T]his is deductive logic. It assumes a fact not supported by evidence and then makes logical assumptions based on that fact. Um, but, you know, we use inductive reasoning which requires observation and experimentation....

What happened in 1450 that changed science forever? ... Remember what I said about those books that were handwritten ...? See, this is one of the differences between the real scientists (inaudible) creationism and evolution, you know. What do evolutionary scientists do every day? They try and disprove the theory of evolution. Every time we find something new, we have to see if that fits with the central organizing theory of biology, which is evolution.

The first time a scientist finds something that can't be explained, you know, in evolution, it may not be thrown out, but it is undermined. And, actually, when they do the research, they're not looking to prove evolution. They're looking to disprove it. That's what the moral hypothesis is. You try and disprove it. And the more you try and disprove it and the more you fail, the more you believe it.

Contrast that with creationists. They never try to disprove creationism. They're all running around trying to prove it. That's deduction. It's not science. Scientifically, it's nonsense. In the case of the printing press, the printing press gives us the opportunity to share ideas. Scientists wrote ... an essay of some scientific theory that you found, and other people are going to be able to read it. And they'll be able to test what you did and see if it's true....

Farnan also focuses on a statement Corbett made about a lawsuit filed against him and the District nearly 20 years ago by a fellow teacher, John Peloza, who had been directed by the school not to teach creationism in his science class. The suit was ultimately resolved in favor of Corbett and the District in an opinion by this court holding that requiring science teachers to teach evolution does not violate the First Amendment. See Peloza v. Capistrano Unified Sch. Dist., 37 F.3d 517, 521–22 (9th Cir.1994) (per curiam). During class a student asked Corbett about the controversy involving Peloza, and Corbett said the following:

I was the adviser to the student newspaper. In his classes, [Peloza] was not telling the kids the scientific truth about evolution. He was hinting to kids in his class that there's another explanation, and he invited kids to his home so they could hear the truth, the Biblical truth about all this. And he came in at lunch and had meetings at lunch with kids who wanted to believe in creationism. And, anyway, my editor wrote an editorial in which she inferred [sic] that [Peloza] was not teaching science in his biology classroom. Instead, he was teaching religion.

He sued me as the advisor to the paper for five million, as a matter of fact. He also, on another issue, sued several other members of the faculty here because he claimed that he had the right under rules of academic freedom, because he was a fully qualified biology teacher, to teach biology any way he saw fit as a qualified teacher....

[T]he school district hired an attorney to defend us. And at the first meeting, the school district's attorney, my attorney, said, "First thing we need you all to do, we do not need to make any more public statements about this until the lawsuit is over." At that point, I stood up and said, "I'll tell you what. I will sign a statement giving you— you do not have to defend me, but I will not leave John [Peloza] alone to propagandize kids with this religious, superstitious nonsense.... John wanted to talk about creation as a science and all that stuff, but you get involved in that argument, you just lose because it's just nonsense....

Based on these statements and others discussed in the district court order, see Farnan I, 615 F.Supp.2d at 1142–53, Farnan filed suit under 42 U.S.C. §§ 1983 and 1988 alleging that Corbett and the District violated the Establishment Clause. He sought declaratory and injunctive relief and nominal damages. Corbett and the District answered the operative first amended complaint in March 2008, but Corbett's answer made no mention of qualified immunity. The following month, the district court granted the motion of the California Teachers Association and Capistrano Unified Education Association to intervene as defendants, and these intervenors filed an answer raising Corbett's entitlement to qualified immunity as an affirmative defense.

The parties filed cross-motions for summary judgment on the constitutionality of the challenged statements in March 2009. Without considering whether Corbett was entitled to qualified immunity, the district court granted Farnan's motion for summary judgment as to the comment regarding John Peloza's lawsuit, but granted summary judgment to the defendants as to all other challenged statements after concluding that they did not violate the Establishment Clause. See id. ... Corbett subsequently moved to amend the scheduling order and requested leave to file an amended answer asserting the defense of qualified immunity. See C.F. v. Capistrano Unified Sch. Dist., 656 F.Supp.2d 1190, 1192 (C.D.Cal. 2009) ("Farnan III"). The district court granted these motions and ultimately held that, although the Peloza comment violated the Establishment Clause, the law was not clearly established, so Corbett was protected by qualified immunity. See id. at 1203–07.

The parties filed timely cross-appeals in October 2009. Farnan challenges the district court's (1) rejection of his Establishment Clause challenge to all the statements except the Peloza comment ... and grant of qualified immunity to Corbett. Corbett appeals the grant of summary judgment to Farnan as to the unconstitutionality of the Peloza comment....

DISCUSSION

1.

The Establishment Clause applies "not only to official condonement of a particular religion or religious belief, but also to official disapproval or hostility toward religion." Am. Family Ass'n v. City & Cnty. of S.F., 277 F.3d 1114, 1120–21 (9th Cir.2002); see also McCreary Cnty. v. ACLU of Ky., 545 U.S. 844, 860 (2005) ("[The Establishment Clause] mandates governmental neutrality between . . . religion and nonreligion." The Supreme Court has long made clear, however, that "the First Amendment does not permit the State to require that teaching and learning must be tailored to the principles or prohibitions of any religious sect or dogma." Epperson v. Arkansas, 393 U.S. 97, 106 (1968). Even statements exhibiting some hostility to religion do not violate the Establishment Clause if the government conduct at issue has a secular purpose, does not have as its principal or primary effect inhibiting religion and does not foster excessive government entanglement with religion. See Am. Family, 277 F.3d at 1121; see also Edwards v. Aguillard, 482 U.S. 578 (1987); Lemon v. Kurtzman, 403 U.S. 602 (1971).

In evaluating a grant of qualified immunity, we ask two questions: (1) whether, taking the facts in the light most favorable to the nonmoving party, the government official's conduct violated a constitutional right, and (2) whether the right was clearly established at the time of the alleged misconduct. See Saucier v. Katz, 533 U.S. 194, 200–01 (2001), overruled in part by Pearson v. Callahan, 555 U.S. 223 (2009). If the answer to either is "no," the official cannot be held liable for damages. See id. We may address the second question first, particularly where "it is plain that a constitutional right is not clearly established but far from obvious whether in fact there is such a right." Pearson, 555 U.S. at 236. We have little trouble concluding that the law was not clearly established at the time of the events in question there has never been any reported case holding that a teacher violated the Establishment Clause by making statements in the classroom that were allegedly hostile to religion. Because the district court's judgment must be affirmed on that basis, we decline to consider the constitutionality of Corbett's statements, and we vacate the district court's decision to the extent it decided the constitutionality of any of Corbett's statements. See id. at 234–37.

2.

"[G]overnmental officials . . . generally are shielded from liability for civil damages insofar as their conduct does not violate clearly established statutory or constitutional rights of which a reasonable person would have known." Deorle v. Rutherford, 272 F.3d 1272, 1285 (9th Cir.2001) (omission in original) (quoting Harlow v. Fitzgerald, 457 U.S. 800, 807 (1982)) (internal quotation marks omitted). In evaluating whether a right is clearly established, we look to the state of the law at the time of the incident in question. See Bryan v. MacPherson, 630 F.3d 805, 832 (9th Cir.2010). "The contours of the right must be sufficiently clear that a reasonable official would understand that what he is doing violates that right." Saucier, 533 U.S. at 202 (quoting Anderson v. Creighton, 483 U.S. 635, 640 (1987)) (internal quotation marks omitted). Courts "do not require a case directly on point, but existing precedent must have placed the statutory or constitutional question beyond debate." Ashcroft v. al-Kidd, 131 S.Ct. 2074, 2083 (2011). That standard is not met here—nothing put Corbett on notice that his statements might violate the Establishment Clause. See Hope v. Pelzer, 536 U.S. 730, 739–41 (2002); Flores v. Morgan Hill Unified Sch. Dist., 324 F.3d 1130, 1136–37 (9th Cir.2003). . . .

The only cases that Farnan argued in his briefs clearly establish the law in the relevant educational context involve claims that school officials were promoting religion rather than expressing hostility toward it, and challenge systemic actions such as state laws and school district policies rather than parsing individual teachers' classroom discussions. See, e.g., Elk Grove Unified Sch. Dist. v. Newdow, 542 U.S. 1, 15–18 (2004) (holding that a father lacked standing to challenge school district policy requiring teacher-led recitation of the Pledge of Allegiance in his daughter's kinder-garten class); Epperson, 393 U.S. at 104–08 (holding that Arkansas statutes prohibiting the teaching of evolution in public schools violated the Establishment Clause); Sch. Dist. of Abington Twp. v. Schempp, 374 U.S. 203, 223–25 (1963) (holding that state laws requiring the reading of Bible verses and recitation of the Lord's Prayer in public school classes violated the Establishment Clause). At oral argument, Farnan's counsel conceded that there is no case directly on point, but argued that the general principles gleaned from the cases cited in his briefs, and from cases involving claims of hostility to religion in noneducational contexts, are sufficient to clearly establish the law. We cannot agree.

The Supreme Court has long recognized the importance of protecting the "robust exchange of ideas" in education, "which discovers truth 'out of a multitude of tongues.' " Keyishian v. Bd. of Regents, 385 U.S. 589, 603 (1967) (quoting United States v. Associated Press, D.C., 52 F.Supp. 362, 372 (S.D.N.Y.1943)). "Teachers and students must always remain free to inquire, to study and to evaluate, to gain new maturity and understanding. . . ." Id. (quoting Sweezy v. New Hampshire, 354 U.S. 234, 250 (1957)) (internal quotation marks omitted); see also Nat'l Sch. Bds. Ass'n, School Board Policies on Academic Freedom 2, 5 (1973) ("Academic freedom is an essential for responsible teachers. . . . To prepare students for adult roles in a democratic society, teachers and the schools must try to maintain an atmosphere of free inquiry."). This academic freedom will sometimes lead to the examination of controversial issues. Both parties agree that AP Euro could not be taught without discussing religion. We have no doubt that the freedom to have a frank discussion about the role of religion in history is an integral part of any advanced history course. Indeed, a collective of organizations including the American Association of School Administrators, American Federation of Teachers, National Edu-cation Association and National School Boards Association, has long acknowledged that "[b]ecause religion plays a significant role in history and society, study about religion is essential to understanding both the nation and the world." Religion in the Public School Curriculum: Questions and Answers, 8 J.L. & Religion 309, 310 (1990); see also Tenn. Educ. Ass'n, A Teacher's Guide to Religion in the Public Schools 2 (2008) (same).

In broaching controversial issues like religion, teachers must be sensitive to students' personal beliefs and take care not to abuse their positions of authority. See Edwards, 482 U.S. at 584 ("Families entrust public schools with the education of their children, but condition their trust on the understanding that the classroom will not purposely be used to advance religious views that may conflict with the private beliefs of the student and his or her family."). But teachers must also be given leeway to challenge students to foster critical thinking skills and develop their analytical abilities. This balance is hard to achieve, and we must be careful not to curb intellectual freedom by imposing dogmatic restrictions that chill teachers from adopting the pedagogical methods they believe are most effective. Cf. Keyishian, 385 U.S. at 604. At some point a teacher's comments on religion might cross the line and rise to the level of unconstitutional hostility. But without any cases illuminating the " 'dimly perceive[d] . . . line[ ] of demarcation' " between permissible and impermissible discussion of religion in a college level history class, we cannot conclude that a reasonable teacher standing in Corbett's shoes would have been on notice that his actions might be unconstitutional. Mueller v. Allen, 463 U.S. 388, 393 (1983) (quoting Lemon, 403 U.S. at 612). We therefore affirm the district court's decision that Corbett was entitled to qualified immunity.

CONCLUSION

"[T]he Establishment Clause presents especially difficult questions of interpretation and application," and we cannot expect Corbett to have divined the law without the guidance of any prior case on point. Id. at 392. Because we conclude that Corbett is entitled to the protection of qualified immunity, we affirm the district court's judgment granting qualified immunity. Because we do not reach the constitutionality of any of Corbett's statements, we vacate the district court's judgment in that respect. Each party shall bear its own costs on appeal.

NOTES AND QUESTIONS

1.   Does the Establishment Clause impose any limits on what a public-school teacher can say in class? Decisions dating at least as far back as *Epperson* have uniformly held that public schools cannot advance or endorse a religious view of origins over a scientific one. This rule applies regardless of whether teachers are acting on their own, as in *Webster* or *LeVake*, or pursuant to state or school-board policy, as in *McLean* or *Hendren*. Since the standard interpretation of the Establishment Clause holds that a government action may not have the primary effect of either advancing *or inhibiting* religion, it should follow that public-school teachers are no freer to discredit religion than to

endorse it. In a related context, Judge Danny Boggs wrote in *Mozert* that the state "may not teach as truth that the religions of others are just as correct as religions as plaintiffs' own." Of course, teaching about Darwinism in science classes can never cross this line so long as Darwinism remains the generally accepted scientific theory for the origin of species unless it is taught for the sole purpose or with the primary effect of discrediting religion (rather than providing science education). Did James Corbett cross this line with some of his recorded comments made while teaching AP European History? Certainly Corbett's comments were provocative but did they provoke critical thought or provoke animus toward religion? The court wrote, "At some point a teacher's comments on religion might cross the line and rise to the level of unconstitutional hostility."

2.   Why does the court let Corbett off the hook for his remarks without even deciding if those comments crossed the line of unconstitutional hostility toward religious belief? The court relied on the rule that government officials should only be held liable for violating constitutional or statutory rights if those rights are clearly established and reasonably known beforehand. To satisfy this test, the court noted, existing judicial precedent must place the constitutional or statutory right beyond debate. In this case, even plaintiffs' counsel could not cite prior cases where public-school teachers were sanctioned for inhibiting (rather than promoting) religious belief by their classroom comments. Thus, the court ruled, Corbett enjoyed qualified immunity for his remarks. Does this decision put public-school teachers, administrators, districts on notice that, in the future, they can be held liable for classroom comments that have the sole purpose or primary effect of endorsing or promoting disbelief? At least for now, the Ninth Circuit decision remains the last word on this subject. U.S. Supreme Court declined to hear Farnan's appeal.